Basic Contract Law
for Paralegals

Basic Contract Law for Paralegals

Third Edition

Jeffrey A. Helewitz

Adjunct Faculty of Law
City University of New York
School of Law
Touro College Law Center

Adjunct, Faculty, Paralegal Studies
Marymount Manhattan College

ASPEN
PUBLISHERS

1185 Avenue of the Americas, New York, NY 10036
www.aspenpublishers.com

Permissions
Aspen Publishers
1185 Avenue of the Americas
New York, NY 10036

Printed in the United States of America

ISBN 0-7355-1736-3

4 5 6 7 8 9 0

Library of Congress Cataloging-in-Publication Data

Helewitz, Jeffrey A.
 Basic contract law for paralegals / Jeffrey A. Helewitz.—3rd ed.
  p. cm.
  Includes index.
  ISBN 0-7355-1736-3
  1. Contracts—United States. 2. Legal assistants—United States—Handbooks, manuals, etc. I. Title.

KF801.Z9 H36 2000
346.7302—dc21

00-046883
CIP

About Aspen Publishers

Aspen Publishers, headquartered in New York City, is a leading information provider for attorneys, business professionals, and law students. Written by preeminent authorities, our products consist of analytical and practical information covering both U.S. and international topics. We publish in the full range of formats, including updated manuals, books, periodicals, CDs, and online products.

Our proprietary content is complemented by 2,500 legal databases, containing over 11 million documents, available through our Loislaw division. Aspen Publishers also offers a wide range of topical legal and business databases linked to Loislaw's primary material. Our mission is to provide accurate, timely, and authoritative content in easily accessible formats, supported by unmatched customer care.

To order any Aspen Publishers title, go to *www.aspenpublishers.com* or call 1-800-638-8437.

To reinstate your manual update service, call 1-800-638-8437.

For more information on Loislaw products, go to *www.loislaw.com* or call 1-800-364-2512.

For Customer Care issues, e-mail CustomerCare@aspenpublishers.com; call 1-800-234-1660; or fax 1-800-901-9075.

Aspen Publishers
A Wolters Kluwer Company

To Sarah—my first, and best, teacher

Summary of Contents

Contents   *xi*
Acknowledgments   *xxi*
Introduction   *xxiii*

Chapter 1 Overview of Contracts   1
Chapter 2 Offer   29
Chapter 3 Acceptance   53
Chapter 4 Consideration   81
Chapter 5 Legality of Subject Matter and Contractual
           Capacity   109
Chapter 6 Contractual Intent   133
Chapter 7 Contract Provisions   157
Chapter 8 The Uniform Commercial Code   189
Chapter 9 Third Party Contracts   231
Chapter 10 Discharge of Obligations   263
Chapter 11 Remedies   287
Chapter 12 Drafting Simple Contracts   319

Appendix A   Sample Contracts   335
        Antenuptial Agreement (Simple Form)   336
        Assignment   337
        Bill of Sale (Simple Form)   338
        Consulting Agreement   339
        Employment Contract (Simple Form)   341
        Employment Contract   343
        Equipment Lease Agreement   348
        General Partnership Agreement (Simple Form)   353

Limited Partnership Agreement   356
Promissory Note   376
Purchase Order   377
Real Estate Lease   378
Release   379
Shareholders Agreement   380
Subscription Agreement (Limited Partnership)   388

Appendix B   Supplemental Cases   393
   K. D. v. Educational Testing Service   393
   Fiege v. Boehm   398
   Bartus v. Riccardi   405
   Schwinghammer v. Alexander   407
Glossary   411
Index   419

Contents

Acknowledgments	*xi*
Introduction	*xxiii*

Chapter 1
OVERVIEW OF CONTRACTS   **1**

Chapter Overview	1
Contract Defined	2
Basic Contract Requirements	2
Offer	2
Acceptance	3
Consideration	3
Legality of Subject Matter	4
Contractual Capacity	4
Contractual Intent	5
Classification of Contracts	6
Type of Obligation: Bilateral or Unilateral	6
Method of Creation: Express, Implied, or Quasi-Contracts	7
Type of Form: Formal and Informal Contracts	9
Timing: Executory and Executed Contracts	10
Enforceability: Valid, Void, Voidable, and Unenforceable	11
Sample Clauses	12
Chapter Summary	14
Synopsis	15
Key Terms	15
Exercises	16
Cases for Analysis	17
Duplex Envelope Co., Inc. V. Baltimone Post Co.	17

Questions   23
Childs v. Kalgin Island Lodge   23
Questions   28
Suggested Case References   28

Chapter 2
OFFER   29

Chapter Overview   29
Offer Defined   30
    Present Contractual Intent   31
    Communication to the Offeree   31
    Certainty and Definiteness in the Terms of the Offer   33
Essential Terms of an Offer   33
    Price   34
    Subject Matter   35
    Parties   38
    Time of Performance   39
    Two Related Concepts   40
Sample Offers   41
Chapter Summary   43
Synopsis   43
Key Terms   43
Exercises   44
Cases for Analysis   44
    Alligood v. Procter & Gamble Co.   44
    Questions   46
    Rogus v. Lords   47
    Questions   50
Suggested Case References   50

Chapter 3
ACCEPTANCE   53

Chapter Overview   53
Acceptance Defined   53
    Varying the Terms of the Offer   54
    Silence as Acceptance   55
    Who May Accept   56
Method of Acceptance   58
    Acceptance of a Bilateral Contract   58
        Mailbox Rule   59
    Rejection of a Bilateral Contract   60
        Rejection and the Mailbox Rule   60

Acceptance of a Unilateral Contract   61
Termination of the Ability to Accept   62
   Revocation of Bilateral Contracts   63
   Revocation of Unilateral Contracts   63
   Termination by Operation of Law   65
Effect of Termination of Offer   65
Sample Clauses   66
Chapter Summary   66
Synopsis   67
Key Terms   68
Exercises   69
Cases for Analysis   69
     Marchiondo v. Scheck   69
     Questions   72
     University Emergency Medicine Foundation v.
       Rapier Investments, Ltd. and Medical Business
       Systems, Inc.   72
     Questions   78
Suggested Case References   79

Chapter 4
CONSIDERATION   81

Chapter Overview   81
Consideration Defined   82
   Benefit Conferred   82
   Detriment Incurred   83
What Is Not Consideration   83
Sufficiency of the Consideration   87
Promissory Estoppel   88
Special Agreements   90
   Accord and Satisfaction   90
   Charitable Subscription   91
   Debtor's Promises   91
   Guarantees   92
   Formal Contracts   93
Sample Clauses   94
Chapter Summary   95
Synopsis   95
Key Terms   96
Exercises   97
Cases for Analysis   97
     Don King Productions, Inc. v. Douglas   97
     Questions   102
     Cohen v. Cowles Media Co.   102

Questions   107
Suggested Case References   107

Chapter 5
LEGALITY OF SUBJECT MATTER
AND CONTRACTUAL CAPACITY   109

Chapter Overview   109
Legality of the Subject Matter   110
    Malum in Se   110
    Malum Prohibitum   111
Contractual Capacity   114
    Age   114
    Mental Capacity   115
    Alcohol and Drugs   116
Chapter Summary   116
Synopsis   117
Key Terms   117
Exercises   118
Cases for Analysis   118
    United States v. Yazell   118
    Questions   120
    Matter of Baby M   120
    Questions   131
Suggested Case References   131

Chapter 6
CONTRACTUAL INTENT   133

Chapter Overview   133
Contractual Intent Defined   134
Fraud and Misrepresentation   134
Duress   136
Mistake   139
Chapter Summary   141
Synopsis   141
Key Terms   142
Exercises   142
Cases for Analysis   143
    Francois v. Francois   143
    Questions   149
    Brown v. L. V. Marks & Sons Co.   149
    Questions   155
Suggested Case References   155

Chapter 7
CONTRACT PROVISIONS   157

Chapter Overview   157
The Statute of Frauds   158
    Contracts for an Interest in Real Estate   159
    Contracts in Consideration of Marriage   160
    Contracts Not to Be Performed Within One Year   161
    Guarantees   162
    Contracts for the Sale of Goods   163
    Executor's Promise to Pay Decedent's Debts   163
    What the Statute of Frauds Is Not   163
Covenants   164
Conditions   164
    Conditions Precedent   165
    Conditions Subsequent   166
    Conditions Concurrent   166
    Express Conditions   167
    Implied-in-Fact Conditions   167
    Implied-in-Law Conditions   168
Court Doctrines: Rules of Construction and the Parol
   Evidence Rule   168
Sample Clauses   171
Chapter Summary   172
Synopsis   173
Key Terms   173
Exercises   174
Cases for Analysis   174
       Nestle Food Co. v. Miller   174
       Questions   181
       Loyal Erectors, Inc. v. Hamilton & Son, Inc.   182
       Questions   187
Suggested Case References   187

Chapter 8
THE UNIFORM COMMERCIAL CODE   189

Chapter Overview   189
General Background   190
Article I, General Provisions   191
    Basic Guidelines   191
        Law of the State Applies   191
        Parties May Agree to Vary UCC Provisions   191
        UCC Provisions Are to Be Liberally Construed   192
    Obligations Imposed by Article I   192

Article II, Sales   194
  General Background   194
  Types of Contracts Covered by Article II   194
    Goods   194
    Leases   196
    Contracts for the Sale of Goods Between
      Merchants   196
  Contractual Provisions   198
    Warranties   198
    Risk of Loss   200
  Remedies   202
    Remedies Available to Seller   203
    Remedies Available to Buyer   204
    Written Assurances   205
  Summary   205
Article IX, Secured Transactions   206
  Secured Transaction Defined   206
  Requirements to Create a Security Interest   207
  Priorities   210
Sample Clauses   211
Chapter Summary   212
Synopsis   213
Key Terms   214
Exercises   216
Cases for Analysis   216
    Hong v. Marriott Corp.   216
    Questions   220
    In re Peregrine Entertainment, Ltd.   220
    Questions   230
Suggested Case References   230

Chapter 9
THIRD PARTY CONTRACTS   231

Chapter Overview   231
Third Party Beneficiary Contracts: Generally   232
Third Party Creditor Beneficiary Contracts   234
Third Party Donee Beneficiary Contracts   237
Assignment   240
  Creating the Assignment   240
  Consent of the Promisor   242
  Effect of Assignment   243
  Multiple Assignees   245
Delegation   246
Sample Clauses   247
Chapter Summary   248

Synopsis   249
Key Terms   250
Exercises   251
Cases for Analysis   251
     Artist Management Office, Inc. v. Worldvision
        Enterprises Inc.   *251*
        Questions   255
        Matter of Gosmire Estate   *256*
        Questions   261
Suggested Case References   261

Chapter 10
DISCHARGE OF OBLIGATIONS   263

Chapter Overview   263
Methods of Discharge   264
   Excuse of Conditions   264
   Performance   268
   Breach of Contract   269
   Agreement of the Parties   271
   Impossibility of Performance   273
   Supervening Illegality   274
   Death of the Parties or Destruction of the Subject
      Matter   274
   Frustration of Purpose   275
Sample Clauses   275
Chapter Summary   277
Synopsis   277
Key Terms   278
Exercises   279
Cases for Analysis   279
     Dunaj v. Glassmayer   *279*
     Questions   282
     Broome Construction Co. v. Beaver Lake
       Recreation Center, Inc.   *282*
     Questions   285
Suggested Case References   285

Chapter 11
REMEDIES   287

Chapter Overview   287
Legal Remedies   288
   Compensatory Damages   288

Punitive Damages   290
Consequential Damages   290
Liquidated Damages   291
Equitable Remedies   293
Injunction   294
Specific Performance   294
Rescission and Restitution   295
Reformation   296
Quasi-contractual Remedies   296
Quantum Meruit   296
Quantum Valebant   297
Waivers and Their Effect   297
Arbitration Provisions   298
Sample Clauses   298
Chapter Summary   299
Synopsis   300
Key Terms   301
Exercises   302
Cases for Analysis   302
Guard v. P & R Enterprises, Inc.   302
Questions   306
Edens v. Goodyear Tire & Rubber Co.   306
Questions   317
Suggested Case References   318

Chapter 12
DRAFTING SIMPLE CONTRACTS   319

Chapter Objective   319
Checklist of Clauses   320
Description of the Parties   321
Description of the Consideration   321
Security Agreement   324
Warranties   324
Title   325
Risk of Loss   325
Waivers   326
Assignments   326
Delegation   327
Terminology   327
Special Provisions and Clauses   328
Covenant Not to Compete   328
Duties   328
Pronouns   328
Severability   328
Successors   328

Time of the Essence   328
Trade Secrets   329
Work Product   329
Duration and Termination   329
Remedies   330
Choice of Law   330
Arbitration   331
Submission to Jurisdiction   331
Signatures   332
Chapter Summary   332
Exercises   333

Appendix A
SAMPLE CONTRACTS   335

Antenuptial Agreement (Simple Form)   336
Assignment   337
Bill of Sale (Simple Form)   338
Consulting Agreement   339
Employment Contract (Simple Form)   341
Employment Contract   343
Equipment Lease Agreement   348
General Partnership Agreement (Simple Form)   353
Limited Partnership Agreement   356
Promissory Note   376
Purchase Order   377
Real Estate Lease   378
Release   379
Shareholders Agreement   380
Subscription Agreement (Limited Partnership)   388

Appendix B
SUPPLEMENTAL CASES   393

K. D. v. Educational Testing Service   393
Fiege v. Boehm   398
Bartus v. Riccardi   405
Schwinghammer v. Alexander   407

Glossary   411
Index   419

Acknowledgments

I have been extremely fortunate to have had the kind assistance of several people in the preparation of this project. Joyce E. Larson, a Legal Assistant Coordinator in the Mutual Funds division of Brown & Wood, generously provided succinct and helpful criticism of the work in progress and continual encouragement throughout the writing of this book. Maria Montgomery, a corporate Legal Assistant and translator of international contracts at Stroock & Stroock & Lavan, spent many devoted hours commenting on and editing the manuscript. Words cannot express my gratitude to these two kind and intelligent women, without whose help this book never would have been possible.

I wish to thank all of the people at Little, Brown and Company who worked on the First Edition of this text, especially Betsy Kenny, Carolyn O'Sullivan, Kerry Vieira, and Lisa Wehrle. In addition, I would like to thank Linda Richmond and Lai T. Moy at Aspen Law & Business for their work on the Second and Third Editions respectively.

Introduction

This book provides the paralegal student and practitioner with a quick, simple, and straightforward text on the law of contracts. It helps to clarify this very complex area of law using numerous practical examples of how to draft and interpret different types of contracts. This book is not intended to discuss every nuance of contract law, nor is it designed as a casebook for law students. *Basic Contract Law for Paralegals* is meant to be an easy-to-use, readable reference tool for the legal assistant.

The reader should be aware of the fact that there are two legal sources of law with respect to contract formation and interpretation. The first, and traditional source, is the common law, that law that has developed over the centuries based on judicial precedent (and sometimes codified by specific state statute). The second source of contract law is the Uniform Commercial Code (UCC), a form of which has been adopted by every jurisdiction in the country. The UCC regulates contracts for the sale of goods and contracts between merchants. Contracts for services or between non-merchants are still governed by the common law. Throughout the text the distinction between these two sources, whenever significant, will be specifically addressed.

The most important aspect of all laws is the relationship between the parties in dispute. The law is primarily concerned with relationships between and among individuals. In contract law, the value of the contract in monetary terms is of secondary importance; the relationship between the contract parties is the most important determining factor. The simple contract for the sale of a morning newspaper and the multipage document for the development of a $20 million shopping center both involve indentical legal principles. Because the law is concerned with principles and relationships, the logical starting point for the analysis of any legal problem is the legal relationship of the litigants.

The most common problem encountered in analyzing a legal situation is that everyone immediately wants to jump to the end result—"What can I get"—rather than discerning the actual rights and liabilities of the parties. It is more important to identify each element of the relationship to determine whether or not a legal dispute exists.

Contracts is only one area of law that defines particular relations between persons; it is not the exclusive area of law applicable to a given situation. To determine a person's rights and liabilities, first you must determine what area of law—for instance, contracts, torts, bankruptcy—best applies to the problem. Then you must determine that all of the requisite elements of the legal relationship, as defined by that area of the law, exist. You cannot bend the law to fit the facts; if the facts do not fit into a particular legal theory, that theory is incorrect and a new one must be found. Keeping this general principle in mind will help analysis of all legal problems.

The role of the paralegal with respect to contracts is multidimensional. A paralegal is often called on to draft the initial agreement for the client and, as negotiations develop, to see that all subsequent changes are incorporated into the document. If a problem arises, the paralegal is generally responsible for making the initial analysis of the contract in dispute to determine all potential rights and liabilities of the client. And finally, the legal assistant will work with the attorney to determine the appropriate remedies available to the client. To perform these tasks, the legal assistant must be conversant with all of the elements of basic contract law and drafting.

Basic Contract Law
for Paralegals

1 Overview of Contracts

CHAPTER OVERVIEW

This chapter discusses the six basic requirements for every valid contract and then indicates the various classifications into which all contracts fall. The chapter is intended to give a general overview of, and introduction to, contract law. The specific details involved in analyzing contractual situations are covered in the following 11 chapters.

The law of contracts is one of the most complex and important areas of substantive law taught in law school. Every law school in the country teaches contracts as part of the first year of required courses because, more than any other course of law, contracts affect everyone's daily existence.

Think of everything that you do each day: You wake up in your home, brush your teeth, dress, eat breakfast, read the morning newspaper, and travel to work or to school. Each of these activities involves contract law. Rent or mortgage payments involve a contract with a landlord or lender; brushing your teeth requires the purchase of a toothbrush and toothpaste; getting dressed is accomplished only after buying the clothes worn; buying the newspaper is a simple sales transaction; and even taking public transportation involves a contract with the municipality. Every aspect of normal life is dominated by contractual principles, but few people realize the extent to which they are, in fact, contracting parties. To the nonlaw professional, a contract is a long and complicated legal document that is drafted by an attorney and involves huge sums of money. Yet, in reality, most contracts involve little, if any, written documentation, no lawyer, and only small amounts of money (if money is involved at all).

It is this all-pervasive element of contracts that makes contract law both interesting and challenging.

Contract Defined

A **contract** is a legally enforceable agreement that meets certain specified legal requirements between two or more parties in which each party agrees to give and receive something of legal value. It is distinguishable from a gift in that each party gives and receives something. In a gift situation only one party gives; the other one receives. Also, a contract is more than just an agreement. An agreement may not meet all of the specific requirements needed to create a contract; hence it will not be legally enforceable under a contractual claim.

Basic Contract Requirements

To determine whether a contractual relationship exists between two persons, it is necessary to ascertain that all six of the requisite elements of a valid contract exist. If *all* of these elements are not present, the parties do not have a contractual relationship (although they may have a relationship described by some other theory of law, which, if true, then would have to be addressed). Even if all of the elements are present in the agreement, the contract may be unenforceable because of some other statutory reason, such as the Statute of Frauds or the Statute of Limitations.

The six requisite elements of every valid contract are

1. offer;
2. acceptance;
3. consideration;
4. legality of subject matter;
5. contractual capacity; and
6. contractual intent.

Offer

An **offer** is a proposal by one party to another manifesting an intention to enter into a valid contract. Every valid contractual relationship starts with an offer.

EXAMPLE:

One student asks another, "Will you buy my used Contracts book for $5?" The student has stated a proposal to sell a particular object (the used book) at a particular price ($5). Without this initial proposition, the two students could not possibly develop a contractual relationship.

The offer defines the boundaries of the potential relationship between the parties and empowers the other party to create the contract by accepting the proposition.

Acceptance

To create the contract, the party to whom the offer is made must **accept** the proposal. If she does not, then no contract comes into existence. The law will not force a person to fulfill an obligation to which she has not agreed.

 EXAMPLE:

The paralegal student in the example above says "OK, I'll take the book." In this case a contract has been created because the student has agreed to the proposal of the seller.

The concepts of offer and acceptance go hand in hand in determining whether a contract exists. The offer and acceptance together form the **mutual assent** of the parties—the agreement that they do intend to be contractually bound to each other. Without this meeting of the minds, no matter what else may exist, there is no valid contract.

Consideration

Consideration is the subject matter of the contract; it is the thing for which the parties have bargained. Most people assume consideration to be the price, but that is not completely accurate. Although money may be part of the bargain, it is not always the complete bargain. Nor is money itself always necessary. The crucial aspect of consideration is that each party both gives and receives consideration. Each must give something of value.

EXAMPLE:

In the example given above, the consideration is both the $5 and the book itself. The seller is bargaining for the money; the buyer is bargaining for the book.

Consideration is deemed to be anything of legally significant value—monetary worth is not the ultimate determining factor of legal value.

EXAMPLE:

In the example above, instead of asking for $5, the student says "Will you exchange your used Torts book for my used Contracts book?" If the second student agrees, a contract is formed. In this instance the books themselves are consideration—no money changes hands.

These first three elements—offer, acceptance, and consideration—are the three most important aspects of every valid contract because they form the provisions of the contract itself. Without these three components there can be no contract.

Legality of Subject Matter

To be valid, a contract can only be formed for a legal purpose and must fulfill any statutory regulations with respect to form.

EXAMPLE:

Acme, Inc., a major producer of automobile tires, enters into an agreement with Goodyear to run Dunlop out of business by fixing prices. Although this contract may meet all of the other contractual requirements, it is not enforceable because it violates U.S. antitrust laws. This contract is not formed for a legal purpose.

Contractual Capacity

Contractual capacity refers to the ability of a person to enter into a valid contract. The most typical examples of capacity (or rather, the lack of capacity) deal with the age of the party and the person's mental condition.

EXAMPLE:

John, a precocious 14-year-old, wants to buy some woodland for potential real estate development. Although it may be a good idea and may possibly bring in millions of dollars, the law considers a 14-year-old incapable of entering into a contract. His age and presumable lack of experience make him contractually incapable.

Contractual Intent

Contractual intent is the last of the requisite elements of a valid contract, but the one that is all pervasive. Even if the contract meets all of the other requirements enumerated above, if it can be shown that the parties did not subjectively intend to form a contractual relationship, there will be no contract. Many times this aspect of intent is not readily discernible by the words of the parties themselves, and surrounding circumstances must be analyzed to determine whether a contract exists.

 EXAMPLES:

1. Kevin agrees to sell Bruce his house for $50,000. The contract is in writing, describes the house, and specifies the method and terms of payment. On the face of it, the contract appears valid. But what if it were shown that Kevin had been forced to sign the contract at gun point? Under these circumstances, Kevin obviously did not willingly intend to enter into the contractual relationship with Bruce.

2. William agrees to pay Sally $500 a week to be his housekeeper. Once again, on its face, this appears to be a valid contract. However, what if William were 85 years old, and Sally had convinced him that none of his relations wanted anything to do with him? She also told him that if he didn't hire her, he'd be all alone and helpless. Under these circumstances, it would appear that William was the victim of mental coercion. Consequently, his intent to enter the contract of his own free will is suspect.

The above-mentioned six elements must exist if there is to be a valid contract. Each of these elements will be discussed in detail in the following chapters. The foregoing is intended only as a general overview. However, it is necessary to keep all six of these elements in mind when discussing contracts because each one is necessarily intertwined, regardless of the type of contract created.

Classification of Contracts

All contracts fall into a certain number of classifications, or types. Generally, it is a good idea to classify the contract in question prior to analyzing its validity and provisions. This classification process is like making selections from a restaurant menu. Take one item from each category, and when completed, a meal (that is, a contract) is formed.

Type of Obligation: Bilateral or Unilateral

The type of obligation refers to the kind of duty imposed on the parties to the contract. This category defines every contract as belonging to one of two classifications.

All contracts are either **bilateral** or **unilateral**. A bilateral contract is a promise for a promise. A unilateral contract is a promise for an act. This division into bilateral or unilateral is important with respect to what performance is expected from the parties and at what point the contract comes into existence. With a bilateral contract, the parties are expecting a mutual exchange of promises, with the performance to be carried out only after the promises have been given. Most contracts are bilateral, even though it is rare that the parties actually use the word "promise" (except in the most formal of situations).

 EXAMPLE:

In the situation discussed above, with respect to the sale of the used text book, the actual words used were "Will you buy my used Contracts book for $5"? "OK." These words created a bilateral contract. What the parties legally said were: "Will you promise to pay me $5 if I promise to sell you my used Contracts book"? "I promise to pay you $5 if you promise to sell me your used Contracts book." The contract was created when the promises were given. The performance—the exchange of the book for the money—is intended to take place *after* the agreement has been made.

Conversely, in a unilateral contract, the contract is only created when one side has performed a requested act. Instead of an exchange of mutual promises a unilateral contract is an exchange of a promise for an act.

 EXAMPLE:

Allison promises to pay Tim $1500 if Tim paints her apartment on Wednesday. In this instance, Allison is requesting a specific act: Tim's painting the apartment on Wednesday. Allison does not want Tim's promise that he will do the painting; she wants to see the job done. Until Wednesday arrives, and Tim actually paints the apartment, no contract exists. When Tim does the painting, Allison must fulfill her promise to pay him $1500.

There tends to be a lot of confusion in identifying a contract as bilateral or unilateral, simply because most ordinary contracts are formed and completed simultaneously. Consequently, it is difficult to distinguish between the promise and the act. This determination is crucial, however, because it times the start of the contractual relationship. If the contract is bilateral, the relationship is formed at the exchange of promises. The parties are entitled to contractual remedies if one side does not fulfill his promise. (This is the "What can I get?" as discussed in the Introduction.) On the other hand, if the contract is unilateral, the contractual relationship is only formed when one side actually performs the requested act. Until that time, no contractual remedies are available to the parties. If, in the example above, Tim does not paint the apartment on Wednesday, Allison has no recourse to sue him because he is under no contractual obligation.

To determine whether a contract is bilateral or unilateral, it is necessary to determine the intent and the specified wishes of the parties involved. Courts will generally go along with what the parties could most reasonably expect under the circumstances because that would indicate the true meeting of the parties' minds with respect to the manner of acceptance sought. Note that the law is generally pro-contract; that is, it favors contractual relationships and consequently presumes contracts to be bilateral. This creates the contractual relationship sooner than in a unilateral contractual situation.

Method of Creation: Express, Implied, or Quasi-Contracts

How does a contract come into existence? A contract is formed either by the words or conduct of the parties and is classified accordingly.

An **express** contract is one in which the mutual assent of the parties is manifested in words, either orally or in writing. An **implied-in-fact** contract is one in which the promises of the parties are inferred from their actions or conduct as opposed to specific words being used.

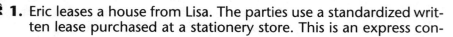 **EXAMPLES:**

1. Eric leases a house from Lisa. The parties use a standardized written lease purchased at a stationery store. This is an express contract because the rights and obligations of the parties are described in written words.

2. In the previous example of the sale of the used Contracts book, the parties have entered into an express contract. Their promises are given orally.

3. Louise goes to a newsstand to buy her morning paper. She picks up the paper and gives the news agent 50 cents. Louise and the news agent have completed an implied-in-fact contract. The contract was entered into by their actions, and no words were used or necessary.

In addition to express and implied-in-fact contracts, the law has also created another category known as **implied-in-law,** or **quasi-contracts.** As the term "quasi" might indicate, these are situations that look like a contract, but, in truth, are not contracts because one of the requisite elements is missing. However, in the interests of fairness, the law has determined that a party should be entitled to some remedy if injured by such a situation.

Whenever the words "quasi" or "estoppel" are used, terms that will be discussed in subsequent chapters, the court is using its equitable jurisdiction. The difference between law and equity is basically the difference between justice and mercy. There are times and situations in which the legal result might be "just" under the laws of society—that is, reasonable under the circumstances—but it would not be "fair"—a party would be injured without recourse. In these situations, the concept of **equity** takes over. Equity was designed to right wrongs, to prevent unfairness and unjust enrichment. Equity was created specifically for those situations in which the application of the law would result in an injured party still suffering. For a more complete discussion of the equity courts, see Chapter 11, Remedies.

With respect to the classification of contracts, the courts have created the concept of quasi-contractual situations, situations in which the parties do not have a contractual relationship but in which it would be most fair to treat them as though a contract did exist. For a quasi-contractual situation to arise, it must be shown that one party unjustly benefited from the other party under circumstances in which a mutual benefit had been expected.

 EXAMPLES:

1. Joan has just completed her paralegal training, but before she starts work she receives a telephone call from her elderly aunt in the Midwest. Her aunt tells Joan that she is very ill, not long for this world, and needs someone to take care of her. The aunt promises Joan that if Joan comes to the Midwest and looks after her, she'll remember Joan in her will.

Based on the foregoing, Joan moves to the Midwest, and for the next ten years cooks, cleans, and takes care of her aunt. When her aunt finally dies, Joan is simply "remembered fondly" in the aunt's will. All the aunt's cash goes to her cat Fluffy.

Can Joan sue the estate for breach of contact? No. Why? Because no contract existed—the aunt merely said she would remember Joan in the will—there was no mutual benefit, and no consideration given to Joan, despite what Joan might have hoped for.

In this instance, the court will probably apply the doctrine of quasi-contract and permit Joan to recover the value of the services she provided for the aunt. Because Joan never intended to make a gift of her services to her aunt, if the aunt received them without compensating Joan, the aunt would be unjustly enriched. This would be unfair to Joan.

2. Sal opens the door to his house one morning and discovers a newspaper on his doorstep. He picks it up and takes it to work with him. For the next week every morning a newspaper appears at his door. At the end of the week Sal receives a bill from the publisher for the newspapers.

Does Sal have a contract with the publisher? No. However, the court, applying the doctrine of quasi-contract, will permit the publisher to recover the cost of the papers. Sal accepted the benefit of the papers by taking them and reading them, and now must pay. If Sal did not want the papers, it was his responsibility to contact the publisher to stop delivery.

Note that there are laws that would make the outcome different if the U.S. mail were used to deliver the goods. Several years ago a statute was enacted stating that if the mail is used to send unsolicited merchandise, the recipient may keep the merchandise as a gift. Also, many states have consumer protection laws prohibiting the delivery of unsolicited goods.

To apply the concept of quasi-contract, it must be shown that no contract exists because a requisite element is missing and one party is unjustly enriched at the expense of the other.

Type of Form: Formal and Informal Contracts

A **formal** contract is a contract that, historically, was written and signed under seal. The concept derives from a time when few people could read or write, and the solemnity of a seal gave importance to a document. The seal was used as the consideration for the agreement.

Nowadays, seals are no longer used, and this term refers to a limited group of contracts that different states have declared valid and enforceable if certain statutory requirements are met. Some examples of formal contracts are negotiable instruments (such as checks, and certificates of deposit) and guarantees.

EXAMPLE:

Fidelity Bank issues printed checks to its customers, which the customers use to pay their bills. These checks do not contain the words and elements of a contract, but they are enforced as a formal contract because of statutory regulations. The contract is between the bank and its customers.

Informal contracts are, simply put, all non-formal contracts. Despite the terminology, informal contracts are agreements that meet all the requirements of valid contracts; they can be quite specific and stylized in and of themselves.

EXAMPLE:

The contract for the sale of the used Contracts book is an example of an informal contract. All the contractual requirements are present, and its form is not regulated by a statute.

Timing: Executory and Executed Contracts

One of the most crucial questions for the parties to a contract involves the timing: "*When* are the contractual obligations to be performed?" This timing element indicates when the parties have enforceable rights and obligations. Contracts are categorized by indicating whether or not the parties have uncompleted duties to carry out. An **executory** contract is a contract in which one or both of the parties still have obligations to perform. An **executed** contract is complete and final with respect to all of its terms and conditions.

EXAMPLE:

When the two paralegal students discussed above agree to the terms for the sale of the used Contracts book, the contract is formed but it is still executory. Once the book and the money have changed hands, the contract is complete with respect to all of its terms, and is now completely executed. (Note that the term "executed" is also used to indicate the signing of a document; in that context the obligations are still executory even though the contract is executed (signed).)

Enforceability: Valid, Void, Voidable, and Unenforceable

Finally, getting to the "What can I get?" element, the law classifies contracts in terms of their enforceability. Can a party to a contract have that agreement enforced in a court of law, and which party to the contract has that right of enforceability.

A **valid** contract is an enforceable contract that meets all of the six requirements discussed above: There is a proper offer and acceptance; legally valid consideration is given and received; the parties have the legal capacity to enter into a contract; the contract is for a legal purpose; and the parties genuinely intend to contract—it is complete under the law. Either party can bring suit for the enforcement of a valid contract.

A **void** contract is, in reality, a contradiction in terms because there is no contract, and therefore the law does not entitle the parties to any legal remedy. The agreement has not met the contractual requirements.

In a **voidable** contract a party to the agreement has the option of avoiding his legal obligation without any negative consequences, but who could, if he wished, affirm his obligation and thereby be contractually bound. A contract entered into by a minor is an example of a voidable contract. Legally, a minor does not have contractual capacity and can avoid fulfilling contracts into which he has entered. (There are exceptions for certain types of contracts. See Chapter 5.) However, if, on reaching majority, the former minor affirms the contract, he will be contractually bound.

 EXAMPLE:

Seventeen-year-old Gene enters into a contract with Bob, an adult, to buy Bob's used car. If Gene changes his mind, he can avoid the contract. However, if, on Gene's eighteenth birthday, Gene affirms his promise to Bob by giving Bob a payment, the contract will be totally enforceable. The option of avoidance is with Gene who is under the disability, not with Bob who is not.

A voidable contract may become valid and enforceable if the party under the disability—a minor, or a person induced by fraud, duress, or like condition to enter the agreement—later affirms his obligation when the disability is removed. A void contract, on the other hand, can never be made enforceable, regardless of what the parties do; any addition to the agreement that the parties attempt in order to meet contractual requirements actually creates the contract at that time; it does not validate what was void.

An **unenforceable** contract is a valid contract for which the law offers no recourse or remedy if its obligations are not fulfilled. For instance, a contract may exist in which one party failed to meet her contractual obligation; by the time the aggrieved party decides to sue, the Statute of Limitations has run, meaning that the law has determined that the proponent has waited so long to bring the suit that the court will not hear the question. Or, parties agree to open a store at a particular location, but before the contract can be fulfilled, the town rezones the area for residential use only. Even though the contract is valid, it can no longer be enforced because of a subsequent change in the law that makes its purpose incapable of being legally performed.

In classifying any given contract, remember that it will consist of elements of each type discussed above. The following chart summarizes these five types:

Type of Obligation	Method of Creation	Form	Timing	Enforceability
Bilateral Unilateral	Express Implied in fact Implied in law (quasi)	Formal Informal	Executory Executed	Valid Void Voidable Unenforceable

Every contract will have one item from each of these five categories; the terms are not mutually exclusive.

SAMPLE CLAUSES

1

Dear Irene,

Pursuant to our telephone conversation yesterday, I hereby agree to buy the pearl necklace you inherited from your Grandmother Rose for $500. Come to my house for dinner next Monday, and I'll give you a check.

Love,
Jeannette

P.S. Don't forget to bring the necklace.

The above letter constitutes an example of a bilateral contract between Jeannette and Irene. Irene made an offer for the sale of her necklace, which Jeannette has acknowledged and accepted in writing. The consideration Irene is giving is the necklace; the consideration Jeannette is giving is the $500. In terms of classification, this is an informal bilateral express contract that is executory until the consideration changes hands. Remember that to be legally enforceable, a contract does not have to take any particular form or include words of overt legality. Even a handwritten note may constitute a valid contract.

2

This contract dated the _____ day of _____, 20 ____, is made between Samuel Smith, hereinafter Smith, whose address is _____, and Peter Jones, hereinafter Jones, whose address is _____.

Jones hereby agrees to paint the exterior of Smith's house, located at _____, on the _____ day of _____, 20 ____, in consideration for which Smith hereby agrees to pay Jones the sum of $2500, inclusive of all expenses, upon the completion of said painting.

In Witness Whereof, the undersigned have executed this contract the date and year first above written.

_____

Samuel Smith

_____

Peter Jones

The preceding is a more formalized version of a simple bilateral contract, this time for services instead of for the sale of goods. Why is it bilateral instead of unilateral, since services are being requested? The answer is that both parties are making present promises to each other: Jones to paint the house, and Smith to pay for Jones' painting services. The contract is formed on the date indicated; performance is merely delayed until the date specified. Whenever there is a mutual exchange of promises, the contract is bilateral.

Note that Smith has included the cost of all of Jones' expenses in the contract price. This means that the $2500 is all that Smith is liable for, and Jones is responsible for paying for all paints, brushes, and so forth, that are required to do the work. This is a written example of an informal express, executory, bilateral contract.

3

Dear Mr. Whitson:

This concerns the parcel of land I bought from you last month. On making a personal inspection of the property, I noticed that

the drainage ditch was clogged. I will be out of state for the next two
months and can't clear it myself. Please clear the ditch for me and send
a bill to my office for $500.

Sincerely,
Alfred Brace

The following week Mr. Whitson cleared the drain and sent Mr.
Brace a bill for $500.

This is an example of an express unilateral contract. Mr. Brace has
requested a service from Mr. Whitson and has agreed to pay Whitson
upon completion of the requested task. Mr. Whitson accepted the offer
by doing the act requested and now is waiting for payment. The contract
is still executory because Mr. Whitson has not yet received Mr. Brace's
check.

This example differs from Sample 2 in that here the offering party
has requested an act, not a promise, and the offer became a contract when
the other party accepted by cleaning the ditch. Once again, the corre-
spondence was more informal than a signed and printed document. This
does not negate the fact that it is a binding contract between the parties.

In analyzing information that is presented, always go through the
checklist of five contract classifications given above to determine the exact
form of the documents you are handling. Do not be put off or swayed
by the physical appearance of the materials. Handwritten letters, notes,
and typed agreements all may be valid contracts, depending on the substance of the material itself. Remember, the classifications only help to
organize the material; they do not determine the agreement's legal effect
or the relationship created between the parties. That determination involves a minute examination of the six contractual requirements examined earlier in the chapter.

CHAPTER SUMMARY

The law of contracts is one of the most complex, yet most ele-
mental, of all areas of the law. Contract law forms the basis of most people's daily existence and therefore is of paramount importance as a field
of study.

To create a valid contract, the agreement must contain the following
six elements: offer, acceptance, consideration, legality of the subject matter, contractual capacity of the parties, and the contractual intent of the
parties. Without these elements, the parties are not in a contractual relationship and, if injured, must rely on a different legal relationship to resolve the dispute.

All contracts can be classified according to five different categories, and in analyzing a contractual situation, it is best to classify the agreement prior to determining the rights and liabilities of the parties. The five classifications are: type of obligation (bilateral or unilateral); method of creation (express, implied in fact, or quasi); type of form (formal or informal); timing of obligation (executory or executed); and enforceability (valid, void, voidable, or unenforceable). Once the situation has been appropriately classified, analysis of the specific provisions can begin.

SYNOPSIS

Six requirements of every valid contract
  1. Offer
  2. Acceptance
  3. Consideration
  4. Contractual capacity
  5. Legality of subject matter
  6. Contractual intent
Classifications of contracts
  1. Type of obligation
       a. Bilateral
       b. Unilateral
  2. Method of creation
       a. Express
       b. Implied
       c. Quasi
  3. Type of form
       a. Formal
       b. Informal
  4. Timing
       a. Executory
       b. Executed
  5. Enforceability
       a. Valid
       b. Void
       c. Voidable
       d. Unenforceable

Key Terms

Acceptance: manifestation of assent to the offer proposed
Bilateral contract: a contract in which a promise is exchanged for a promise
Consideration: the bargain of the contract; a benefit conferred or detriment incurred at the request of the other party

Contract: a legally enforceable agreement between two or more parties in which each agrees to give and receive something of legal value

Contractual capacity: the legal ability of a person to enter into a contractual relationship

Contractual intent: the purposefulness of forming a contractual relationship

Equity: the branch of the law that deals with fairness and mercy to prevent unjust enrichment

Executed contract: a contract that is complete and final with respect to all of its terms and conditions

Executory contract: a contract in which one or both of the parties still have obligations to perform

Express contract: a contract manifested in words, oral or written

Formal contract: historically, a written contract under seal; currently, any contract so designated by a state statute

Implied-in-fact contract: a contract in which the promises of the parties are inferred from their actions as opposed to specific words

Implied-in-law contract: see Quasi-contract

Informal contract: any nonformal contract

Mutual assent: agreeing to the same terms at the same time; the offer and acceptance combined

Offer: a proposal by one party to another manifesting an intent to enter into a valid contract

Quasi-contract: a legal relationship that the courts, in the interest of fairness and equity, treat in a manner similar to a contractual relationship, even though no contract exists

Unenforceable contract: a contract that is otherwise valid but for a breach of which there is no remedy at law

Unilateral contract: a contract in which a promise is exchanged for an act

Valid contract: an agreement that meets all six contractual requirements

Void contract: a situation in which the parties have attempted to create a contract, but in which one or more of the requisite elements are missing, so no contract exists

Voidable contract: a contract that one party may avoid at his option without being in breach of contract

EXERCISES

1.   Give three examples of bilateral contracts from your everyday life that are not mentioned in the text.
2.   What elements would you look for to determine that an agreement is an enforceable contract?
3.   Why would a valid contract be unenforceable? Give examples.
4.   Create a bilateral contract for a situation that involves barter.
5.   How would you attempt to prove the existence or nonexistence of contractual intent?

Cases for Analysis

To elucidate certain points discussed in the chapter, the following judicial decisions are included. The first case, **Duplex Envelope Co. v. Baltimore Post Co.** highlights requirements incident to the creation of a valid contract. **Childs v. Kalgin Island Lodge** discusses express and implied contracts with respect to employment law.

Duplex Envelope Co., Inc. v. Baltimore Post Co.
163 Md. 596 (1933)

The plaintiff has long been established in the business of supplying religious bodies with a special form of envelopes for use in weekly church collections. In the development of this enterprise, the plaintiff adopted the device of printing on the backs of the envelopes exhortations, with the twofold object of stimulating a constant attendance at church services and a liberal and regular contribution for church purposes. The content of this printed matter was different every Sunday; it was introduced by an appropriate text from the Bible, and its composition was by eminent divines or competent writers. In 1929 the plaintiff attempted a further development by selling this printed matter to selected newspapers for publication every week as a part of the section of the newspaper that was customarily allotted to the printing of matter relating to the various religious denominations of the place of publication. The plan was for the plaintiff to furnish the subscribing newspaper, during the year of its subscription, with 52 full page mats containing the weekly printed matter which would appear on the back of the collection envelopes, and the advertisements, which were to be printed in association with this printed matter. From this mat or mold as the matrix, the contents for publication were readily stereotyped for the weekly printing. In addition, the plaintiff furnished printed copies of this page, in order that the publishers of the newspapers would have it for exhibition in the solicitation by them of advertisements for appearance on the page to be published; and the plaintiff further supplied a list of the churches, with the names of their respective ministers, treasurers, and members, which used their collection envelopes, and other information and suggestions, which would all be informative and valuable to the newspapers, and which would give them access to a group of desirable prospective advertisers or readers, with a plausible reason for their approach and solicitation in the concerted effort by the representatives of the newspapers to obtain advertisements. The particular newspaper was to be paid for the advertisements printed in its journal by the advertisers whose names would be published as sponsors of the page. Thirteen of the weekly mats would be shipped by the plaintiff at a time so that the advertising for a quarter of the year would be available at one time.

The further details of this plan need not be set forth, as its nature, advantages, and appeal are sufficiently disclosed. In brief, the plan of campaign was furnished by the plaintiff, and its execution was the task of the subscribing newspaper.

The defendant is a corporation engaged in publishing a daily newspaper in Baltimore City, and is one of a number of associated newspapers known as the Scripps-Howard chain of newspapers. On August 6th, 1929, the plaintiff sent a lengthy communication to the defendant outlining the plan, and offered it for the consideration of the defendant as a means of selling advertising space. A form of a proposed contract was inclosed [sic], along with specimens of what would be supplied by the plaintiff in fulfillment of the contract. In the form of contract which the plaintiff had sent were these terms:

"For this service the subscriber agrees to pay the Duplex Envelope Company ten per cent (10%) of subscriber's local noncontract page rate, due and payable in monthly installments on the first day of each month commencing February 1, 1930.

If any installment remains delinquent for a period of thirty (30) days, the entire amount of the contract shall become immediately due and payable at the option of the Duplex Envelope Company.

In consideration of contracting for the entire Scripps-Howard chain of newspapers, the Duplex Envelope Company agrees to allow twenty-five per cent (25%) discount off its gross billing to the subscriber, and in addition agrees to use advertising space in the paper below listed, at some time during the year, in the aggregate of one (1) full page, and agrees to accept billing for this page at the foreign rate as published in the rate book of the Standard Rate and Data Service. Payment for this advertising to be made by deducting the amount of the bill from the final amount due The Duplex Envelope Company under this agreement, for its service.

The foregoing to equal, after charges and allowances and deductions have been made, the sum of _____.

It is understood that all agreements are merged in this contract, and that it is not subject to cancellation."

The defendant considered the matter and sent to the plaintiff on August 13th, 1929, this telegram:

> Your contract calls for ten per cent. local noncontract page rate. We have special church rate, is it satisfactory for us to change this to local church contract page rate on your contract.

The next day the plaintiff replied by this telegram to the defendant:

> Satisfactory to substitute in contract ten per cent of local church rate providing this will net us not less than twenty dollars a week, after deducting 25 per cent. and cost on full page advertising to be taken by us.

After this telegram was received by the defendant, a letter under date of August 14, 1929, was mailed to and received by the plaintiff. It is as follows:

The Baltimore Daily Post
Baltimore, Md., August 14, 1929.

Mr. M. O. Jones, Presdt., Duplex Envelope Co., Inc., Richmond, Va.

Dear Mr. Jones: I am enclosing in this letter signed contracts changed to read local Church Contract Page Rate in accordance with your telegram of the 14th.

This will assure you of not less than $20 a week, after deducting 25%, if all the Scripps-Howard Newspapers subscribe. If not enough to cover cost of full page advertisement to be taken by you, we will work this out satisfactorily with you.

I believe your proposition will go over very successfully in Baltimore, and you can rest assured we will go the limit to make it productive for all concerned.

In your original presentation you mentioned that you would send us the list of Churches using these envelopes, also Pastors in charge and possibly the leading members of the Vestry.

I might suggest, if you secure data on the way some of the papers are putting this over in their fields, it will be valuable to the rest of us so that we may profit by the experience of others.

Very truly yours,
The Baltimore Post,
J. C. Flagg, Business Manager.

The duplicate contracts forwarded with this letter were signed and dated on August 14th, 1929, by the defendant, the Baltimore Post, with the change to "local church contract page rate" inserted, and were received in due course of mail on August 15th, 1929, when the plaintiff wrote the defendant an acknowledgment and forwarded the defendant one of the duplicate contracts which the plaintiff had executed after its receipt from the defendant.

The importance of this letter requires it to be reproduced:

August 15th, 1929.

Mr. J. C. Flagg, The Baltimore Post, Business Manager, Baltimore, Maryland.

Dear Mr. Flagg: We have and thank you for your letter of August 14th, enclosing signed contract for the Duplex National Church Advertising Campaign, one copy of which we have executed and are returning herewith.

This is with the understanding that the net cost to you is not less than $20 per week or $1,040 for the year after deduction of 25% discount special allowance for the Scripps-Howard papers and the cost of one full page advertisement to be used by us.

For billing purposes, will you please advise what your local contract church rate is, which information you did not give us in your letter?

We will send you today two copies each of all of the material to be used by your solicitors, and will have tomorrow a list of our customer churches in Baltimore, with the name of the pastor; and will also send you then a suggested plan for solicitation of the sponsors, which we believe will be of great value and make it easy to sell the page.

We are delighted to have The Baltimore Post with us in this campaign, and we hope that the campaign will be productive of much good to the city of Baltimore generally.

> With all good wishes, we are
> Cordially yours,
> The Duplex Envelope Company.
> SGM: IM
> S. G. Mason, Director of Service.

The plaintiff shipped to the defendant the mats in accordance with the contract. The plaintiff never received any notice that any of the mats or supplies which had been shipped by the plaintiff to the defendant were not accepted or had been returned by the defendant. In fact, the defendant wrote the plaintiff under date of December 29th, 1929.

> Received the mats shipped us November 13th in A1 shape. Am just wondering if you will forward me as soon as possible half-dozen sets of the original presentation on the Church Pages.
> Incidentally, if you have any additional ideas as result of putting this campaign over in other cities since original prospectus was sent out, will appreciate your forwarding me all information possible as we are having considerable difficulty here in Baltimore.

In compliance with the request, the plaintiff forwarded the desired articles and gave the requested information.

Again, in reply to the plaintiff's request, the defendant wrote to the representative of the plaintiff this letter, bearing date April 11th, 1930:

> Mr. E. L. Tignon, Duplex Envelope Co., Richmond, Va.
> Dear Mr. Tignon: Frankly, Mr. Tignon, I have been holding up the remittance on the Church Page due to our inability to get the page over in Baltimore. I understood all of our papers are having this same difficulty. I haven't given up the 'ghost,' I have had three different parties and I am still hoping we can get enough to enable us to start the feature.
> I know you are just as interested as we are in putting this feature over and I am wondering if you have any suggestions or can offer me any assistance.
> > Very truly yours,
> > The Baltimore Post,
> > J. C. Flagg, Business Manager.

Then when the plaintiff, through C. W. Page Company, its advertising agent, forwarded to the defendant the one full page of advertising which, according to the stipulations between the parties, was to be published in the newspaper of the defendant for the benefit of the plaintiff as a part of the consideration or purchase price of the service sold by the plaintiff to the defendant, the latter declined to publish the advertisement and wrote this letter of refusal:

July 31st, 1930.

C. W. Page Co., Adv., Richmond, Va.

Dear Mr. Page: I am returning herewith your order No. 11147 and copy full page in the Baltimore post, on the Duplex Envelope Co. of Richmond, Va., which we are unable to accept due to the fact that the original provision involved in this proposition has been impossible of fulfilment.

Very sincerely yours,
The Baltimore Post,
M. C. Roher, National Advertising Mgr.

The negotiations between the parties centered upon the question of the compensation to be paid by the defendant to the plaintiff. An early agreement had been reached that the original form of the contract should be altered so that the basis of calculation should be the defendant's local church contract page rate, but the plaintiff made this conditional upon a minimum compensation being named. The conclusion of the treaty between the parties on this term was reached when the plaintiff wrote its letter of August 15th, 1929, and accepted the written contract, which had been signed by the defendant, upon the understanding, expressed in writing, that the net cost to the defendant under the contract is not less than $20 per week or $1,040 for the year, after deduction of twenty-five percent. Special allowance for the Scripps-Howard papers and the cost of one full page advertisement to be used by the plaintiff. The legal effect of the plaintiff's signing of the written contract, which had been previously signed by the defendant, as modified in writing by the letter of August 15th, and sending the two back to the defendant, was a rejection of the next preceding offer of the defendant and a new offer on the part of the plaintiff which was communicated to the defendant by the receipt of the two paper writings. Williston on Contracts, §77.

When this offer was made, the matter was in treaty, and, for a contract to result, an unqualified and unequivocal acceptance of the particular offer was requisite. The defendant did not formally accept, but an acceptance may be indicated by acts as well as by words. The defendant received and kept the paper writing, which had been signed by both parties, and the letter of August 15th, which contained the changes in the terms of the paper writing.

The testimony tends to prove that the plaintiff delivered the mats and supplies to the defendant, which accepted, used, and retained them, and that the defendant actively engaged in the prosecution of an organized effort to secure the advertisements pursuant to the plan contemplated by the contract, and held back the remittance to the plaintiff because of the inability of the defendant to carry the idea to a successful issue. From these and other pregnant facts there is no doubt that there was legally sufficient evidence for the jury to find that the defendant had accepted the offer made by the plaintiff in its letter of August 15th. Equitable Endowment Ass'n. v. Fisher, 71 Md. 430, 438, 18 A. 808; Read

Drug & Chemical Co. v. Nattans, 130 Md. 465, 471, 100 A. 736. So the question of acceptance should have been submitted to the finding of a jury, and, if the jury had found an acceptance, the contract would be evidenced by the paper writing, which had been signed by both the plaintiff and defendant, and by the letter of the plaintiff to the defendant bearing date August 15th, when read as a single document. Noel Construction Co. v. Atlas Portland Cement Co., 103 Md. 209, 63 A. 384; Amer. Law Inst., Restatement of Contracts, §§235(c), 228.

Furthermore, there was evidence from which the jury could have found that, although the plaintiff was able, ready, and willing to perform, and did perform, so far as was permitted, its promises, the defendant repudiated the contract. Consequently the plaintiff was entitled to recover at least nominal damages, and there was error in granting a prayer to take the case from the jury. Whether or not the plaintiff sustained and proved substantial damages depends upon the terms of the contract as interpreted by the court.

The record does not disclose that any other newspaper in the Scripps-Howard group had made a similar contract, nor that the defendant had agreed that any or all of these newspapers would contract, so no contention could be made that the condition had been fulfilled for the allowance of the specified discount of 25 percent within the meaning of the contract. Therefore, on the proof and under the terms of the contract, the plaintiff was merely entitled to the minimum amount as prescribed by the contract. The agreement of the parties clearly fixed this minimum at $20 per week or $1,040 for the year and the cost of one full page advertisement in the newspaper of the plaintiff at the foreign rate, as published in the rate book of the Standard Rate and Data Service. These stipulations express the intention of the parties when the signed document and the letter of the plaintiff under date of August 15th are interpreted together and as a whole. Amer. Law Inst., Restatement of Contracts, §235(c). While it is true that there is a provision in the original draft of a proposed contract that stipulated for the payment for the single publication of a full page advertisement of the plaintiff in the paper of the defendant by deducting the amount of the bill from the final amount due the Duplex Envelope Company under the agreement for its services, yet the retention of this provision in the contract produces no uncertainty in meaning, because this was and remains a subsidiary term to the next succeeding paragraph, whose paramount nature and effect arises from the fact that, notwithstanding to what residue all the antecedent amounts payable to the plaintiff might, after all charges and allowances and deductions have been made, be reduced, a minimum sum was to be inserted and to be paid to the plaintiff under any circumstance. The letter of August 15th was a completion of the blank space left in the paragraph last mentioned, and simply supplied and fixed the minimum sum payable by the defendant to the plaintiff no matter what the financial result might prove to be. Amer. Law Inst., Restatement of Contracts, §236(a) (c) (e). The office of a term providing a minimum compensation is to assure this amount of compensation in any event. From its nature it must prevail, since it has effect in but one contingency, whereupon it supersedes all else.

In consequence of what has been said, the testimony offered tended to show the making of a contract between the plaintiff and the defendant, a performance by the plaintiff of that contract, and a breach of it by the defendant that had resulted in substantial damages to the plaintiff; and the instruction given by the trial court taking the case from the jury was prejudicial error.

Questions

1. What was the purpose of the court reprinting the various communications between the parties?
2. How does the court determine that an acceptance was effectuated?
3. What was the nature of the breach of contract?

Childs v. Kalgin Island Lodge

779 P.2d 310 (Alaska 1989)

Opinion

The issue in this appeal is whether the Alaska Workers' Compensation Board (Board) applied the correct legal test in deciding that Donald Childs was not an employee of Kalgin Island Lodge (Lodge) after he performed various work-related tasks for the Lodge. Childs claims that he was injured in an auto accident while employed by the Lodge. He filed a claim under the Alaska's Workers' Compensation Act (Act), but was denied coverage by the Board. It concluded that Childs had no contract of hire with the Lodge because the formal hiring process was not complete, and no contract could be implied because no emergency situation existed.

Childs appealed to the superior court, which affirmed the Board's decision. It noted that "all steps of the interview and negotiation process must be complete" before an employee/employer relationship could be formed.

I. Facts and Proceedings

In July 1986, Childs, a professional pilot, sought employment with the Lodge as a pilot and guide. In order to obtain employment, Childs contacted Charles Tulin (Tulin), who interviews and recommends pilots to be employed by the Lodge. Even though Tulin was not the owner of the business which operated the Lodge, he apparently owned certain Lodge facilities and was the co-owner of the real property, improvements and equipment used by the Lodge, including all airplanes.

The Board found that the final hiring decisions normally rested with the Lodge's corporate president and board of directors. It is unclear, however, whether Tulin also had authority, actual or apparent, to hire Childs without their prior approval. However, it is clear from the record that Tulin's recommendations to the Lodge regarding hiring were given at least great weight and would be seriously considered. The corporate president and owner of the business was Tulin's son, Don Tulin.

On or about June 30, 1986, Tulin requested that Childs come to Tulin's law office for an interview. Following the interview, Tulin asked Childs to call him after the July 4th weekend. Childs called as instructed and was invited to lunch on July 7, 1986.

Childs testified that at lunch, Tulin offered to employ him for $3,500 per month, which he accepted. Tulin testified that no such offer was made. Tulin instructed Childs to report to his office the next day. Childs did so at this time, Tulin informed the insurance agent for the Lodge, both by mail and by phone, that Childs should be added to the Lodge's insurance coverage. Tulin directed Childs to hand-carry the insurance agent's letter to the post office to insure prompt delivery and response, which Childs did.

Later that day, at Tulin's request, Childs drove to Lake Hood, where Tulin introduced Childs to various Lodge employees. While there, Childs assisted in loading a plane for a flight to the Lodge, pumped the plane's floats and filled it with 25 gallons of fuel. He then signed for the fuel on behalf of the Lodge. Childs testified that on this occasion, he was instructed to inspect the Lodge's planes and begin making a list of the repairs that needed to be completed for the upcoming winter. He further testified that he was instructed to begin setting up maintenance schedules for the Lodge's planes and programs for pilot selection and training. Later that day, Childs gassed and changed the oil on another of the Lodge's airplanes. He paid for the gas and oil with a Lodge check, given him by Tulin's wife.

Childs was informed by Tulin that he would accompany Tulin out to the Lodge on either July 10 or July 11. On July 10, Childs prepared gear and readied himself for the trip to the Lodge. He was told the trip would be the following day.

On July 11, 1986, Tulin introduced Childs to Don Tulin. Childs testified that he was instructed by both men to use Tulin's law office facilities to work on a marketing program for the Lodge. At this time, Childs made several phone calls in furtherance of marketing for the Lodge.

At about 4 P.M., Childs either volunteered or was asked by Tulin to go to a sporting goods store to pick up two fishing rods. The rods were to be bought with a personal check from Tulin. On the way to the store, while driving Tulin's car, Childs was involved in an auto accident and was injured. He filled a worker's compensation claim after submitting his Notice of Occupational Injury to Tulin.

After depositions and hearings, the Board denied Childs' claim. The Board based its decision on its conclusion that no express contract existed between the Lodge and Childs, because not all of the formal hiring process had been completed at the time of the accident. The Board further concluded that because no emergency situation existed during the time in question, Childs was not an emergency employee and therefore could not receive the benefits of the Act. One member of the Board dissented on the ground that Childs was in a "tryout" period and the Act's coverage should apply under the emergency exception.

Childs appealed to the superior court, which affirmed the Board's decision. The court concluded that the Board applied the correct law and that there was substantial evidence to support its findings of fact. Thus, because no emergency existed and no express contract was made, no relationship existed between the parties which would entitle Childs to coverage under the Act. Therefore, the superior court concluded that workers' compensation benefits were properly denied, and the Board's decision was affirmed. Childs appeals.

II.   Discussion

To determine the issue presented before this court, we need only consider whether the Board applied the proper legal test to reach its conclusions. Ostrem v. Alaska Workmen's Compensation Bd., 511 P.2d 1061, 1063 (Alaska 1973); Burgess Constr. Co. v. Smallwood, 623 P.2d 312, 317 (Alaska 1981). This court has consistently maintained that it will not vacate findings of the Board when supported by substantial evidence. However, if the Board's decision rests on an incorrect legal foundation, review is not so limited. Hewing v. Alaska Workmen's Compensation Bd., 512 P.2d 896, 898 (Alaska 1973). In such cases, independent review of the law is proper. Simon v. Alaska Wood Prods., 633 P.2d 252, 254 (Alaska 1981); M-K Rivers v. Schleifman, 599 P.2d 132, 134 (Alaska 1979).

The Act provides that an employee is a person employed by an employer, and an employer is, in part, "a person employing one or more persons in connection with a business or industry."

The Board correctly recognized that before an employee/employer relationship exists under the Act, an express or implied contract of employment must exist. Whitney-Fidalgo Seafoods, Inc. v. Beukers, 554 P.2d 250, 252 (Alaska 1976). The Board also correctly recognized that employment generally begins after a meeting of the minds has been reached between the employee and the employer, for it is at the point that a contract is formed. See 1C A. Larson, The Law of Workmen's Compensation §47.10 (1986) (hereinafter Larson). Furthermore the Board correctly noted that volunteer work, standing alone, does not necessarily establish an employee/employer relationship for the purposes of the Act.

However, in applying the above law, the Board incorrectly concluded that employee/employer relationships exist only when an express contract for hire is finalized by completion of the hiring process, or an implied contract is formed based on emergency circumstances. The superior court followed the same analysis.

Situations arise in which employee/employer relationships exists without either an express contract or an emergency situation. See, e.g., County of Los Angeles v. Workers' Compensation Appeals Bd., 30 Cal. 3d 391, 637 P.2d 681, 179 Cal. Rptr. 214 (1981). This court has never declared that express contracts are formed only after the formal hiring process is complete, nor have we adopted the view that only emergency situations may sustain implied contracts for hire. Because it is obvious that the Board failed to apply the correct legal analysis under which an employee/employer relationship can be created, we must remand the case to the Board for consideration in light of the following.

A.   Express Contract

As noted in Fjeldahl v. Homer Coop. Ass'n, 11 Alaska 112, 135 (D. Alaska 1946), "to employ" means to make use of the services of another. "To be employed in anything means not only the act of doing it, but also to be engaged to do it; to be under contract or orders to do it." Id. (citations omitted). We agree with the holding of the New Mexico Supreme Court that mere formalization of a contract for hire is not the controlling factor in determining whether an employment contract exists. Roan v. D.W. Falls, Inc., 72 N.M. 464, 384 P.2d 896, 899 (1963).

The formation of an express contract requires an offer encompassing its essential terms, an unequivocal acceptance of the terms by the offeree, consideration and an intent to be bound. Hall v. Add-Ventures, Ltd., 695 P.2d 1081, 1087 n.9 (Alaska 1985) (citing 1 W. Jaeger, Williston on Contracts §64, at 211, §72, at 235, §73, at 128 (3d ed. 1957)).

The Board failed to determine whether Tulin had authority to hire Childs. If so, the Board failed to determine whether Tulin offered Childs a pilot/guide position for $3,500 a month and whether Childs accepted Tulin's offer. The Board also failed to consider the possibility that Childs offered to work for Tulin or the Lodge at $3,500 per month, and Tulin accepted. The Board's failure to determine whether an offer and acceptance was made, regardless of whether the formal hiring process was complete, leads us to conclude that the correct express contract analysis was not considered.

B.   Implied Contract

An implied employment contract is formed by a relation resulting from "the manifestation of consent by one party to another that the other shall act on his behalf and subject to his control, and consent by the other so to act." 9 W. Jaeger, Williston on Contracts §1012, at 4–5 (3d ed. 1967) (quoting Zehr v. Wardall, 134 F.2d 805 (6th Cir. 1943)). Cf. Martens v. Metzgar, 524 P.2d 666, 672 (Alaska 1974).

The Board should make its determination whether an implied contract was formed by considering all the factors in light of the surrounding circumstances. See City of Seward, 413 P.2d at 936 n.13. This court has adopted the position that "ordinarily no single feature of the relation is determinative . . . and each case must depend upon its own facts." Id. (citing Crepps v. Indus. Comm'n, 402 Ill. 606, 85 N.E.2d 5, 9 (1949)). Furthermore, words and acts of the parties should be given such meaning as reasonable persons would give them under all the facts and circumstances present at the time in question.

There is sufficient evidence here from which it may be found that the Lodge employed Childs, even though no express contract is found. By utilizing his services and by controlling the time, manner and location of his work, the Lodge knowingly allowed Childs to act on its behalf, performing many of the job-related skills for which he was being considered. The Board erred when it failed to consider these factors and their implications under the circumstances. Thus, the correct implied contract analysis was also not considered.

C. Tryout Exception

Finally, it is apparent that the Board failed to consider the tryout exception to the general rule that a contract for hire must exist before benefits can be awarded. "Since Workmen's Compensation law is primarily interested in the question when the risks of the employment begin to operate, it is appropriate, quite apart from the strict contract situation, to hold that an injury during a tryout period is covered, when injury flows directly from employment activities or conditions." 1A Larson §26.20, at 5–299 (1985).

The California Supreme Court, in deciding a similar case, concluded that the fundamental purpose of workmen's compensation is to protect individuals from the "special risks" of employment. *Laeng*, 494 P.2d at 8–9. Therefore, when an employer exposes potential employees to risks inherent in a tryout period and the applicant is under his direction or control, and injury resulting during such a period is compensable as a matter of law. Id.

The Lodge argues that the tryout exception analysis is inappropriate to this case because Childs was on a personal errand for Tulin and the Lodge did not control the time, manner, and method of work. We cannot accept this argument. These facts were disputed at the hearing and never decided by the Board.

It is not this court's task on review to reweigh conflicting evidence or substitute its judgment for that of the Board. Whaley v. Alaska Workers' Compensation Bd., 648 P.2d 955, 957 (Alaska 1982). Nor is it within the province of this court to reweigh witness credibility and competing inferences from testimony because those functions are reserved to the Board. See Delaney v. Alaska Airlines, 693 P.2d 859, 863 (Alaska 1985). Accordingly, this court may not ascertain the facts of this case. However, it is sufficient to note, as suggested by the dissenting board member, that a tryout period may have been initiated.

III. Conclusion

The decision of the superior court is reversed and the case is remanded to the superior court with directions to remand it to the Board for further proceedings consistent with this opinion.

Questions

1. How does the court distinguish between an express and an implied contract?

2. How does the court decide whether or not an implied contract existed?

3. What is your opinion of the decision?

Suggested Case References

1. For a discussion of express and implied contracts, as well as promissory estoppel, read Tuttle v. ANR Freight System, 797 P.2d 825 (Colo. App. 1990).

2. Can a unilateral contract become a bilateral contract? Cook v. Johnson, 37 Wash. 2d 19, 221 P.2d 525 (1950).

3. To see how the federal court sitting in New York defines consideration, read Banque Arabe et Internationale D'Investissement v. Bulk Oil (USA), 726 F. Supp. 1411 (S.D.N.Y. 1989).

2 Offer

CHAPTER OVERVIEW

This chapter focuses on the creation of the contractual relationship. It describes the process and requirements of the first essential element of every valid contract: the offer. For a contract to be deemed valid, the parties to the contract must manifest to each other their mutual assent to the same bargain at the same time. A contract is the meeting of two minds for one purpose. Therefore, the law expects the parties to indicate to each other that they are of the same mind. Without this mutuality of purpose, the parties would have misplaced expectations.

This contractual process of agreement begins with the party known as the offeror, who first proposes the contractual relationship. It is the offeror's function to initiate the contract process, and to determine the boundaries of that agreement under the common law. The terms of the contract are entirely determined by the words or actions of the offeror except for contracts for the sale of goods between merchants pursuant to the provisions of the Uniform Commercial Code. See infra. It is the offeror who creates all the provisions of the contract.

In order to guarantee that there is, in fact, a meeting of the minds between the offeror and the person to whom the offer is made, the offeree, the common law requires that the offer be definite and certain in all of its relevant terms. The relevant terms are price, subject matter, parties to the contract, and the time of performance of the contractual provisions. The law will not countenance an offer that is so indefinite in its provisions that a reasonable person would be unable to recognize and understand the relevant terms of the contract.

Offer Defined

An **offer** is a proposal by one party, the **offeror**, to a second party, the **offeree**, manifesting an intention to enter into a valid contract. The offer creates a power in the offeree to establish a contract between the parties by making an appropriate acceptance.

The offeror, the one making the proposal, is the creator and the initiator of the contractual process under the common law. It is the offer itself that determines all of the relevant provisions of the contract. The terms of the offer are the terms of the contract. Once the offer has been made, the power or ability to create the contract rests with the offeree. This is the key element of all contractual relationships. The offeror proposes; the offeree disposes. Without the assent of the offeree, no contract can exist.

 EXAMPLE:

Jessica proposes to sell her car to Elizabeth so that she can use the money for a vacation. Jessica's asking price is $1200. Elizabeth, when she hears the price, thinks the price is too high, and declines. No contract exists. Elizabeth, the offeree, has refused to accept the terms of the contract that Jessica has proposed.

Not all proposals are considered to be legal offers. For instance, in the example above, if Jessica did not mention a price for the car, how could Elizabeth accept? Elizabeth would not know the terms of the contract she was accepting. Furthermore, what if Jessica simply said she would sell the car to Elizabeth for $1200, but Elizabeth was not around to hear the proposal? How could someone accept a proposition of which she was unaware?

Consequently, the common law requires that the following three conditions be met for a proposal to qualify as a contractual offer:

1. the offeror must manifest a present contractual intent;
2. the offer must be communicated to the offeree; and
3. the offer must be certain and definite with respect to its terms.

Unless these requirements are met, the proposal may exist, but it will not be considered an offer to contract. It must be noted that now contracts for the sale of goods between merchants are governed by the Uniform Commercial Code (UCC), a statute that has made significant changes to the common law for contracts that come within its purview. Therefore, throughout the text, where appropriate, these differences will be addressed.

Present Contractual Intent

The element of intent is a basic requirement of all contractual relationships. Unlike other aspects of life and law, a contract cannot be thrust upon an unsuspecting person. For the offer to have legal validity, it must appear to an objective, reasonable person that the offeror actually intended to make an offer. How is this element of intent determined? Intent is shown by taking into consideration all of the circumstances surrounding the proposal. The more serious the words and expressions used, the more likely it is that the element of intent can be demonstrated. The court will always attempt to find the most reasonable interpretation of the facts based on the circumstances presented.

 EXAMPLES:

1. Philip is showing a group of friends a valuable watch he inherited from his grandfather. While joking around about how old-fashioned the watch is, Philip laughingly offers to sell it for an inexpensive up-to-date plastic sports watch. If one of his friends attempts to accept by giving Philip a plastic watch, there would be no contract. Under these circumstances, reasonable persons would assume Philip was joking, not making a valid offer.

2. Darren, having constant trouble with his car, kicks the wheels and says out loud that for two cents he'd sell the car. John, overhearing him, gives Darren two pennies and tries to drive off with the car. There is no contract. Under the circumstances, it is unreasonable to assume that Darren intended to offer his car for sale for two cents. Words spoken in jest or frustration lack the requisite element of intent.

Communication to the Offeree

For an offer to be capable of acceptance, the offer must be communicated to the offeree. It is the offeree who has the power to create a valid contract by making the appropriate acceptance, but that acceptance can occur only if the offeree is aware of the offer.

The precise method of communication is left to the discretion of the offeror. The law supposes that the offerer will use effective means of communicating an offer to the offeree so that a contract can come into existence. Oral, written, telephonic, and mechanical means of communication are all considered legally sufficient methods of communication. The offeror is not limited to making the offer specifically to just one person. An offer can be made to a group, or class, of persons, any of whom is capable of accepting the offer.

The effect of a valid communication is to give the person to whom it was communicated the ability to accept. The method of acceptance is discussed in detail in Chapter 3, Acceptance.

 EXAMPLES:

1. Mildred leaves a message on Kate's answering machine offering to sell Kate a used Real Property textbook for $10. This offer has been validly communicated to Kate, even though the words were not spoken to her directly.

2. Upset at her grade in a Litigation course, Mildred screams out in her room that she'd sell her litigation text for $2. Walter, passing by Mildred's window, hears her scream, and tries to buy the book. There is no contract. Not only is it unlikely that Mildred intended an offer, but the proposal was not effectively communicated. Merely making a statement in the presumptive privacy and solitude of one's own room does not constitute communication of an offer.

3. In the school newspaper, Mildred inserts a notice offering to sell her used Torts book for $10. This is a valid offer that has been communicated to anyone who reads the paper.

Take careful note that although the above example illustrates a valid communication of an offer via the newspaper, not all newspaper advertisements are considered to be offers. Courts have determined that in many instances newspaper ads are merely "invitations" to the public to make an offer, or to patronize a particular establishment. The distinguishing factors between a valid offer and a mere invitation turn on intent of the advertisers and the certainty and definiteness of the terms employed. The more certain and definite the words used by the advertiser, the more likely it is that the ad will be considered an offer.

 EXAMPLE:

An advertisement to sell a particular named product at 25–50 percent below the listed price is not an offer to the public, but is an invitation to the public to negotiate for the item. Why? Because the terms of the ad are not sufficiently definite. The presumed intent of the seller is not to make an offer but to invite the public to bid for the product in a range from 25–50 percent below the listed price.

Certainty and Definiteness in the Terms of the Offer

Because the offeror creates the terms of the contract by what is expressed in the offer, the court carefully scrutinizes the terms specified in the proposal. As previously discussed, the more certain and definite the proposal, the more likely it is that the court will construe the proposal as an offer to create a valid contract.

To determine that the terms are indeed definite and certain, the law looks for the presence of four essential elements:

1. the price of the contract;
2. the subject matter of the contract;
3. the parties to the contract; and,
4. the time of performance for fulfilling the contract.

The more certain and definite these elements, the more likely it is that the proposal will be considered an offer under the common law; conversely, the more indefinite or ambiguous these terms, the less likely it is that the proposal will be considered a valid offer. Because the parties are required to demonstrate mutual assent, it would be impossible to have the assent if the parties did not know or were uncertain as to what they were agreeing.

To ascertain that these four elements exist, the court will examine all the circumstances surrounding the creation of the offer. It will consider all the statements made by the parties, all preliminary negotiations that may have existed, and any other documentation that can indicate the intent, certainty, and communications of the parties.

Essential Terms of an Offer

Contracts are a matter of private concern between the contracting parties themselves, and, unless the contract includes some aspect of life that is governmentally regulated, the law leaves the creation of the contract terms completely up to the parties.

Under the common law, when drafting the provisions of an offer, the offeror must be as specific as possible with respect to price, subject matter, parties, and timing of performance. The law requires that these terms be certain, definite, and capable of being readily understood by a reasonable person. If the offeror indicates terms that are not objectively definite but are vague and ambiguous, the offer will not be considered valid.

As a general rule, the courts will not correct vague terms mentioned in an offer in order to create a valid contract. To uphold contracts, however, and consequently the legal expectations of the parties, the court will, under certain circumstances, apply the concept of "reasonableness" with respect to a contract provision that the parties have neglected to include. On the other hand, the court will not insert "reasonable" terms if the parties themselves have attempted to specify a term but have done so badly. In sum, the court can sometimes correct omissions but can never change the terms the parties themselves have used.

How all this fits together will be analyzed in the following discussion of the four essential terms of an offer.

Price

The price stated in the contract is an example of contractual consideration. **Consideration** is the bargain of the contract; it is the benefit conferred or the detriment incurred. Both sides must give and receive something of legal value to make the contract valid. Price—that is, money—is the most typical example of consideration, but it is not the only one. For a detailed discussion of consideration, see Chapter 4, Consideration.

If the parties are intending the sale of a good or service, usually the good or service is exchanged for cash or a cash equivalent such as a check or money order. Because this forms part of the consideration, a requisite element of every valid contract (see Chapter 1), the law requires that the price be specified in the offer itself. If the parties indicate in the offer that the price will be left for future negotiations, no offer or contract exists, even if every other contractual requirement has been met. Why? Because without knowing an essential term, the parties cannot have mutual assent.

EXAMPLE:

Sam agrees to sell Hank three roasting chickens, to be delivered Friday morning, for a price to be determined at the time of delivery. There is no contract. Hank might have thought that the price would be 29 cents per pound, whereas Sam might have thought $3 per chicken was fair. There is no mutual assent to this offer despite what the parties might have thought.

Under certain circumstances, the price of a contract can be determined by a court inserting the element of reasonableness and thereby salvaging an otherwise void contractual agreement. If the parties completely neglect to mention a specific price, the court can interpret a "reasonable price," and then entertain evidence as to what the reasonable price would be. The court can only apply the reasonableness rule if the term has not been mentioned at all, or the parties state "reasonable price" themselves. On the other hand, if the parties attempt to state a price but indicate one that is vague or uncertain, as in the example given above, the court's hands are tied; the contract will fail on grounds of indefiniteness. The court cannot vary the terms the parties have stated.

Note that for contracts for the sale of goods covered by the Uniform Commercial Code exceptions to the common law rule have been carved out. For contracts for the sale of goods between commercial traders, the UCC will permit contracts to be formed even if the price is not quoted, provided that the parties have a history of past dealings and some objective standard can be used to determine a price.

The parties do not have to specify a particular dollar amount to have a definite price. If the parties refer to some objective standard by which the price can be determined, then the offer will stand. Should the parties refer to some subjective measure, the offer will fail."

 EXAMPLES:

1. After completing her paralegal program, Rosa starts looking for a job. Rosa remains unemployed for several months. Finally, the firm of Hacker & Slacker agrees to hire her. Nervously, Rosa asks what her salary is to be, and Hacker says they'll pay her what they think she's worth. There is no contract. The determination of "worth" has been left up to Hacker's subjective evaluation; therefore, the offer lacks the essential term of price.

2. In the situation above, when Rosa asks about her salary, Hacker says he'll pay her the average starting salary paid to new paralegals at mid-size law firms in their city. This is a valid offer. Hacker has specified an objective standard for determining price, and that price can be proven by analysis of salaries in the area.

Any attempt by the parties to create a situation in which one side has total discretion with respect to filling in the terms will fail because of vagueness and indefiniteness. What one person considers "fair" may be deemed unjust by the other party. Terms such as a "fair profit," "fair price," or "fair rate of interest" are too uncertain to be enforceable. "Fair" is a subjective term. The court can only interpret "reasonableness." It can not cure defects created by the specific words of the parties themselves.

Subject Matter

The subject matter of a contract is another example of the consideration for the contract. If one side is providing the price, the other side is usually providing a good or service, such as a textbook or paralegal services, which is that party's consideration for the contract.

Under strict common law principles, if the offer is to be deemed valid, the subject matter of the contract must be specifically described, not only in terms of content but in terms of quantity as well. How many textbooks of which subject are offered for sale? How many hours per week is the paralegal expected to work, and what are her functions? Any description of the subject matter that is inconclusive, vague, or ambiguous will cause the contract to fail.

Some typical problems that are encountered regarding the subject matter are discussed below.

Ambiguity.   If the subject matter is described in terms that are capable of more than one interpretation, the offer is deemed ambiguous and will not stand.

EXAMPLE:

Celeste offers to sell Bonnie her brooch for $100. Celeste has three brooches and fails to specify which brooch is meant in the offer. No contract exists. The subject matter has been ambiguously described.

As in the example given above, if the subject matter is described in words that are ambiguous, the offer will not stand. The offeror must be sufficiently descriptive in her choice of words so that any reasonable person should be able to determine the subject matter of the contract. Ambiguity destroys the certainty of the terms of the offer.

EXAMPLE:

Andy offers to sell his house in Los Angeles to Jim for $500,000. Andy has two houses in L.A., one worth $450,000, the other worth $3 million. Which house is meant? Andy may mean the less valuable house; Jim may assume the more valuable one. The offer is too ambiguous to stand.

If neither party is aware that the language is ambiguous, and both intend the same object, the court will let the offer stand because there is a meeting of the minds. Both parties intend the same object. On the other hand, if only one party is aware of the ambiguity, the court may uphold the offer based on the intention of the innocent party. In other words, the court won't let one party "pull a fast one" on the other.

EXAMPLES:

1. Aaron offers to sell his house in Chicago to Brian for $500,000. Unknown to Aaron, Aaron's uncle has died and left him a house in Chicago worth $5 million. Brian hears of the uncle's death, agrees to the offer, and then sues Aaron to have Aaron convey the more expensive property. There is no contract. Because Aaron, at the time of making the offer, did not know the term was ambiguous (he thought he only owned one house in Chicago), the court will find the offer refers to the less expensive house.

2. In the same situation described above, both Aaron and Brian intend the contract to be for the sale of the less expensive house. Because both parties intend the same subject matter, the offer is valid.

Alternate Offers. The offeror may offer to the offeree alternative subject matter. Making alternative proposals does not necessarily mean that the offer is uncertain. Provided that each alternative is certain and definite, the offeror is considered to be making two offers. Acceptance of one cancels the other.

 EXAMPLE:

Louise offers to sell Sophie her house in Maryland for $500,000, or her house in Delaware for $350,000. Assuming that Louise only owns one house in each state, the offer is definite in its terms, but gives Sophie a choice. Sophie can agree to buy either house, or neither. This constitutes a valid offer.

Note that in the example above, had either alternative been vague or ambiguous (Louise owns two houses in Delaware), there would have been only one valid offer capable of acceptance.

Output Contracts. Just as with the element of price discussed above, the offer will stand if the quantity or quality of the subject matter can be sufficiently determined by an objective standard to which the parties have agreed both under the common law and the UCC.

The calculation of Rosa's salary by reference to average salaries in the area is a case in point. Another example of this type of agreement is known as an **output** contract. In an output contract, one party agrees to purchase all of the output of the other party for a specified price. If one party agrees to purchase from a supplier all supplies actually used during a given period, this is known as a **requirements** contract. Even though the exact amount of the product that is the subject of the contract is uncertain, the parties have specified an objective standard that can be used to fill in the uncertain term.

EXAMPLES:

1. A juice manufacturer agrees to buy all of the oranges Farmer Brown grows in a given season at the price of $10 per bushel. This agreement is a valid contract because the amount of oranges can be determined by an objective standard: how many oranges are actually grown during the season.

2. Acme Inc., offers to buy all the coal it will need for its factory furnaces from Ace Mining Company for the next six months at a price of $10 per ton. This is a valid offer because the actual use of the factory furnaces can be mathematically determined.

Just as with the price discussed above, if one of the parties retains the absolute discretion to determine the standard for measuring the quantity or quality of the subject matter, the offer will fail for vagueness. The key is whether the standard used by the parties in the term of description is objective or subjective. Only an objective standard will create a valid offer.

EXAMPLE:

Bijoux Jewelers offers to buy from Beta Diamond Mines for $1000 per carat all of the diamonds Beta cuts from its mines for the next six months that Bijoux finds of an acceptable grade for its customers. The offer is invalid. Bijoux has retained the right to determine which diamonds are acceptable to its customers; it is not purchasing all of Beta's output. The standard used is subjective.

Parties

The requirement that the parties be specifically described in the offer generally refers only to the offerees. Usually the identity of the offeror is readily ascertainable because he or she is making the proposal. In rare circumstances, a particular offeror may wish her identity to be unknown in order to have a better bargaining position, and this will usually not affect the validity of the offer. If the identity of the offeror is a prime concern of the offeree, as in the example of a contract for personal services, then identity must be revealed for the offer to be deemed valid. For example, Pavarotti might wish to accept an offer to sing at the New York Metropolitan Opera, but he might not want to accept an offer to sing at the National Opera of Costa Rica. Here the identity of the offeror is of great importance.

The offer creates a power of acceptance in the offeree. Therefore it is important to determine who is capable of accepting the offer. Only the offeree may accept a valid offer, but the offeree does not have to be particularly identified in the offer, provided that his identity can be determined by an objective standard.

And, unless the offeror expressly identifies the intended offeree, any person or persons to whom the offer is communicated is an offeree. The intended offeree may be an individual or a group of persons known as a **class** and any member of the class may accept the offer.

 EXAMPLES:

1. Sid offers to buy 100 shares of Gamma, Inc., stock for $3 a share from the first shareholder who accepts. He Makes this offer to all Gamma shareholders. Gamma shareholders are the class, and the first shareholder to accept creates a valid contract.

2. Rhonda offers to sell her bicycle for $50. She makes the offer in front of three of her friends but specifies that the offer is made only to Sue. In this instance, only Sue is capable of accepting, even though several other people are aware of the offer.

Time of Performance

The fourth essential element of a valid offer is the aspect of the timing of the performance. Offers are not expected to last indefinitely, nor are contracts intended to be performed forever. Some words of limitation must be expressed by the offeror. Only in this manner can the parties know when the contract is to be fulfilled and, conversely, know when the parties have not lived up to their obligations.

Just as with a missing price term, if the parties neglect to mention time, the court will interpret "reasonable time" as the intent of the parties. On the other hand, if the parties attempt to designate a time period but do so imperfectly, the offer will fail.

 EXAMPLE:

Farmer White offers to sell five bushels of apples for $10 a bushel to Anne, time of delivery to be determined later. Anne intends to use the apples to bake pies for a church sale. The offer is not valid. Since

the delivery time may be too late for Anne's purposes, unless the
time is specified in the offer there can be no meeting of the minds.

If time is an important element for the parties—for example, in a
contract involving the sale of perishable goods or involving parties who
need the goods for a specific purpose—the element of time must be made
a specific term of the offer. Such provisions are known as **time of the
essence** clauses. They create a specific enforceable duty on the part of the
deliverer to convey the goods by the specified time or be in breach of
contract. These clauses are used in circumstances in which "reasonable
time" would be too late for one of the parties.

"Reasonable time" is one of those terms that is determined by general custom or usage, and may vary depending on the specific circumstances in a particular area, business, or transaction. The court will
consider all the surrounding circumstances to determine what is reasonable for a given situation.

 EXAMPLE:

Jim is having a house built and contracts with Richard to deliver
piping so the builder can install it. The builder can only do the work
on a specific day, and if the pipe isn't there at that time, Jim will have
to wait another two weeks to have the pipe installed. This delay will
incur additional expense for Jim. In this instance, delivery time of the
pipe would be of the essence and should be specified in the contract
as such.

Two Related Concepts

Two specific concepts must be mentioned at this point with respect
to all of the foregoing. The first deals with the **Uniform Commercial
Code**. The Uniform Commercial Code (UCC) is a model law adopted in
whole or in part by each state as a statutory enactment that, among other
things, has codified certain contractual concepts with respect to the sale
of goods. For the most part, contract law still remains an area of law
ruled by common law, but the UCC has made several significant changes
to the common law of contracts. A complete discussion of the UCC is
found in Chapter 8, but at this point one UCC provision should be noted.

If the contract is a contract for the sale of goods between merchants,
the contract must comply with the provisions of the UCC. The purpose
of the UCC is to promote commerce. To achieve this end, the UCC states
that the absence of one or more of the preceding elements of an offer will
not render the offer invalid. This exception is based on the presumption
that the merchants intend a contract and, as business professionals, are

best able to determine the essential requirements of their contracts. But remember, this exception applies only to contracts for the sale of goods between merchants, *not* for service contracts or contracts between non-merchants. (See Chapter 8.)

 EXAMPLE:

Oscar, a fabric manufacturer, agrees to sell Barbara, a clothing designer, ten bolts of fabric. No mention is made of timing of delivery or price, but Oscar has sold fabric to Barbara in the past. There is a valid contract. Because they are both merchants, and the contract is for the sale of goods, the UCC will let the offer stand. It is assumed that the parties know how to transact business, and time and price can be determined by their past business practices or other UCC provisions.

The second concept worthy of mention is that, regardless of any defect in the terms of the offer, if the parties to the agreement have performed or have started to perform, any defect can be cured by their actual actions. The parties' acts will be construed as creating the specifics of the vague term.

 EXAMPLE:

Return to the example given above involving Rosa and the law firm. If Rosa had gone to work for Hacker, even though the salary was left up to Hacker's discretion, and received a paycheck for $300 at the end of the week, the defect of the offer would have been cured by Hacker's actions. The contract would now be interpreted as providing Rosa a salary of $300 per week.

However, if the parties' performances cure one defect but leave other terms indefinite or vague, the offer will still fail.

SAMPLE OFFERS
| 1 |
For Sale

One blue 1956 Chevy convertible. Excellent condition. Only used by an elderly man to drive three blocks to church on Sundays. Price: $1200. Nonnegotiable. If interested, call Ray: 555-1234.

This simple notice for the sale of an automobile constitutes a valid offer. All of the essential terms for an offer have been met. Remember, it is the elements of an offer that are paramount, not the form that the offer takes. However, should the advertisement have requested offers or said it would sell for the best price, the notice would not be an offer, but rather would be an invitation to bid or to make an offer. The person who answered that type of ad would, in, fact, become the offeror.

2

To: William Smith
        Acme, Inc., hereby offers to sell to William Smith 500 yards of decorative copper piping at the price of $.25 per inch, to be delivered by the 15th of next month. To be effective, acceptance of this offer must be sent via certified mail by _____, 20____.

                                        Signature
                                        President, Acme, Inc.

The above example constitutes a sample offer for the sale of goods in which the offeror, Acme, Inc., has specified the means of acceptance for William Smith. As indicated above, the offeror establishes the terms of the contract, the offeree creates the contract by giving the appropriate acceptance. As will be discussed in the next chapter, the offeree must accept in the manner requested by the offeror in order to make a valid contract.

| 3 | **Offer**
|---|

_____, hereinafter Offeror, hereby agrees to sell to _____, hereinafter Offeree, the following items for the price indicated next to each item so mentioned.

(FILL IN ITEMS AND PRICES)

The above constitutes a simple form offer, once again for the sale of goods. If the contract were for the sale of services, the services would be specified in the offer where the items and prices are now. As demonstrated, the wording of an offer may be quite simple, provided that the subject matter of the contract and its price are sufficiently described. Precision of wording, as opposed to any particular words, is the key to drafting a valid offer.

CHAPTER SUMMARY

The first requirement of every valid contract is that the parties manifest to each other their mutual assent to the *same* bargain at the *same* time. The process by which this assent is manifested starts with an offer. An offer is a proposal by one party (the offeror) to the other party (the offeree) manifesting an intent to enter into a valid contract and creating a power in the offeree to create a contract between the parties by making an appropriate acceptance.

It is the offer that establishes all of the terms of the contract. Consequently, the law requires that the offer manifest a present contractual intent, that it be communicated to the offeree, and that it be certain and definite in all of its essential terms. It is only by meeting these requirements that the offeree knows what he is agreeing to, thereby creating the contract between the parties.

There are four essential elements with respect to the terms of an offer: the offer must be certain and definite with respect to the contract price, subject matter, parties, and time of performance. If the offer's terms are indefinite or ambiguous, the offer cannot create a valid contract because the offeree would be uncertain as to what she was accepting. Generally, the courts will not fix terms inaccurately stated by the offeror; however, should the offer fail completely to mention time or price, the courts usually will infer a "reasonable" time and "reasonable" price in order to uphold the contract. Any defect in the terms of the offer can be cured by the actions of the parties themselves. If they begin to perform the contract, their performance creates the certainty of the indefinite term.

Finally, when dealing with contracts for the sale of goods between merchants, the UCC has provided exceptions to the foregoing, permitting the merchants to determine the terms in their own contracts in order to further and advance commercial transactions.

SYNOPSIS

Three requirements of an offer
1. Manifestation of present contractual intent
2. Communication to offeree
3. Certainty and definiteness as to terms

Four required terms
1. Price
2. Subject matter
3. Parties
4. Time of performance

UCC exception: Sale of goods between merchants

Key Terms

Class: group of persons identified as a group rather than as named individuals

Consideration: the bargain of the contract; a benefit conferred or a detriment incurred

Offer: proposition made by one party to another manifesting a present intention to enter into a valid contract and creating a power in the other person to create a valid contract by making an appropriate acceptance

Offeree: the person to whom an offer is made; the one who has the power to create a valid contract by making an appropriate acceptance

Offeror: the person who initiates a contract by proposing the offer

Output contract: an agreement whereby one person agrees to buy or sell the goods produced by the other party

Requirements contract: agreement whereby one person agrees to buy all his supplies during a given period from one supplier

Time of the essence clause: contractual clause in which a specified time for performance is made a key element of the contract

Uniform Commercial Code: statutory enactment codifying certain areas of contract law, specifically with respect to sales contracts between merchants

EXERCISES

1.   Take an advertisement from your local newspaper and argue that it is an offer.
2.   Using the same ad as above, argue that it is an invitation to bid.
3.   What is your opinion of the UCC exceptions to general contract law?
4.   Write an offer to sell a piece of your own personal property.
5.   Draft an offer that is capable of being accepted by a specified class.

Cases for Analysis

The following case, Alligood v. Procter & Gamble Co., discusses a catalog ad as an offer or bid to offer. In Rogus v. Lords, the Arizona Court discusses membership in a professional association as creating a contractual relationship.

Alligood v. Procter & Gamble Co.
72 Ohio App. 3d 309 (1991)

On May 1, 1989, two groups of plaintiffs filed separate complaints against defendant-appellee, the Procter & Gamble Company ("P & G"), alleging breach of contract arising from a catalog promotion advertised on boxes of Pampers diapers. The plaintiffs-appellants sought class-action certification and representation, which was granted on June 27, 1989.

On June 16 and June 29, 1989, P & G filed motions to dismiss, requesting that they be treated as motions for summary judgment. Following oral argument, the court of common pleas granted summary judgment to P & G on October 30, 1989.

P & G began the Pampers catalog promotional offer in 1981. A statement on each box of Pampers explained that by saving the teddy bear proof-of-purchase symbols on packages of Pampers diapers, a customer could order various baby items from the Pampers Softouches Baby Catalog at a reduced cost. The catalog would be sent free to consumers upon request.

Included in the catalog were pictures of the items for sale and the designated amount of teddy bear symbols and cash necessary for purchase. All sale terms, including the dates during which the offer was in effect, were described in each catalog. The only method for ordering merchandise was the use of the specific order form included in each catalog.

Around April 1989, P & G sent out its final catalog. On the front of the catalog was a statement that it was the final catalog and that the offer would expire on February 28, 1990.

The plaintiffs had cut out and saved the teddy bear symbols. The plaintiffs claim that each package of Pampers contained an offer to enter into a unilateral contract which they accepted by purchasing Pampers and saving the teddy bear proof-of-purchase symbols. The plaintiffs specifically argue that their claim arises solely from the language on the Pampers packages and has nothing to do with any of the language and terms contained within the catalog.

In their single assignment of error, the plaintiffs allege that the trial court erred by finding that no valid contract existed between the plaintiffs and P & G and by granting summary judgment to P & G. We find the assignment to be without merit and affirm the judgment of the trial court.

The precise language of the advertisement printed on packages of Pampers states as follows:

> Save these Teddy Bears points and use them to save money on toys, clothes, furniture, and lots of other baby things when you shop the Pampers Baby Catalog. For your free copy of the Catalog, send your name, complete address and youngest baby's date of birth to:
>
> Pampers Baby Catalog
> P.O. Box 8634,
> Clinton, Iowa 52736.

It is basic contract law that to have an enforceable contract, there must be a meeting of the minds of the parties to the contract. Noroski v. Fallet (1982), 2 Ohio St.3d 77, 442 N.E.2d 1302. A valid contract must also be specific as to its essential terms, such as the identity of the parties to be bound, the subject matter of the contract, consideration, a quantity term, and a price term. See Mr. Mark Corp. v. Rush, Inc. (1983), 11 Ohio

App. 3d 167, 464 N.E.2d 586; 18 Ohio Jurisprudence 3d (1980), Contracts, Sections 17 and 140. If it can be determined that the parties intend to be bound, a court may fashion less essential terms that were omitted, in order to reach a fair and just result. Litsinger Sign Co. v. American Sign Co. (1967), 11 Ohio St.2d 1, 227 N.E.2d 609.

However, the Ohio Supreme Court has stated that: "It is settled law that if the parties' manifestations taken together as making up the contract, when reasonably interpreted in the light of all the circumstances, do not enable the court to determine what the agreement is and to enforce it without, in effect, 'making a contract for the parties,' no enforceable obligation results." Id. at 14, 227 N.E.2d at 619.

Clearly, this is the situation before us. The language printed on the boxes of Pampers, which the plaintiffs insist makes up the complete contract with P & G, is sorely lacking in all the requirements necessary to create a valid contract. Only one of the parties, P & G, can be identified. The subject matter of the alleged contract, as well as the consideration required of the offeree, is too vague to be discernible. The advertisement states no price term or quantity term. As one Ohio court has stated, "a contract indefinite at the time of its making is not binding." Preston v. First Bank of Marietta (1983), 16 Ohio App. 3d 4, 473 N.E.2d 1210. Without question, the advertisement at issue does not rise to the level of a legally enforceable contract.

Even if we considered the advertisement in conjunction with the Pampers catalog, which the plaintiffs have specifically asked us not to do, and even if the expiration date in the catalog had not passed, the advertisement and the catalog taken together would not constitute an offer to enter into a contract. They create only an offer to receive offers, an invitation to order from the catalog. Erlich v. Willis Music Co. (1952), 93 Ohio App. 246, 51 113 N.E.2d 252; Craft v. Elder & Johnston Co. (1941), 34 Ohio Law Abs. 603, 38 N.E.2d 416. As such, no legal obligations are created for which P & G can be held responsible.

Upon review of a summary judgment, the evidence must be construed in favor of the nonmoving party and when the evidence is so viewed, if reasonable minds can come only to one conclusion against the nonmoving party, summary judgment was properly granted. Hounshell v. American States Insurance Co. (1981), 67 Ohio St.2d 427, 424 N.E.2d 311; Temple v. Wean United, Inc. (1977), 50 Ohio St.2d 317, 364 N.E.2d 267. In the case before us, we hold that in viewing all the evidence in the plaintiffs' favor, reasonable minds must conclude in favor of P & G and that P & G is entitled to judgment as a matter of law. The decision of the trial court is, therefore, affirmed.

Judgment affirmed.

Questions

1. How does the court determine that there was a meeting of the minds?
2. What is your opinion of this case?

Rogus v. Lords
804 P.2d 133 (Ariz. App. 1991)

The sole issue we address in this appeal is whether appellants presented sufficient evidence of a contractual relationship between themselves and appellees arising out of their mutual membership on a board of realtors that would entitle appellants to damages against appellees for breach of v contract.

Facts

We review the facts in the light most favorable to sustaining the judgment. Klensin v. City of Tucson, 10 Ariz. App. 399, 401, 459 P.2d 316, 318 (1969).

At all relevant times, all of the parties were licensed real estate salespersons or brokers, and all were members of the Mesa-Chandler-Tempe Board of Realtors. In 1985, appellee David Lords solicited offers to purchase a certain parcel of real property from another real estate broker, appellant Sylvia Waters. Although Lords did not have a written listing agreement, he did have a verbal listing agreement from the owners. Waters later obtained a written offer from Walter Bush to purchase the property. The offer contained Bush's name, address, and phone number, and provided for payment of a real estate commission in the amount of six percent, one-half of which was to be paid to appellants and one-half to appellees.

Waters gave the written offer to Lords, who submitted it to the owners. The owners then contacted Bush directly and negotiated a sale of the property to Bush on terms virtually identical to those contained in the original offer, except that the commission provision had been deleted.

No real estate commission was ever paid in connection with the sale of the property to Bush. Appellants brought this action against appellees, seeking to recover approximately $66,000.00—the commission they would have received based on Bush's original offer to purchase the property. The case was tried to the court. After appellants rested their case, the trial court granted appellees' motion to dismiss. This appeal followed.

Discussion

Appellants' primary contention on appeal is that the parties' mutual membership in the Mesa-Chandler-Tempe Board of Realtors (Board) gave rise to a contractual relationship that would entitle appellants to bring a claim for breach of contract. In support of this contention, appellants rely on Savoca Masonry Co. v. Homes & Son Constr. Co., 112 Ariz. 392, 542 P.2d 817 (1975), which involved an action by one masonry company against another for the latter's breach of contract established by the by-laws of the Arizona Masonry Association. The Savoca court stated:

Unquestionably the bylaws of a voluntary, unincorporated association constitute a contract between the association and its members and the rights and duties of the members as between themselves and in their relation to the association in all matters affecting its internal government and the management of its affairs are measured by the terms of such bylaws.

Id. at 395, 542 P.2d at 820. See also Rowland v. Union Hills Country Club, 157 Ariz. 301, 304, 757 P.2d 105, 108 (App. 1988) (articles of incorporation and bylaws of voluntary association constitute a contract between members and the organization, and among the members themselves); Aspell v. American Contract Bridge League, 122 Ariz. 399, 402, 595 P.2d 191, 193 (App. 1979).

In this case, however, neither the bylaws, constitution, nor any rules or regulations of the Board were submitted as evidence to the trial court. Rather, appellants introduced only the National Association of Realtors' Code of Ethics and the Standards of Practice Relating to Articles of the Code of Ethics (Code of Ethics) as proof of the terms of the alleged contract. Consequently, we focus our inquiry on whether the terms of this document created a contractual relationship between the parties based on which appellants could maintain an action against appellees for their breach thereof.

For an enforceable contract to exist, there must be an offer, an acceptance, consideration, and sufficient specification of terms so that the obligations involved can be ascertained. K-Line Builders, Inc. v. First Fed. Sav. & Loan Ass'n, 139 Ariz. 209, 212, 677 P.2d 1317, 1320 (App. 1983), citing *Savoca*, 112 Ariz. at 394, 542 P.2d at 819. The requirement of certainty is relevant to the ultimate element of contract formation, i.e., whether the parties manifested assent or intent to be bound. Schade v. Diethrich, 158 Ariz. 1, 9, 760 P.2d 1050, 1058 (1988). See generally 6 Am. Jur. 2d Associations and Clubs §20 (1963) (whether the bylaws or other rules of an organization form a contract between the members themselves depends on the intention of the parties).

A California court has held that the bylaws of a plumbing association did not constitute a contract between its members so that one member could maintain an action against another for failure to abide by the bylaws. Scott v. Lee, 208 Cal. App. 2d 12, 24 Cal. Rptr. 824 (1962). The Scott court stated:

It is doubtless true that parties may, as among themselves, assume a contractual obligation to comply with the bylaws and rules of a voluntary association. Whether the by-laws themselves constitute such an agreement turns on whether the elements of a contract are present.

24 Cal. Rptr. at 826. Noting that mutual consent is an essential element of a contract, the court found that the bylaws on their face negated assent to contractual obligations:

It is much more closely related to a fraternal oath than to the business agreement. The pledge is "on my sacred word and honor," and "on my honor as a man," phrases which, cynically or not, have come to be construed as expressing "moral obligation" as distinguished from business agreement.

Id.

Similarly, in our opinion, the Code of Ethics of the Board was intended by the realtor members to constitute a noncontractual pledge of moral conduct rather than a contract that would give rise to enforceable rights between the members. The preamble to the Code of Ethics provides, in part:

> Under all is the land. Upon its wise utilization and widely allocated ownership depend the survival and growth of free institutions and of our civilization. . . .

The REALTOR, therefore, is zealous to maintain and improve the standards of his calling and shares with his fellow REALTORS a common responsibility for its integrity and honor. The term REALTOR has come to connote competency, fairness, and high integrity resulting from adherence to a lofty ideal of moral conduct in business relations.

The preamble further sets forth the "Golden Rule" as a guide in interpreting the obligations set forth therein: "Whatsoever ye would that men should do to you, do ye even so to them." In our opinion, these provisions clearly are evidence of the Board members' intent to impose a moral, not a contractual, obligation upon themselves with respect to their relations with the public and each other. See generally *Scott*, supra.

Moreover, in order to be binding, an agreement must be definite and certain so that the liability of the parties may be exactly fixed. Pyeatte v. Pyeatte, 135 Ariz. 346, 350-351, 661 P.2d, 200-201 (App. 1982) (essential terms and requirements of agreement not sufficiently definite so that obligations of the parties could be determined). Not only are the obligations set forth in the Code of Ethics generally aspirational in nature, there simply are no terms providing for specific enforcement of any ethical violations by an individual member against another member, nor are there any terms relating to financial obligations assumed by the members. We believe that the lack of specificity in the terms of the Code of Ethics is evidence of the parties' intent not to be contractually bound thereby.

We hold that the Code of Ethics did not constitute a contract between the parties that would enable appellants to bring an action for damages against appellees. Because the Code of Ethics was the only evidence presented to establish a contractual relationship between the parties, the trial court properly granted appellees' motion to dismiss.

Attorneys' Fees

Appellants also argue that the trial court abused its discretion in awarding appellees their attorneys' fees and costs pursuant to A.R.S. §12-341.01. An award of attorneys' fees and costs under §12-341.01 is left to the sound discretion of the trial court and will not be reversed on appeal absent an abuse of discretion. Wheel Estate Corp. v. Webb, 139 Ariz. 506, 508, 679 P.2d 529, 531 (App. 1983).

Initially, we note that appellants make an oblique argument that, because the trial court held that no contract existed between the parties, this was not a case "arising out of contract" under §12-341.01. However, a prevailing party is entitled to its fees under §12-341.01 when sued on a contract even if the judgment is based on the absence of any contract. Lacer v. Navajo County, 141 Ariz. 392, 394, 687 P.2d 400, 402 (App. 1984).

Appellants also argue that the award was erroneous because appellees did not establish a "just defense." Section 12-341.01(B) provides:

> The award of reasonable attorney's fees awarded pursuant to subsection A should be made to mitigate the burden of the expense of litigation to establish a just claim or a just defense. . . .

Appellants contend that, even if no contract existed between the parties, appellees violated not only the Code of Ethics but also certain Arizona statutes, and therefore appellees came to the court with "dirty hands." However, appellees clearly established a "just defense" to appellants' claim of breach of contract: the trial court found that no contractual obligations existed between appellants and appellees. The claim that Lords acted unethically was presented to the trial court, and we find it within the court's discretion to reject that claim.

Conclusion

The judgment of the trial court is affirmed. We grant appellees' request for attorneys' fees on appeal pursuant to A.R.S. 12-341.01, upon compliance with Rule 21(c), Arizona Rules of Civil Appellate Procedure.

Questions

1.   The Court states that membership in a voluntary organization creates a contract between the members. Discuss the merits of this legal conclusion.

2.   What factors does the court use to ascertain that the valid elements of a contract exist?

3.   Do you agree with the court's conclusion? Why or why not?

Suggested Case References

1.   In a newspaper advertisement, a department store advertised mink coats for sale for $150. The ad is a misprint; the store meant to say $1500. A customer came into the store and agreed to buy the coat for $150. Is there a valid offer and acceptance? Read the Georgia court's opinion in Georgian Co. v. Bloom, 27 Ga. App. 468 (1921).

2. A judicial interpretation of the concept of good faith in making a valid offer is discussed by the court in Phoenix Mut. Life Ins. Co. v. Shady Grove Plaza, Ltd., 734 F. Supp. 1181 (D. Md. 1990).

3. For an analysis of the terms necessary to create a valid offer read Patton v. Mid-Continent Systems, 841 F.2d 742 (7th Cir. 1988).

3 Acceptance

CHAPTER OVERVIEW

As discussed in the preceding chapter, the offeror creates a power in the offeree to establish a valid contract by giving the appropriate acceptance. The acceptance is the second major component of every valid contract, and the offer and acceptance together are what constitute the mutual assent.

This chapter discusses the actual formation of the contract when the offeree gives the appropriate assent. To be valid under the common law the acceptance must correspond exactly to the terms established by the offeror in the offer; any variance in these terms may prevent the creation of a contract between the parties. For contracts covered by the Uniform Commercial Code different legal rules apply.

The manner of the acceptance is dependent on the nature of the contract contemplated: bilateral or unilateral. For bilateral contracts, the offeree must manifest a promise to perform; for unilateral contracts, the offeree must actually perform the requested act.

However, the offeree cannot wait indefinitely to accept or reject the offer. Each offer must be either accepted or rejected in a reasonable time or before circumstances make fulfillment of the contract unlikely or impossible. Unless the offeror has accepted something of value to keep the offer open, the offeror may terminate the offeree's power of acceptance by revoking the offer.

Acceptance Defined

The law is concerned with relationships between persons, and the threshold question in analyzing every legal problem is to determine the exact legal relationship between the parties. Therefore, if a party is attempting to assert a contractual claim, one must be certain that a contract does in fact exist. By giving an appropriate acceptance, the offeree not only creates the contract, but also establishes the moment at which the parties to the contract have enforceable rights and obligations, provided all other elements of a valid contract exist. This element of the acceptance cannot be stressed too strongly; it determines whether the parties have a contract claim against each other, or whether the injured party must seek remedies under a different legal concept.

What is an **acceptance**? Legally defined, acceptance is the manifestation of assent in the manner requested or authorized by the offeror. In making the offer, the offeror may specify exactly how he or she wishes to receive a response. Acceptance requires the offeree to make some affirmative gesture, either by words or actions, depending on the nature of the prospective contract. For the acceptance to be valid, the acceptance must be both unequivocal and unqualified. In other words, the offeree must respond to the *exact* terms stated by the offeror.

Varying the Terms of the Offer

The typical method used to accept an offer is to restate the exact words of the offer or merely to say "I accept." Any change in the terms of the offer or any conditioning of the acceptance on another event ("I accept, provided that I have enough money by the date of the sale") will be interpreted as a counteroffer (or **cross-offer**). A **counteroffer** is a response by an offeree that so significantly changes the terms of the original offer that the roles of the parties are reversed; the offeree becomes the offeror of the new terms. A counteroffer, in effect, rejects the original offer and terminates the original offeree's power of acceptance. A new power of acceptance is created in the original offeror to agree to the terms of the offeree's counteroffer.

 EXAMPLES:

1. Peter offers to sell Rob his home in downtown Los Angeles for $350,000, and Rob attempts to accept by saying "I agree to buy your home in Los Angeles for $325,000." Rob has not accepted the original offer but has made his own offer for the house at a lower price.

2. In the situation above, if Rob says to the homeowner, "I will think about your offer, but do you think you might be willing to accept less than $350,000," Rob has not made a counteroffer but has merely inquired as to whether the offeror would consider changing the terms while still keeping the original offer open.

3. In the same situation, if Rob had responded by saying "I accept your offer to sell me your house in Los Angeles for $350,000, provided that you have a title sufficient to transfer to me a good title to the property," once again this is not deemed to be a counteroffer because having title sufficient to transfer the property is an implicit condition of the homeowner's ability to make the offer.

What can be gleaned from the foregoing? *First,* to be valid, the acceptance must parrot exactly the terms of the offer. This is known as the **mirror image rule.** *Second,* any variance in the terms of the offer creates a counteroffer, which rejects and therefore terminates the original offer. On the other hand, a mere inquiry, couched in terms of a hypothetical proposal, does not create a counteroffer. *Third,* if the variance is merely a term that is implicit in the original offer, that variance will not constitute a cross-offer.

An exception is made under the Uniform Commercial Code for contracts for the sale of goods between merchants. Because the purpose of the UCC is to promote commerce, the Code permits merchants to vary the terms of the offer in their response without falling into the category of counteroffer. Under the UCC, if the merchant offeror wishes to have the offer accepted exactly as stated, he or she must state that it is an "iron clad offer, take it or leave it." Under these circumstances the common law rules apply. Absent such a restriction on the part of the offeror, the offeree may vary the terms and that variance will form a part of the contract unless its provisions materially change the offer. If the offeror does not wish to have the new terms made part of the contract, he or she must object within ten days. What constitutes a "material" alteration is determined on a case-by-case basis. The terms that appear in the last communication between the merchant traders become the contractual provisions. The situation is sometimes referred to as the battle of the forms. (See infra.) For a complete discussion of the UCC provisions, see Chapter 8.

Although the preceding section involved bilateral contracts (a promise for a promise), the same rules apply to unilateral contracts. If the offeree attempts a performance that varies from the requested act, no contract is formed.

EXAMPLE:

Jack offers Jill $2 if she will bring him a cup of coffee. Jill brings tea. Jill has not accepted this unilateral offer.

Silence as Acceptance

If making changes in the terms of the offer constitutes a counteroffer, (except under the UCC, as noted above) what is the effect of silence on the part of the offeree? The basic rule is that silence is not an acceptance, even if the offeror says that silence will constitute acceptance.

 EXAMPLE:

Jeff writes to Brittany offering to sell his used answering machine for $30. In the letter, Jeff says that if he does not hear from Brittany to the contrary within two weeks, he will send the machine. Jeff cannot assume acceptance by Brittany's silence. As the recipient of an offer, Brittany has the right to speak but not the obligation.

However, silence may constitute an acceptance in two situations:

1. if the offer was solicited by the offeree; or
2. the contract is implied in fact (Chapter 1).

Also note that under the UCC a merchant trader may accept simply by shipping the goods ordered. No actual words of acceptance are required.

 EXAMPLES:

1. Imogene admires Jane's antique ring and says, "Will you offer to sell me that ring for $100?" In this example, the offeree has asked Jane to make her an offer she couldn't refuse. Response becomes superfluous, and the contract is created. This is an example of a solicited offer.

2. Sal goes into the grocery store to buy a can of peas. He places the can on the counter, and the clerk rings up the sale. No words were spoken by either party, but their actions created an offer and acceptance. The contract is implied in fact.

Who May Accept

While at first glance it may appear that only the person to whom the offer is made, the offeree, may accept the offer, this is not always the case. The offer need not specifically identify an individual as the offeree. It may refer just as easily to a class or group of persons, any of whom is capable of accepting the offer. The most typical example of this type of offer is a catalog sale. The "person" who is capable of accepting is anyone who is cognizant of the catalog, subject to any limitations the offeror might have made (for example, offer available only to the first 100 customers).

EXAMPLE:

Howard sees a J. Crew catalog on the lobby floor of his apartment building. He looks through the catalog and decides to order a shirt. Even though the catalog was addressed to Howard's neighbor, Howard is capable of accepting because J. Crew is making an offer to anyone who sees the catalog, not only to the specified addressee.

There are two exceptions to this rule. The first exception relates to options. An **option** is a situation in which, for consideration, an offeror agrees to hold the offer open exclusively for the option holder, or his transferee, for a specified period of time.

EXAMPLE:

Rashid wants to buy Clio's house and gives her $1000 as a binder for one month. During this time period, Clio is prohibited from selling her house to any other person. However, Rashid, as the option holder, can transfer his right to purchase to someone else. The option only binds the person who has received the tangible consideration.

The second exception to the general rule that only the person to whom the offer is made may accept the offer is the case of the **undisclosed principal**.

To understand the undisclosed principal, first you must understand the **principal-agent** relationship. Briefly, an *agent* is one who acts for and in the place of another, known as the *principal*, in order to enter into contracts with third persons on the principal's behalf. The consequence of these contracts is to bind the principal to the third person. The agent is merely the conduit for the negotiation and completion of the contract. Consequently, when a third person makes an offer to an agent, it is in fact the principal who has the power to accept. Even when an agent does not disclose to the offeror who the principal is, it is still only the principal who has the ability to create the contract.

 EXAMPLE:

A famous actress wants to buy a Van Dyke painting; however, she knows that the price will go up if the current owner finds out that she is the buyer. She has her sister Lee go to the owner as her agent to negotiate the sale. Lee tells the owner she represents someone who doesn't want her identity known. When the owner makes an offer to Lee as the agent, the actress is actually the purchaser. Only the actress has the power to accept the offer.

Method of Acceptance

The appropriate method of acceptance depends on the type of contract contemplated: bilateral or unilateral. As stated in Chapter 1, a **bilateral** contract exchanges a promise for a promise, and a **unilateral** contract exchanges a promise for an act. To accept a bilateral contract, the offeree must make the promise requested. In contrast, the only way that a unilateral contract can be accepted is by performing the act requested.

The preceding idea may seem quite simple, yet it is extremely important because it is the acceptance that creates the contract. All contract rights and obligations flow from and are dependent on the existence of a valid contract. Consequently, the timing of the acceptance is crucial to the determination of the rights of the parties.

Acceptance of a Bilateral Contract

Whenever the offeree gives the promise requested, the bilateral contract comes into existence (assuming all other contractual requirements are met). As long as the offeree outwardly manifests an intent to accept the offer, the contract is formed, regardless of the offeree's subjective intent. Even if the offeree is not serious in her intent, as long as her outward appearance gives no indication to a reasonable person that she does not intend to accept, she will be bound by the contract. If all the circumstances lead the offeror to reasonably believe that the offeree was manifesting contractual intent, then the offeror's expectation that a contract exists is usually given full weight. Of course, the "reasonableness" of the situation is crucial to this determination and can only be ascertained by particular facts in a given circumstance.

Not only may a bilateral offer be accepted by giving the requested promise, it may also be accepted impliedly by *doing* the act promised. Action, as well as words, may be used to create a binding contract. See the above reference to the tax UCC.

 EXAMPLE:

A customer sends an order for buying goods. The seller may respond either by promising to sell the goods at the offered price or by shipping the goods, thereby implying his promise by fulfilling his obligation. In either instance, it is a bilateral contract that is formed.

To give the appropriate acceptance, the offeree must be conversant with all of the terms of the offer. The offeree's incomplete knowledge of the terms of the offer would preclude his ability to give a valid acceptance. How can one accept what he doesn't know? There would be no mutual assent in this situation.

As indicated above, the timing of this manifestation of assent is imperative in determining whether a contract has come into existence. Obviously, if the offer and acceptance are made verbally by each party to the other, there would be no question whether the contract was formed; the parties were face to face at that moment. However, what if another method of communication is used? How are the parties to know at what precise moment in time the contract was created?

Mailbox Rule

Back in the days before the telephone, telegram, and fax machines, the postal service was the typical method of communication used by persons living some distance from each other. From those times a rule was formulated to help determine the moment of the creation of a contract. The **mailbox rule** states that the acceptance of an offer of a bilateral contract is effective when properly dispatched by an authorized means of communication. The moment the acceptance is dropped in the mailbox, the contract is formed.

The mailbox rule requires that the letter be "properly dispatched" and that the means of communication be "authorized." If the letter is incorrectly addressed or does not contain sufficient postage, it would not be "properly dispatched." Also, if the offeror specifies an answer by letter only, an attempt to answer by telegram would not be an authorized means of communication. In these instances, the acceptance would only be effective when actually received by the offeror, and only if he agreed to the variance.

EXAMPLE:

On Monday Janet offers to sell Brenda her Ming vase for $10,000, provided that Brenda accepts in writing by Friday. At 11:00 on Friday morning, Brenda mails a letter to Janet accepting her offer. On Saturday, Janet agrees to sell the vase to someone else. Does Brenda have a contract with Janet? Can Brenda force Janet to convey the vase to her? The answer to both questions is yes. Even though Brenda's letter doesn't reach Janet until Monday, because she dispatched the acceptance on Friday according to the terms of the offer a contract was formed.

There is an exception to the mailbox rule for option contracts. Acceptance of an option is only effective on receipt. This exception exists because of the nature of an option—a contract to limit the offeror's ability to sell the item to someone else, even though the offeree has not yet accepted the sale itself. Because of the limiting nature of the option, the offeror must actually receive the acceptance to be bound.

Rejection of a Bilateral Contract

If a person is not interested in accepting a specific offer, the offeree has the ability to reject. Be aware, however, that the offeree's rejection terminates the offeree's ability to accept, thus ending that particular offer.

EXAMPLE:

Jaime offers to sell his used Contracts book to Mitch for $10. Mitch thinks he can get a better price at the bookstore and turns Jaime down. Later, realizing that Jaime's offer was a bargain, Mitch attempts to accept. He cannot. Once rejected, the offer cannot be revived. Mitch's attempted acceptance to Jaime constitutes a counteroffer.

The general rule with respect to the rejection of bilateral contracts is that rejection is effective only when actually received. The offeror does not actually have to have read the rejection for it to be effective. Only receipt is required.

Rejection and the Mailbox Rule

Historically, the mailbox rule and the rule of rejection under contract law have created certain conflicting situations.

EXAMPLE:

In the example posited above with Brenda, Janet, and the Ming vase, what if Brenda decides that she really didn't need a Ming vase? On Friday morning at 9:00 she writes to Janet rejecting her offer. However, at 10:00 A.M. her neighbor mentions to Brenda that he is in the market for a Ming vase and will pay $15,000 for one. Immediately Brenda writes to Janet accepting the offer, mailing the acceptance at 11:00 A.M. The rejection arrives at Janet's on Monday morning; Monday afternoon she sells the vase. Tuesday morning Brenda's acceptance arrives. Does Brenda have a contract right against Janet?

Under the historical interpretation, Janet would be in breach of contract because the contract was formed on Friday at 11:00 A.M. when Brenda dispatched the acceptance. The rejection is effective only on receipt—Monday—so clearly the acceptance occurred first. Therefore, Janet and Brenda have a contract, which Janet breached by selling the vase on Monday afternoon.

Under modern standards, however, this solution would not be fair to Janet. Consequently, the modern approach to the problem is to determine the reasonable expectations of the offeror. In this situation, it is reasonable that Janet would have assumed that Brenda rejected her offer, and so the rejection would take precedence over the mailbox rule.

What if Janet still had the vase on Tuesday, not having agreed to sell it to anyone else. Would Brenda then have a contract with Janet? Probably, because Janet had not changed her position in reliance on Brenda's rejection.

Acceptance of a Unilateral Contract

Unlike bilateral contracts, where the contract is formed before either side has performed any of the promised acts, a unilateral contract may only be accepted by the offeree by actually performing the act requested. Only when the requested act has been performed is the contract accepted.

EXAMPLES:

1. Hilary promises to pay Lorraine $75 if Lorraine types Hillary's term paper this afternoon. If Lorraine does not do the typing, Hillary

has no legal recourse. She requested an act, not a promise, and until the act is performed no contract exists.

2. Jeanne's mother promises to give Jeanne $1000 if Jeanne quits smoking for two years. Until Jeanne completes two smoke-free years, no enforceable contract exists.

Usually, the law imposes no duty on the offeree to notify the offeror that the act has been performed. However, there are three exceptions to this general rule with respect to notification.

1.   The offeree must notify the offeror if the offeror has requested such notification as part of the offer.
2.   The offeree must notify the offeror of the performance if the offeror would have no other way of knowing that the act has been performed.

 EXAMPLE:

Sara, who lives in Illinois, offers Frank $1500 to paint her summer house in Vermont. If she weren't told that the house had been painted, she wouldn't know the contracted had been accepted.

3.   The offeree must notify the offeror in a reverse unilateral contract. In a **reverse unilateral contract** the performer makes the offer rather than the promisor.

 EXAMPLE:

Eric says to Jeff, "I will paint your house if you promise to pay me $1500." The offer proposes that an act be exchanged for a promise, and the offeree must accept by giving the promise (the giving of the promise constitutes the "notice"). This is an unusual situation, but it is interesting to note.

Because unilateral contract offers are only accepted by performance of the act, they are much easier to analyze than bilateral contract offers. One must merely pinpoint the moment at which the act was completed to determine the moment the contract is formed.

Termination of the Ability to Accept

The ability of the offeree to accept the offer exists only for as long as the offer remains open. The law does not anticipate that offerors will keep their offers open indefinitely. Therefore, either by an act of the parties or by operation of law, every offer will have a finite period during which it is capable of acceptance. After that period, the offer is viewed as terminated, and any attempt on the part of the offeree to accept constitutes a counteroffer. A terminated offer cannot be revived unless *both* parties agree to the revival.

To terminate an offer by an act of the parties, either the offeree must reject the proposal or the offeror must **revoke** the offer. An offeror may revoke an offer anytime prior to acceptance by the offeree. Once the offeree has accepted, a contract is formed, and any attempt by the offeror to revoke could be construed as a breach of his contractual obligations (see Chapter 10).

Revocation of Bilateral Contracts

For bilateral contracts, the offeror may revoke any time prior to the offeree giving her promise, the acceptance. However, there are four situations in which the offeror may not revoke an offer prior to acceptance by the offeree.

First, an offeror may not revoke an offer prior to acceptance in the case of an option contract. As discussed previously, one of the peculiar elements of an option is the obligation of the offeror to keep the offer open for a specified period of time. Because the offeror has received consideration for this promise, he is automatically bound to fulfill it.

Second, an offeror may not revoke an offer prior to acceptance if the offeree has detrimentally relied on the offer, even though he has not yet accepted.

 EXAMPLE:

Lil offers to sell her house to Isobel, and gives her two weeks in which to accept. During this time Isobel receives an offer for her own house, and sells it based on Lil's offer. If Lil were to revoke her offer within this two week period, Isobel would be homeless, and consequently, the court would not permit Lil to revoke.

Third, an offeror may not revoke an offer prior to acceptance in an auction without reverse. An **auction without reserve** is a situation in which the property owner agrees to auction her property and specifically to accept as selling price whatever is the highest bid. Because of the specific promise on the part of the property owner and the expectations of the auction dealer and the bidders, the parties are precluded from revoking. Note that this is not the case if the property is put up at an **auction with reserve**, which gives the parties the right to revoke at any time before the gavel finally comes down.

Fourth, under the UCC a merchant offeror may not revoke a **firm offer** for a period of 90 days, even if such offer is not supported by consideration.

Revocation of Unilateral Contracts

The general rule true for bilateral contracts—that the offeror has the power to revoke an offer any time prior to acceptance by the offeree—is just as true for unilateral contracts. However, the time element is different with a unilateral contract because an act must be completed rather than a promise given. Only when the offeree completes the act is the offer considered accepted and a contract created.

 EXAMPLE:

On Monday, Steven offers to pay Cal $2000 if Cal will paint his house on Friday. Steven is to supply all the paints and brushes. On Wednesday, Steven revokes the offer. No contract exists between Cal and Steven because the requested act has not yet been performed, and neither party has suffered any damages. But what if Steven revokes on Friday afternoon, after Cal has already painted half the house? What if Cal were supposed to buy the paints and brushes, which he did on Monday afternoon, and Steven revokes on Wednesday? In these instances, would Cal have a cause of action against Steven?

To resolve the questions in the above example, it would help to know about a case decided many years ago that answered similar problems: the case of Jimmy the Human Fly.

 EXAMPLE:

As an advertising gimmick, a store owner put an ad in the newspaper offering "Jimmy the Human Fly" $10,000 if he would climb to the very top of the Washington Monument on a particular day and time. Jimmy was a performer for the circus who claimed he could climb any surface.

On the day in question, a large crowd gathered, and the store owner handed out circulars about a sale at his store. At the appropriate moment, Jimmy arrived and started up the edifice. Just before he reached the very top of the monument, the store owner screamed, "I revoke!"

Jimmy sued the store owner for the $10,000, and won. The court held that because Jimmy had made a *substantial beginning* on the performance, the offeror no longer had the ability to revoke. Although Jimmy hadn't completely accepted at that point (because he had not reached the very top), it would be unfair to him if the offeror could terminate the offer at that point.

Back to Cal and Steven. Based on the foregoing, it would appear that after Cal had painted half of Steven's house, Steven would no longer be able to revoke his offer. If he revoked after Cal bought the paints and brushes but before he started painting, the purchase of the equipment would probably not be considered a "substantial beginning," and therefore there would not be a contract. Would Cal lose the money he spent on the paint and brushes? Probably not, because he only made these purchases in reliance on the offer. Steven would most probably have to reimburse Cal for the purchases. If Cal could prove that the paints and brushes could only be used for Steven's project, and that he had no other need for the materials, it would be unjust to Cal not to have Steven reimburse the money Cal had expended in reliance of the proposed contact with Steven.

Termination by Operation of Law

An offer may also be terminated by operation of law. **Operation of law** is a legal term for the circumstance in which one event has a legal effect on a second, unconnected event. With respect to the law of contracts, there are four circumstances, or events, that terminate offers by operation of law:

1. *Lapse of time.* If the offeree takes an unreasonable length of time to respond, the offer is considered terminated by operation of law. The courts do not expect offers to be kept open indefinitely, and the offeree's attempt to accept after a long delay constitutes a new offer to the original offeror.
2. *The death or destruction of the subject matter.* For example, it is impossible to sell a horse to stud if the horse has died, and substitution in this instance is not possible.
3. *The death or insanity of the offeror or offeree.* Death would appear to be self-explanatory, and insanity falls under the capacity of the parties to enter into a valid contractual relationship (see Chapter 5).

4. *Supervening illegality.* **Supervening illegality** means that the contract was legal at the time of the offer, but prior to acceptance a statute or court decision makes the subject matter illegal.

 EXAMPLE:

Dot is offered a contract to operate a gambling casino in Atlantic City, New Jersey. Prior to acceptance, the town officials of Atlantic City decide that having gambling on the boardwalk is not a good idea and rescind the ordinance permitting gambling in the city. Dot would no longer be able to accept such an offer because the subject matter of the contract, managing a gambling casino, is now illegal.

Effect of Termination of Offer

Once an offer has been terminated, either by act of the parties or by operation of law, it can no longer be accepted. Any attempt on the part of the offeree to accept after that point constitutes a new offer to the original offeror. The roles of the parties are then reversed, and all of the rules with respect to offers and acceptance apply in reverse. The original offeree is now the offeror and must make her offer according to the dictates of the law with respect to offers. The power of acceptance now rests with the erstwhile offeror, who must follow the guidelines of this chapter. This is an important concept because it relates to the issue of whether, and when, a contractual relationship has been created between the parties.

The entire series of events must now be analyzed. Was the original offer valid? Was it terminated before acceptance? Does the acceptance, after termination, convey sufficient precision so as to constitute a valid offer? How can the new offer be accepted? Always remember that every action and word of the parties in a contractual situation has specific legal meaning and ramifications. Never assume a result until a full analysis has been made.

SAMPLE CLAUSES

Unlike other sections of contractual negotiations, there are no specific clauses that one can point to and say, "That is an acceptance!" As a general rule, the offer and acceptance merge into the basic terms of the contract. The offeror creates the contract terms; the offeree merely agrees to those terms. This agreement can take the form of signing the completed contract, agreeing to the terms orally, or, for a unilateral contract, performing the act. No words other than the ones used by the offeror can

be used to accept. Any variance in the offeror's stated terms may constitute an offer to the offeror and thus do not form an acceptance except for
contracts between merchants for the sale of goods covered by the UCC.

CHAPTER SUMMARY

Acceptance is the manifestation of assent in the manner requested or authorized by the offeror under the common law. To be effective, the acceptance must be unequivocal and unqualified; any variance
in the terms, except those implicit in the offer, may constitute a counteroffer (or cross-offer). This common law rule has been changed significantly for contracts for the sale of goods between merchant traders where
changes in the offeree's terms, except for an iron clad offers, act to modify
the original offer. Acceptance requires an affirmative act, either in words
or deeds. Silence, except in solicited offers or implied-in-fact contracts, is
never deemed to be assent. The offer and acceptance together constitute
the requisite mutual assent to form a contract.

An offer may be accepted only by the person or group to whom it
has been made, and the offeree must know all the material terms of the
offer to make a valid acceptance. A bilateral contract is accepted by giving
a promise or by implying the promise by performing the promised act.
A unilateral contract is accepted by performing an act. At the moment
acceptance is validly given, the contract is formed, and the parties are
thereby obligated to its terms.

Bilateral contracts are accepted when the acceptance is properly dispatched by an authorized means of communication (the mailbox rule).
Rejection of a bilateral contract is only effective when actually received
by the offeror. But, in any event, the court will uphold the reasonable
expectations of the parties as determined by the particular factual situation.

Unilateral contracts are accepted whenever the offeree performs the
act requested. The offeree of a unilateral contract, except in special circumstances, has no duty to communicate with or notify the offeror of his
performance of the requested act. The act itself is sufficient acceptance.

An offer may no longer be accepted if it is terminated by the parties.
An offeree terminates his ability to accept by rejecting the offer. An offeror
terminates the offer by revoking the offer prior to the acceptance. In unilateral contracts, the offeror may not revoke once the offeree has made a
substantial beginning on the requested performance.

An offer may also terminate, not by act of the parties, but by operation of law (lapse of time, destruction of the subject matter, death or
insanity of the parties, or supervening illegality). Any attempt to accept
an offer after it has terminated does not revive the offer but creates a new
offer extending from the original offeree to the original offeror.

The key questions with respect to acceptance are:

1. Is the acceptance timely and valid?
2. At what point does the contract come into existence?
3. Has the offer terminated?
4. What are the reasonable expectations of the parties?
5. Is the contract covered by the UCC?

SYNOPSIS

Acceptance
    1. Must be unequivocal and unqualified
    2. Must be in the exact manner and form indicated by the offeror
    3. Any variance in terms of the offer is a counteroffer
    4. Silence is not an acceptance
Method of acceptance
    1. Bilateral
        a. Give promise
        b. Mailbox rule
    2. Unilateral
        a. Do act
        b. Substantial beginning
Termination of offers
    1. Rejection
    2. Revocation
    3. Varying terms
    4. Operation of law

Key Terms

Acceptance: manifestation of assent in the manner requested or authorized by the offeror

Auction with reserve: parties have the right to revoke any time before gavel comes down

Auction without reserve: property owner relinquishes the right to revoke

Bilateral contract: a contract that exchanges a promise for a promise

Counteroffer: a variance in the terms of the offer that constitutes a rejection of the original offer and a creation of a new offer

Cross-offer: see Counteroffer

Firm offer: offer made under the UCC that remains open for a reasonable period of time but in no event more than 90 days

Iron clad offer: under the UCC, an offer whose terms may not be altered by the offeree

Mailbox rule: rule stating that the acceptance of a bilateral contract is effective when properly dispatched by an authorized means of communication; formulated to help determine the moment of creation of a contract

Mirror image rule: to be valid, the acceptance must correspond exactly to the terms of the offer

Operation of law: the manner in which one event has a legal effect on a second, unconnected event

Option: a contract to keep an offer open for a specified time that is secured by consideration

Principal-agent: an agent is one who acts for and on behalf of another, the principal, for the purpose of entering into contracts with third persons

Rejection: to refuse an offer

Reverse unilateral contract: a contract in which the performer, rather than the promisor, makes the offer

Revocation: to recall an offer

Supervening illegality: a law that renders a once-legal activity illegal

Undisclosed principal: a person, represented by an agent, who is party to a contract but has not revealed his or her identity to the other party

Unilateral contract: a contract that exchanges a promise for an act

EXERCISES

1. What elements make an attempted acceptance a counteroffer?
2. Give two examples in which the actions of the offeree reject a written offer.
3. Compose an offer that specifically limits the offeree's ability to accept.
4. Using the example of Jimmy the Human Fly, argue the case for the store owner.
5. Discuss the circumstances that would terminate a person's ability to accept a valid offer.

Cases for Analysis

The first case summary that follows highlights the concept of the right to revoke a unilateral offer, Marchiondo v. Scheck. The second poses an intriguing variation on the mailbox rule by discussing University Emergency Medicine Foundation v. Rapier Investments, Ltd., and Medical Business Systems, Inc.

Marchiondo v. Scheck
78 N.M. 440, 432 P.2d 405 (1967)

Opinion

The issue is whether the offeror had a right to revoke his offer to enter a unilateral contract.

Defendant, in writing, offered to sell real estate to a specified prospective buyer and agreed to pay a percentage of the sales price as a commission to the broker. The offer fixed a six-day time limit for acceptance. Defendant, in writing, revoked the offer. The revocation was received by the broker on the morning of the sixth day. Later that day, the broker obtained the offeree's acceptance.

Plaintiff, the broker claiming breach of contract, sued defendant for the commission stated in the offer. On the above facts, the trial court dismissed the complaint.

We are not concerned with the revocation of the offer as between the offeror and the prospective purchaser. With certain exceptions (see 12 C.J.S. Brokers §95(2), pp. 223–224), the right of a broker to the agreed compensation, or damages measured thereby, is not defeated by the refusal of the principal to complete or consummate a transaction. Southwest Motel Brokers v. Alamo Hotels, 72 N.M. 227, 382 P.2d 707 (1963).

Plaintiff's appeal concerns the revocation of his agency. As to that revocation, the issue between the offeror and his agent is not whether defendant had the power to revoke; rather, it is whether he had the right to revoke. 1 Mechem on Agency, §568 at 405 (2d ed. 1914).

When defendant made his offer to pay a commission upon sale of the property, he offered to enter a unilateral contract; the offer was for an act to be performed, a sale. 1 Williston on Contracts, §13 at 23 (3d ed. 1957); Hutchinson v. Dobson-Bainbridge Realty Co., 31 Tenn. App. 490, 217 S.W.2d 6 (1946).

Many courts hold that the principal has the right to revoke the broker's agency at any time before the broker has actually procured a purchaser. See Hutchinson v. Dobson-Bainbridge Realty Co., supra, and cases therein cited. The reason given is that until there is performance, the offeror has not received that contemplated by his offer, and there is no contract. Further, the offeror may never receive the requested performance because the offeree is not obligated to perform. Until the offeror receives the requested performance, no consideration has passed from the offeree to the offeror. Thus, until the performance is received, the offeror may withdraw the offer. *Williston*, supra, §60; Hutchinson v. Dobson Bainbridge Realty Co., supra.

Defendant asserts that the trial court was correct in applying this rule. However, plaintiff contends that the rule is not applicable where there has been part performance of the offer.

Hutchinson v. Dobson-Bainbridge Realty Co., supra, states:

> A greater number of courts, however, hold that part performance of the consideration may make such an offer irrevocable and that where the offeree or broker manifests his assent to the offer by entering upon performance and spending time and money in his efforts to perform, then the offer becomes irrevocable during the time stated and binding upon the principal according to its terms. . . .

Defendant contends that the decisions giving effect to a part performance are distinguishable. He asserts that in these cases the offer was of an exclusive right to sell or of an exclusive agency. Because neither factor is present here, he asserts that the "part performance" decisions are not applicable.

Many of the decisions do seem to emphasize the exclusive aspects of the offer. See Garrett v. Richardson, 149 Colo. 449, 369 P.2d 566 (1962) where a listing agreement for a definite period of time was held to imply an exclusive right to sell within the time named.

Such emphasis reaches its extreme conclusion in Tetrick v. Sloan, 170 Cal. App. 2d 540, 339 P.2d 613 (1959), where no effect was given to the part performance because there was neither an exclusive agency, nor an exclusive right to sell.

Defendant's offer did not specifically state that it was exclusive. Under §70-1-43, N.M.S.A. 1953, it was not an exclusive agreement. It is not the exclusiveness of the offer that deprives the offeror of the right to revoke. It is the action taken by the offeree which deprives the offeror of that right. Until there is action by the offeree—a partial performance pursuant to the offer—the offeror may revoke even if his offer is of an exclusive agency or an exclusive right to sell. Levander v. Johnson, 181 Wis. 68, 193 N.W. 970 (1923).

Once partial performance is begun pursuant to the offer made, a contract results. This contract has been termed a contract with conditions or an option contract. This terminology is illustrated as follows:

> If an offer for a unilateral contract is made, and part of the consideration requested in the offer is given or tendered by the offeree in response thereto, the offeror is bound by a contract, the duty of immediate performance of which is conditional on the full consideration being given or tendered within the time stated in the offer, or, if no time is stated therein, within a reasonable time. Restatement of Contracts, §45 (1932).

Restatement (Second) of Contracts, §45, Tent. Draft No. 1, (approved 1964, Tentative Draft No. 2, p. vii) states:

> (1) Where an offer invites an offeree to accept by rendering a performance and does not invite a promissory acceptance, an option contract is created when the offeree begins the invited performance or tenders part of it.
>
> (2) The offeror's duty of performance under any option contract so created is conditional on completion or tender of the invited performance in accordance with the terms of the offer.

Restatement (Second) of Contracts, §45, Tent. Draft No. 1, comment (g), says:

> This Section frequently applies to agency arrangements, particularly offers made to real estate brokers. . . .

See Restatement (Second) of Agency, §446, comment (b).

The reason for finding such a contract is stated in Hutchinson v. Dobson-Bainbridge Realty Co., supra, as follows:

This rule avoids hardship to the offeree, and yet does not hold the offeror beyond the terms of his promise. It is true by such terms he was to be bound only if the requested act was done; but this implies that he will let it be done, that he will keep his offer open till the offeree who has begun can finish doing it. At least this is so where the doing of it will necessarily require time and expense. In such a case it is but just to hold that the offeree's part performance furnishes the 'acceptance' and the 'consideration' for a binding subsidiary promise not to revoke the offer, or turns the offer into a presently binding contract conditional upon the offeree's full performance.

We hold that part performance by the offeree of an offer of a unilateral contract results in a contract with a condition. The condition is full performance by the offeree. Here, if plaintiff-offeree partially performed prior to receipt of defendant's revocation, such a contract was formed. Thereafter, upon performance being completed by plaintiff, upon defendant's failure to recognize the contract, liability for breach of contract would arise. Thus, defendant's right to revoke his offer depends upon whether plaintiff had partially performed before he received defendant's revocation. In re Ward's Estate, 47 N.M. 55, 134 P.2d 539, 146 A.L.R. 826 (1943), does not conflict with this result. Ward is clearly distinguishable because there the prospective purchaser did not complete or tender performance in accordance with the terms of the offer.

What constitutes partial performance will vary from case to case since what can be done toward performance is limited by what is authorized to be done. Whether plaintiff partially performed is a question of fact to be determined by the trial court.

The trial court denied plaintiff's requested finding concerning his partial performance. It did so on the theory that partial performance was not material. In this the trial court erred.

Because of the failure to find on the issue of partial performance, the case must be remanded to the trial court. State ex rel. Reynolds v. Board of County Comm'rs., 71 N.M. 194, 376 P.2d 976 (1962). We have not considered, and express no opinion on the question of whether there is or is not substantial evidence in the record which would support a finding one way or the other on this vital issue. Compare Geeslin v. Goodno, 75 N.M. 174, 402 P.2d 156 (1965).

The case is remanded for findings on the issue of plaintiff's partial performance of the offer prior to its revocation, and for further proceedings consistent with this opinion and the findings so made.

It is so ordered.

Questions

1. How does this case tally with the case of "Jimmy the Human Fly" discussed in the chapter?

2. Discuss this case in light of the mailbox rule and its effect on unilateral contracts.

University Emergency Medicine Foundation v. Rapier Investments, Ltd. and Medical Business Systems, Inc.
197 F.3d 18 (1st Cir. 1999)

Rapier Investments Ltd. ("Rapier") and Medical Business Systems, Inc., ("MBS") (collectively, the "appellants") appeal from the summary judgment entered in favor of plaintiff-appellee, University Emergency Medicine Foundation ("Emergency Medicine"), declaring effective Emergency Medicine's notice to terminate a service contract with appellants. This case calls upon us to decide whether notice of termination is effective pursuant to the law of Rhode Island where: (1) the notice is mailed in advance of, but received after, the expiration of the contractual notice period; and (2) a separate contractual notice provision invites notice by mail to a certain address, but notice is sent to, and actually received by, the noticee at a different address. Because we agree with the trial court that such notice was effective, we affirm.

I

As this is an appeal from an entry of summary judgment, we recount the pertinent facts in the light most favorable to the non-moving party, the appellants. See Reich v. John Alden Life Ins. Co., 126 F.3d 1, 6 (1st Cir. 1997). Emergency Medicine is a non-profit Rhode Island corporation that provides physicians' services to emergency departments at several Rhode Island hospitals. Pursuant to a series of contracts spanning more than ten years, MBS, a subsidiary of Rapier, performed coding, billing, collection and accounts receivable services for Emergency Medicine.

On October 1, 1995, Emergency Medicine and Rapier executed a contract (the "Agreement") calling for MBS to service Emergency Medicine for one year, and further providing that this Agreement shall be automatically extended for additional one (1) year period [sic] ("additional terms") unless and until either party electsto terminate this Agreement as of the end of the initial term or any additional term by giving at least four (4) months written notice that it elects to have this Agreement terminated, without cause.

A separate paragraph entitled "Notices," (the "notice paragraph"), prescribes a method by which notice may be "effectively given":

> Any notices given pursuant to this Agreement shall be deemed to have been effectively given if sent by registered or certified mail to the party to whom the notice is directed at the address set forth for such party herein above or at such other address as such party may hereafter specify in a notice given in accordance with this paragraph.

The only addresses "set forth" in the Agreement are Rapier's principal office, 7 Wells Avenue, Newton, Massachusetts, and Emergency Medicine's principal place of business, 593 Eddy Street, Providence, Rhode Island.

During the contract's first year, neither party terminated, and it automatically renewed for an additional year, ending September 30, 1997. On Friday, May 30, 1997, Annamarie Monks of Emergency Medicine mailed two letters intended to notify Rapier that Emergency Medicine planned to terminate the Agreement before it renewed for a third year. She sent one letter certified mail to Alan Carr-Locke of Rapier at 1238 Chestnut Street, Newton, Massachusetts. Because the letter was incorrectly addressed, it was returned undelivered on June 10, at which point Emergency Medicine mailed the notice to 7 Wells Avenue, Newton, Massachusetts. She sent the second letter certified mail to JoAnn Barato-Mills of MBS, the employee who had negotiated and signed the Agreement on behalf of Rapier, at her place of business, 20 Altieri Way, Warwick, Rhode Island. Ms. Barato-Mills received the letter the following Monday, June 2, 1997.

In the months following Emergency Medicine's notice of nonrenewal, MBS continued to perform services under the Agreement. Meanwhile, Emergency Medicine solicited bids for a new service contract and, although MBS submitted a bid, Emergency Medicine awarded the new contract to a different service provider. MBS then asserted that, because Emergency Medicine's termination notice had been invalid, the Agreement had already extended automatically for an additional year, ending September 30, 1998.

Emergency Medicine filed a complaint seeking, inter alia, a declaration that its notice had effectively terminated the Agreement. The parties filed cross-motions for summary judgment on the validity of the termination notice, and the trial court granted judgment in favor of Emergency Medicine. This appeal ensued.

II

The Agreement entered into by Emergency Medicine and Rapier expressly reserved to either party the power to terminate the contract before it automatically renewed. Termination provisions are standard fare in modern contracts, see 1A Corbin on Contracts, §265, at 531, and such provisions often require that the terminating party fulfill certain conditions before termination is effective, see 6 Corbin, §1266 at 55-56. Where "the power to terminate is a conditional power," termination is not effective until the party seeking termination can show that the condition has been fulfilled. See id. at 56. According to Rapier, Emergency Medicine did not fulfill the condition required for termination under the Agreement because it failed to provide Rapier with at least four months written notice. We are asked therefore to evaluate the effectiveness of Emergency Medicine's termination notice pursuant to the contract.

A.   The Mailbox Rule

The Agreement expressly conditions a party's right to terminate on that party "giving at least four (4) months written notice" to the other party. Where, as here, such "a condition is required by the agreement of the parties . . . a rule of strict compliance traditionally applies." Farnsworth, Contracts §8.3 at 571 (1990) (emphasis added). "Strict compliance" means that "the notice to terminate, to be effective, must be given at the stipulated time." Fred Mosher-Grain, Inc. v. Kansas Co-op. Wheat Mktg. Ass'n, 136 Kan. 269, 15 P.2d 421, 425 (Kan. 1932); see also 6 Corbin §1266 at 65-66 (where the contract expresses a time period for notice, it is presumed that "time is of the essence"). As one court cautioned more than 75 years ago, "the difference of one day in the giving of notice is small, in one view, but it is the distance across a necessary boundary in relations under the contract, and must be taken as decisive, or there can be no boundary." Brown Method Co. v. Ginsberg, 153 Md. 414, 138 A. 402, 403-404 (Md. 1927). Accordingly, we must strictly enforce the four-month notice period bargained for by Rapier and Emergency Medicine.

The Agreement, as extended by renewal for one additional year, was set to expire on September 30, 1997. Counting back exactly four months, the last day on which Emergency Medicine had the power to terminate was May 31, 1997. Although Emergency Medicine mailed notice letters on May 30, these letters were not received until after the notice period had expired. Thus, the timeliness of Emergency Medicine's notice turns on whether notice of termination is effective upon mailing, or upon receipt.

At common law, the default rule—i.e., the rule that governs unless the parties contract for different terms—makes notice effective only upon receipt, not mailing. See 1A Corbin §265 at 532 ("If the agreement merely provides that one party may terminate by giving notice, the notice will be effective only when received, and not when it is started by mail or otherwise."); Kantrowitz v. Dairymen's League Co-Op. Ass'n, Inc., 272 A.D. 470, 71 N.Y.S.2d 821, 822 (N.Y. App. Div. 1947) ("Where a contract requires notice, but does not specify the manner in which the notice is to be given, the mere mailing of notice is not sufficient unless it is received within the time specified.")

However, the parties may override the default rule by contract. See 6 Corbin §1266 at 65 ("The time and manner of exercising a power of termination may be specified in the contract. . . ."). In particular, the parties may contract to permit notice by mail. If they do, notice becomes effective upon mailing pursuant to the time-honored "mailbox rule." See 1 Merrill on Notice §633 (1956); Kantrowitz, 71 N.Y.S.2d at 822; cf. Larocque v. Rhode Island Joint Reinsurance Ass'n, 536 A.2d 529, 531 (R.I. 1988) ("Where the [insurance] policy provides that cancellation may be effected by mailing notice, the general rule is that notification is fulfilled by proof of mailing.").

Here, the Agreement unquestionably authorizes notice by mail. The notice paragraph expressly invites notice "sent by registered or certified mail." This paragraph therefore triggers the "mailbox rule," making notice effective upon mailing. Accordingly, Emergency Medicine's notice letters, mailed on May 30, 1997, took effect on that date, and were timely under the Agreement's four-month notice period, which did not expire until May 31, unless the use of an address other than the one specified in the contract deprived Emergency Medicine of the benefit of the mailbox rule.

B. The Mailing Address

The notice paragraph states that notice "shall be deemed to have been effectively given if sent . . . to the party to whom the notice is directed at the address set forth for such party herein above or at such other address as such party may hereafter specify. . . ." The address "set forth" in the Agreement was Rapier's principal office located at 7 Wells Avenue, Newton, Massachusetts. Emergency Medicine, however, mailed its May 30 notices to Rapier at an incorrect Massachusetts address and to MBS at a Rhode Island address.

The trial court concluded that the notice paragraph, written in nonexclusive language, only set forth one method by which notice could be "effectively given." See University Emergency Med. Found. v. Rapier Inv., Ltd., 1998 U.S. Dist. LEXIS 22722, No. 97-549-T, slip op. at 4-5 (D.R.I. October 15, 1998) (order granting summary judgment). The court then noted that, as a general rule, notice given by a method different from the one provided for in the contract "is effective if it is actually received unless the method by which notice is given is an essential element of the transaction." Id. (citing 1 Merrill, §603, at 662-663). Finding that Emergency Medicine's notice was actually received (and, impliedly, that the contractual method for providing notice was not an "essential element" of Rapier and Emergency Medicine's transaction), the court ruled that notice was effective. See id. at 6.

We accept the trial court's conclusion that the notice was effective, but disagree slightly with its underlying reasoning. Although the notice paragraph is non-exclusive, permitting notice in any other way recognized by law, Emergency Medicine must rely on the notice paragraph on the facts of this case because it is only this paragraph that invites notice by mail, and, consequently, as discussed above, it is only by virtue of this paragraph that Emergency Medicine's notice was timely. Because Emergency Medicine must rely on the notice paragraph as its authority for invoking the "mailbox rule," we must inquire whether Emergency Medicine's notice letters complied with the terms and conditions of valid notice under that paragraph.

In doing so, we are mindful of the principle, so fundamental in the law of contracts, that we must give effect to the intent of the parties. See McCarthy v. Azure, 22 F.3d 351, 355 (1st Cir. 1994); Brady v. Norwich Union Fire Ins. Soc., Ltd., 47 R.I. 416, 133 A. 799, 799 (R.I. 1926). Here, the critical question is whether the parties intended the use of the mailing address specified in the contract to be a condition precedent to valid termination. We conclude that they did not. Rather, we find that the parties identified specific addresses for the mailing of notice merely as a convenient means of ensuring timely delivery.

First, we note the obvious difference in import of the four-month notice provision and the mailing address provision. A notice period reflects the amount of time deemed necessary by the parties to adapt to the other's termination. For the service provider, it includes the time needed to procure new clients or reallocate staff and equipment; for the service recipient, it includes the time needed to replace its former service provider. By contrast, the mailing address does not, in itself, confer any benefit upon either party. It is merely a collateral term intended to enhance the probability that mailed notice will arrive promptly in the proper hands. Cf. Palo Alto Town & Country Village, Inc. v. BBTC Co., 11 Cal. 3d 494, 521 P.2d 1097, 1100, 113 Cal. Rptr. 705 (Cal. 1974) (in bank) (an option contract's provision that notice be given personally or by prepaid registered mail is a "mere suggestion of a permissive method of communication," not "a prescribed requirement or an absolute condition."). Thus, by its very nature, the stipulation that notice be sent to a particular address is not the type of term ordinarily bargained for, nor is it the type of term intended to allow one party to extinguish the other's contractual rights based on a failure of strict compliance. Indeed, courts have held that mailed termination notice is valid so long as it is actually received by the noticee, even where it is mailed to an incorrect address, see U.S. Broad. Co. v. National Broad. Co., 439 F. Supp. 8, 9-10 (D. Mass. 1977), or where the form of the mailing is technically defective, see Southern Sanitation Co. v. City of Shreveport, 308 So. 2d 848, 849 (La. Ct. App. 1975) (letter addressed incorrectly to "P.O. Box 3326" rather than "3328"); Barbier v. Barry, 345 S.W.2d 557, 562 (Tex. Civ. App. 1961) (letter sent by regular rather than registered mail). But see Prudential Carolinas Realty v. Cambridge Dev. Corp., 872 F. Supp. 256, 261 (D.S.C. 1994) aff'd, 42 F.3d 1386 (4th Cir. 1994) (per curiam).

Second, the overall structure of the Agreement indicates that the parties did not intend the mailing address to be a condition of valid termination. See Aneluca Assoc. v. Lombardi, 620 A.2d 88, 92 (R.I. 1993) (construing the parties' intent by looking to the contract as a whole). The paragraph of the Agreement delineating termination rights appears five pages before the paragraph describing "notice" by mail. The only conditions of termination expressed within the paragraph on termination rights are that notice be given in writing and at least four months in advance of the Agreement's year-end date. Moreover, as the trial court correctly found, the notice by mail paragraph is written in non-exclusive language, suggesting that any method of written notice valid under law would be effective. See University Emergency Med. Found., No. 97-549-T, slip op. at 4-5; see also Southern Region Indus. Realty, Inc. v. Chattanooga Warehouse and Cold Storage Co., 612 S.W.2d 162, 164 (Tenn. 1980) (finding that the contractual address "merely suggests a permitted place and method of giving notice and does not preclude sending notice to other offices . . . "). If the parties had intended the use of the address specified in the contract to be a condition of valid termination, like the four-month notice period, they presumably would have located the address requirement next to the notice period in the paragraph defining termination rights. Moreover, if the address was an essential term of the bargain, the parties would have made notice sent to that address the exclusive means of providing written notice, rather than just one method among many that would have been effective. Thus, the overall structure of the Agreement supports our conclusion that the parties intended the mailing address as a convenient means of effectuating delivery and not as a condition precedent to valid termination.

To be sure, a party that fails to use the address identified in the contract for mailing notice risks losing the benefit of the mailbox rule. The contract provision at issue in this case, which states that notice of termination may be given effectively by registered or certified mail sent to a particular address, allocated the risk of non-delivery of a notice sent in strict compliance with the contract. Cf. Worms v. Burgess, 620 P.2d 455, 457 (Okla. Ct. App. 1980) (observing that in the offer-acceptance context the mailbox rule shifts the risk of loss during transmission to the offeror); Farnsworth, Contracts §3.22 at 184 ("The mailbox rule has been used to allocate the risk of transmission. . . ."). That is, if Emergency Medicine chose to give timely notice of termination by registered or certified mail sent to the specified address, and the notice was undelivered because of a failure by the postal service, Emergency Medicine would have still given timely notice of termination despite the non-delivery. Cf. Restatement (Second) of Contracts §63 ("Unless an offer provides otherwise, . . . an acceptance made in a manner and by a medium invited by an offer is operative . . . without regard to whether it ever reaches the offeror. . . ."). If, however, Emergency Medicine directed its otherwise timely notice of termination to the wrong address and there were no delivery, Emergency Medicine would lose the benefit of the mailbox rule. In situations where there is delivery despite the use of a wrong address, and the circumstances indicate that the parties intended the address as merely a collateral term designed to enhance the timely delivery of notice, the continuing availability of the mailbox rule to the sender requires an assessment of the particular facts of the case.

In the case at hand, Emergency Medicine risked losing the benefit of the mailbox rule with respect to both of its improperly addressed May 30 mailings. That risk arguably materialized in the case of the letter mailed to Rapier's Alan Carr-Locke, which was returned undelivered, and finally arrived at Rapier more than 10 days after it was originally sent. However, the letter mailed to MBS's JoAnn Barato-Mills arrived in her hands just one business day after it was mailed (the letter was mailed on Friday and arrived on Monday), within the ordinary time period expected for delivery by mail. Under these circumstances, Emergency Medicine retained the benefit of the mailbox rule despite the improper address, and this second letter placed Rapier on written notice of Emergency Medicine's intent to terminate the Agreement before it automatically renewed for a third year. Therefore, we conclude that Emergency

Medicine provided Rapier with four months written notice of its intent to terminate as required under the Agreement.

Affirmed.

Questions

1.   What is your opinion of the court's application of the mailbox rule to these facts?

2.   Why does the law require the offeree to accept or reject an offer only in the manner requested by the offeror? How does this tally with modern technology?

Suggested Case References

1.   The case that established the mailbox rule is Adams v. Lindsell, 1 B & Ald. 681 (1818). Read and analyze the case. Do you agree with the court's decision? What factors did the court consider determinative to its final conclusion?

2.   You are staying at a hotel and, while unpacking your clothes, you find a diamond brooch in the closet. Being honest, you inform the front desk and discover that a reward was offered by the guest who lost the brooch to anyone who found it. Are you entitled to the reward? Is this an example of a unilateral contract? Can you accept terms of which you are unaware? Read Vitty v. Eley, 51 A.D. 44, 64 N.Y.S. 397 (1900).

3.   To see how a New York court interpreted silence as acceptance (or not), read Joseph Schultz & Co. v. Camden Fire Ins. Co., 304 N.Y. 143 (1952).

4 Consideration

CHAPTER OVERVIEW

Consideration is the third essential element of every valid contract. It is the bargain that supports the entire contractual relationship. Without consideration no contract can exist. An agreement unsupported by consideration may legally bind the parties to each other, but the parties' legal relationship is not a contractual one.

What is "consideration"? Consideration is the subject matter of the agreement over which the parties have negotiated. It is the used textbook the student wants to sell, the paralegal services the attorney wants to employ, the land that the developer wants to buy. For a contract to be valid, both parties to the contract must give *and* receive consideration. If consideration flows only to one person, then it most probably is intended as a gift. The basic premise of a contractual relationship is a bargain, an element lacking if both sides do not receive something of value.

The monetary value of the object of the contract is, for the most part, irrelevant to the law. A 5¢ piece of gum may have as much legal significance as a $5 million piece of real estate, whereas, under certain circumstances, a $1 million diamond necklace may not be considered sufficient to support a contract. (The adequacy of the consideration may involve questions of capacity. See Chapter 5.) The law is looking for proof of the bargain: It must be evidenced that the parties truly wanted and bargained for the object or service in question.

Consideration Defined

Consideration is something that has legal value. It is generally defined as a benefit conferred or a detriment incurred at the behest of the other party. Because consideration is the subject matter of a bargain, there must be **mutuality of consideration**—each side must give and receive something of legal value (the **quid pro quo**).

In bilateral contracts, the mutuality of the consideration is evidenced by the promise each side makes to the other. Mutuality of consideration in unilateral contracts is evidenced by giving the promise and performing the act. The act is consideration, and its performance creates a duty to perform on the part of the promisor.

The monetary value of the consideration is of little importance. Because the law is looking for the bargain, the only requirements are that the consideration have legal value (benefit or detriment) and be valuable to the person requesting it.

Benefit Conferred

The benefit-conferred concept of consideration is the easier of the two to understand. Simply stated, it is the exchange of the exact object or service described in the contract. Usually it is a good or service that one side is selling and the other side is purchasing. The exchange of goods or services is the most typical type of consideration encountered in everyday contracts.

 EXAMPLES:

1. Ted offers to sell, and William agrees to buy, a used textbook for $10. The consideration is both the book and the money. Ted gives the book and receives the $10. William gives the $10 and receives the book. There is a mutuality of consideration.

2. Irene offers to exchange her gold earrings for Denise's pearl earrings, and Denise agrees. Each side gives and receives something of value. Each party has conferred "benefit" (earrings) on the other. The consideration is valid.

3. Leroy is employed as a legal assistant by the law firm of Smith & Jones, P.C., for a salary of $300 per week. Leroy is conferring on the firm his paralegal services, and the firm is conferring on Leroy a salary. There is mutuality of consideration.

Detriment Incurred

Conceptualizing consideration as a detriment incurred at the request of the other party is generally more difficult to comprehend. Most people look for objects, services, or money as consideration because these things are tangible and easily identified as having value. But of what value is a detriment?

For a "detriment" to qualify as consideration, the person incurring the detriment must

1. give up a legal right,
2. at the request of the other party,
3. in exchange for something of legal value.

All three elements must coexist for the detriment to qualify as consideration.

 EXAMPLES:

1. Maria's mother is worried about Maria's smoking. Mom offers Maria $1000 if Maria quits smoking for a year, and Maria agrees. There is a contract. This is an example of a detriment incurred. Maria is giving up her legal right to smoke at her mother's request in exchange for $1000. On the other hand, if Maria quits smoking for her own health concerns or simply to please her mother, there would be no contract because she would bargain nothing of legal value for her forbearance.

2. Lisa's mother is worried about Lisa smoking marijuana. Mom offers Lisa $1000 if she quits smoking marijuana for a year. Lisa agrees. There is no contract. This is not an example of a detriment incurred because Lisa has no legal right to smoke marijuana. Consequently, Lisa is not giving up a right at the request of the other party in exchange for something of value. Because no legal right exists, it cannot be offered as contractual consideration.

Usually consideration is specifically noted in the contract. The important factors to ascertain are that the consideration mentioned has legal value and that both parties give and receive consideration.

What Is Not Consideration

Far more difficult than determining what is consideration is determining what it is *not*. In making this determination, the court uses the following rules and guidelines.

"Past consideration is no consideration." Even if the object or service mentioned by the parties has legal value, it must be shown that it was meant to be exchanged as part of the present contract. Former gifts or consideration given in prior contracts cannot be consideration for a current contract simply because the parties wish it. It must satisfy legal principles as well. In some jurisdictions past consideration may be deemed sufficient consideration if that fact is put in writing by the party to be charged. Each state's law must be analyzed to determine whether this situation is available for a given contract.

EXAMPLE:

Three years ago John gave Dorothy a mink coat. Two years ago he gave her a trip around the world. Last year he gave her a diamond watch. Now he wants to use these items as consideration for Dorothy's current domestic services as his housekeeper. The law says no. John must offer new, current consideration.

"Moral consideration is no consideration." Simply because someone feels morally obligated to another person it does not follow that the moral obligation is sufficient to form the consideration of a contract. The parties must demonstrate that they bargained with each other, not simply that one felt indebted to the other.

EXAMPLES:

1. Hassan's parents pay for his school tuition. When he graduates, Hassan says he will repay his parents with interest. There is no contract. Hassan's parents did not intend to loan the money to Hassan, and the fact that he feels morally obligated to promise to repay them does not mean that they have a contractual relationship. They did not bargain with each other.

2. Leslie cannot afford school tuition and so gets a job to save money, thereby delaying her schooling. Leslie's parents offer to loan Leslie the tuition, with repayment to be made after graduation at 5 percent interest. This is a contract. Even though Leslie may feel morally obligated to repay her parents, more importantly she is legally obligated to them because the tuition was bargained for, and Leslie's parents expect its return with interest.

"A gift can never be legal consideration." Just because the parties use words that, on their face, would appear to represent consideration, no contract will be formed if it can be shown that under the circumstances

the true intent of the parties was to confer a gift. The courts will review all the surrounding circumstances to ascertain that the element and intent of a bargain exist.

 EXAMPLE:

Mr. and Mrs. Jones offer to sell their four bedroom house to Mr. and Mrs. Smith for $10,000, and the Smiths agree. Is there a contract? That would depend on the surrounding circumstances. Consider two different scenarios:

1. The Joneses are the parents of Mrs. Smith. The house has a market value of $450,000
2. The Joneses have to move to another state for job reasons. They have to sell the house as quickly as possible, and their employers have agreed to compensate them for any loss they incur on the sale. The Joneses have never met the Smiths prior to the sale.

In the first example there would be no contract. It would appear that Mrs. Smith's parents intended to make a gift of the house but used words of consideration to make it appear like a contract (probably for tax advantages).

In the second example, although it may appear the Joneses have made a bad deal, a mutual exchange of bargains has occurred. A contract has been created.

"Illusory promises are never consideration." Recall Chapter 2, Offer, in which the concept of the certainty and definiteness of the terms of an offer was discussed. If a party to the contract retains the discretionary right to determine the subject matter of the contract, the offer will fail. This is an example of an illusory promise. Even if words of consideration are used, the "consideration" is legally inadequate because it cannot be objectively determined what is to be given.

 EXAMPLE:

The law firm of Smith & Jones, P.C. agrees to pay Emmet what they think he's worth in consideration for his employment as a paralegal. The firm's promise is illusory. There is no determinable consideration, and so there is no valid offer or contract.

To prove an illusory promise, it must be shown that one party has subjective control over its terms. If the term can be objectively determined, like an output contract discussed previously, and can be objectively quantified, it is not illusory.

"Promises to do that which one is already bound to do are not consideration." If one is under a preexisting duty to perform, either because of a contractual or other obligation, a promise to fulfill that obligation is insufficient consideration. The other party has received nothing of value. This is known as the **preexisting duty rule**. However under certain circumstances, a preexisting duty may be consideration for a new agreement:

1.   if new or different consideration is given
2.   the purpose is to ratify a voidable obligation
3.   the duty is owed to a third person, not the promisee
4.   unforeseen circumstances make the duty more difficult to fulfill

 EXAMPLES:

 1. Officer Green promises to catch the burglar who robbed Mr. White's house in exchange for Mr. White's promise to give her $300. There is no contract. The police officer is already obligated by virtue of her job to find the thief and has given nothing of additional value to induce Mr. White's promise. She has a preexisting duty to assist Mr. White.

 2. Chris owes Fred $200. Chris asks Fred to accept $100 in full payment of the debt. There is no consideration for Fred to take less than he is already owed. However, if Chris asks Fred to accept $100 now and $110 at a later date, the compromised agreement would be valid because Fred received something of value in addition to what he was previously entitled.

 3. Phyllis and Lupe have a contract for the sale of Lupe's computer for $300. After the contract is signed, Phyllis tries to change the contract to include Lupe's computer programs for the same price. The second agreement is invalid. Lupe received no new or additional consideration for giving Phyllis the programs. Every contract must be individually supported by consideration, and any modification to an existing contract must be supported by additional consideration.

Under the UCC merchant traders may modify their prior contractual obligations without new or different consideration provided that the modification is made "in good faith." This rule substantially changed the common law concepts for contracts for the sale of goods between merchants.

Sufficiency of the Consideration

The concept of the **sufficiency of the consideration** concerns itself, once again, with the element of the bargain. The law is only interested in the legal value of the bargain, not its monetary worth. For this reason, not only must the object, service, or detriment itself be analyzed, but it is also necessary to analyze all of the circumstances surrounding the making of the agreement to determine that a bargain, not a gift, was intended. So, although the value of the consideration per se is not important, it remains a factor in determining whether a bargained-for exchange has occurred.

Does it matter that a party to a contract makes a "bad" bargain—that she does not receive consideration monetarily equivalent to what was given? No. The law does not concern itself with insuring the fairness of every contractual relationship. Obviously, persons only enter into a contract because each thinks he is making a good deal. Unless some other factors exist that would make the contract invalid (see Chapter 6), the law applies the doctrines of **caveat emptor** and **caveat venditor**—"Let the buyer beware" and "Let the seller beware." The only factors that the law looks at are the legal value of the consideration, the mutuality of the consideration, and the element of the bargain.

 EXAMPLE:

Horace offers to sell an old trunk for $25. The trunk has been around for years, Horace doesn't like it, and he wants the space it takes up in the attic. Joanne agrees to buy the trunk, which she needs for storage. Later, Joanne finds out the trunk is an antique worth $1000. The contract is valid, and Joanne has made an exceptionally good purchase. Both Horace and Joanne received what they wanted for the contract; Joanne just made a better deal.

Nominal consideration, consideration that has such an obviously small monetary value relative to the consideration for which it is exchanged, is always immediately suspect by the law. Even though the monetary value is never a primary concern of the law, and the courts usually leave the parties to their own devices when it comes to bargaining powers, the law wants to make sure that a bargain does exist. Consequently, the courts will usually inquire into the surrounding circumstances if the bargain, on its face, appears to be overly one-sided. If a bargain can be proved, however, the contract will stand.

 EXAMPLE:

An advertisement in the newspaper offers one mint condition Rolls Royce for $1 to the first person who presents the cash to the seller at a given day and time. Is the $1 legally sufficient consideration for a Rolls Royce?

The background of the notice is this: A wealthy man dies, and his will names his wife as executrix. All of the deceased's property is left to his wife, except for the proceeds of the sale of his Rolls Royce, which was to go to his mistress. In this instance, the consideration is sufficient. The widow truly wants the least amount of money possible for the car. She may violate a fiduciary obligation to the mistress, but the person who bought the car has a valid contract.

Sham consideration is consideration that, on its face, appears to have no true value at all. The concept typically applies to gifts. One party intends to make a gift to the other but phrases the exchange in words of contract for some private purpose. For example, a statement such as "In consideration of $1 plus other good and valuable consideration" represents sham consideration. Terms such as "good and valuable consideration," without being specifically defined, are legally insignificant and tend to indicate lack, rather than presence, of consideration. The circumstances surrounding the contract, not just the words used, may also indicate sham consideration.

Conditional promises are not necessarily insufficient simply because they involve an element of doubt. A conditional promise is dependent on the happening, or nonhappening, of some event that would trigger the obligation. (See Chapter 7, Contract Provisions.) Provided that the consideration promised has legal sufficiency, the contract will be valid.

EXAMPLE:

Shirley agrees to buy Pam's house for $250,000, provided that she can get financing within 30 days. This is a valid contract. Both the house and the money are legally sufficient; simply because Shirley's obligation to pay is conditioned on her getting a mortgage does not mean the consideration is not sufficient, only that the right to receive the money may not come to Pam.

Promissory Estoppel

Promissory estoppel is a doctrine originally established by the courts of equity. Equity courts, as opposed to law courts, were designed to remedy situations in which the "legal" result might be just but was unfair or unduly hard on one of the parties. Equity provides "mercy" to persons when the legal result appears unfair. (See Chapter 11, Remedies.)

The doctrine of promissory estoppel arises in certain situations in which a person reasonably believes that he has entered into a contract, even though no contract exists. Relying on this reasonable belief that there is a contract, the promisee materially changes his position. This circumstance arises when the promise made by the presumptive offeror is illusory—what has been promised cannot be objectively defined or is left to the discretion of the promisor. These are not contractual relationships, even though at first glance it might appear that a contract was intended. If it can be shown that the promisee has materially changed his position in reasonable reliance on the promise, the law will not allow him to suffer. The promisor will be obligated to compensate the promisee. The promisor is barred, or estopped, from avoiding a promise because to do so would be unjust to the promisee.

The concepts of promissory estoppel and gifts are very closely related; however, with promissory estoppel the element of donative intent is lacking. For a gift to exist, it must be shown that a gift was intended. For promissory estoppel to exist, it must be shown that the promisee detrimentally relied on the promise, and that the promisor never intended to give the promisee a gift.

 EXAMPLES:

1. Simone promises to give Loretta $100,000, so that she will not have to work anymore. Based on this promise, Loretta quits her job. Here there is no mutuality of consideration because Simone did not promise the money in exchange for Loretta's promise not to work; she simply promised the money so that Loretta *would not have* to work.

But because Loretta quit her job based on Simone's promise, she can sue Simone under the doctrine of promissory estoppel to recover her lost wages. The court will not give her the full $100,000, but will compensate her for her actual loss based on Simone's promise.

2. Simone promises to pay for Loretta's college education. Based on this promise, Loretta enrolls in school. There is no contract. Simone didn't exchange her promise for Loretta's promise to go to college, but based on her promise Loretta has incurred the expense of tuition. The court will permit Loretta to recover her tuition from Simone because she acted in reliance on Simone's promise.

3. Simone promises to convey her farm in Vermont to Loretta so that Loretta won't have to live in the city anymore. Based on this promise, Loretta sells her house in the city, packs her belongings, and moves to Vermont. The court will enforce Simone's promise. Even though there was no mutuality of consideration, and thus no contract, Loretta has detrimentally relied on Simone's promise by changing her entire living condition. It would be unjust to let her suffer.

In each of the foregoing situations, Loretta has changed her position based on her reasonable belief that Simone would adhere to her promise. There is no specific indication that Simone intended a gift, and in no example did Simone receive anything of legal value, so there is no contract. However, under the court's equitable jurisdiction, these types of promises will be enforced to prevent injustice. Be aware, though, that under the doctrine of promissory estoppel, even though the promise is enforced, it is only enforced to the extent the promisee relied on the promise. Take note of the fact that if the promise is not relied on by the promisee to her detriment, the doctrine of promissory estoppel will not apply. It is an equitable doctrine designed to prevent injustice. If the promisee cannot prove detrimental reliance on the promise, it would be unfair to the promisor to force him to fulfill his promise when no injury was sustained.

To determine whether contract law or promissory estoppel exists, look for the mutuality of consideration, the intent of the offeror, and the possible illusory nature of the promise. If mutuality or legally sufficient consideration and contractual intent can be shown, a contract exists. It is not a situation to which the theory of promissory estoppel applies.

Special Agreements

There are several other types of agreements that ordinarily would fail as valid contracts for lack of consideration but that, because of the formality of the circumstances and the dictates of public policy, stand as enforceable obligations.

Accord and Satisfaction

An **accord and satisfaction** is a very particular type of agreement that results from a disagreement between the parties to an existing contract. One (or both) of the parties disputes that he has received the consideration promised in the contract; however, rather than litigating to have the court decide the parties' respective rights, they agree to modify their original agreement. Ordinarily there would be no consideration for the parties to rewrite an existing obligation; however, both sides have agreed to forgo their legal right to sue in court. This mutual detriment (forbearance of the right to sue) constitutes sufficient consideration for the new agreement.

EXAMPLE:

Farmer Green has a contract to sell 1000 bushels of Grade A oranges to Ace Supermarkets for $10 a bushel. On delivery day, Ace claims the oranges are Grade B, and is unwilling to pay more than $8 a bushel. Rather than sue, Green and Ace enter into an Accord and Satisfaction, and agree to a price of $9 per bushel, making no comment about the grade of the oranges.

In the example above, each side could have sued under the original contract, and, presumably, the accord and satisfaction gives each party less than he was promised under the original contract. But because each has forborne the lawsuit and has saved the expense of litigation, the accord and satisfaction will stand.

The requirements for a valid accord and satisfaction are

1. a valid contract;
2. a dispute between the parties with respect to that contract; and
3. an agreement to compromise the dispute rather than sue.

Accord and satisfactions are typically entitled as such on the top of the agreement.

Charitable Subscription

A **charitable subscription** is a pledge made to a charitable organization. Under most theories of law, it should be identified as a gift. However, as a matter of public policy, the law has mandated that these pledges are enforceable by the charities. Unlike the promisee in promissory estoppel who is limited to his actual loss, the charity will get the full pledge, not just what it lost in reliance on the promise.

EXAMPLE:

Every year the Muscular Dystrophy Foundation has a telethon to raise money. In the heat of the moment, Vivica calls in a pledge of $250. When the charity moves to collect the money, Vivica says she has changed her mind. The foundation can sue Vivica to redeem her pledge because it is a charitable subscription.

Debtor's Promises

A debtor who has been discharged of his obligation by the legal system is under no further duty to repay his creditors. A person can be legally discharged from his debt by going through bankruptcy or because the statute of limitations on the claim has expired.

If a debtor, under the above circumstances, voluntarily agrees to re-pay the debt, this gratuitous promise is enforceable against her even though the promise is not supported by consideration. Again, the law has determined that, as a matter of public policy, it is beneficial to encourage people to repay their debts. Therefore, even though the consideration is only moral consideration, the law will hold the debtor to her promise.

If the debt has been deemed unenforceable due to bankruptcy, the Bankruptcy Act imposes certain additional requirements to make the promise enforceable. The act requires the debtor to reaffirm the promise prior to final discharge by the court and to receive the court's consent. On the other hand, if the debt is barred only by the statute of limitations, the promise itself is generally considered sufficient to make the contract enforceable.

 EXAMPLE:

Floyd has been judicially declared bankrupt, and his creditors are being paid 50¢ on the dollar. Feeling very guilty about his creditors' losses, Floyd promises Jennifer, one of his creditors, that he will pay her back all that he owes her within six months. He gets the court's approval. Jennifer now has a legally enforceable claim against Floyd for the full amount.

Guarantees

A **guarantee** is a written promise to answer for the debts of another that is enforceable against the **guarantor.** The guarantee is given at the same time the debtor receives the subject consideration.

Under general contract law principles, it would appear that the guar-antor is not legally bound because she has not received any benefit from the promise. However, this is an example of a statutorily created *formal contract* designed to promote business and industry.

For the guarantee to be valid, the following requirements must be met:

1. a valid contract is entered into between two or more parties;
2. the guarantor creates the guarantee at the time the contract is executed; and
3. the guarantee is in writing.

 EXAMPLE:

Joanne wants to buy a house, but her credit record is poor. The bank agrees to give her a mortgage if her parents guarantee the loan.

When Joanne takes out the loan, her parents sign the mortgage contract as Joanne's guarantors. This is a valid guarantee.

Note that in the example given above, Joanne's parents are merely agreeing to answer for Joanne's payments *if* Joanne does not pay. This is to be contrasted with **co-signers.** Co-signers are persons who agree to be *equally* bound with the obligor, and the creditor can go after a co-signer *instead* of the actual obligor because each is equally liable. With co-signers, a joint and several liability is incurred: The mortgagee can sue either Joanne, or her parents, or all three of them together.

For the guarantee to be valid, the obligor must receive consideration at the time the guarantee is given.

 EXAMPLE:

In the circumstances given above, assume Joanne has an excellent credit history, and the bank loans her the money on her own signature. Two years later, Joanne loses her job, and the bank, worried about the mortgage payments, asks Joanne to have her parents come in to guarantee the loan. Joanne's parents agree to sign the mortgage. However, because Joanne already received the consideration and became obligated prior to the guarantee, the guarantee is not enforceable against her parents.

For the above guarantee to be enforceable against Joanne's parents, the bank must give Joanne some additional consideration at the time the guarantee is given, such as extending the time for payments, reducing the interest rate, or giving her additional money to increase the overall mortgage. Unless the guarantee is given at the time the obligation is incurred, the guarantee will not be enforceable.

Formal Contracts

A **formal** contract is a contract that meets special statutory requirements and as such is valid even though no consideration is mentioned. The statutory formality of these agreements gives them special status under the law and creates a special situation with respect to consideration. (See Chapter 1.) Each state's statutes indicate what is to be deemed a formal contract.

SAMPLE CLAUSES

| 1 |

Accord and Satisfaction

In Accord and Satisfaction of all claims arising out of the contract between Farmer Green and Ace Supermarkets dated _____, 20 _____ (Copy affixed hereto), the parties agree that the price for the oranges shall be $9 per bushel, payable in 30 days from this date.

| 2 |

Bill of Sale

Know all men by these presents that I, _____, of _____, in consideration of One Hundred Dollars ($100.00) to me paid by _____ of _____, have bargained and sold to said _____ the following goods and chattels, to wit:

(Specify goods and chattels)

Witness by hand and seal this _____ day of _____, 20 _____.

(Signatures)

_____

In drafting any contract, always be sure to specify all consideration.

| 3 |

Guarantee

In consideration of the mortgage entered into this _____ day of _____, 20 _____, between _____ of _____, and _____ bank, we, the undersigned, do hereby guarantee all payments due under said mortgage should said mortgagor be found in default.

(Signatures)

_____

CHAPTER SUMMARY

Consideration is the third major element of every valid contract. It is the subject matter of the contract for which the parties have bargained.

Consideration is generally defined as a benefit conferred or a detriment incurred at the request of the other party. For the contract to be enforceable each party to the contract must give and receive consideration. This is known as mutuality of consideration.

The actual market value of the consideration is not important; it simply must be something legally sufficient to support the contract. The law is not concerned with the market value of the good, service, or forbearance described in the contract; it is only concerned with whether the consideration is actually bargained for and is not intended to mask a gift.

Past consideration, moral consideration, gifts, and illusory promises are never sufficient to support a contractual agreement. However, there are certain situations in which the law has determined that in the interests of public policy, a contract will be found even though consideration is lacking. These situations are accord and satisfaction agreements, charitable subscriptions, debtors' gratuitous promises to pay otherwise unenforceable debts, written guarantees, and statutorily defined formal contracts.

Closely associated with the concept of contractual consideration is the doctrine of promissory estoppel, which the court uses to enforce a promise for reasons other than lack of consideration, even though no contract exists. This occurs when the promises made are unsupported by consideration, but the promisee has materially changed his position in reasonable reliance on those promises. In this instance, the court will permit the promisee to recover what he has lost based on the promise.

For a contract to be enforceable, the consideration must always be definite, certain, and specifically described.

SYNOPSIS

Consideration
1. Benefit conferred
2. Detriment incurred
3. Each side must give and receive bargained-for consideration

What is not consideration
1. Past consideration
2. Moral obligations
3. Gifts
4. Illusory promises
5. Legal duties

Sufficiency of consideration
Must be sufficient to support the contract

Promissory estoppel
      Illusory promises enforced by the court if detrimentally relied on
Special agreements
      1.   Accord and satisfaction
      2.   Charitable subscription
      3.   Debtor's promises
      4.   Guarantees
      5.   Formal contracts

Key Terms

Accord and satisfaction: a special agreement in which the parties to a
      disputed contract agree to new terms in exchange for forbearing
      to sue under the original contract
Caveat emptor: Latin phrase meaning "Let the buyer beware"
Caveat venditor: Latin phrase meaning "Let the seller beware"
Charitable subscription: pledge or promise to donate money to a char-
      ity; given the enforceability of a contract under law
Conditional promise: a promise dependent on the happening or non-
      happening of a future event
Consideration: a benefit conferred or a detriment incurred; a basic re-
      quirement of every valid contract
Co-signer: person who agrees to be equally liable with a promisor un-
      der a contract
Formal contract: written contract under seal specifically enforced by
      statute
Guarantee: an enforceable written promise to answer for the debts of
      another
Guarantor: person who agrees to be responsible to answer for the debts
      of another should the debtor default
Mutuality of consideration: the bargain element of a contract that re-
      quires each side to give and receive something of legal value
Nominal consideration: consideration of insufficient legal value to sup-
      port a contract
Preexisting duty rule: promises to do what one is already bound to do
      is not consideration
Promissory estoppel: doctrine in which promises not supported by con-
      sideration are given enforceability if the promisee had detrimen-
      tally relied on the promises
Quid pro quo: Latin phrase meaning "this for that"; the mutuality of
      consideration
Sham consideration: legally insufficient consideration used to mask a
      gift in words of contract
Sufficiency of the consideration: doctrine that each party to a contract
      must contribute something of legal value for which he has bar-
      gained

EXERCISES

1. Give two examples of consideration as a detriment incurred not discussed in the chapter.
2. Discuss mutuality of consideration with respect to your contract with your school.
3. Under what circumstances would a person argue the doctrine of promissory estoppel?
4. Find out what contracts are considered formal contracts in your jurisdiction.
5. Find and analyze a contract that requires a co-signer.

Cases for Analysis

The concept of consideration is generally one of the most confusing in contract law. To expand the previous discussion, the cases of Don King Productions, Inc. v. Douglas, and Cohen v. Cowles Media Co. are included.

Don King Productions, Inc. v. Douglas
742 F. Supp. 741 (S.D.N.Y. 1990)

. . . Indefiniteness of Consideration

According to Johnson and Douglas, the Promotion and Bout Agreements are unenforceable because they are indefinite as to the essential term of consideration. The facts are undisputed: the Promotion Agreement provided for payment of $25,000 to Douglas in return for his granting DKP the exclusive right to promote his bouts for a stated term. Compensation for the individual bouts that were contemplated by the Promotion Agreement (numbering no fewer than three per year, with the exception of the first contract year) was made subject to further negotiation and agreement, with the agreed-to terms to be set forth in the individually-negotiated bout agreements. The Promotion Agreement specified a floor level of compensation of $25,000, plus $10,000 in training expenses, for these fights, except that in the case of a title bout or defense of such a bout, no floor (or ceiling) was provided, the purse to be "negotiated and mutually agreed upon between us."

One such subsequent agreement as to Douglas' purse for a title fight was reached, as set forth in the Bout Agreement executed for the match with then-world champion Tyson. The Bout Agreement stated that "in full consideration of [Douglas'] participation in the [Tokyo] Bout and for all of the rights herein granted to Promoter," Douglas would be paid $1.3 million. That agreement further provided that with respect to Douglas'

first three fights post-Tokyo, upon which DKP was given an exclusive
option, the purse per fight would be $1 million, unless Douglas was the
winner in Tokyo, in which case the amount would be subject to negotiation with that sum of $1 million as a floor.

In the face of this contractual language, Douglas and Johnson are
forced to take the position that "although a minimum purse of $1,000,000
was specified, this is insufficient to render the contract sufficiently definite
for enforcement" because "the 'minimum' consideration is obviously a
token, at best." The factual predicate for the argument is that the market
at present values the world champion heavyweight fighter at considera-
bly more than one million dollars a pop (Johnson states he has received
offers as high as $50 million for Douglas to fight, and King apparently
offered him $15 million plus a percentage of gross receipts). Therefore,
the contractually-specified million dollar compensation floor is asserted
to be nothing other than the proverbial "peppercorn" of consideration.

Assuming the factual premise as to Douglas' present value, the argument, nevertheless, suffers once one considers that the appropriate
yard-stick for making the judgment. Whether one million dollars is token
consideration must be assessed by reference to Douglas' expected future
value as a fighter at the time the agreement was entered into, i.e., before
his unexpected defeat of Tyson. No one has contended on this record that
$1 million was a "mere token" vis-à-vis Douglas' value at the time he,
Johnson and their lawyer Enz, negotiated the Bout Agreement, and, in
fact, the parties, after such negotiations, fixed a figure reasonably proxi-
mate to that—$1.3 million—for services to be rendered in a title fight with
an undefeated heavy-weight champion. Thus, when Douglas and Johnson
signed the Bout Agreement they evidently did not regard one million
dollars as a "peppercorn," even if they did not regard it as the full (as
opposed to minimum) value to be affixed to Douglas' services when defending a championship. The subsequent change in Douglas' relative for-
tunes does not provide a legal basis now to disregard his prior agreement
as to the reasonable floor at which to begin discussion of the value of his
services as defending heavyweight champion.

It is standard contract law that a contract, to be binding, must address without "impenetrable vagueness" the terms material to its subject
matter. Joseph Martin, Jr. Delicatessen, Inc. v. Schumacher, 52 N.Y.2d 105,
109, 436 N.Y.S.2d 247, 249, 417 N.E.2d 541, 543 (1981). Just as well settled
is the proposition that

> to render a contract enforceable, absolute certainty is not required; it is
> enough if the promise or agreement is sufficiently definite and explicit so
> that the intention of the parties may be ascertained "to a reasonable cer-
> tainty." Varney v. Ditmars, 217 N.Y. 223, 228, 111 N.E. 822, 824, Ann. Cas.
> 1916B, 758. A contract cannot be ignored as meaningless, except as a last
> resort. "Indefiniteness must reach the point where construction becomes
> futile." Cohen & Sons v. M. Lurie Woolen Co., 232 N.Y. 112, 114, 133 N.E.
> 370, 371.

Here, the Promotional Agreement and Bout Agreement addressed their essential subject matter in a manner that is far from impenetrable. While leaving certain terms open to future negotiation, the contracts were explicit and definite about Douglas' commitment to fight only for DKP during the life of those contracts and about the minimum consideration he could receive for making that commitment. Thus, the contracts, at least with respect to their exclusivity terms, are much more than "mere agreements to agree." Joseph Martin, Jr. Delicatessen, 52 N.Y.2d at 109, 436 N.Y.S.2d at 249, 417 N.E.2d at 543.

The parties agreed to leave open the compensation that would be payable under certain contingencies, such as after Douglas' becoming world champion (in contrast to the fixed purse for title fights against another champion, which were priced at $1 million a bout) and this may have repercussions as to Douglas' obligation to fight a particular title defense at a particular price named by King, since no separate bout agreement has been executed for such fight pursuant to the process of negotiation contemplated by the Promotion Agreement for fights to be held under its provisions. Nevertheless, the writing manifests in definite language Douglas and DKP's agreement to deal exclusively with one another with respect to title defenses and to negotiate in an effort to reach a mutual understanding as to the open price term for such a defense.

For that reason, the exclusivity provisions of the Agreements are not void *ab initio* on grounds of price indefiniteness. See R. S. Stokvis & Sons v. Kearney & Trecker Corp., 58 F. Supp. 260, 267 (S.D.N.Y. 1944) (agreement containing definite grant of "exclusive representation" valid as to that term, notwithstanding that agreement contained "no provisions with respect to quantities, prices, deliveries, payments, or even discounts," all of which were "left 'to be arranged separately.'"). Whether $1 million turns out to be a definite default price—or merely a minimum price— simply does not control the question of whether Douglas and Johnson have violated the definite right they granted to DKP to exclusively "secure and arrange all [of Douglas'] professional boxing bouts" and their definite duty under the Agreement to refrain from "render[ing][] services as a professional boxer to any person, firm or entity" other than DKP. That is because the minimum price terms, together with DKP's upfront payment of $25,000 and its commitments to hold a set number of bouts, clearly did provide an expectancy of compensation for Douglas that was sufficiently definite to induce his promise to fight exclusively for DKP. Accordingly, Douglas/Johnson fail to sustain their burden as movants seeking dismissal of the complaint on the ground that the underlying instruments are too illusory to be breached.

Adequacy of the Term

Douglas and Johnson next urge that this case is an appropriate one for application of the maxim that "an option actually intended by the parties to run for an unlimited time, i.e., forever is void." Mohr Park Manor, Inc. v. Mohr, 83 Nev. 107, 424 P.2d 101 (1967).

The Promotional Agreement and Bout Agreement do not fall into that class of contracts, as both contain clauses explicitly addressing duration and neither contemplates an indefinite term. The former provides that it shall run for three years and shall be "automatically extended to cover the entire period [Douglas is] world champion and a period of two years following the date on which [Douglas] thereafter cease[s], for any reason, to be so recognized as world champion." So extensive a commitment of one's services might be questioned as excessive, but clearly does not suffer from indefiniteness or ambiguity. Nor does the Bout Agreement: it grants DKP an exclusive option on the promotion of Douglas' "next three fights," which must be exercised within thirty days of the Tokyo bout.

Both are contracts "of the type . . . which do provide for termination or cancellation upon the occurrence of a specified event," Payroll Express Corp. v. Aetna Casualty & Sur. Co., 659 F.2d 285, 291 (2d Cir. 1981), and are therefore not jeopardized by the void-for-indefiniteness rule. Id. Contracts which "provide no fixed date for the termination of the promisor's obligation but condition the obligation upon an event which would necessarily terminate the contract" remain in force until that event occurs. Warner-Lambert Pharmaceutical Co. v. John J. Reynolds, Inc., 178 F. Supp. 655 (S.D.N.Y. 1959), aff'd, 280 F.2d 197 (2d Cir. 1960) (upholding contract entered into in 1881 that lacked termination date but which obligated pharmaceutical manufacturer to pay royalties on every gross of "Listerine" made and sold by it as long as it continued to manufacture the product); Ketcham v. Hall Syndicate, Inc., 37 Misc. 2d 693, 236 N.Y.S.2d 206, 212-213 (Sup. Ct. 1962) (agreement for syndication of cartoons sufficiently definite as to term where duration of contract was made subject to termination in event artist's share of revenue fell below stipulated amount), aff'd, 19 A.D.2d 611, 242 N.Y.S.2d 182 (1st Dep't 1963). . . .

The Unconscionable Contracts Defense

Douglas and Johnson plead as an affirmative defense that the contracts they entered into with DKP are unconscionable. Under New York law, a determination of unconscionability

> requires a showing that the contract was both procedurally and substantively unconscionable *when made*—i.e., "some showing of an 'absence of meaningful choice on the part of one of the parties together with contract terms which are unreasonably favorable to the other party.'"

Gillman v. Chase Manhattan Bank, N.A., 73 N.Y.2d 1, 10, 537 N.Y.S.2d 787, 791, 534 N.E.2d 824, 828 (1988) (citations omitted and emphasis supplied). The factual contentions set forth in the Douglas/Johnson interrogatories to support the unconscionability defense—that the Tokyo conduct of King was unconscionable, that King is a powerful promoter, and that exclusive, extendable terms of the contracts are unreasonably favorable to King—are as a matter of law insufficient.

The Douglas/Johnson contention that the contracts "became unconscionable" *after* their inception owing to King's conduct during the Tokyo fight is unavailing, as the underlined language in Gillman illustrates. The doctrine of unconscionability implicates the circumstances and terms of a contract at the time of formation—not the parties' subsequent performance under it. See State v. Avco Financial Service of New York, Inc., 50 N.Y.2d 383, 390, 429 N.Y.S.2d 181, 185, 406 N.E.2d 1075, 1079 (1980) (referring to "circumstances existing at the time of the making"). The Tokyo performance by King is, of course, relevant to whether King breached his obligations of good faith and fair dealing under the contracts, an issue discussed at length in the May 18 Opinion and which has been reserved for trial to a jury. That conduct has, however, absolutely no bearing on the defense of unconscionability, which relates to substantive and procedural fairness of a contract "when made." *Gillman*, 73 N.Y.2d at 10, 537 N.Y.S.2d at 791, 534 N.E.2d at 828.

Douglas/Johnson next contend that King so dominates promotion of heavyweight fights that the Douglas-King contracts are inherently procedurally unconscionable. That assertion, if true, sounds more probative of an antitrust claim for monopolization than it is demonstrative of the particularized showing of an unfair bargaining process that is requisite to the defense of unconscionability. Douglas/Johnson make no allegation here that deceptive or high-pressure tactics were employed in concluding the contracts, that contract terms were concealed in fine print, or that there was a gross asymmetry in the experience and education of the parties, each of whom was represented by counsel throughout the course of their arms-length negotiations. See May 18 Opinion at 747; cf. *Gillman*, 73 N.Y.2d at 11, 537 N.Y.S.2d at 791, 534 N.E.2d at 828 (identifying relevance of these and other factors to establishment of procedural unfairness).

At least as stated in the responses to the contention interrogatories, the unconscionability defense does not here implicate its primary use as "a means with which to protect the commercially illiterate consumer beguiled into a grossly unfair bargain by a deceptive vendor or finance company." Marvel Entertainment Group, Inc. v. Young Astronaut Council, No. 88-5141, 1989 WL 129504 (S.D.N.Y. October 27, 1989). Without some definite allegation of a defect in the contract negotiation process apart from King's stature in the boxing field, which alone does not suggest "inequality so strong and manifest as to shock the conscience and confound the judgment," id. (quoting Christian v. Christian, 42 N.Y.2d 63, 71, 396 N.Y.S.2d 817, 823, 365 N.E.2d 849, 855 (1977)), defendants have failed to create an issue of procedural unconscionability requiring resolution by jury.

The contention that the contracts require Douglas to fight exclusively for DKP for the extendable terms of such contracts, which could amount to the rest of the boxer's professional life, equally fails to satisfy the requirement of substantive unconscionability. Only in "exceptional cases" is "a provision of [a] contract . . . so outrageous as to warrant holding it unenforceable on the ground of substantive unconscionability alone." *Gillman*, 73 N.Y.2d at 12, 537 N.Y.S.2d at 792, 534 N.E.2d at 829 (omitting-citations); see also *Marvel Entertainment* (citing Christian v. Christian, 42 N.Y.2d 63, 71, 396 N.Y.S.2d 817, 823, 365 N.E.2d 849, 855 (1977)) (terms must be "such as no [person] in his senses and not under delusion would make on one hand, and no honest and fair [person] would accept on the other").

Douglas and Johnson fail to make any proffer as to what makes this term of their contract so exceptional as to fit within in the line of cases referred to in *Gillman*, and they cite to no case considering or holding an exclusive services contract unconscionable on grounds of duration. . . . The court therefore declines to revisit its prior legal determinations that the contract durational terms were definite in nature and the contracts were supported by sufficiently-definite price consideration to induce Douglas' promise to fight exclusively for DKP. See May 18 Opinion at 761-764. The unconscionability defense accordingly shall be stricken, there having been no proffer or allegation sufficient to establish either its procedural or substantive elements. . . .

Questions

1. Do you think the contract was fair to Douglas? Why, or why not?
2. What do you think of the court's analysis of the indefiniteness of the contract?
3. Do you believe that the contract is unconscionable? Why, or why not?
4. If your firm was representing Douglas, what other arguments might you propose?

Cohen v. Cowles Media Co.

445 N.W.2d 248, *review granted, aff'd in part, rev'd in part,*
457 N.W.2d 199 (Minn. App. 1990)

SIMONETT, Justice.

This case asks whether a newspaper's breach of its reporter's promise of anonymity to a news source is legally enforceable. We conclude the promise is not enforceable, neither as a breach of contract claim nor, in this case, under promissory estoppel. We affirm the court of appeals' dismissal of plaintiff's claim based on fraudulent misrepresentation, and reverse the court of appeals' allowance of the breach of contract claim.

Claiming a reporter's promise to keep his name out of a news story was broken, plaintiff Dan Cohen sued defendants Northwest Publications, Inc., publisher of the St. Paul Pioneer Press Dispatch (Pioneer Press), and Cowles Media Company, publisher of the Minneapolis Star and Tribune (Star Tribune). The trial court ruled that the First Amendment did not bar Cohen's contract and misrepresentation claims. The jury then found liability on both claims and awarded plaintiff $200,000 compensatory damages jointly and severally against the defendants. In addition, the jury awarded punitive damages of $250,000 against each defendant.

The court of appeals (2-1 decision) agreed that plaintiff's claims did not involve state action and therefore did not implicate the First Amendment; further, that even if First Amendment rights were implicated, those rights were outweighed by compelling state interests and, in any event, such rights were waived by the newspapers. The appeals panel ruled, however, that misrepresentation had not been proven as a matter of law and, therefore, set aside the punitive damages award. The panel upheld the jury's finding of a breach of contract and affirmed the award of $200,000 compensatory damages. Cohen v. Cowles Media Co., 445 N.W.2d 248 (Minn. App. 1989). We granted petitions for further review from all parties. . . .

Promising to keep a news source anonymous is a common, well-established journalistic practice. So is the keeping of those promises. None of the editors or reporters who testified could recall any other instance when a reporter's promise of confidentiality to a source had been over-ruled by the editor. Cohen, who had many years' experience in politics and public relations, said this was the first time in his experience that an editor or a reporter did not honor a promise to a source.

[On] October 28, 1982, both newspapers published stories and both articles published Cohen's name. Under the headline, *Marlene Johnson arrests disclosed by Whitney ally*, the Star Tribune identified Cohen as a "political associate of IR gubernatorial candidate Wheelock Whitney" and named the advertising firm where Cohen was employed. . . .

The same day as the two newspaper articles were published, Cohen was fired by his employer. The next day, October 29, a columnist for the Star Tribune attacked Cohen and his "sleazy" tactics, with, ironically, no reference to the newspaper's own ethics in dishonoring its promise. A day later the Star Tribune published a cartoon on its editorial page depicting Dan Cohen with a garbage can labeled "last minute campaign smears."

Cohen could not sue for defamation because the information disclosed was true. He couched his complaint, therefore, in terms of fraudulent misrepresentation and breach of contract. We now consider whether these two claims apply here.

I

First of all, we agree with the court of appeals that the trial court erred in not granting defendants' post-trial motions for judgment not withstanding the verdict on the misrepresentation claim.

For fraud there must be a misrepresentation of a past or present fact. A representation as to future acts does not support an action for fraud merely because the represented act did not happen, unless the promisor did not intend to perform at the time the promise was made. Vandeputte v. Soderholm, 298 Minn. 505, 508, 216 N.W.2d 144, 147 (1974). Cohen admits that the reporters intended to keep their promises, as, indeed, they testified and as their conduct confirmed. Moreover, the record shows that the editors had no intention to reveal Cohen's identity until later when more information was received and the matter was discussed with other editors. These facts do not support a fraud claim. For this reason and for the other reasons cited by the court of appeals, we affirm the court of appeals' ruling. Because the punitive damages award hinges on the tort claim of misrepresentation, it, too, must be set aside as the court of appeals ruled.

II

A contract, it is said, consists of an offer, an acceptance, and consideration. Here, we seemingly have all three, plus a breach. We think, however, the matter is not this simple.

Unquestionably, the promises given in this case were intended by the promisors to be kept. The record is replete with the unanimous testimony of reporters, editors, and journalism experts that protecting a confidential source of a news story is a sacred trust, a matter of "honor," of "morality," and required by professional ethics. Only in dire circumstances might a promise of confidentiality possibly be ethically broken, and instances were cited where a reporter has gone to jail rather than reveal a source. The keeping of promises is professionally important for at least two reasons. First, to break a promise of confidentiality which has induced a source to give information is dishonorable. Secondly, if it is known that promises will not be kept, sources may dry up. The media depend on confidential sources for much of their news; significantly, at least up to now, it appears that journalistic ethics have adequately protected confidential sources.

The question before us, however, is not whether keeping a confidential promise is ethically required but whether it is legally enforceable; whether, in other words, the law should superimpose a legal obligation on a moral and ethical obligation. The two obligations are not always coextensive.

The newspapers argue that the reporter's promise should not be contractually binding because these promises are usually given clandestinely and orally, hence they are often vague, subject to misunderstanding, and a fertile breeding ground for lawsuits. See Ruzicka v. Conde Nast Publications, Inc., 733 F. Supp. 1289, 1300-01 (D. Minn. 1990) (a promise not to make a source identifiable found too vague to be enforceable). Perhaps so, and this may be a factor to weigh in the balance; but this objection goes only to problems of proof, rather than to the merits of having such a cause of action at all. Moreover, in this case at least, we have a clear-cut promise.

The law, however, does not create a contract where the parties intended none. Linne v. Ronkainen, 228 Minn. 316, 320, 37 N.W.2d 237, 239 (1949). Nor does the law consider binding every exchange of promises. See, e.g., Minn. Stat. ch. 553 (1988) (abolishing breaches of contract to marry); see also Restatement (Second) of Contracts §§189-191 (1981) (promises impairing family relations are unenforceable). We are not persuaded that in the special milieu of media newsgathering a source and a reporter ordinarily believe they are engaged in making a legally binding contract. They are not thinking in terms of offers and acceptances in any commercial or business sense. The parties understand that the reporter's promise of anonymity is given as a moral commitment, but a moral obligation alone will not support a contract. See Cruickshank v. Ellis, 178 Minn. 103, 107, 226 N.W. 192, 194 (1929). Indeed, a payment of money which taints the integrity of the newsgathering function, such as money paid a reporter for the publishing of a news story, is forbidden by the ethics of journalism.

What we have here, it seems to us, is an "I'll-scratch-your-back-if you'll-scratch-mine" accommodation. The source, for whatever reasons, wants certain information published. The reporter can only evaluate the information after receiving it, which is after the promise is given; and the editor can only make a reasonable, informed judgment after the information received is put in the larger context of the news. The durability and duration of the confidence is usually left unsaid, dependent on unfolding developments; and none of the parties can safely predict the consequences of publication. See supra note 4. Each party, we think, assumes the risks of what might happen, protected only by the good faith of the other party.

In other words, contract law seems here an ill fit for a promise of news source confidentiality. To impose a contract theory on this arrangement puts an unwarranted legal rigidity on a special ethical relationship, precluding necessary consideration of factors underlying that ethical relationship. We conclude that a contract cause of action is inappropriate for these particular circumstances.

III

But if a confidentiality promise is not a legally binding contract, might the promise otherwise be enforceable? In Christensen v. Minneapolis Mun. Employees Retirement Bd., 331 N.W.2d 740, 747 (Minn. 1983), we declined to apply a "conventional contract approach, with its strict rules of offer and acceptance" in the context of public pension entitlements, pointing out this approach "tends to deprive the analysis of the relationship between the state and its employees of a needed flexibility." We opted instead for a promissory estoppel analysis. The doctrine of promissory estoppel implies a contract in law where none exists in fact. According to the doctrine, well-established in this state, a promise expected or reasonably expected to induce definite action by the promisee that does induce action is binding if injustice can be avoided only by enforcing the promise.

In our case we have, without dispute, the reporters' unambiguous promise to treat Cohen as an anonymous source. The reporters expected that promise to induce Cohen to give them the documents, which he did to his detriment. The promise applied only to Cohen's identity, not to anything about the court records themselves.

We are troubled, however, by the third requirement for promissory estoppel, namely, the requirement that injustice can only be avoided by enforcing the promise. Here Cohen lost his job; but whether this is an injustice which should be remedied requires the court to examine a transaction fraught with moral ambiguity. Both sides proclaim their own purity of intentions while condemning the other side for "dirty tricks." Anonymity gives the source deniability, but deniability, depending on the circumstances, may or may not deserve legal protection. If the court applies promissory estoppel, its inquiry is not limited to whether a promise was given and broken, but rather the inquiry is into all the reasons why it was broken.

Lurking in the background of this case has been the newspapers' contention that any state-imposed sanction in this case violates their constitutional rights of a free press and free speech. Under the contract analysis earlier discussed, the focus was more on whether a binding promise was intended and breached, not so much on the contents of that promise or the nature of the information exchanged for the promise. See Restatement (Second) of Contracts, ch. 8, introductory note (1981) ("In general, parties may contract as they wish, and courts will enforce their agreements without passing on their substance."). Thus, the court of appeals, using a contract approach, concluded that applying "neutral principles" of contract law either did not trigger First Amendment scrutiny or, if it did, the state's interest in freedom of contract outweighed any constitutional free press rights. 445 N.W.2d at 254-257. Because we decide that contract law does not apply, we have not up to now had to consider First Amendment implications. But now we must. Under a promissory estoppel analysis there can be no neutrality towards the First Amendment. In deciding whether it would be unjust not to enforce the promise, the court must necessarily weigh the same considerations that are weighed for whether the First Amendment has been violated. The court must balance the constitutional rights of a free press against the common law interest in protecting a promise of anonymity.

For example, was Cohen's name "newsworthy"? Was publishing it necessary for a fair and balanced story? Would identifying the source simply as being close to the Whitney campaign have been enough? The witnesses at trial were sharply divided on these questions. Under promissory estoppel, the court cannot avoid answering these questions, even though to do so would mean second-guessing the newspaper editors. See, e.g., Miami Herald Pub. Co. v. Tornillo, 418 U.S. 241, 258, 94 S. Ct. 2831, 2839, 41 L. Ed. 2d 730 (1974) ("The choice of material to go into a newspaper . . . constitute[s] the exercise of editorial control and judgment," a process critical to the First Amendment guarantees of a free press.). Of critical significance in this case, we think, is the fact that the promise of anonymity arises in the classic First Amendment context of the quintessential public debate in our democratic society, namely, a political source involved in a political campaign. The potentiality for civil damages for promises made in this context chills public debate, a debate which Cohen willingly entered albeit hoping to do so on his own terms. In this context, and considering the nature of the political story involved, it seems to us that the law best leaves the parties here to their trust in each other.

We conclude that in this case enforcement of the promise of confidentiality under a promissory estoppel theory would violate defendants' First Amendment rights. In cases of this kind, the United States Supreme Court has said it will proceed cautiously, deciding only in a "discrete factual context." The Florida Star v. B.J.F., — U.S. —, —, 109 S. Ct. 2603, 2607, 105 L. Ed. 2d 443 (1989). We, too, are not inclined to decide more than we have to decide. There may be instances where a confidential source would be entitled to a remedy such as promissory estoppel, when the state's interest in enforcing the promise to the source outweighs First Amendment considerations, but this is not such a case. Plaintiff's claim cannot be maintained on a contract theory. Neither is it sustainable under promissory estoppel. The judgment for plaintiff is reversed.

Affirmed in part and reversed in part.

Questions

1. Why does the court hold that the reporter's promise constitutes consideration for a contract?

2. Why does the court hold that the reporter's promise does not constitute promissory estoppel?

3. Do you think the result is fair to the plaintiff?

Suggested Case References

1. Does having a contract under seal negate the necessity of having consideration? Read what the Massachusetts court said in Thomas v. Kiendzior, 27 Mass. App. Ct. 370, 538 N.E.2d 66 (1989).

2. Can forbearance of right to assert a valid and mature claim be consideration for a promise? First Texas Sav. Ass'n v. Comprop Inv. Properties, Ltd., 752 F. Supp. 1568 (M.D. Fla. 1990).

3. For a definition of consideration by an Arkansas court, read Bass v. Service Supply Co., Inc., 25 Ark. App. 273, 757 S.W.2d 189 (1988).

5 Legality of Subject Matter and Contractual Capacity

CHAPTER OVERVIEW

The first three elements of a valid contract—offer, acceptance, and consideration—discussed in the preceding chapters focus on the actual terms of the agreement itself. The last three requisite elements of a valid contract are concerned with the circumstances surrounding the agreement—the legality of the subject matter, the ability of the parties to enter into enforceable contractual agreements, and the intent of the parties. This chapter examines the fourth and fifth requirements: legality and capacity.

For a contract to be valid and enforceable, the contract must be formed for a legal purpose. If the subject matter of the agreement violates statutory law or public policy, the court would be unable and unwilling to permit its provisions to be carried out. Consequently, even though all the other elements of a valid contract may be present, if the subject matter of the contract is illegal, no enforceable agreement can exist.

In addition to the legality of the subject matter, the law is also concerned with the legal ability of the parties to create a valid contract. The law has decided that under certain circumstances and conditions a person is legally incapable of forming a valid contract. These standards of contractual capacity are based on the person's age and mental condition at the moment the contract is entered into.

Legality of the Subject Matter

Contracts that are entered into for an illegal purpose are not enforceable. The reason is obvious. How can a court, designated to uphold the law, enforce an agreement that purports to break the law?

However, not all laws involve heinous actions, and the law has divided "illegality" into two broad categories. The first category contains laws that support the very nature and fabric of society. Violation of these rules go against all public policy, and contracts violating them are completely void and unenforceable. The second category includes minor illegalities, those laws created by statute that bar actions which are not, in and of themselves, morally reprehensible. Contracts that violate this second category may still permit the injured party some form of **quasi-contractual** relief.

Malum in Se

The first category of illegality, those contracts that violate public policy, are deemed **malum in se**—bad in and of themselves. The actions prohibited by these laws are considered to be morally reprehensible, and contracts formed for purposes *malum in se* are entirely unenforceable. Typical examples of these types of laws are felonies, contracts in restraint of trade, contracts found to discriminate against a protected category of citizen (race, age, sex, national origin, and so forth), and contracts that are deemed unconscionable.

 EXAMPLES:

1. Wally enters into a contract with Eddie, promising Eddie $10,000 if Eddie can find a hit man to kill Wally's business partner. Although all the other requisite elements of a valid contract may exist, in this instance the contract is still unenforceable because murder is considered *malum in se*.

2. Gamma, Inc. and Beta Corp. enter into a contract to fix their prices, thus driving all other competition out of their market. This contract is unenforceable because its purpose is to restrain trade, which is *malum in se*.

3. Violet needs a new secretary and hires an employment agency to find her a suitable employee. Violet makes it a condition of her agreement with the agency that they find her only white male secretaries. This contract is unenforceable. The provisions are meant to discriminate against persons based on race and sex, which is *malum in se*.

Malum Prohibitum

The second category of illegal subject matter encompasses actions that are not morally reprehensible or against public policy but are still minor violations of the law. This category is known as **malum prohibitum**—a prohibited wrong, or something prohibited by statutory regulation. Although contracts that are *malum prohibitum* are unenforceable, some quasi-contractual relief may be available if the aggrieved party can demonstrate that to deny recovery would unjustly enrich the other party to the agreement. The following is a sample list of contracts that are viewed as *malum prohibitum*. Every state code has its own statutory prohibitions, and you should review each state's laws independently.

Contracts that Violate the Statute of Frauds.   The **Statute of Frauds** is a law that requires certain types of contracts to be in writing in order to be enforceable. Typically, six types of contracts come within the provisions of the Statute of Frauds:

1. contracts for an interest in realty;
2. contracts that are not to be performed within one year;
3. contracts in consideration of marriage;
4. guarantees;
5. sale of goods valued at over $500; and
6. executors' promises to pay the decedent's debts.

A complete discussion of the Statute of Frauds appears in Chapter 7, Contract Provisions.

Although the statute requires these types of contracts to be in writing, if the parties actually perform under the oral agreement, their performances will take the contract out of the Statute of Frauds and make it enforceable.

 EXAMPLES:

1. In consideration of her promise to marry him, Donald promises to give $5 million to Marla. For this contract to be enforceable in a court of law, Marla had better get the promise in writing. Otherwise it violates the Statute of Frauds and is *malum prohibitum*.

2. Cathy and LaWanda enter into an oral agreement whereby LaWanda agrees to buy Cathy's summer home for $25,000. Because the agreement is for the sale of an interest in real estate, the Statute of Frauds applies, and the parties can avoid the agreement because it is *malum prohibitum*.

3. Cathy and LaWanda enter into an oral agreement whereby LaWanda agrees to buy Cathy's summer home for $25,000. Two weeks after the agreement was reached, LaWanda gives Cathy a check for the purchase price. The next day Cathy changes her mind and tries to avoid the agreement by saying it violates the Statute of Frauds. Because LaWanda has already performed, the court would most probably decide that LaWanda's performance has taken the contract out of the category of *malum prohibitum*.

Usury.   **Usury** laws regulate the legal rate of interest that can be charged for extending credit. A contract for the loan of money that indicates a rate of interest above the legal limit is *malum prohibitum* because it is usurious and therefore unenforceable. If the lender has already performed, some courts will permit him to receive the legal rate of interest; to do otherwise would mean the borrower received the money interest-free, which would be unfair to the lender. (In some states, the usurer cannot even collect the principal. Each state statute must be specifically checked).

EXAMPLE:

Rhonda agrees to lend Lennie $2000 at an annual rate of interest of 50 percent. The contract is unenforceable as being *malum prohibitum*. However, if Rhonda actually gave the money to Lenny, Lenny may be required to repay the loan at the legal rate of interest.

Gambling.   Gambling, except in certain locations and under certain prescribed situations, is illegal. Consequently, a contract entered into for the purpose of betting is *malum prohibitum*.

EXAMPLE:

Saul leases a building to operate a gambling casino in downtown St. Louis. Gambling is not permitted in Missouri, and so the contract is *malum prohibitum*. The lease may still be operative if the building can be used for a legal purpose.

Licensing Statutes.   State and local communities have various licensing statutes, laws that require certain types of occupations or enterprises to receive a governmental permission to operate. Any contract that would violate the government licensing statute is *malum prohibitum*.

EXAMPLE:

Sherree and Latoya enter into an agreement to open and operate a beauty and hair salon. Beauticians and hairdressers are required to be licensed by the state. If neither Sherree nor Latoya is licensed, the contract is *malum prohibitum*.

Laws that impose licensing requirements are created either to protect the public or to provide the government with income from the licensing fees. If the agreement violates a licensing law designed to protect the public, no recovery at all is possible. If the purpose of the licensing statute is merely to raise revenue, some quasi-contractual remedy may be available.

EXAMPLES:

1. Ernie goes to Veronica for medical assistance. Although Veronica holds herself out to be a doctor, she, in fact, is not a doctor. Therefore, Veronica's agreement with Ernie for a fee is *malum prohibitum*. In this instance, Veronica cannot recover the value of her services to Ernie. To do so would potentially endanger the public.

2. La Dolce Vita, an Italian restaurant, serves alcohol and wine to its customers. The restaurant does not have a liquor license. In this instance, even though the contract for the sale of liquor is *malum prohibitum*, the restaurant may be allowed to recover the cost of the alcohol it sold. This statute is designed to raise revenue for the government.

As indicated above, contracts that are *malum prohibitum* are not considered as seriously wrong as those that are *malum in se*, although neither category creates a valid contract. But because the law generally favors contractual relationships, it does sometimes permit an agreement that has both legal and illegal provisions to be **severed:** that is, the legal portion of the contract, if possible, is separated from the illegal portion and upheld, whereas the illegal portion remains unenforceable. This concept was exemplified above in the examples where portions of the agreement were permitted to stand, such as the lease of the building in St. Louis and the loan of the money.

Contractual Capacity

Contractual capacity, the fifth requisite element of every valid contract, refers to the parties' legal ability to enter into a binding contractual relationship. In reality, the concept of contractual capacity is concerned more with defining contractual incapacity than it is with defining contractual capacity. There are four major areas of contractual capacity, which are discussed below.

Age

Age is the most common capacity issue to arise. The law divides a person's age into two major categories: *adulthood* (or **majority**) and **minority**.

An *adult* is anyone over the *age of consent*, which most states designate to begin at age 18. (Some statutes, however, may establish younger limits for the age of consent.) Adults are considered contractually capable with respect to age.

A *minor* is anyone under the age of consent pursuant to state statute. Minors are further subdivided into **natural infants** and **children of tender years**. A natural infant, a child younger than 7, is considered totally incapable of entering into any contract because of extreme youth. A child of tender years, a minor between the ages of 7 and 14, is usually considered too young to form a valid contract, but that decision is based on the particulars of the contract in question.

Those persons between puberty and the age of consent, the group inbetween the above-mentioned categories, are deemed to be minors. As mentioned in Chapter 1, minors are generally considered to lack contractual capacity. It is this age group that causes the most concern with respect to the capacity of a person to enter into a valid contract. Minors may avoid contracts they enter into at any point up to reaching their majority without being in breach of contract. The contracts entered into by minors are considered **voidable** at the option of the minor, which is why most people who contract with minors require that an adult, usually the minor's parent, guarantee the contract.

 EXAMPLE:

Floyd, a 17-year-old, has just received several CDs as a holiday present. Floyd doesn't own a CD player, but he sees one advertised at a price he can afford. If he enters into a contract with the store owner to buy the CD player, Floyd can rescind his acceptance anytime prior to reaching age 18 without being in breach of contract. However,

Floyd may be charged for the use of the CD player until his disavowal of the agreement.

There are certain categories of contracts that the law has determined that minors cannot avoid. These contracts are contracts to provide the minor with **necessaries**—items deemed essential to support life such as food, clothing, shelter, and medical aid. Be aware, though, that some states require only **emancipated** minors to be bound to contracts for necessaries. Emancipated minors are those no longer under the legal care of an adult; they are responsible for all their own actions. These situations are usually treated as quasi-contracts; that is, the reasonable value of the item, not necessarily the contract price, may be recovered.

In addition, many states prohibit a minor from avoiding contracts for education or marriage, and the federal government has determined that minors cannot avoid their voluntary military enlistment simply because of age.

 EXAMPLE:

Nick graduates high school at age 17 and decides to enlist in the army to fulfill a lifelong dream of becoming a soldier. After 8 days of boot camp, Nick regrets his decision and tells his sergeant he wants out. Too late. A minor may not avoid his contract for enlistment with Uncle Sam.

Mental Capacity

A mentally deficient person lacks contractual capacity. If the person is in a mental institution, this lack of capacity exists until such time as he is adjudged mentally competent by an appropriate authority. If, on the other hand, the person merely suffers occasional mental lapses and is not confined, his mental capacity is determined by the nature of the contract, and whether or not he understands the nature of what he is undertaking. Any question dealing with a person's mental capacity is always determined on the facts and circumstances of each individual situation.

 EXAMPLE:

Marvin hears voices that tell him what clothes to wear and what horses to bet on. After placing a bet with his bookie, Charlotte, Marvin gets hungry and goes to a fast food restaurant for a hamburger and fries. The contract with the restaurant is valid. Marvin's mental state has no affect or relationship to this particular contract.

Alcohol and Drugs

A person who is under the influence of alcohol or drugs is incapable of entering into a valid contract. The incapacity is only temporary, however. When the effect of the alcohol or drug wears off, provided no other problems exist, the person is considered to be contractually capable once again. Any contract entered into during the period of incapacity may be reaffirmed and made valid once the temporary incapacity is removed. As with mental incapacity, the determination as to the person's mental state at the moment of contract is determined on a case-by-case basis.

 EXAMPLE:

Bess is 80 years old and takes medication whenever she has a heart palpitation. As a side effect of the drug, Bess becomes dizzy and disoriented. During the period of disorientation, an encyclopedia salesperson rings Bess's doorbell and convinces her to buy a set of encyclopedias. The next day, when the effect of the medicine wears off, Bess realizes what she has signed but feels the books would be a good gift for her son. Bess can either avoid the contract, because of her drug-induced mental state at the time of the signing, or affirm the contract now that the medicine has worn off.

CHAPTER SUMMARY

Even if an agreement possesses the elements of a valid offer and acceptance and is supported by legally sufficient consideration, the contract will still fail if it is formed for a legally proscribed purpose or if one of the parties lacks contractual capacity.

A contract is considered formed for an illegal purpose if the subject matter is either *malum in se* or *malum prohibitum*. Agreements that are *malum in se* are those formed for purposes that go against the moral grain of society. Such contracts are unenforceable as a matter of public policy. Some examples of *malum in se* agreements are agreements to commit crimes, to discriminate, or to restrain trade.

By comparison, a contract is considered *malum prohibitum* if its subject matter violates some less serious prohibition. This type of illegality is not considered morally reprehensible, and, consequently, if injury can be shown, the court will permit the injured party some remedy based on a quasi-contractual claim. Some examples of *malum prohibitum* agreements are those that violate the Statute of Frauds, usury or licensing laws, or gambling statutes.

Each state has determined the legal age of contractual consent for its citizens. If a contract is entered into by someone considered a minor under the appropriate state statute, that contract is voidable by the minor any time until the minor reaches majority. Although the contract is voidable, on reaching majority the minor may choose to affirm the contract, thereby making it enforceable. Note that exceptions to this rule are made for contracts entered into by minors for necessaries, marriage, and enlistment in the armed services.

In addition to the age of the party to a contract, the law also looks to the person's mental state at the time of contracting. Persons who are mentally incapable lack contractual capacity. Persons who are under the influence of drugs or alcohol are considered to be temporarily incapable, but they may affirm the contract once the temporary infirmity is removed.

In any instance, anytime a person has performed his contractual obligation, except for contracts *malum in se* or when the person is totally incapable, that performance will usually entitle him to some form of legal recovery so as to avoid injury and to prevent unjust enrichment.

SYNOPSIS

Legality of subject matter
1. *Malum in se*: Unenforceable
2. *Malum prohibitum*: Quasi-contractual recovery may be permitted
Contractual capacity
1. Age
2. Mental condition
3. Alcohol
4. Drugs
Contracts formed when a party is incapable may be affirmed once the incapacity is removed

Key Terms

Children of tender years: children between the ages of seven and fourteen
Contractual capacity: the statutory ability of a person to enter into a valid contract
Emancipation: a minor no longer under the legal care of an adult
Majority: adulthood; above legal age of consent
Malum in se: bad in and of itself; against public morals
Malum prohibitum: regulatory wrong; violates statute
Minority: person under the legal age of consent
Natural infant: a child under the age of seven

Necessaries: food, clothing, shelter, medical aid

Quasi-contract: implied-in-law contract (see Chapter 1)

Severability: ability to separate a contract into its legal and illegal portions

Statute of Frauds: statute requiring certain types of contracts to be in writing (see Chapter 7)

Usury: rate of interest higher than the rate allowed by law

Voidable contract: a contract capable of being avoided without being in breach of contract (see Chapter 1)

EXERCISES

1. Check your own state statutes for the age of consent and contracts that are deemed to be *malum in se* and *malum prohibitum*.
2. Why can a person receive some remedy even if the contract is *malum prohibitum*?
3. What factors would determine a person's lack of mental capacity?
4. Are there circumstances in which a person's physical, not mental, state can cause her to lack contractual capacity? Why?
5. Dr. Doe firmly believes in the terminally ill's right to die. He has contracts to assist Richard Roe, an 80-year-old man dying of cancer, in committing suicide. The fee agreed on is $1000. After Mr. Roe's death, Dr. Doe requests the fee from the Roe estate, which refuses to pay him. Argue for and against the legality of the contract.

Cases for Analysis

For the most part, it is the moral conscience of a society that determines the legality of the subject matter of a contract. In the following case summaries, the courts are called on to decide whether the marital status of a woman may be in violation of general public policy with respect to contractual capacity, United States v. Yazell, and whether certain parental rights may not be relinquished, Matter of Baby M.

United States v. Yazell
334 F.2d 454 (5th Cir. 1964)

This appeal is by the United States from a judgment sustaining the appellee's defense of coverture on a note executed under a contract entered into under a federal program authorized by congress for the aiding of small business. The suit was against appellee and her husband, and the judgment against the husband is not appealed from. The sole issue was and is whether the law of Texas, where the contract was made, that a married woman is protected by coverture from personal liability upon a contract, is controlling here, or whether, since the transaction was a transaction with the federal government, the Texas law of coverture is nullified and abrogated.

The district judge, sustaining Mrs. Yazell's plea of coverture, followed Texas law as it has been uniformly declared:

> With the adoption of the common law as the rule of decision in this state, in 1840, our married women were rendered unable to bind themselves by contract. Kavanaugh v. Brown, 1 Tex. 481. And although by statute we retained the Spanish law rule that the wife can own property, our adoption of the common law meant that she can contract with respect to it or otherwise only for a purpose pointed out by law and only in such manner as our statutes may permit.

The Texas law of coverture is the controlling law. This applies just as well to government groups and the United States as to anybody else. In short, this is not a case like the cases relied on by the United States of federal commercial paper issued by and as an obligation of the United States. This is a simple case of trying to hold a married woman liable on a contract which under the laws of Texas she was incapable of making, and the claim is no more reasonable than to hold that a minor, or one of unsound mind, could be held liable on a contract despite his disability merely because the United States was a party to it. There is nothing in this view, and we are in no doubt that the decision of the district judge should be affirmed.

The contention of the United States, that because the promissory note sued on was payable to The Small Business Administration, the Texas law as above set forth is not controlling here, is completely unfounded, and we reject as without authority here the opinion of the Sixth Circuit, in United States v. Helz, 314 F.2d 301, as we reject appellant's contention that the fact that the Small Business Administration is a party to the note sued on nullifies or has any effect on the incapacity of Mrs. Yazell to bind herself by contract.

The district judge was right in his decision. His judgment is affirmed.

Dissent

Mrs. Yazell and her husband, trading as a partnership, borrowed money from the Federal Government through the Small Business Administration. They signed a note for the loan. They also signed, as security for the loan, a chattel mortgage on the merchandise in their store. They could not pay, and the Government foreclosed on the security. A deficiency remained. The Government sued on the note, praying judgment for the balance of the loan. Mrs. Yazell moved for summary judgment on the ground that she is a married woman and so, in Texas, no personal judgment and no judgment affecting her separate estate can be rendered against her, with a few exceptions not here material. The District Court judge agreed with her, and so do my brethren on this court. I am contrari-minded.

A loan from the Federal Government is a federal matter and should be governed by federal law. There being no federal statute on the subject, the courts must fashion a rule. This is the clear holding of Clearfield Trust Co. v. United States.

To effectuate the policy of the Small Business Act, loans of many hundreds of thousands of dollars each year to businesses must be made throughout the country. These loans can be made only under conditions which will reasonably assure repayment. I think the Act should be of uniform application throughout the country. If local rules are to govern federal contracts in respect to the capacity of married women to contract, so too should local rules as to all other features of contractual capacity govern such contracts. Chaos which would nullify federal programs for disaster relief would arise. And of course there is no reason to restrict this decision to loans under the Small Business Act. It would necessarily apply with equal force to every other federal program which involves contracts between the Federal Government and individuals. A multitude of programs will be frustrated by it.

It seems to me that, if a person has capacity to get money from the Federal Government, he has the capacity to give it back. The present lawsuit does not involve a general liability for debt; it involves merely the obligation to repay to the Government specific money borrowed from the Government. It seems to me that if a person borrows a horse from a neighbor he ought to be required to give it back if the owner wants it back, whether or not the borrower is a married woman. I suppose the Texas law, by nullifying repayments by married women, tends to minimize ill-advised borrowing. But I think the federal rule ought to be that you must repay what you borrow.

It seems to me that United States v. Helz was correctly decided by the Sixth Circuit and that it applies here. I would follow it.

Questions

1.   What is your opinion of "marital status" and gender being factors in determining contractual capacity?

2.   Do you agree with the majority opinion of the dissent? Why?

Matter of Baby M
109 N.J. 396 (1988)

Wilentz, C. J.

In this matter the Court is asked to determine the validity of a contract that purports to provide a new way of bringing children into a family. For a fee of $10,000, a woman agrees to be artificially inseminated with the semen of another woman's husband; she is to conceive a child, carry it to term, and after its birth surrender it to the natural father and his wife. The intent of the contract is that the child's natural mother will thereafter be forever separated from her child. The wife is to adopt the child, and she and the natural father are to be regarded as its parents for all purposes. The contract providing for this is called "surrogacy contract," the natal mother inappropriately called the "surrogate mother."

We invalidate the surrogacy contract because it conflicts with the law and public policy of this State. While we recognize the depth of the yearning of infertile couples to have their own children, we find the payment of money to a "surrogate" mother illegal, perhaps criminal, and potentially degrading to women. Although in this case we grant custody to the natural father, the evidence having clearly proved such custody to be in the best interests of the infant, we void both the termination of the surrogate mother's parental rights and the adoption of the child by the wife/step-parent. We thus restore the "surrogate" as the mother of the child. We remand the issue of the natural mother's visitation rights to the trial court, since that issue was not reached below and the record before us is not sufficient to permit us to decide it *de novo*.

We find no offense to our present laws where a woman voluntarily and without payment agrees to act as a "surrogate" mother, provided that she is not subject to a binding agreement to surrender her child. Moreover, our holding today does not preclude the Legislature from altering the current statutory scheme, within constitutional limits, so as to permit surrogacy contracts. Under current law, however, the surrogacy agreement before us is illegal and invalid. . . .

Invalidity and Unenforceability of Surrogacy Contract

We have concluded that this surrogacy contract is invalid. Our conclusion has two bases: direct conflict with existing statutes and conflict with the public policies of this State, as expressed in its statutory and decisional law.

One of the surrogacy contract's basic purposes, to achieve the adoption of a child through private placement, though permitted in New Jersey "is very much disfavored." Sees v. Baber, 74 N.J. 201, 217 (1977). Its use of money for this purpose—and we have no doubt whatsoever that the money is being paid to obtain an adoption and not, as the Sterns argue, for the personal services of Mary Beth Whitehead—is illegal and perhaps criminal. N.J.S.A. 9:3-54. In addition to the inducement of money, there is the coercion of contract: the natural mother's irrevocable agreement, prior to birth, even prior to conception, to surrender the child to the adoptive couple. Such an agreement is totally unenforceable in private placement adoption. *Sees*, 74 N.J. at 212-214. Even where the adoption is through an approved agency, the formal agreement to surrender occurs only *after* birth (as we read N.J.S.A. 9:2-16 and 9:2-17, and similar statutes), and then, by regulation, only after the birth mother has been offered counseling. N.J.A.C. 10:121A-5.4(c). Integral to these invalid provisions of the surrogacy contract is the related agreement, equally invalid, on the part of the natural mother to cooperate with, and not to contest, proceedings to terminate her parental rights, as well as her contractual concession, in aid of the adoption, that the child's best interests would be served by awarding custody to the natural father and his wife—all of this before she has even conceived, and, in some cases, before she has the slightest idea of what the natural father and adoptive mother are like.

The foregoing provisions not only directly conflict with New Jersey statutes, but also offend long-established State policies. These critical terms, which are at the heart of the contract are invalid and unenforceable; the conclusion therefore follows, without more, that the entire contract is unenforceable.

Conflict with Statutory Provisions

The surrogacy contract conflicts with: (1) laws prohibiting the use of money in connection with adoptions; (2) laws requiring proof of parental unfitness or abandonment before termination of parental rights is ordered or an adoption is granted; and (3) laws that make surrender of custody and consent to adoption revocable in private placement adoptions.

(1) Our law prohibits paying or accepting money in connection with any placement of a child for adoption. N.J.S.A. 9:3-54a. Violation is a high misdemeanor. N.J.S.A. 9:3-54c. Excepted are fees of an approved agency (which must be a non-profit entity, N.J.S.A. 9:3-38a.) and certain expenses in connection with childbirth. N.J.S.A. 9:3-54b.

Considerable care was taken in this case to structure the surrogacy arrangement so as not to violate this prohibition. The arrangement was structured as follows: the adopting parent, Mrs. Stern, was not a party to the surrogacy contract; the money paid to Mrs. Whitehead was stated to be for her services—not for the adoption; the sole purpose of the contract was stated as being that "of giving a child to William Stern, its natural and biological father"; the money was purported to be "compensation for services and expenses and in no way . . . a fee for termination of parental rights or a payment in exchange for consent to surrender a child for adoption"; the fee to the Infertility Center ($7,500) was stated to be for legal representation, advice, administrative work, and other "services." Nevertheless, it seems clear that the money was paid and accepted in connection with an adoption.

The Infertility Center's major role was first as a "finder" of the surrogate mother whose child was to be adopted, and second as the arranger of all proceedings that led to the adoption. Its role as adoption finder is demonstrated by the provision requiring Mr. Stern to pay another $7,500 if he uses Mary Beth Whitehead again as a surrogate, and by ICNY's agreement to "coordinate arrangements for the adoption of the child by the wife." The surrogacy agreement requires Mrs. Whitehead to surrender

Baby M for the purposes of adoption. The agreement notes that Mr. *and* Mrs. Stern wanted to have a child, and provides that the child be "placed" with Mrs. Stern in the event Mr. Stern dies before the child is born. The payment of the $10,000 occurs only on surrender of custody of the child and "completion of the duties and obligations" of Mrs. Whitehead, including termination of her parental rights to facilitate adoption by Mrs. Stern. As for the contention that the Sterns are paying only for services and not for an adoption, we need note only that they would pay nothing in the event the child died before the fourth month of pregnancy, and only $1,000 if the child were stillborn, even though the "services" had been fully rendered. Additionally, one of Mrs. Whitehead's estimated costs, to be assumed by Mr. Stern, was an "Adoption Fee," presumably for Mrs. Whitehead's incidental costs in connection with the adoption.

Mr. Stern knew he was paying for the adoption of a child; Mrs. Whitehead knew she was accepting money so that a child might be adopted; the Infertility Center knew that it was being paid for assisting in the adoption of a child. The actions of all three worked to frustrate the goals of the statute. It strains credulity to claim that these arrangements, touted by those in the surrogacy business as an attractive alternative to the usual route leading to an adoption, really amount to something other than a private placement adoption for money.

The prohibition of our statute is strong. Violation constitutes a high misdemeanor, N.J.S.A. 9:3-54c, a third-degree crime, N.J.S.A. 2C:43-1b, carrying a penalty of three to five years imprisonment. N.J.S.A. 2C:43-6a(3). The evils inherent in baby-bartering are loathsome for a myriad of reasons. The child is sold without regard for whether the purchasers will be suitable parents. N. Baker, Baby Selling: The Scandal of Black Market Adoption 7 (1978). The natural mother does not receive the benefit of counseling and guidance to assist her in making a decision that may affect her for a lifetime. In fact, the monetary incentive to sell her child may, depending on her financial circumstances, make her decision less voluntary. Id. at 44. Furthermore, the adoptive parents may not be fully informed of the natural parents' medical history.

Baby-selling potentially results in the exploitation of all parties involved. Ibid. Conversely, adoption statutes seek to further humanitarian goals, foremost among them the best interests of the child. H. Witmer, E. Herzog, E. Weinstein, & M. Sullivan, Independent Adoptions: A Follow-Up Study 32 (1967). The negative consequences of baby-buying are potentially present in the surrogacy context, especially the potential for placing and adopting a child without regard to the interest of the child or the natural mother. . . .

The provision in the surrogacy contract stating that Mary Beth Whitehead agrees to "surrender custody . . . and terminate all parental rights" contains no clause giving her a right to rescind. It is intended to be an irrevocable consent to surrender the child for adoption—in other words, an irrevocable commitment by Mrs. Whitehead to turn Baby M over to the Sterns and thereafter to allow termination of her parental rights. The trial court required a "best interests" showing as a condition to granting specific performance of the surrogacy contract. 217 N.J. Super. at 399–400. Having decided the "best interests" issue in favor of the Sterns, that court's order included, among other things, specific performance of this agreement to surrender custody and terminate all parental rights.

Mrs. Whitehead, shortly after the child's birth, had attempted to revoke her consent and surrender by refusing, after the Sterns had allowed her to have the child "just for one week," to return Baby M to them. The trial court's award of specific performance therefore reflects its view that the consent to surrender the child was irrevocable. We accept the trial court's construction of the contract; indeed it appears quite clear that this was the parties' intent. Such a provision, however, making irrevocable the natural mother's consent to surrender custody of her child in a private placement adoption, clearly conflicts with New Jersey law.

Our analysis commences with the statute providing for surrender of custody to an approved agency and termination of parental rights on the suit of that agency. The two basic provisions of the statute are N.J.S.A. 9: 2-14 and 9:2-16. The former provides explicitly that

> [e]xcept as otherwise provided by law or by order or judgment of a court of competent jurisdiction or by testamentary disposition, no surrender of the custody of a child shall be valid in this state unless made to an approved agency pursuant to the provisions of this act . . .

There is no exception "provided by law," and it is not clear that there could be any "order or judgment of a court of competent jurisdiction" validating a surrender of custody as a basis for adoption when that surrender was not in conformance with the statute. Requirements for a voluntary surrender to an approved agency are set forth in N.J.S.A. 9:2-16. This section allows an approved agency to take a voluntary surrender of custody from the parent of a child but provides stringent requirements as a condition to its validity. The surrender must be in writing, must be in such form as is required for the recording of a deed, and, pursuant to N.J.S.A. 9:2-17, must

> be such as to declare that the person executing the same desires to relinquish the custody of the child, acknowledge the termination of parental rights as to such custody in favor of the approved agency, and acknowledge full understanding of the effect of such surrender as provided by this act.

If the foregoing requirements are met, the consent, the voluntary surrender of custody

> shall be valid whether or not the person giving same is a minor and shall be irrevocable except at the discretion of the approved agency taking such surrender or upon order or judgment of a court of competent jurisdiction, setting aside such surrender upon proof of fraud, duress, or misrepresentation. [N.J.S.A. 9:2-16.]

The importance of that irrevocability is that the surrender itself gives the agency the power to obtain termination of parental rights—in other words, permanent separation of the parent from the child, leading in the ordinary case to an adoption. N.J.S.A. 9:2-18 to 9:2-20.

This statutory pattern, providing for a surrender in writing and for termination of parental rights by an approved agency, is generally followed in connection with adoption proceedings and proceedings by DYFS to obtain permanent custody of a child. Our adoption statute repeats the requirements necessary to accomplish an irrevocable surrender to an approved agency in both form and substance. N.J.S.A. 9:3-41a. It provides that the surrender "shall be valid and binding without regard to the age of the person executing the surrender," ibid.; and although the word "irrevocable" is not used, that seems clearly to be the intent of the provision. The statute speaks of such surrender as constituting "relinquishment of such person's parental rights in or guardianship or custody of the child *named therein* and consent by such person to adoption of the child." Ibid. (emphasis supplied). We emphasize "named therein," for we construe the statute to allow a surrender only after the birth of the child. The formal consent to surrender enables the approved agency to terminate parental rights.

Similarly, DYFS is empowered to "take voluntary surrenders and releases of custody and consents to adoption[s]" from parents, which surrenders, releases, or consents "when properly acknowledged . . . shall be valid and binding irrespective of the age of the person giving the same, and shall be irrevocable except at the discretion of the Bureau of Childrens Services [currently DYFS] or upon order of a court of competent jurisdiction." N.J.S.A. 30:4C-23. Such consent to surrender of the custody of the child would presumably lead to an adoption placement by DYFS. See N.J.S.A. 30:4C-20.

It is clear that the Legislature so carefully circumscribed all aspects of a consent to surrender custody—its form and substance, its manner of execution, and the agency or agencies to which it may be made—in order to provide the basis for irrevocability. It seems most unlikely that the Legislature intended that a consent not complying with these requirements would also be irrevocable, especially where, as here, that consent falls radically short of compliance. Not only do the form and substance of the consent in the surrogacy contract fail to meet statutory requirements, but the surrender of custody is made to a private party. It is not made, as the statute requires, either to an approved agency or to DYFS.

These strict prerequisites to irrevocability constitute a recognition of the most serious consequences that flow from such consents: termination of parental rights, the permanent separation of parent from child, and the ultimate adoption of the child, See Sees v. Baber, supra, 74 N.J. at 217. Because of those consequences, the Legislature severely limited the circumstances under which such consent would be irrevocable. The legislative goal is furthered by regulations requiring approved agencies, prior to accepting irrevocable consents, to provide advice and counseling to women, making it more likely that they fully understand and appreciate the consequences of their acts. N.J.A.C. 10:121A-5.4(c).

Contractual surrender of parental rights is not provided for in our statutes as now written. Indeed, in the Parentage Act, N.J.S.A. 9:17-38 to 59, there is a specific provision invalidating any agreement "between an alleged or presumed father and the mother of the child" to bar an action brought for the purpose of determining paternity "[r]egardless of [the contract's] terms." N.J.S.A. 9:17-45. Even a settlement agreement concerning parentage reached in a judicially-mandated consent conference is not valid unless the proposed settlement is approved beforehand by the court. N.J.S.A. 9:17-48c and 9:17-48d. There is no doubt that a contractual provision purporting to constitute an irrevocable agreement to surrender custody of a child for adoption is invalid.

In Sees v. Baber, supra, 74 N.J. 201, we noted that a natural mother's consent to surrender her child and to its subsequent adoption was no longer *required* by the statute in private placement adoptions. After tracing the statutory history from the time when such a consent had been an essential prerequisite to adoption, we concluded that such a consent was now neither necessary nor sufficient for the purpose of terminating parental rights. Id. at 213. The consent to surrender custody in that case was in writing, had been executed prior to physical surrender of the infant, and had been explained to the mother by an attorney. The trial court found that the consent to surrender of custody in that private placement adoption was knowing, voluntary, and deliberate. Id. at 216. The physical surrender of the child took place four days after its birth. Two days thereafter the natural mother changed her mind, and asked that the adoptive couple give her baby back to her. We held that she was entitled to the baby's return. The effect of our holding in that case necessarily encompassed our conclusion that "in an unsupervised private placement, since there is no statutory obligation to consent, there can be no legal barrier to its retraction." Id. at 215. The only possible relevance of consent in these matters, we noted, was that it *might* bear on whether there had been an abandonment of the child, or a forsaking of parental obligations. Id. at 216. Otherwise, consent in a private placement adoption is not only revocable, but, when revoked early enough, irrelevant. Id. at 213-215.

The provision in the surrogacy contract whereby the mother irrevocably agrees to surrender custody of her child and to terminate her parental rights conflicts with the settled interpretation of New Jersey statutory law. There is only one irrevocable consent, and that is the one explicitly provided for by statute: a consent to surrender of custody and a placement with an approved agency or with DYFS. The provision in the surrogacy contract, agreed to before conception, requiring the natural mother to surrender custody of the child without any right of revocation is one more indication of the essential nature of this transaction: the creation of a contractual system of termination and adoption designed to circumvent our statutes.

Public Policy Considerations

The surrogacy contract's invalidity, resulting from its direct conflict with the above statutory provisions, is further underlined when its goals and means are measured against New Jersey's public policy. The contract's basic premise, that the natural parents can decide in advance of birth which one is to have custody of the child, bears no relationship to the settled law that the child's best interests shall determine custody. See Fantony v. Fantony, 21 N.J. 525, 536-537 (1956); see also Sheehan v. Sheehan, 38 N.J. Super. 120, 125 (App. Div. 1955) ("Whatever the agreement of the parents, the ultimate determination of custody lies with the court in the exercise of its supervisory jurisdiction as *parens patriae.*"). The fact that the trial court remedied that aspect of the contract through the "best interests" phase does not make the contractual provision any less offensive to the public policy of this State.

The surrogacy contract guarantees permanent separation of the child from one of its natural parents. Our policy, however, has long been that to the extent possible, children should remain with and be brought up by both of their natural parents. That was the first stated purpose of the previous adoption act, L. 1953, c. 264, §1, codified at N.J.S.A. 9:3-17 (repealed): "it is necessary and desirable (a) to protect the child from unnecessary separation from his natural parents. . . ." While not so stated in the present adoption law, this purpose remains part of the public policy of this State. See, e.g., Wilke v. Culp, 196 N.J. Super. 487, 496 (App. Div. 1984), *certif. den.*, 99 N.J. 243 (1985); In re Adoption by J.J.P., supra, 175 N.J. Super. at 426. This is not simply some theoretical ideal that in practice has no meaning. The impact of failure to follow that policy is nowhere better shown than in the results of this surrogacy contract. A child, instead of starting off its life with as much peace and security as possible, finds itself immediately in a tug-of-war between contending mother and father.

The surrogacy contract violates the policy of this State that the rights of natural parents are equal concerning their child, the father's right no greater than the mother's. "The parent and child relationship extends equally to every child and to every parent, regardless of the marital status of the parents." N.J.S.A. 9:17-40. As the Assembly Judiciary Committee noted in its statement to the bill, this section establishes "the principle that regardless of the marital status of the parents, all children *and all parents* have equal rights with respect to each other." Statement to Senate No. 888, Assembly Judiciary, Law, Public Safety and Defense Committee (1983) (emphasis supplied). The whole purpose and effect of the surrogacy contract was to give the father the exclusive right to the child by destroying the rights of the mother. . . .

The only legal advice Mary Beth Whitehead received regarding the surrogacy contract was provided in connection with the contract that she previously entered into with another couple. Mrs. Whitehead's lawyer was referred to her by the Infertility Center, with which he had an agreement to act as counsel for surrogate candidates. His services consisted of spending one hour going through the contract with the Whiteheads, section by section, and answering their questions. Mrs. Whitehead received no further legal advice prior to signing the contract with the Sterns. . . .

Under the contract, the natural mother is irrevocably committed before she knows the strength of her bond with her child. She never makes a totally voluntary, informed decision, for quite clearly any decision prior to the baby's birth is, in the most important sense, uninformed, and any decision after that, compelled by a pre-existing contractual commitment, the threat of a lawsuit, and the inducement of a $10,000 payment is less than totally voluntary. Her interests are of little concern to those who controlled this transaction.

Although the interest of the natural father and adoptive mother is certainly the predominant interest, realistically the *only* interest served, even they are left with less than what public policy requires. They know little about the natural mother, her genetic makeup, and her psychological and medical history. Moreover, not even a superficial attempt is made to determine their awareness of their responsibilities as parents.

Worst of all, however, is the contract's total disregard of the best interests of the child. There is not the slightest suggestion that any inquiry will be made at any time to determine the fitness of the Sterns as custodial parents, of Mrs. Stern as an adoptive parent, their superiority to Mrs. Whitehead, or the effect on the child of not living with her natural mother.

This is the sale of a child, or, at the very least, the sale of a mother's right to her child, the only mitigating factor being that one of the purchasers is the father. Almost every evil that prompted the prohibition on the payment of money in connection with adoptions exists here.

The differences between an adoption and a surrogacy contract should be noted, since it is asserted that the use of money in connection with surrogacy does not pose the risks found where money buys an adoption. Katz, "Surrogate Motherhood and the Baby-Selling Laws," 20 Colum. J.L. & Soc. Probs. 1 (1986).

First, and perhaps most important, all parties concede that it is unlikely that surrogacy will survive without money. Despite the alleged selfless motivation of surrogate mothers, if there is no payment, there will be no surrogates, or very few. That conclusion contrasts with adoption; for obvious reasons, there remains a steady supply, albeit insufficient, despite the prohibitions against payment. The adoption itself, relieving the natural mother of the financial burden of supporting an infant, is in some sense the equivalent of payment.

Second, the use of money in adoptions does not *produce* the problem —conception occurs, and usually the birth itself, before illicit funds are offered. With surrogacy, the "problem," if one views it as such, consisting of the purchase of a woman's procreative capacity, at the risk of her life, is caused by and originates with the offer of money.

Third, with the law prohibiting the use of money in connection with adoptions, the built-in financial pressure of the unwanted pregnancy and the consequent support obligation do not lead the mother to the highest paying, ill-suited, adoptive parents. She is just as well-off surrendering the child to an approved agency. In surrogacy, the highest bidders will presumably become the adoptive parents regardless of suitability, so long as payment of money is permitted.

Fourth, the mother's consent to surrender her child in adoptions is revocable, even after surrender of the child, unless it be to an approved agency, where by regulation there are protections against an ill-advised surrender. In surrogacy, consent occurs so early that no amount of advice would satisfy the potential mother's need, yet the consent is irrevocable.

The main difference, that the unwanted pregnancy is unintended while the situation of the surrogate mother is voluntary and intended, is really not significant. Initially, it produces stronger reactions of sympathy for the mother whose pregnancy was unwanted than for the surrogate mother, who "went into this with her eyes wide open." On reflection, however, it appears that the essential evil is the same, taking advantage of a woman's circumstances (the unwanted pregnancy or the need for money) in order to take away her child, the difference being one of degree.

In the scheme contemplated by the surrogacy contract in this case, a middle man, propelled by profit, promotes the sale. Whatever idealism may have motivated any of the participants, the profit motive predominates, permeates, and ultimately governs the transaction. The demand for children is great and the supply small. The availability of contraception, abortion, and the greater willingness of single mothers to bring up their children has led to a shortage of babies offered for adoption. See N. Baker, Baby Selling: The Scandal of Black Market Adoption supra; Adoption and Foster Care, 1975; Hearings on Baby Selling Before the Subcomm. On Children and Youth of the Senate Comm. on Labor and Public Welfare, 94th Cong. 1st Sess. 6 (1975) (Statement of Joseph H. Reid, Executive Director, Child Welfare League of America, Inc.). The situation is ripe for the entry of the middleman who will bring some equilibrium into the market by increasing the supply through the use of money.

Intimated, but disputed, is the assertion that surrogacy will be used for the benefit of the rich at the expense of the poor. See, e.g., Radin, "Market Inalienability," 100 Harv. L. Rev. 1849, 1930 (1987). In response it is noted that the Sterns are not rich and the Whiteheads not poor. Nevertheless, it is clear to us that it is unlikely that surrogate mothers will be as proportionately numerous among those women in the top twenty percent income bracket as among those in the bottom twenty percent. Ibid. Put differently, we doubt that infertile couples in the low-income bracket will find upper income surrogates.

In any event, even in this case one should not pretend that disparate wealth does not play a part simply because the contrast is not the dramatic "rich versus poor." At the time of trial, the Whiteheads' net assets were probably negative—Mrs. Whitehead's own sister was foreclosing on a second mortgage. Their income derived from Mr. Whitehead's labors. Mrs. Whitehead is a homemaker, having previously held part-time jobs. The Sterns are both professionals, she a medical doctor, he a biochemist. Their combined income when both were working was about

$89,500 a year and their assets sufficient to pay for the surrogacy contract arrangements.

The point is made that Mrs. Whitehead *agreed* to the surrogacy arrangement, supposedly fully understanding the consequences. Putting aside the issue of how compelling her need for money may have been, and how significant her understanding of the consequences, we suggest that her consent is irrelevant. There are, in a civilized society, some things that money cannot buy. In America, we decided long ago that merely because conduct purchased by money was "voluntary" did not mean that it was good or beyond regulation and prohibition. West Coast Hotel Co. v. Parrish, 300 U.S. 379, 57 S. Ct. 578, 81 L. Ed. 703 (1937). Employers can no longer buy labor at the lowest price they can bargain for, even though that labor is "voluntary," 29 U.S.C. §206 (1982), or buy women's labor for less money than paid to men for the same job, 29 U.S.C. §206(d), or purchase the agreement of children to perform oppressive labor, 29 U.S.C. §212, or purchase the agreement of workers to subject themselves to unsafe or unhealthful working conditions, 29 U.S.C. §§651 to 678. (Occupational Safety and Health Act of 1970). There are, in short, values that society deems more important than granting to wealth whatever it can buy, be it labor, love, or life. Whether this principle recommends prohibition of surrogacy, which presumably sometimes results in great satisfaction to all of the parties, is not for us to say. We note here only that, under existing law, the fact that Mrs. Whitehead "agreed" to the arrangement is not dispositive.

The long-term effects of surrogacy contracts are not known, but feared—the impact on the child who learns her life was bought, that she is the offspring of someone who gave birth to her only to obtain money; the impact on the natural mother as the full weight of her isolation is felt along with the full reality of the sale of her body and her child; the impact on the natural father and adoptive mother once they realize the consequences of their conduct. Literature in related areas suggests these are substantial considerations, although, given the newness of surrogacy, there is little information. See N. Baker, Baby Selling: The Scandal of Black Market Adoption, supra; Adoption and Foster Care, 1975: Hearings on Baby Selling Before the Subcomm. on Children and Youth of the Senate Comm. on Labor and Public Welfare, 94th Cong. 1st Sess. (1975).

The surrogacy contract is based on principles that are directly contrary to the objectives of our laws. It guarantees the separation of a child from its mother; it looks to adoption regardless of suitability; it totally ignores the child; it takes the child from the mother regardless of her wishes and her maternal fitness; and it does all of this, it accomplishes all of its goals, through the use of money.

Beyond that is the potential degradation of some women that may result from this arrangement. In many cases, of course, surrogacy may bring satisfaction, not only to the infertile couple, but to the surrogate mother herself. The fact, however, that many women may not perceive surrogacy negatively but rather see it as an opportunity does not diminish its potential for devastation to other women.

In sum, the harmful consequences of this surrogacy arrangement appear to us all too palpable. In New Jersey the surrogate mother's agreement to sell her child is void. . . .

We have found that our present laws do not permit the surrogacy contract used in this case. Nowhere, however, do we find any legal prohibition against surrogacy when the surrogate mother volunteers, without any payment, to act as a surrogate and is given the right to change her mind and to assert her parental rights. Moreover, the Legislature remains free to deal with this most sensitive issue as it sees fit, subject only to constitutional constraints. . . .

The judgment is affirmed in part, reversed in part, and remanded for further proceedings consistent with this opinion.

Questions

1. What do you think of the result of this decision?

2. How could the parties have phrased a surrogate parenting contract so as not to be in violation of the law?

3. Do you agree with the court that the contract was designed for the sale of a baby? How do the rights of the natural father, one of the contracting parties, fit into this analysis?

Suggested Case References

1. May a person who is suffering from a progressive mental disease still be mentally competent to contract? Read Butler v. Harrison, 578 A.2d 1098 (D.C. App. 1990).

2. May an elderly person suffering from great mental lapses still have capacity to contract? Read Brown v. Resort Developments, 238 Va. 527, 385 S.E.2d 575 (1989).

3. Contracts for the sale of sexual favors are *malum in se*, at least in Oregon. State v. Grimes, 85 Or. App. 159, 735 P.2d 1277 (1987).

6 Contractual Intent

CHAPTER OVERVIEW

The sixth, and final, requisite element of every valid contract is the contractual intent of the parties. For the contract to be enforceable, the parties to the agreement must intend to enter into a binding contractual relationship. Even if all of the other requirements are satisfied, if the parties do not objectively intend to contract, there is no binding agreement.

The intent of the parties relates back to the concept of mutual assent. If a person does not freely and voluntarily agree to the terms of a contract, regardless of how clear and specific those terms appear, there is no valid consent. Generally, the genuineness of a person's assent to a contract may be suspect in three situations: one, if the person is induced to enter the relationship by fraud; two, if the person is coerced or forced into agreeing to the terms of the contract; or three, if the parties are in some way mistaken about the terms of the agreement.

A contract is fraudulently entered into if the innocent party is purposely misled or lied to in order to induce his contractual promise. The law will not enforce a contract that is induced by fraud.

If the person is forced to agree to a contractual relationship, by threats of physical, emotional, or economic duress, the person obviously lacks voluntary contractual intent.

Finally, if the parties to the contract are mistaken as to the subject matter of the contract, no contract exists because there is no meeting of the minds. This is true even though the mistake is an innocent one. As long as the parties to the agreement do not contemplate the same subject matter, no contract can be formed.

Just as with the requirements of contractual capacity and legality of subject matter, this final requirement of intent concerns the circumstances surrounding the agreement, not the terms of the agreement itself. On its face, an agreement may appear to meet all of the formalities of contract law, but if the parties do not truly intend to contract, the agreement will fail.

Contractual Intent Defined

As introduced in Chapter 1, there must be a meeting of the minds before an agreement can be deemed an enforceable contract. The parties to the contract must actually intend to enter into a contract for the same bargain at the same time. If it can be demonstrated that a contract was not intended by one, or both, of the parties, no contract can exist because there is no mutual assent.

 EXAMPLE:

Susan and Jon have been friends since childhood. Susan has to turn in a book report for school tomorrow, and asks Jon to come to her house to help her. To induce his promise, Susan offers him $10,000 for his help, and Jon laughingly accepts. There is no contract. The parties did not intend a contractual relationship; as friends they were merely agreeing to help one another.

The example given above is a situation in which the parties are joking with each other, based on a long-standing relationship. The intent to contract is obviously missing. As in most cases when contractual intent is called into question, it is the circumstances surrounding the transaction that determine intent.

Generally, when determining the contractual intent of an agreement, there are three areas of possible concern: fraud, duress, and mistake. Each of these situations will be discussed below.

Fraud and Misrepresentation

In **fraud**, one party to an agreement tricks a second party into entering the agreement. Only if all five of the elements of fraud are shown will a contract fail. The five elements of contractual fraud are

1. the misrepresentation
2. of a material fact
3. made with the intent to deceive and
4. relied on by the other party
5. to his or her detriment.

If an agreement is induced by fraud, the innocent party has the option either to avoid the contract, because she lacked the requisite intent, or to fulfill the contract.

What, however, would be the result if the deception is innocent—that is, the person making the statements does not intend to deceive the other party? In this instance, there is no fraud, but there is a **misrepresentation**. If a material fact (a fact that goes to the heart of the transaction) is misrepresented, the injured party is entitled to the same relief she would be granted if she had been defrauded.

EXAMPLES:

1. Paul is walking down the street when he sees a man selling watches. The man tells Paul the watches are Cartier's and offers to sell one to Paul for $50. Paul buys the watch, but two days later it breaks down. He brings the watch to a licensed Cartier dealer for repairs and discovers the watch is not a Cartier, but a cheap imitation. If Paul can ever find that man on the street again, he can get his money back. The contract was induced by fraud. The man lied about the subject matter to Paul to induce Paul's assent to the contract, and Paul was economically injured.

2. Lola is in the market for a Van Gogh painting. Charles is an art dealer selling a painting said to be a Van Gogh, although he has not bothered to check its origins. Charles sells the painting to Lola, who discovers that the painting is a forgery. This is an example of misrepresentation. Charles was negligent in not establishing the genuineness of the painting, but he did not intend to deceive Lola. There is no mistake, because the genuineness of the painting could have been checked had Charles not been careless. Lola can get her money back.

3. In a recent trial decision, a man sued his ex-wife for fraud. After many years of marriage, the wife admitted to the husband that she never loved him. After the divorce, the former husband sued the wife for fraud in the marriage contract and won. The wife purposely misled the husband by saying that she loved him in order to induce the marriage. This constitutes a fraud, because marriage is a contract. The detriment the husband suffered was the property the wife acquired from him during the marriage.

A contract that is induced by fraud or misrepresentation is **voidable** by the innocent party. This means that even though the innocent party was misled into entering the contract, if he wishes to complete the agreement, he may do so. The innocent party may also avoid the obligation because of the other party's fraudulent actions. Fraud and misrepresentation are determined by the facts of each individual situation.

Duress

Duress connotes some form of force or coercion exercised over one party to the contract in order to induce that party's promise to contract. Because the innocent party is forced to enter into the agreement, there is no contract. The party did not freely intend to contract.

Duress can take several forms. The most obvious example of duress would be **physical duress**. Physical duress occurs when one party forces the other to enter into the contract by threatening physical harm.

 EXAMPLE:

Bill holds a gun to Morris' head and tells him to sign a contract deeding over Blackacre to Bill for a stated price. There is no contract. Morris was forced to sign the contract at gun point, and so he did not freely intend to contract. Note that on its face the contract itself would appear to be valid; it is the surrounding circumstances that invalidate the agreement.

Another form of duress is **economic duress**, wherein a person is induced to contract for fear of losing some monetary benefit. At the turn of the century, before unionism, this concept was exemplified by the saying, "If you don't come in Sunday, don't come in Monday." Workers were forced to work a seven-day week or lose their jobs. They did not agree to work seven days of their own free will but were forced to come in for fear of losing their livelihoods entirely. Any form of economic force used to induce agreement to a contract is economic duress.

 EXAMPLE:

Iris receives a letter from her state tax department stating that she has underpaid her taxes and ordering an audit of her returns. Under the state law, the tax department can only audit returns for the previous three years. When Iris goes to the audit, the agent tells her that if she doesn't sign a waiver to permit an audit of all of her previous returns he will order all of her assets frozen until a final determination of her tax liability is made. Iris agrees to the waiver. This is an example of economic duress, and the waiver is invalid.

A third type of duress is **mental duress**, wherein a person is coerced to enter into a contract by psychological threats. As with all forms of duress, the ability of a particular threat to induce a party to contract is determined on a case-by-case basis. It is the impact on the particular party that is conclusive of the duress.

One important factor that goes into this determination is the relationship of the threatening party to the innocent party. The greater the degree of psychological control the threatening person exercises, the more likely it is to be found that the contract was induced by mental duress. When the mental duress is exercised by someone who is in a close relationship with the innocent party, it is known as **undue influence**.

 ## EXAMPLES:

1. Maxwell is 92 years old and lives in a nursing home. The owner of the home convinces Maxwell to sign over all of his property to the home in consideration of all of the loving care the home gives him. This contract is invalid because it was induced by the undue influence the owner of the home exercised over Maxwell.

2. Mary and David are getting divorced. David convinces Mary to sign a joint custody agreement for their three children by threatening to take the children out of the country if she refuses. The contract is unenforceable. Mary was coerced into signing the agreement because of the fear of never seeing her children again. This is mental duress.

3. Hilda is 80 years old and frail. A real estate developer convinces her to sell her house by telling her that, because of her frail health, the state is going to take her house away and put her in a home. There is no contract. This is an example of both mental duress and fraud.

A type of contract known as a **contract of adhesion** also falls under the category of duress. A contract of adhesion is a contract in which one side has an unfair bargaining position, a position that is so unequal that the other party's assent is suspect. Even though no actual duress exists, because of the inequality of the parties the contract is called into question. These types of contracts are voidable by the innocent party because of the unconscionable aspect of the other side's bargaining position.

Generally, if a contract of adhesion can be shown, the party with the weaker bargaining position can avoid his obligation. The unequal bargaining position can come about because of lack of competition in the area, forceful salesmanship, or because the innocent party perceives the other person as having special knowledge or expertise and is relying on that person's greater experience.

EXAMPLES:

1. Leo lives in a small town, and there is only one car dealership within a 100-mile radius. When Leo is talked into buying a car for several thousand dollars more than he wanted to spend, the contract may be deemed a contract of adhesion because, if Leo wants a car, he really has no other choice. The dealer is in an unfair bargaining position.

2. Sylvio, having put on a few pounds over the last several years, walks into a health club to inquire about joining. The club salesman, a powerfully built young man, walks Sylvio around the facility, takes him into his office, and tells him about a "special deal" only available for that day. If he signs up right now, he saves $300; if he doesn't sign immediately, he loses the opportunity. The salesman also tells Sylvio that he is not getting any younger, and the longer he waits the harder it will be to take off the weight. Sylvio signs up for a three-year membership and immediately regrets it. This is a contract of adhesion. Because of aggressive salesmanship, Sylvio was put in a position of signing an agreement without having a chance to consider the possibilities. He can avoid this contract. Be aware that many states have special consumer protection laws specifically dealing with health club memberships because of the clubs' sales techniques.

3. Wanda, the wistful widow of Winnetka, wants to put more fun in her life, and so she signs up for dance lessons. Her instructor is young and handsome Raoul. After the initial ten sessions are over, Raoul convinces Wanda to sign up for the advanced course because of her great dance potential. Halfway through the advanced course, Wanda attends a community dance where all of her partners comment on how badly she dances. Wanda sues to get her money back from the dance school. Wanda will prevail. Because of his perceived expertise, Raoul was able to convince Wanda to spend money on dance lessons. This is a contract of adhesion.

When dealing with any form of duress or with contracts of adhesion, it is the perception of the party involved that determines intent. If, under the circumstances, the innocent party reasonably believed that she was threatened, no contract will exist, even if the fear seems unfounded. Also, a contract of adhesion may be enforceable if the injured party wishes to fulfill the contract. It is voidable or enforceable at the election of the innocent party.

Mistake

The third situation that brings into question the parties' intent to contract is **mistake**. Mistake occurs when one (or both) of the parties is under a misconception as to the subject matter of the contract. Mistake is distinguishable from contractual fraud in that, with mistake, there is no intent to deceive or misrepresent; the mistake is due to the honest and innocent belief of the parties.

Contractual mistakes are divided into two broad categories: **mutual mistake** and **unilateral mistake**. A mutual mistake concerns the underlying consideration of the contract itself.

 EXAMPLES:

1. Sheila and Kathleen enter into a contract for the sale of Sheila's summer house, but unknown to both parties, the house is destroyed by a hurricane. There is no contract because the basic assumption of the contract, that the house exists, is mistaken.

2. Edward agrees to lease some property to Eve so that Eve can operate a retail store at that location. Unknown to both Edward and Eve, the town council passes a zoning ordinance restricting the use of the area in question to residential use only. There is no contract. Both parties are mistaken with respect to a basic assumption underlying the agreement, that is, that the property could be used for commercial purposes. This is an example of mutual mistake.

A mutual mistake is a defense to contract formation if the mistake goes to a basic assumption of the agreement, the mistake has a material adverse effect on the parties, and the mistake was of the type that could not be foreseen.

A unilateral mistake usually concerns a situation in which only one party to the contract is mistaken because of some typewritten or computation error. In this instance, the contract may still be enforceable by the innocent party, the one who neither caused nor knew that there was in fact a mistake.

EXAMPLE:

Arnold submits a contracting bid to Ace, Inc., for the construction of a warehouse. Arnold makes a mistake in computing his expenses, and the bid is $2000 lower than it should be. Ace accepts. There is a contract. This is an example of a unilateral mistake in which Ace, the innocent party, has no way of knowing that Arnold has miscalculated his bid, and so a valid contract exists. Note, however, that if Arnold's bid had itemized all his expenses and only the total was incorrect, there would be no contract at the low bid because Ace could see the mistake simply by doing the totals itself. Also, if Arnold realized his error before Ace accepted and he notified Ace, Ace could not accept the low bid because it would then be aware of the error.

A similarity exists between the concept of mistake and the concept of the ambiguity of the terms discussed in Chapter 2, Offer. There are circumstances in which the ambiguity of the language used by the parties can create mistaken impressions. In those instances, the law will go with the most reasonable and most legally fair interpretation of the parties' intent. Generally, ambiguities are held against the party who drafted the contract.

Take careful note of the fact that the concept of mistake does not concern itself with the risk of contracting, that is, the risk that one or both of the parties may not get the bargain for which he or she had hoped. As discussed previously in Chapter 4, Consideration, the law is not the insurer of every contractual agreement. It cannot and will not guarantee that every contract will be as economically beneficial as the parties had hoped. However, the law will guarantee that the parties do receive the object or service for which they bargained.

EXAMPLES:

1. Sophie offers to sell Lindsay a blue stone she has in her possession for $100. Sophie thinks the stone is a blue quartz; Lindsay thinks the stone is a sapphire. Lindsay agrees to the contract. Later, Lindsay discovers the stone is a blue quartz, and wants her money back, claiming she was mistaken as to the object of the contract. The contract is valid. Because the parties only contracted for the sale of a "blue stone," the fact that a party was mistaken as to its value is irrelevant. She received exactly what she bargained for. Let the buyer beware!

2. Sophie offers to sell Lindsay a blue stone designated as a blue quartz she has in her possession for $100. Sophie and Lindsay both think the stone is a blue quartz. Lindsay agrees to the contract for the sale of a blue quartz. Later, Lindsay finds out the

stone is a sapphire worth $10,000. The contract is not valid. So-
phie sold a blue quartz, but Lindsay received a sapphire. In these
circumstances, since the contract specified the blue quartz, the
contract is not enforceable.

As indicated above, when dealing with a contractual mistake it is
important to differentiate between a mutual mistake and a unilateral mistake. With a mutual mistake, both parties are intending different subject
matter, and so no contract exists because there is no meeting of the minds.
With a unilateral mistake, only one party to the contract is mistaken, and
the contract can be enforced by the innocent party (the one who did not
cause the error).

CHAPTER SUMMARY

For a contract to be deemed enforceable, it must be shown that
both parties actually intended to enter into a contractual relationship. If
it can be demonstrated that this requisite element of contractual intent is
missing, then no contract is formed.

Just as with the legality of the subject matter and contractual capacity, the contractual intent is concerned with the circumstances surrounding the formation of the agreement, not the provisions of the agreement
itself. Even if the contract meets all of the other five requirements to create
a valid contract, if the intent to contract is lacking, there is no contract.

Contractual intent is a concept that is always determined by the facts
and circumstances of each individual situation. If it can be shown that
the particular party lacked contractual intent, even though such a situation would seem unreasonable, there is no contract.

There are three major legal concepts associated with intent: fraud,
duress, and mistake. If a party to an agreement is defrauded into entering
the agreement, no contract exists. If the party is coerced into entering the
agreement, no contract exists. And finally, if the parties are mistaken as
to the subject matter of the contract, no contract exists.

SYNOPSIS

No contract exists if the contract is induced by fraud, duress, or mistake
Fraud
1. A misrepresentation
2. of a material fact,
3. made with the intent to deceive and
4. relied on by the other party
5. to his or her detriment

Duress
1. Physical
2. Economic
3. Mental (undue influence)
4. Contracts of adhesion: Unfair bargaining position
Mistake
1. Mutual mistake: No contract
2. Unilateral mistake: May be enforced

Key Terms

Contract of adhesion: contract entered into where one party has an unfair bargaining position; voidable
Duress: force or coercion used to induce agreement to contract
Economic duress: threatening loss of economic benefit to induce a person to contract
Fraud: a misrepresentation of a material fact made with the intent to deceive; relied on by the other party to his or her detriment
Mental duress: psychological threats used to induce a person to contract
Misrepresentation: misstatement of a material fact relied on by the other party to his or her detriment; no intent to defraud
Mistake: misconception of the subject matter of a contract
Mutual mistake: misconception of the subject matter of a contract by both parties; unenforceable
Physical duress: threatening physical harm to force a person to contract
Undue influence: mental duress by a person in a close and particular relationship to the innocent party
Unilateral mistake: misconception of the subject matter of a contract by only one party to the contract; may be enforceable
Voidable contract: a contract that one party may void at his option without being in breach of contract

EXERCISES

1. A salesman tells you that the diamond ring you want to purchase is "the best quality diamond he has in the entire store and, in fact, is the best diamond he has ever seen." After you buy the diamond you discover that the diamond is a very low grade. Have you been defrauded? Why?
2. Give two examples of contracts of adhesion not discussed in the chapter.
3. Explain the difference between a mutual mistake and ambiguity.
4. Explain the difference between misrepresentation and fraud.
5. Give an example of a contract induced by economic duress not discussed in the chapter.

Cases for Analysis

To highlight the concepts of fraud, undue influence, and duress, the following case summaries are presented for analysis. Francois v. Francois concerns duress with respect to a property settlement agreement and Brown v. L. V. Marks & Sons, Co. concerns fraud in the procurement.

Francois v. Francois
599 F.2d 1286 (3d Cir. 1979)

Opinion of the Court

We are asked in this appeal to assess whether the district court properly relieved a husband from the disastrous financial consequences of a "Property Settlement and Separation Agreement" (agreement) entered into with his wife. The plaintiff, Victor H. Francois, instituted an action in the district court against his wife, A. Jane Francois, seeking rescission of the agreement and various real and personal property transfers made pursuant to that agreement. The district court declared the agreement and the conveyances to be null and void on the grounds, Inter alia, that Jane Francois had exerted undue influence over her husband. The district court restored title to one parcel of real property and various securities to Victor Francois in his name alone. From the final order of the district court, Jane Francois appeals alleging that the district court improperly invalidated the agreement and reconveyed properties to her husband. We affirm.

I

The controversy before us arises out of the troubled and relatively brief marriage of the parties. Victor H. Francois (Victor) and A. Jane Francois (Jane) were married on May 13, 1971 after a brief courtship of several months. At the time of the wedding, Victor was fifty years old, a bachelor residing with his elderly mother. Jane was thirty years old, twice divorced, and the mother of two minor children, one approximately sixteen years old, and the other, thirteen. Victor was relatively secure financially, possessing an acre lot, Lilliendal and Marienhoj, St. Thomas, V.I. (Lilliendal), with a two story, five bedroom building containing two apartments, a one-fourth interest in his family's hardware business, thirty shares of a family close corporation (Francois Realty), four shares of stock in a multi-family close corporation (21 Queen's Quarter), a portfolio of publicly held stock valued at between $18,000 and $19,000, and two bank accounts. Victor also received income from his job as manager of the family hardware business. Jane was gainfully employed at the time of the marriage but ceased working shortly thereafter. She apparently brought no money or property to the marriage.

The couple began to experience difficulties not long after the marriage. A series of events over the next four years centering on financial disputes led to the deterioration and eventual collapse of the marital relation. Within months of the wedding, Jane began to express anxiety over her financial security in the event that Victor died. To allay his wife's fears, Victor opened a joint savings account into which he deposited $5,000 for her use.

Jane also expressed a continuing desire for a marital homestead. In response, in March of 1972, Victor purchased a fairly large house with a swimming pool (Misgunst) for a sum of $107,000. Victor supplied a $37,000 downpayment from his assets and undertook the responsibility for the monthly mortgage payments in excess of $860 per month. Title was taken by the entireties. The same year, Victor filed a petition seeking adoption of Jane's two children. The court granted the petition after Victor acknowledged under oath that he voluntarily assumed responsibility for the children.

In the fall of 1973, the couple's finances became further consolidated. Victor conveyed all of his interest in his Lilliendal property to Jane and assigned to her a half interest in both his thirty shares of Francois Realty stock and four shares of 21 Queen's Quarter stock. He also gave Jane a power of attorney over his portfolio of publicly held stock. Jane also insisted on having a boat. Victor sold $18,000 of his stock in order to purchase a boat for Jane in her name at the cost of $17,000. Jane sold this boat approximately a year later for $16,000 and personally invested the proceeds for herself. The couple also executed reciprocal wills leaving the entirety of the marital estate to the surviving spouse or, if no spouse survived, to the children.

In September of 1974 a domestic quarrel precipitated the demise of the marriage. The dispute centered on an incident in which Victor allegedly embarrassed Jane by his behavior in front of one of Jane's friends. As a result of the incident, Jane determined to divorce Victor and on October 8, 1974, contacted an attorney, Harold Monoson, to draw up divorce papers. Victor was unaware of his wife's decision to terminate the marriage. Two days later, Jane, without any explanation, invited Victor to accompany her to Monoson's office where Victor, to his complete surprise, was presented for his signature a "Property Settlement and Separation Agreement." Monoson advised Victor that he would need an attorney, but Victor's choice was vetoed by his wife's insistence that this attorney was unacceptable. Monoson then asked a lawyer with an office in the same building, Gregory Ball, to come into the office. Ball read the agreement, which interestingly already had his name on it as Victor's counsel. Ball strenuously advised Victor not to sign the agreement because it would commit him to "financial suicide." When Victor persisted in his determination to sign, Ball informed him that he could not represent him in the matter, and left the office.

Victor, relying on representations made to him by Monoson and Jane, was persuaded that only by signing the agreement could he preserve his marriage. Victor signed the agreement and several related documents apparently in hope of saving his marriage. He conveyed to Jane his one-half interest in the marital home, Misgunst, and assigned to her his stock portfolio and his remaining stock interest in both close corporations. In addition, the agreement required Victor to pay $300 per month in alimony to his wife.

After signing the agreement, however, the parties resumed cohabitation for approximately one year. But early in 1975, Jane informed Victor that she had sold the entire portfolio of publicly held stock for around $20,000. In October of 1975, Jane informed Victor that she had sold the Misgunst and Lilliendal properties in exchange for properties owned in California by AD'M Enterprises, a limited partnership. In mid-October Jane also summarily informed Victor that she was leaving him permanently and promptly left the Virgin Islands. AD'M took title to the properties by a single deed dated October 15, 1975 but before it could record the deed, Victor instituted these proceedings. Apparently when AD'M learned of this litigation, it never recorded the deed but instead sued Jane for rescission of the conveyance.

Victor's suit against Jane and AD'M sought rescission of the agreement and reconveyance of all properties transferred to Jane. AD'M was duly served but never appeared and a default judgment was entered against them from which no appeal has been taken. The case was tried to the court without a jury.

Chief Judge Christian, the trial judge, declared the Property Settlement and Separation Agreement to be null and void as the result of: 1) the cohabitation of the parties subsequent to the signing of the agreement; 2) the undue influence exerted by Jane over Victor in connection with the signing of the agreement; 3) fraud and misrepresentation on the part of Jane; and 4) the unconscionable terms of the agreement. Judge Christian also declared the deed of October 10, 1974 transferring sole title in the Misgunst property to Jane to be null and void and awarded title to the property solely in Victor's name. The court held the attempted transfer of Misgunst and Lilliendal properties by Jane to AD'M to be null and void. The court likewise voided the assignment made to Jane, pursuant to the agreement of Victor's stock in the two close corporations, Francois Realty and 21 Queen's Quarters, and restored sole title to the stock to Victor. The court decreed that title to the Lilliendal property remain in Jane's name because "the circumstances of that transfer were not explicated before the court in the testimony." The court, however, placed a lien against the Lilliendal property to secure Victor's reimbursement for the value of the stock and monies converted by Jane in early 1975. Finally, the district court awarded costs and attorneys fees to Victor.

II

Jane's first contention on appeal is that the district court erred in setting aside the Property Settlement and Separation Agreement. She challenges each of the four theories underpinning the district court's order of nullification. Because we agree that the district court properly voided the agreement on the grounds of undue influence exerted by Jane over her husband, we need not examine Jane's contentions relating to the three other theories supporting the district court's judgment.

We turn then to the issue of undue influence. The district court found that a confidential relationship existed between Jane and Victor. The court further found that Jane was the dominant partner in the marriage and that Victor was extremely susceptible to her influence. The court noted that the evidence was replete with instances in which Jane was able to secure her wishes by simply badgering Victor into submission. The court held that because a confidential relationship existed between the parties, the burden of proof was on Jane to demonstrate the fairness of the agreement. The court found that Jane deliberately misrepresented and misled Victor into believing that his signature on the agreement could save their marriage. The court concluded that Jane had failed to establish the fairness of the transaction and declared the agreement to be null and void.

Jane argues that the district court erred in placing the burden of proof on her to demonstrate the fairness of the transaction. She contends that a husband-wife relationship does not necessarily give rise to a relation of confidence. Even if such a confidential relationship existed, Jane maintains that the burden of proof is on the person seeking to void the transaction to show undue influence. She asserts that because Restatement law is authoritative in the Virgin Islands, n1 Restatement of Contracts §497 on undue influence, read in conjunction with Restatement §498 on fiduciary relations mandates the conclusion that only in fiduciary relationships does the burden of proof shift to the party benefiting from the transaction to prove its fairness. Jane concludes that because husbands and wives do not stand in fiduciary relation to each other, the burden of proof rested on Victor to prove the unfairness of the Property Settlement and Separation Agreement. Appellant's interpretation of the Restatement, however, is erroneous and misconstrues the law of undue influence.

We believe that this case is controlled by the law of constructive trusts although neither side briefed or argued it on this theory. A constructive trust is an equitable remedy utilized by courts to prevent unjust enrichment. Restatement of Restitution §160; Scott on Trusts, §462. It is an established principle of equity that "(w)here the owner of property transfers it, being induced by fraud, duress or undue influence of the transferee, the transferee holds the property upon a constructive trust for the transferor." Restatement of Restitution §166. See also, Yohe v. Yohe, 466 Pa. 405, 353 A.2d 417, 421 (1976). A common context in which undue influence may be exerted so as to warrant the imposition of a constructive trust is when a party to a confidential relationship abuses that relation to secure personal advantages. See *Scott*, §469 at 3441; Stauffer v. Stauffer, 465 Pa. 558, 351 A.2d 236, 241-242 (1976); Buchanan v. Brentwood Federal Savings and Loan Ass'n, 457 Pa. 135, 320 A.2d 117, 127 (1974). A confidential relationship may arise as a matter of law; but it is usually a question of fact in each case. *Buchanan*, supra 320 A.2d at 127.

A confidential relation exists between two persons when one has gained the confidence of the other and purports to act or advise with the other's interest in mind. A confidential relation may exist although there is no fiduciary relationship; it is particularly likely to exist where there is a family relationship. . . .

Restatement (Second) of Trusts §2, at 7 (1959). See also, Restatement of Restitution §166, Comment (d) at 676-677 (1937); Restatement of Contracts §497, Comment (a), at 954-955 (1932).

The key inquiry in the case before us is whether Jane and Victor Francois, as husband and wife, also enjoyed a confidential relationship. The marital relation does not automatically give rise to a confidentially relation, but it "arises when one party places confidence in the other with a resulting superiority and influence on the other side." *Yohe*, supra 353 A.2d at 421. Thus, each marriage must be examined on its own facts to determine if a confidential relation exists.

The district court unequivocally found that a confidential relationship existed between Jane and Victor Francois and that Jane was clearly the dominant partner. The district court found the evidence to be "replete with instances" in which Jane was able to secure her wishes simply by badgering Victor into submission. The record reveals that Victor, very early in the marriage, began to turn over the management of his finances to Jane who subsequently used her position to gain control incrementally over most of Victor's assets. The evidence supports the district court's findings that the relationship between the parties was one in which Victor reposed total trust and confidence in Jane who used her superior position in the marriage to Victor's financial detriment.

The existence of a confidential relationship does not automatically give rise to the imposition of a constructive trust. Rather, "its effect is simply to impose a burden upon the party benefiting from the transaction of proving that he took no unfair advantage of his relationship with the other." *Stauffer*, supra 351 A.2d at 242. Williston states that if the person alleging undue influence can prove that "he was the servient member of a confidential relationship, . . . (courts) hold that this raises a rebuttable presumption of undue influence requiring the dominant party to come forward with proof of the fairness of the transaction." Williston on Contracts, §1625 at 800 (3d ed. 1970) (footnotes omitted). We also have held in Joseph v. Eastman, 344 F.2d 9, 12, 5 V.I. 201, 207 (3d Cir. 1965), that in relationships of trust or confidence the burden of proof shifts to the person seeking to uphold the transaction to demonstrate the absence of undue influence. Thus, Jane's contention that the trial court incorrectly shifted the burden of proof to her to show the lack of undue influence is meritless. The trial court, after determining the existence of a confidential relation quite properly allocated the burden of proof to Jane.

We must now consider whether Jane met her burden of proof to rebut the charge of undue influence. If she failed, a constructive trust may be imposed on the couple's properties in order to prevent Jane's unjust enrichment.

Undue influence is not a concept susceptible of unitary definition. The essence of the idea is the subversion of another person's free will in order to obtain assent to an agreement.

If a party in whom another reposes confidence misuses that confidence to gain his own advantage while the other has been made to feel that the party in question will not act against his welfare, the transaction is the result of undue influence. The influence must be such that the victim acts in a way contrary to his own best interest and thus in a fashion in which he would not have operated but for the undue influence.

Williston on Contracts, §1625 at 776-777 (3d ed. 1970) (footnotes omitted).

The degree of persuasion that is necessary to constitute undue influence varies from case to case. The proper inquiry is not just whether persuasion induced the transaction but whether the result was produced by the domination of the will of the victim by the person exerting undue influence. Restatement of Contracts §497, Comment c. Hence, the particular transaction must be scrutinized to determine if the agreement was truly the product of a free and independent mind. In this respect, the fairness of the agreement must be shown by clear and convincing evidence. Id. §1627B at 823, *Buchanan*, supra 320 A.2d at 127.

Jane claims that the factual findings of the court distorted the true relationship between the parties and that no undue influence was present. First, we note that the district court's fact-finding cannot be disturbed unless it "(1) is completely devoid of minimum evidentiary support displaying some hue of credibility, or (2) bears no rational relationship to the supporting evidentiary data." Krasnov v. Dinan, 465 F.2d 1298, 1302 (3d Cir. 1972). We believe that the evidence in this case amply supports the district court's finding of undue influence.

The district court found that Jane alone caused the agreement to be made and that she alone benefited from it. The district court described the circumstances under which Victor was urged to obtain legal advice as a charade. There is no evidence that the independent advice received by Victor was from an attorney of his choosing. In fact, the meeting with Attorney Ball was arranged spontaneously and without an opportunity for a full and private consultation. Ball's name was already on the agreement as Victor's counsel. (For importance of independent counseling, see *Williston*, supra §1625 at 778.) Victor was apparently surprised by his wife's decision to terminate the marriage and there is evidence that Monoson and/or Jane misled him into believing that by signing the agreement, the marriage could be salvaged. The district court also found that Jane, at the time the agreement was signed, had no real intent to save the marriage.

The terms of the agreement were hardly fair. Attorney Ball's assessment that the agreement was financial suicide for Victor was accurate. On this record, we conclude that the district court was correct in its finding that Jane had failed to rebut the presumption of undue influence.

We thus have a classic situation in which a constructive trust should be imposed over all the assets acquired by Jane. The district court properly used its equitable power to declare the agreement to be null and void. Equity should fully protect one spouse from exploitation through the exercise of undue influence by the other in whom confidence and trust has been innocently reposed. . . .

The judgment of the district court will be affirmed.

Questions

1. What act of duress was exerted in this case?
2. What was the fraud and misrepresentation with respect to the agreement as discussed by the court?
3. Does this case influence your thinking about the validity of antenuptial agreements? Discuss.

Brown v. L. V. Marks & Sons Co.
64 F. Supp. 352 (E.D. Ky. 1946)

The defendant is a manufacturer of ladies shoes. For many years it has operated two factories in Kentucky. One of them at Augusta, the other at Vanceburg. The plaintiff was the superintendent of the Vanceburg plant. He had been connected with the shoe manufacturing business for many years before he was employed by the defendant. His employment by the defendant commenced in 1934 or 1935.

In 1938 he devised certain new features in connection with the sole of the shoe which produced a cushion or resilient effect. These new features were disclosed to the officers of the defendant company, who became enthusiastic about them. With the plaintiff's consent the defendant secured patents on these inventions. The patents were issued in the name of the plaintiff, Mark L. Brown, and Emanuel S. Marks as co-inventors, both of whom executed assignments of the patents to the defendant. In all there were three different new features covered by three separate patents. Patent No. 2,207,437 was issued on July 9, 1940, covering the invention used in what is designated as the "Aerotized" shoe. Patent No. 2,300,739, issued on November 3, 1942, was utilized in the construction of a shoe called "Cushomatic" insole. Patent No. 2,320,321, issued May 25, 1943, was a development and new feature for the "welt" type construction.

My conclusions in this case affect all of these patents alike so there is no need to identify them further for distinguishing features.

It is alleged by the plaintiff that at the time of the assignments of the inventions, the defendant, in consideration of the assignments, agreed to pay him a reasonable royalty on each pair of shoes sold.

The shoes were well accepted by the trade and were in such demand that both plants were almost immediately converted to the exclusive manufacture of the Aerotized and Cushomatic shoes.

It should be pointed out that while the patents were issued in the names of Emanuel S. Marks and Mark L. Brown as coinventors, Marks had but little to do with the invention and I find was not in fact coinventor. The whole new ideas embraced in the patented articles came from Brown and the few simple suggestions from Marks do not entitle him to any credit for the ultimately patented articles.

The plaintiff seeks to have the assignments set aside because of fraud in the procurement, asks for an accounting for the sale of all shoes manufactured under the patents, and that the defendant be perpetually enjoined from further manufacture of shoes under the patents.

The defendant rests its defense on three main issues: First, that there was no contract either express or implied to pay royalty. Second, that it is entitled to "shop rights," since the invention was conceived and perfected by the plaintiff on the defendant's time and with the use of its materials. Third, that any claim which the plaintiff may have had is barred by laches.

I must conclude from the record that there was an express contract to pay the plaintiff a reasonable royalty. The conclusion is based on the positive testimony of the plaintiff, which is corroborated by subsequent events about which there is no dispute. The defendant spends much time arguing that the invention added little or nothing to the art. This argument can hardly be accepted. When the idea was presented to Emanual Marks, who in turn took it to the home office in Cincinnati, for examination by other executives and responsible employees of the company, it was received with enthusiasm. The defendant immediately set about to have patents issue[d] and to have an assignment to it of exclusive rights in the invention. The defendant's witness, McGovern, a stockholder and chief salesman of the company, testified that at the Boston shoe show in 1938 the idea of a cushioned or resilient soled shoe was 'in the air' and all the talk among shoe men. Therefore, due to the initiative and inventive genius of the plaintiff, the defendant was enabled to take advantage of this 'stir' in the industry and put on the market, ahead of competitors, the new idea in shoe construction. Further, it is significant that the defendant abandoned entirely any other type of construction and converted both of its plants into the manufacture of Aerotized and Cushomatic shoes. Neither is the defendant in a very enviable light in attempting now to minimize the novelty in this construction. When it was seeking the patent it was strenuously urging that this was a radical change in shoe construction previously unknown to the art. At that time the defendant was sufficiently plausible in the advocacy of the Aerotized and Cushomatic shoes to have patents issue on them. It further appears from the record that the defendant company had for 'four or five years' licensed a large manufacturer of shoes under these patents and had received royalties for the license granted.

There is another fact which I think infers that there must have been some understanding between the parties that the plaintiff should be compensated for making the assignments of the patents. The plaintiff, a resident of Vanceburg during his employment as the defendant's superintendent, decided to build a house. He purchased from the defendant a building lot in the town of Vanceburg for the sum of $800 and paid $100 down. Later after conference between executives and stockholders of the company the $100 was refunded and a deed to the lot was executed and delivered to the plaintiff and his wife as a gift. This was in June 1940, after the shoes were in production. This fact strongly indicates an effort to placate the plaintiff and to forestall any claim under the agreement. It is not a strong circumstance but one to be considered in the light of other facts.

On the whole case the plaintiff has sustained the burden of proving by a preponderance of evidence through testimony and all reasonable inferences that may be drawn from it that there was an express agreement to pay a reasonable royalty for the assignment of the exclusive patent rights.

Having established that there was such a contract, the plaintiff assumes the burden of proving that it was procured by fraud and asks that because of the fraud it be annulled and the assignment cancelled. To establish fraud in the procurement of a contract is one of the most difficult burdens that can be assumed by a litigant. Brown asks the court to cancel his assignment of the patent rights. This valid written obligation is attacked because as he claims there was a preconceived plan on the part of the defendant to defraud him and wrongfully obtain these valuable patents. The plaintiff rests his case upon the following statement of law from 23 Am. Jur. 885, §106 "A majority of American courts hold that fraud may be predicated on promises made with a present intention not to perform them or, as the rule is frequently expressed, on promises made without an intention of performance, and that for such fraudulent promise, relief may be had in equity or law, as the circumstances and issues presented demand. Recourse may therefore be had for such promises, made for the purpose of deceiving the promisee and including him to act, where otherwise he would not do so, in such a way as to affect his legal right or to alter his position to his injury or risk, as by making and entering into disadvantageous contracts or in some way giving over, transferring, or surrendering real or personal property or rights therein to the person who makes the fraudulent promise." The gist of the fraud in such cases is not the breach of the agreement to perform, but the fraudulent intent of the promisor, the false representation of an existing intention to perform where such intent is in fact nonexistent, and the deception of the obligee by such false promise. The generally accepted modern theory categorizes a promise which the promisor does not intend to carry out as a misstatement of material and subsisting fact, recognizing, in the oft-quoted language of Lord Bowen, that: "There must be a misstatement of an existing fact; but the state of a man's mind is as much a fact as the state of his digestion. It is true that it is very difficult to prove what the state of a man's mind at a particular time is, but if it can be ascertained it is as much a fact as anything else. A misrepresentation as to the state of a man's mind is therefore a misstatement of fact."

It is thus seen that he must produce proof of the highest dignity in order to sustain his case. The case of Dolle v. Melrose Properties, 252 Ky. 482, 67 S.W.2d 706, 709, expresses the rule on which the plaintiff rests his case, in the following language: "A charge of fraud may be predicated on the nonperformance of a promise, where the promise is accompanied by a present intention not to perform, and is made to deceive the promisee." Citing, Jones v. Brammer, 229 Ky. 649, 17 S.W.2d 736. See also Kentucky Road Oiling Co. v. Sharp, 257 Ky. 378, 78 S.W.2d 38, and Kentucky Cardinal Coal Corp. v. Delph, 296 Ky. 295, 176 S.W.2d 886.

In order for the court to so find the evidence must be clear, unequivocal and convincing. The evidence must be of such character that it does not leave the court in any doubt that fraud was practiced and the plaintiff acted only because of the fraudulent misrepresentation.

The case insofar as it seeks to establish fraud in the procurement fails. In fact I can find no evidence that remotely suggests that there was an intention on the part of the defendant and its agents to filch the patents from the plaintiff at the time of the assignment. There have been instances in the law in which such a case was established, but the plaintiff fails to make out such a case here. Whatever fraud there may be was in failing to comply with the contract after it was made. The facts here more nearly fall within the latter part of section 106 of American Jurisprudence, volume 23: "In order to render nonperformance of a promise fraudulent, the intention not to perform must exist when the promise is made; and if the promise is made in good faith when the contract is entered into, there is no fraud, even though the promisor subsequently perform. Moreover, there is no inference of fraudulent intent not to perform from the mere fact that a promise made is subsequently not performed."

The Circuit Court of Appeals for the Sixth Circuit has well expressed the rule applicable here in the following quotation with authorities, from Bowen v. B. F. Goodrich Co., 36 F.2d 306, 308: "The issue is thus reduced to a question of veracity between appellant and the witness Eakin, as illuminated by the circumstances disclosed in the record. Before noticing these circumstances we observe that where a complainant seeks a rescission of an executed instrument upon the ground of fraud, he must establish the fraud by evidence that is clear and convincing. Atlantic Co. v. James, 94 U.S. 207, 24 L. Ed. 112; Maxwell Land-Grant Co.), 121 U.S. 325, 7 S. Ct. 1015, 30 L. Ed. 949; Lalone v. United States, 164 U.S. 255, 17 S. Ct. 74, 41 L. Ed. 425."

All Kentucky decisions are in line with this rule. Lincoln-Income Life Ins. Co. v. Kraus, 279 Ky. 842, 132 S.W.2d 318; Lausman et al. v. Brown et al., 293 Ky. 95, 168 S.W.2d 579; T. M. Crutcher Laboratory v. Crutcher, 288 Ky. 709, 157 S.W.2d 314; Pacific Mutual Life Ins. Co. v. Arnold, 262 Ky. 267, 90 S.W.2d 44; Dotson v. Norman et al., 159 Ky. 786, 169 S.W. 527. In Lincoln-Income Life Ins. Co. v. Kraus, supra, the court used this language (279 Ky. 842, 132 S.W.2d 320): "It is likewise well established that a duly executed written contract will not be set aside and ignored, upon the ground of fraud in its procurement, unless the testimony clearly establishes the fraud, and the burden is upon the one asserting it to furnish the evidence necessary for that purpose."

It would serve no good purpose to further review the reported case involving the question of fraud in the procurement.

Since I have found that there was an express contract the question of shop rights is no longer important. There can be no claim for shop rights where the parties have agreed on a royalty basis. However, since the question of shop rights is somewhat related, I am constrained to call attention to the rule stated in United States v. Dubilier Condenser Corp., 289 U.S. 178, 53 S. Ct. 554, 77 L. Ed. 1114, 84 A.L.R. 1488. The cases of Gill v. United States, 160 U.S. 426, 16 S. Ct. 322, 40 L. Ed. 480; Dalzell v. Dueber Watch Case Mfg. Co., 149 U.S. 315, 13 S. Ct. 886, 37 L. Ed. 749; and Standard Parts Co. v. Peck, 264 U.S. 52, 44 S. Ct. 239, 68 L. Ed. 560, 32 A.L.R. 1033, are considered and Mr. Justice Roberts' comprehensive statement of the law in the light of all that has theretofore been said. The rule there stated is (289 U.S. 178, 53 S. Ct. 558): "Recognition of the nature of the act of invention also defines the limits of the so-called shop right, which, shortly stated, is that, where a servant, during his hours of employment, working with his master's materials and appliances, conceives and perfects an invention for which he obtains a patent, he must accord his master a nonexclusive right to practice the invention. McClurg v. Kingsland, 1 How. 202, 11 L. Ed. 102; Solomons v. United States, 137 U.S. 342, 11 S. Ct. 88, 34 L. Ed. 667; Lane & Bodley Co. v. Locke, 150 U.S. 193, 14 S. Ct. 78, 37 L. Ed. 1049. This is an application of equitable principles. Since the servant uses his master's time, facilities, and materials to attain a concrete result, the latter is in equity entitled to use that which embodies his own property and to duplicate it as often as he may find occasion to employ similar appliances in his business. But the employer in such a case has no equity to demand a conveyance of the invention, which is the original conception of the employee alone, in which the employer had no part. This remains the property of him who conceived it, together with the right conferred by the patent, to exclude all others than the employer from the accruing benefits. These principles are settled as respects private employment."

As late as October 9, 1945, the Kentucky Court of Appeals in an opinion referred to the Dubilier case and used this language: "The testimony covered a wide range and tended to establish that the invention was perfected and utilized under such circumstances as to entitle appellant to 'shop rights,' that is, the right to use said invention in its business without the payment of royalty." Ashland Oil & Refining Co. v. Dorton, 300 Ky. 385, 189 S.W.2d 394, 395.

Notwithstanding certain language which is used in earlier cases, I cannot conclude in the light of the Dubilier case that estoppel is longer an essential element in establishing shop rights. Frequently it is present and must strengthen the case but there may be shop rights to a discovery in industry without past development. There is a vested property right which equity fixes in the invention at its inception. Where the employee makes his discovery while working with the employer's tools, machinery, and materials and on the employer's time, the interest or shop right in favor of the employer attaches immediately. I quote the following pertinent language from 32 A.L.R. 1041:

> In addition to the cases cited in the earlier annotation on this question, holding that the employer had, at least, a license or shop right to use the

invention made by the employee, is Wiegand v. Dover Mfg. Co., D.C., 1923, 292 F. 255, in which the court followed the decision in Gill v. United States, 1896, 160 U.S. 426, 16 S. Ct. 322, 40 L. Ed. 480, to the effect that the mere fact that the employee conceived and made the original drawings of the invention on his own free time and at his own home, outside of working hours, would not take the case out of the rule entitling the employer to a license to use the invention, where the same was developed and put into practical operation in the employer's factory and at the latter's expense, the employer, on the principle of an estoppel in pais, being entitled to such a license or shop right. The court said that the entire development and reduction to practice was made at the risk, cost, and expense of the employer; that its accumulated store of experience and its materials and facilities were placed at the disposal of the employee; that it was in this atmosphere, and under the pressure of business necessity, that the inventions were produced, and that whatever originality the employee contributed was only one factor in their evolution; that if the employee's contentions were sound the result would be that he entered the employment with nothing, and three years later left it, the practical owner of the employer's business.

The remaining question of laches as a defense admits of little consideration. This is not a stale claim within the meaning of equity. The plaintiff and defendant began their consideration of these patents in March, 1938, and continued so long as the plaintiff was in the defendant's employ, which lasted until 1942. The action was brought November 10, 1943. The last patent did not issue until May 25, 1943. Negotiations and discussions were being held constantly between the parties. The plaintiff says that he spoke to Emanuel Marks several times about the royalty promise but that Marks stated it was necessary to first see how well the shoes sold and how many "repeat" orders were received by the company. This is a most reasonable explanation. Certainly no chancellor would deny recovery on the ground that the plaintiff had unduly delayed seeking redress. I feel that the record so clearly sustains my finding on this point that citation of authorities is unnecessary. I point out, however, that in Howard v. Howe, 7 Cir., 61 F.2d 577, where the same defense was made, there was a lapse of nineteen years between the assignment of the patent and the claim for remuneration. See also Galliher v. Cadwell, 145 U.S. 368, 12 S. Ct. 873, 36 L. Ed. 738; Northern Pacific R. Co. v. Boyd, 9 Cir., 177 F. 804. In affirming the decision in the Boyd case, 228 U.S. 482, 33 S. Ct. 554, 562, 57 L. Ed. 931, the Supreme Court said: "Unless the nonaction of the complainant operated to damage the defendant, or to induce it to change its position, there is no necessary estoppel arising from the mere lapse of time." There is no indication that the defendant has been damaged by the alleged delay in the case at bar.

The justice of this case demands that the plaintiff should receive a reasonable royalty for his discovery and invention. The defendant has profited through his genius and should not be permitted to exploit the patents and ignore the inventor.

Under the present state of the record the plaintiff's whole case must fail, since I find that no fraud was practiced in the procurement of the assignments and since there is no prayer for a reasonable royalty. The plaintiff is given thirty days to amend his complaint to conform to the proof. Federal Rules of Civil Procedure, rule 15, 28 U.S.C.A. following section 723c; McDowall v. Orr Felt & Blanket Co., 6 Cir., 146 F.2d 136. If at the end of that time no steps are taken, the complaint will be dismissed at the plaintiff's cost.

Findings of fact and conclusions of law are this day filed.

Questions

1. What was the nature of the alleged fraud in this case?
2. What is the "shop right" discussed in the case, and what is its applicability to the instant facts?
3. What is your opinion of this case?

Suggested Case References

1. Contracting for the sale of leases that the seller knows, or has reason to know, have expired is not a mistake, but fraud. Read what the federal court sitting in Texas said in Matter of Topco, 894 F.2d 727, *reh'g denied*, 902 F.2d 955 (5th Cir. 1990).

2. A manufacturer attempts to avoid its collective bargaining agreement with a union. Under the contract, the manufacturer agreed to offer its employees the same insurance plan the employees had with a separate manufacturer, a copy of which was shown to the company. The company now asserts it was mistaken with respect to the clauses of the insurance plan. Is this a mistake permitting avoidance of the contract? Read what the federal court sitting in California had to say in Libby, McNeil & Libby v. United Steelworkers, 809 F.2d 1432 (9th Cir. 1987).

3. Even if both parties to a contract are mistaken as to the value or usefulness of the goods sold, as long as the goods are properly identified, the mistake does not invalidate the contract because it only pertains to the value of the subject matter. Fernandez v. Western Ash Builders, Inc., 112 Idaho App. 907, 736 P.2d 1361 (1987).

4. If a party seeks to avoid a contract induced by duress, must he return the consideration he has received pursuant to that agreement? Read Solomon v. FloWARR Management, Inc., 777 S.W.2d 701 (Tenn. App. 1989).

5. To read what the Delaware court says about the effects of disclaimers see Alabi v. DHL Airways, Inc., 583 A.2d 1358 (Del. Super. 1990).

7 Contract Provisions

CHAPTER OVERVIEW

The preceding six chapters have discussed the general law of contracts that must be kept in mind when analyzing the validity of a contractual agreement. The time has now come to look at the actual provisions of a contract itself.

As indicated in the first chapter, contracts may be valid whether or not they are in writing. However, there is a small group of contracts that the law mandates must be in writing to be enforceable. This requirement exists for agreements that are described in the Statute of Frauds. However, regardless of the form, written or oral, all contract terms are given similar weight and interpretation.

Contracts are composed of various clauses, or paragraphs, that indicate the promises each party has made up to the other. These specific promises form the consideration of the contract and are the parties' contractual obligations. Once there has been a meeting of the minds over the subject matter, these promises form the basis of the parties' enforceable rights. Such provisions are known as **covenants.**

The mere promise to perform is not totally indicative of the moment that the promise becomes enforceable in a court of law. Incident to every covenant is an element of timing: at what point is the promisor obligated to perform, and at what point does the promisee have an enforceable right? Although many everyday contracts lack this timing element, since the promise and the performance occur simultaneously, many contractual situations exist in which the contractual obligation is conditioned on some event that is not a specific part of the contract itself. This timing element, which forms its own clause in the contract, is known as a **condition**. A condition specifies the moment at which the covenant becomes legally enforceable.

Consequently, when analyzing any contract, these two separate elements must be specifically determined: one, what has been promised in the contract; and two, at what point does that promise become enforceable in a court of law. If a disputed provision winds up in court, the court has adopted several rules or guidelines to interpret and prove contract provisions. These guidelines are called **rules of construction** and will be discussed below.

The Statute of Frauds

The law generally makes no distinction between contracts that are written and contracts that are verbal; each is given legal validity. The primary distinction between them deals not with contract law, but with the law of evidence. It is simply easier to demonstrate a contractual promise if the trier of fact can read the contract itself. If the terms of the contract have to be proven by oral testimony, there can be a conflict between what the parties to the agreement remember about the terms, and so an extra burden is placed on the trier of fact. Before he can determine what the parties' contractual rights are, he must fast determine what the contract says.

Despite the preceding, the overwhelming majority of contracts entered into on a daily basis are either oral or implied, not written. Buying a newspaper, taking a bus, buying a cup of coffee, or purchasing clothing are usually effectuated without any written agreement. At most, a person might receive a receipt, which merely memorializes the transaction without meeting any of the requirements of a written contract. However, for historical reasons that will be discussed below, there are six situations in which the law has determined that, to be enforceable, the agreement must be in writing.

The law that requires certain contracts to be in writing is known as the **Statute of Frauds.** Every state has adopted a version of the Statute of Frauds, either legislatively or judicially. The origin of the Statute of Frauds lies in feudal England and is worth some mention.

In feudal times, travel and communication were extremely difficult, and the life expectancy of most people was very short. The major contractual relationships of the day dealt with land ownership and land rights. Consequently, to protect persons over geographic and time spans, the Statute of Frauds was enacted. The Statute of Frauds provided some assurance that the contract in question did in fact exist. The "fraud" in the Statute of Frauds was not the contractual concept of fraud discussed previously, but concerned preventing perjury and fraud with respect to proving contractual clauses. The Statute of Frauds required that, to be enforceable, the following six types of contracts had to be in writing:

1. contracts for an interest in real estate;
2. contracts in consideration of marriage;
3. contracts that are not to be performed within one year;
4. guarantees;
5. contracts for the sale of goods valued over a specified amount; and
6. executor's promises to pay a decedent's debts.

Contracts for an Interest in Real Estate

Because the entire concept of a feudal society was based on land ownership, the Statute of Frauds required that any contract for an interest in real estate be in writing. In medieval times, requiring that deeds be in writing assured persons that ownership could be specifically traced without recourse to faulty memories. Also, contractual terms could be proved even if persons involved in the agreement had died and therefore could not testify about the contract. Land rights were too important to be left to such vagaries, and consequently the statute was enacted.

This provision is still in force today. To be enforceable, every contract for an interest in real estate must be in writing. Contracts for the sale of land are also permanently recorded in governmental offices in the county where the property is located. This insures that the title to the property can be traced and determined.

EXAMPLE:

Joseph agrees to sell the house he inherited in Florida to Mindy. They enter into a written contract for the sale of the house. When each side has performed under the contract—Mindy paying for the house and Joseph conveying the deed—the sale is recorded in the county Recorder's Office in the county where the house is located so that title to the property will read from Joseph to Mindy by contract of sale.

This provision of the Statute of Frauds is only concerned with the land itself. Anything that may be considered the "fruits of the land" (crops, minerals, and so on) are not within the provisions of the statute. Contracts for the sale of crops may be enforceable even if they are oral.

EXAMPLES:

1. Gary agrees to buy all of the potatoes Bob grows on his farm this year for a set price per pound. The agreement between Gary and

Bob is not in writing. The contract is enforceable because the subject matter of the agreement is crops, not the land itself. The Statute of Frauds does not apply.

2. The Greens have just bought a house next to the Richards. To get to the nearest shopping center, it is most convenient for the Greens to pass over a portion of the Richards' property. The Richards orally agree to assign this right over their property (called an *easement*) to the Greens for a nominal fee. This agreement is not enforceable. An easement deals directly with an interest in the land and so comes within the Statute of Frauds. Easements must be in writing.

The determining factor of whether the contract must be in writing is whether the agreement directly concerns the land itself or whether it concerns something that can be removed from the land. If the latter, it is not within the Statute of Frauds.

Contracts in Consideration of Marriage

In feudal times, marriage was more a matter of property transfer than of love and affection. The medieval husband was entitled to a dowry from his intended wife's family, and the law required this dowry to be written down. If the wife's family did not deliver the goods specified in the contract, the groom could sue to have the property transferred or, in certain countries, could return the wife.

Although nowadays dowries are exceedingly rare in the United States, the concept that any promise given in consideration of marriage must be in writing still exists. This usually takes the form of an **antenuptial,** or **prenuptial, agreement.** An antenuptial agreement is a contract between the intended bride and groom specifying each one's property rights in case of death or divorce. It is not unusual for wealthy, well-known persons to have prenuptial agreements, but even persons who are neither wealthy nor famous enter into such contracts.

EXAMPLES:

1. Gussie and Izzy are about to be married. The bride and groom are each in their 70s, it is a second marriage for both of them, and they each have children and grandchildren. Gussie wants to make sure that the money she inherited from her late husband goes to her children on her death, and Izzy feels the same way about his money and family. Consequently, they draw up a written prenuptial agreement specifying that each relinquishes claims to the other's estate in case of death or divorce. The agreement is valid and enforceable. The consideration is the impending marriage.

2. Hedda has agreed to marry Osbert, the unattractive son of a wealthy industrialist. To induce Hedda's promise, Osbert's father has promised to give $100,000 to her after the ceremony. Hedda gets this promise in writing and, after the ceremony, places the written agreement before her father-in-law. This agreement is enforceable, and he must now give Hedda the cash.

Do not get confused between contracts in consideration of marriage and what has become known as **palimony.** Palimony is an invented term used to enforce promises made between persons who are not legally married at the time of their break-up. The theory of law used to enforce these agreements is a contractual one, but it is specifically not based on a promise in consideration of marriage.

Contracts Not to Be Performed Within One Year

In feudal times, human life expectancies were so short that it could not be guaranteed that parties to a contract, or people who knew of the contract, would live long enough to testify about its provisions should a problem arise. Therefore, if the contract in question contemplated that the performance would take more than one year, it was required that the contract be in writing so that its provisions could be analyzed should there be a breach.

Today, this provision of the Statute of Frauds still exists. However, be aware that even though the statute requires the contract to be in writing, if the parties actually perform or make a substantial beginning on the performance, those actions will make the contract enforceable under equitable concepts previously discussed. Also note that for determining the applicability of the statute, the period starts from the day of the agreement, not the date on which the performance is to start.

 EXAMPLES:

1. Maud agrees to buy Stacey's mink coat, which she's always admired. However, Stacey is asking $1500, and Maud doesn't have that much cash on hand. Maud and Stacey enter into an agreement whereby Maud agrees to pay Stacey $100 per month until the coat is paid for. To be valid, the contract must be in writing because the performance will take more than one year.

2. Mark agrees to work as a paralegal on a temporary basis for the firm of Blacke & Blewe, P.C. on February 1. The job that Mark is assigned to do will take eight months and is to start on September 1. This contract does have to be in writing because performance will not be completed in less than one year or the date on which the agreement was made.

3. Kenny agrees to buy Jose's car for $1800. They orally agree on a payment schedule whereby Kenny pays Jose $100 per month until the car is paid for, at which point Jose will transfer the registration. After Kenny makes five payments, Jose changes his mind and tells Kenny the deal is off. Because they have no written agreement, Jose claims there is no contractual obligation. Kenny sues. In court, because Kenny has already made a substantial performance, the contract would most likely be upheld because to do otherwise would be unfair to Kenny.

This provision of the Statute of Frauds is concerned with situations in which it is impossible for the performance to be completed within just one year. If, under *any* conceivable circumstance, the performance could be completed within 12 months, the contract does not come within the statute.

Additionally, if the performance is conditioned on some future uncertain event (say, for example, a life expectancy), the contract does not fall within the statute. Because any uncertain event *may* occur in less than one year, the statute does not apply. The statute will apply if the performance of only one party to the contract will take more than one year.

 EXAMPLE:

Arthur is terminally ill, and Danielle agrees to nurse him for a specified salary as long as he lives. This contract is not within the Statute of Frauds. Arthur could live one month or ten years. Because life expectancy is uncertain, performance of the contract could be performed within one year.

Guarantees

As discussed in an earlier chapter, a **guarantee** is a promise to answer for the debts of another. A guarantee is also a type of formal contract. The concept of a guarantee comes from the Statute of Frauds. Because there is, in fact, no consideration for this promise, it must be in writing to be enforceable. This provision of the statute is still in force today.

Contracts for the Sale of Goods

Historically, contracts for the sale of goods valued above a specified amount (the amount has increased over the years) had to be in writing to be enforceable. The concept evolved from the idea that personal property was not as valuable as real property until a certain value was reached. At that monetary point, the property became sufficiently important for the law to require a writing to protect parties.

Today, this provision of the Statute of Frauds has been absorbed by the **Uniform Commercial Code (UCC)** for most commercial contracts. The UCC, a version of which has been adopted in every jurisdiction, provides that any contract for the sale of goods valued at over $500 must be in writing to be enforceable. The UCC will be fully discussed in Chapter 8; for the moment simply realize that this type of contract is now governed by the UCC, not the Statute of Frauds.

Executor's Promise to Pay Decedent's Debts

Under the Statute of Frauds, an executor's agreement to pay the debts of the deceased out of the executor's own pocket must be in writing. This provision evolved in a manner similar to that of guarantees, and the same theories hold true for both.

This section of the Statute of Frauds concerns estate administration, not contracts, and is most appropriately discussed in a work dealing with that area of law. It is noted here only to complete our discussion of the Statute of Frauds.

What the Statute of Frauds Is Not

Bear in mind that the Statute of Frauds is concerned with the *enforceability* of a contractual agreement, not with the *validity of its terms*. The validity of any contract is determined by its meeting the six requirements mentioned in the earlier chapters. Enforceability is concerned with whether the contract can be given force in a court of competent jurisdiction.

Nor does the Statute of Frauds change the interpretation of the contract clauses. It merely places an additional requirement on the formation of those clauses for certain categories of contracts—the requirement that those contracts be in writing. Aside from that one point, the interpretation given to the clauses is identical, whether written or oral. Either the clauses will represent the enforceable promises of the parties or the timing element with respect to when those promises must be performed.

Regardless of the statute, if the parties have performed or made a substantial beginning on the performance, the contract is taken out of the statute. Also, if the entire contract is not in writing but the parties have made a written memorandum that sufficiently details the provisions of their agreement, that memo will take the contract out of the statute. (Note that a memo will not be sufficient if the contract is for an interest in realty; that must still be a complete written contract.)

Covenants

A **covenant** is defined as an unconditional, absolute promise to perform. It is the contractual promise to which no conditions are attached. If a party fails to fulfill his contractual covenant, it is deemed to be a breach, or violation, of the entire contract per se (in and of itself).

What is an unconditional, absolute promise to perform? It is consideration that the party has promised to give to induce the other side's promise. It is the promise to convey the textbook in a contract for the sale of a book; it is the promise to perform paralegal duties in an employment contract; it is the promise to pay for a mink coat in a sales contract. If a person fails to perform on her covenant, the contract is breached, and she can be sued. Furthermore, the other party is relieved of all other performance promised under the contract.

 EXAMPLE:

Suzanne agrees to work as a paralegal for the firm of White & Lace, P.C. The agreed-on salary is $300 per week, payable every two weeks. At the end of her first two weeks, Suzanne expects a paycheck. When the firm's partner apologizes and says the firm cannot afford to pay her, the firm has breached the contract. Suzanne is no longer obligated to work for the firm, and she can sue them for back wages. In this contract, Suzanne's covenant is to perform paralegal services, and the firm's covenant is to pay Suzanne a salary of $300 per week.

Not every clause in a contract is considered to be a covenant. The covenants are only the specific contractual promises. Consequently, if there are any terms that a party wants to make determinative of contractual rights, they should be phrased as unconditional promises and thus as covenants. Any clause that would otherwise be a condition can be made a covenant by the intent and wording of the parties.

Conditions

The covenant is the specific promise made by the parties to the contract. It is the basis of the contractual agreement. However, as incident to every contractual covenant, the parties must come to some agreement with respect to when the promises are to be performed. This timing element for performance of the covenant is known as a **condition.**

A condition is a fact or event, the happening or nonhappening of which creates or extinguishes an absolute duty to perform. Simply stated, the covenant is what must be performed, and the condition indicates when it is to be performed. In the example given above, with the paralegal Suzanne and the law firm, the covenants were the promises to perform paralegal duties and to pay a salary; the condition was Suzanne's performing for two weeks *before* the firm was to pay her. In other words, Suzanne's performance created the timing element of the contract. If she didn't perform, the law firm would not be obligated to pay her. Conversely, once she had performed for two weeks, the condition or timing element of the contract had been met, and the firm was obligated to pay. Any words modifying a provision contingent on an uncertain event create a condition.

How do you know that a particular contract contains conditions as well as covenants? The answer lies in what the parties themselves have either specifically agreed to, what can be inferred from their actions, or what has been imposed by the law.

Conditions are categorized by *when* they create, or extinguish, the duty to perform the covenant. There are three such categories of conditions:

1. conditions precedent;
2. conditions subsequent; and
3. conditions concurrent.

Conditions are categorized not only by their timing element, as indicated above, but also by *how* the parties have arrived at them. Once again, there are three categories to indicate how the conditions were created:

1. express conditions;
2. implied-in-fact conditions; and
3. implied-in-law conditions.

Each of the six categories of covenants is examined more carefully below.

Conditions Precedent

A **condition precedent** is a condition that must occur before the contractual promise becomes operative and enforceable. The example above, of Suzanne and the law firm, is an example of a condition precedent: Suzanne must perform for two weeks *before* the firm becomes obligated. If Suzanne decides not to work for the firm, the firm is under no contractual obligation.

EXAMPLE:

Karen and Bertram enter into a contract for the sale of Bertram's house. Bertram promises to sell, and Karen promises to buy, the house for $95,000. However, Karen inserts a clause in the contract conditioning the sale on her ability to arrange financing within 30 days of the date of signing the agreement. This is a condition precedent. For the parties to be contractually obligated, Karen must arrange financing. The financing is an external event that gives rise to her enforceable promise to purchase. Should she not be able to arrange financing, the contract for the sale of the house would not come into existence.

Conditions Subsequent

A **condition subsequent** is a condition that extinguishes a previous absolute duty to perform. This type of condition relieves the parties of their contractual obligations without being in breach of contract.

EXAMPLES:

1. Helen buys a blouse on credit at Macy's. When she gets home she decides she doesn't like the blouse, and the next day she goes back to Macy's to return it. Macy's has a return policy that says if an item is returned within seven days of the purchase, with all tags and receipts attached, Macy's will accept the return. Helen has met all of the store's conditions, and the store credits her charge account. This is an example of a condition subsequent. At the time of purchase Macy's was obligated to give Helen the blouse, and Helen was obligated to pay for it. Because of Macy's return policy, Helen has the option of returning the blouse for a full refund; in other words, her returning the item extinguishes her previous duty to pay for the blouse.

2. Dorothy and Jack are getting divorced. As part of the divorce settlement, they agree to alimony payments for Dorothy. The alimony payments are to be paid monthly until Dorothy or Jack dies, or Dorothy remarries. Dorothy's remarriage is an example of a condition subsequent. Jack is obligated to make these payments until the condition (Dorothy's remarriage) extinguishes his absolute duty to perform.

Conditions Concurrent

A **condition concurrent** is the most typical type of condition encountered in everyday contracts. A condition concurrent occurs when the mutual performances of the parties are capable of simultaneous execution, and the parties expect the promise and the performance to occur at the same time. Most contracts are formed and executed at the same time.

EXAMPLES:

1. Hazel agrees to sell, and Olivia agrees to buy, Hazel's textbook for $10. When Olivia gives the money she expects to receive the book; when Hazel gives the book she expects to receive the money. This is an example of a condition concurrent.

2. Raymond goes to his neighborhood grocery store to buy his weekly food supplies. At the checkout counter, Raymond pays for the goods as the checker bags and gives him the items. Once again, the promise and the performance occur simultaneously.

Express Conditions

An **express condition** is a condition that has been specifically manifested in so many words by the parties themselves. This manifestation can either be written or oral, depending on the nature of the contractual agreement.

EXAMPLE:

Leah agrees to purchase Phyllis' used car for $900; however, Phyllis still has $200 outstanding on the loan she took out when she first bought the car. The parties condition the sale on Phyllis' paying off the loan before the sale goes through so that Leah won't have to worry about a problem of title to the automobile. This is an example of an express condition, specifically agreed to by the parties. It is also a condition precedent, because the contract for the sale will not obligate the parties until and unless the prior loan is paid off.

Implied-in-Fact Conditions

An **implied-in-fact condition** comes about out of necessity; it is what the parties would, in good faith, expect from each other. As contrasted with an express condition, in which the parties have specifically manifested some timing element, an implied-in-fact condition comes about because of what the parties could reasonably expect under the circumstances; no words are used at all.

EXAMPLE:

Felix agrees in writing to buy Oscar's house for a certain sum of money. Although nothing is specifically stated, it is reasonable that Felix would assume that Oscar has a transferable title to the house. Although this is not specifically stated by the parties, it is implied in the transaction and, consequently, is deemed an implied-in-fact condition. If Oscar does not have a transferable interest, there is no contractual obligation on Felix's part to buy the house.

Implied-in-Law Conditions

An **implied-in-law condition,** also known as a **constructive condition,** is a condition that the law imposes in the interest of fairness. This category of conditions arises in situations where the parties have not specifically agreed to any definite time element. Its purpose is to give each party to the agreement the same amount of time in which to perform. There are three general rules with respect to constructive conditions:

1. When one party's performance requires time to complete, the other side may take the same amount of time.
2. When a date is set for one party's performance, the other party is expected to perform on that date as well.
3. When the performances can be simultaneous, they will be simultaneous.

As can be seen, implied-in-law conditions impose an element of fairness with respect to the timing of the performances. Of course, the parties themselves are totally free to establish any particular conditions they wish, but if none are expressed or implied in fact, the law gives each side an equivalent amount of time to perform.

Court Doctrines: Rules of Construction and the Parol Evidence Rule

The courts have fashioned several principles to assist them in interpreting and enforcing contract provisions. These rules should always be kept in mind when drafting contracts. Knowing how the court will interpret clauses and what kind of evidence will be permitted to prove clauses is critical for the practitioner in drafting these provisions.

Rules of construction are the guidelines that the courts use to interpret all contractual provisions. The rules of construction attempt, if possible, to uphold contracts as valid and to give proper interpretation to the presumptive intent of the contracting parties. There are four primary rules of construction with respect to analyzing the validity of contractual provisions.

1. *Lengthy communications are viewed as a whole, and any inconsistent words are discarded.* Many contracts form only after a lengthy negotiation process. In the course of this extended negotiation period, the parties may create inconsistent clauses. Because the prime objective of the court is to salvage the contract, the court will examine the entire negotiation and discard any provisions that are inconsistent with the existence of a valid contract.

2. *Contracts are to be interpreted according to business custom and usage.* People in business or business situations contract with certain expectations based on the nature, history, and customs of a particular industry. The court refers to industrywide standards, as well as to the history between the parties, in interpreting the meanings of a contract's provisions.

3. *Words are to be construed according to their ordinary meaning.* Unless the parties stipulate otherwise, the words used in an offer or completed contract are given their ordinary dictionary interpretation. However, the parties are always free to define any words they wish to in the contract itself, and the parties' specific definition will prevail. Consequently, in drafting a contract, it is essential to define specifically any words to which the parties want to give a specialized meaning or that may create definitional problems at a later time.

4. *If there is an inconsistency with words that are printed, typed, or handwritten, handwriting prevails over typing, and typing prevails over mechanical printing.* The purpose behind this rule of construction is to ascertain the exact intent of the parties at the moment of signing the contract. Handwriting presumably would be done at the last moment, and therefore it most clearly reflects the intent at the time of contracting. Typing may be inserted on a preprinted form to make changes or insertions and so, again, indicates intent close to the moment of contracting.

All of these rules exist to help uphold existing contracts, but be careful not to convolute the rules and argue for the existence of a contract where one does not legally exist. These rules are intended to facilitate interpretation, not creation, of contractual clauses.

Another principle adopted by the courts deals with written contracts and how disputes over the terms of those contracts are to be handled. The **parol evidence rule** was created to prevent parties from attempting to change the provisions of a written agreement by offering oral evidence to dispute the terms of a contract. The basic rule states that once a contract is reduced to writing, the writing itself prevails. Oral testimony will not be admitted to vary the terms of a written instrument. It is assumed that the writing will speak for itself.

There are four exceptions to the parol evidence rule that permit a court to accept oral testimony in interpreting a written contract. Although these four instances are called "exceptions" to the Rule, in fact they are not. Exceptions would indicate instances in which oral testimony is permitted to vary the written terms. In the following instances, the oral evidence is not being used to vary the terms of the writing but to show something outside the writing that changes the meaning of the contract.

The first exception involves showing a failure of consideration. Here the contract provision is not being questioned, but the fact that the consideration was not what was promised in the writing.

 EXAMPLE:

A contract says that the buyer paid for the object of the sale by check. Oral testimony shows that the check bounced. Note that the written contract provision isn't being changed at all. It is the failed consideration that the oral testimony addresses.

The second exception permits a party to show that the contract was induced by fraud, duress, or mistake, and therefore the party to the contract lacked the requisite intent to enter into the contractual relationship. If the intent is there, the contract as written will still stand unquestioned.

 EXAMPLE:

Lee holds a gun to Ingrid's head and tells her to sign a contract for the sale of her house. Ingrid's testimony is not used to change the written provision, but to show that she was forced to sign the contract and lacked the intent to contract.

The third exception permits oral testimony to prove the existence of a collateral oral agreement. Again, the written contract isn't being questioned, but the existence of a second, oral contract is being proved. The purpose of this exception is to permit *both* contracts to be considered.

 EXAMPLE:

Connie has a written contract with Bill to sell him her gold bracelet for $100. After the contract is signed, Connie agrees to sell Bill her gold ring as well for a price of $150 for both pieces of jewelry. Oral testimony may be used to show the existence of both these contracts.

Finally, the fourth exception to the parol evidence rule permits oral testimony to explain ambiguities in a written contract. A writing on its face may appear unambiguous, but there may in fact be ambiguities. Consider the offer mentioned about the sale of a house in Los Angeles. On the face of the writing it would appear to indicate only one house, but in fact two could fit the description given. Oral testimony can be used to show this ambiguity.

The preceding rules are rules of the court. They are used when problems arise between the parties to a questionable contract, but they should always be kept in mind when drafting offers and contracts. Knowing how the court will most probably interpret clauses and prove their intent suggests how these clauses should be created.

SAMPLE CLAUSES

| 1 |

In an antenuptial agreement:

All monies or property hereinafter acquired by the above-mentioned parties, or either of them, shall be held in joint or equal ownership.

In the case of the death of one of the above-mentioned parties, all of said property shall, subject to the claims of creditors, vest absolutely in the survivor.

The above two clauses are examples of covenants. Each of the parties has specifically promised that all property acquired during the marriage shall be owned equally and shall go to the survivor upon the death of the other. In this case, the consequence of death is not a condition but is made part of the covenant to which the parties have agreed.

| 2 |

In a construction contract:

Said building shall be completed according to all of the above-mentioned specification by _____, 20 ____, time is of the essence.

In this instance, the date of completion of performance has been made a specific covenant of the contract. It is not merely a condition. How? By the insertion of the term **time is of the essence.** The term "time is of the essence" makes a covenant of a timing element. Whenever there is a specific need that performance be completed by a certain date, these words should be inserted so as to give the parties greater protection. See Chapters 10 and 11.

| 3 |

In a promissory note:

Thirty (30) days after the date of this instrument I hereby promise to pay to the order of _____ the sum of Five Hundred Dollars ($500), in consideration of value received.

This **promissory note** is an example of both a covenant and a condition. The covenant is to repay the loan of $500. The condition is the timing element: 30 days after the date of the note. The promise to perform is only absolute at the end of the 30-day period.

CHAPTER SUMMARY

Contracts are deemed to be valid regardless of whether they are in writing or come about by the oral representations of the parties, provided that they meet the six requirements of all contractual agreements. The only exception to this general statement comes under the Statute of Frauds. The Statute of Frauds states that certain types of contracts, to be enforceable, must be in writing. However, even if the contract should be in writing because of the statute, if the parties actually perform their oral agreement, that performance may make the contract enforceable in a court of law. In other words, the Statute of Frauds generally makes contracts voidable, not necessarily void.

Regardless of how the contract comes into existence, all contractual provisions are classified either as covenants or conditions. A covenant is an absolute, unconditional promise to perform. It is the basis of the contractual agreement, and a party's failure to perform a covenant is deemed to be a breach of contract.

On the other hand, a condition is the timing element of the contract. A condition specifies when, if ever, the parties must perform. With conditions precedent, if the condition does not happen, no covenant comes into existence. With conditions subsequent, when the conditional event occurs, the parties are no longer obligated to perform. With conditions concurrent, the promise and the performance of the contract occur simultaneously.

Conditions are created either by the express words of the parties, by implication of what would be reasonable under the particular circumstances, or are imposed by law in the interest of fairness.

If possible, the court attempts to uphold contracts. To this end the court has established certain guidelines, referred to as rules of construction. It uses these rules to interpret contractual clauses. The four main rules of construction with respect to contracts state: (1) lengthy communications are viewed as a whole, and inconsistent words are discarded; (2) contracts are to be interpreted according to business use and custom; (3) words are construed according to their ordinary meanings; and (4) handwritten words prevail over typewritten ones, and typewritten words prevail over printed ones in construing the final terms of a contract.

In addition to the rules of construction, the court has adopted the parol evidence rule, which states that oral testimony cannot be used to vary the terms of a writing. The written offer, or contract, must stand or fall on its own.

SYNOPSIS

Statute of Frauds: Requires certain types of contracts to be in writing
    1. Contracts for an interest in realty
    2. Contracts in consideration of marriage
    3. Contracts not to be performed within one year
    4. Guarantees
    5. Contracts for the sale of goods over $500 (UCC)
    6. Executor's promise to pay a decedent's debts
Contractual clauses
    1. Covenant: Unconditional promise to perform
    2. Condition
        a. Timing element
            i. Precedent
            ii. Subsequent
            iii. Concurrent
        b. Created
            i. Express
            ii. Implied in fact
            iii. Implied in law
Court doctrines
    1. Rules of construction
    2. Parol evidence rule

Key Terms

Antenuptial agreement: contract entered into prior to marriage determining parties' rights on dissolution of the marriage; must be in writing

Condition: fact or event, the happening or nonhappening of which creates or extinguishes an absolute duty to perform

Condition concurrent: promise to perform and performance occur simultaneously

Condition precedent: fact or event that must occur before an absolute duty to perform is created

Condition subsequent: fact or event that extinguishes an absolute duty to perform; no breach of contract

Constructive condition: Same as implied-in-fact condition

Covenant: an absolute, unconditional promise to perform

Express condition: conditions created by words of the parties

Guarantee: promise to answer for the debts of another; must be in writing

Implied-in-fact condition: condition created by the reasonable expectations of the parties

Implied-in-law condition: condition imposed by law in the interest of fairness

Palimony: payment made to a person under certain circumstances pursuant to the break-up of a nonmarital relationship
Parol evidence rule: oral testimony may not be used to vary the terms of a contract writing
Prenuptial agreement: same as antenuptial agreement
Promissory note: written promise to pay money in repayment of a loan
Rules of construction: court guidelines used to interpret contractual provisions
Statute of Frauds: law requiring certain types of contracts to be in writing to be enforceable
Time of the essence clause: contractual clause that makes a covenant of a timing element
Uniform Commercial Code: statutory enactment that covers the sale of goods valued at over $500, among other things (see Chapter 8)

EXERCISES

1.   Find and analyze your own state's Statute of Frauds.
2.   How can a condition precedent become a condition subsequent? Draft an example.
3.   Must a lease for an apartment be in writing to be enforceable? Why?
4.   Give two examples of implied-in-fact conditions not discussed in the chapter.
5.   How can a condition become a covenant? Draft an example.

Cases for Analysis

One of the most typically encountered provisions in an employment contract is a restrictive covenant. To show how the court enforces such provisions, Nestle Food Co. v. Miller is included. Additionally, the difference between a condition and a covenant is highlighted in Loyal Erectors, Inc. v. Hamilton & Sons, Inc.

Nestle Food Co. v. Miller
836 F. Supp. 69 (D. R.I. 1993)

Plaintiff, Nestle Food Co. ("Nestle") has brought this action seeking injunctive relief and damages against its former salesman, defendant Stephen Miller ("Miller"). Nestle contends that Miller is in breach of an employment agreement that prohibits him from engaging in sales activity on behalf of a direct competitor in his former territory. Nestle also contends that Miller has wrongfully used confidential or "trade secret" information belonging to Nestle in his present employment. After a trial on this matter I find that Miller has breached his agreement with Nestle, and that Nestle is entitled to injunctive relief that reasonably protects Nestle's legitimate interests. Nestle has failed however, to provide any reasonable basis upon which this Court may calculate damages, and therefore, Nestle is entitled to only nominal damages in the amount of one dollar. . . .

Discussion

Miller entered into an employment agreement with Nestle on January 1, 1992, covering the period of January 1, 1992 through December 31, 1992. The relevant provisions of that agreement provide as follows:

Competitive Activity

As a condition of employment, you agree not to engage in or in any way assist any sales or similar related work or services for any third-party fund raising company or third party fund raising products of any kind during your employment and for a period of one year thereafter. . . . The post-employment restriction contained in this paragraph applies to your territory as assigned at termination of your employment.

In the event the Company must resort to legal action as regards post-employment competitive activity, the one-year period referenced above shall be extended so that such period shall begin on the date of termination of your employment and extend to the date which is one year from the date the court grants the Company's request for preliminary injunctive or other relief. . . .

Confidential Information

You acknowledge and agree that customer-related information which you have received and/or will receive from the Company, including but not limited to the names and addresses of customers, key contacts at customers, customers expressions of interest in purchasing Company or other fund-raising products, information regarding customer buying habits and preferences and customer contact reports are confidential and proprietary to the Company whether or not such information (i) is received in written or oral form or (ii) is marked with any restrictive legend. Information regarding the Company's actual and prospective production processes, sales training, development and marketing techniques, pricing, promotional policies and/or terms and conditions of sales similarly is confidential and proprietary to the Company. You agree not to use any information designated in this Agreement as Company property or as confidential and proprietary to the Company for any purpose other than in furtherance of your responsibilities set forth above.

In essence, the agreement restricted Miller from: (1) working for a direct competitor for the period of one year after the termination of his employment in the same territory; and (2) using confidential, customer-related information which Miller came in contact with while at Nestle.

Miller and the other salesmen were required to sign this contract each year or else they would have been terminated by the company. These provisions must be looked at to determine first if they have been violated, and second if they are enforceable against Miller in the factual context of this case.

1.   Competitive Activity Provision

The "Competitive activity" provision in the January 1, 1992 agreement between Miller and Nestle restricted Miller from working for a direct competitor in the fund-raising sales market within the territory that Miller covered for Nestle at the time of his termination for a period of one year after his leaving Nestle. The facts as established by the testimony and exhibits clearly establish that this provision has been violated. Upon leaving Nestle, Miller worked for Hebert Candies, a direct competitor of Nestle, in the same territory, comprising Rhode Island and parts of southeastern Massachusetts. The issue now becomes whether this provision is legally enforceable.

This analysis must begin with mention that, under Rhode Island law, noncompetitive covenants are not favored by the courts, and are carefully scrutinized. Such covenants are enforceable only to the extent they are reasonable. The standard adopted by the Rhode Island Supreme Court is set forth in section 188 of the Restatement (Second) of Contracts. Section 188 provides: A promise to refrain from competition that imposes a restraint that is ancillary to an otherwise valid transaction or relationship is unreasonable in restraint of trade if (a) the restraint is greater than is needed to protect the promisee's legitimate interest, or (b) the promisee's need is outweighed by the hardship to the promisor and the likely injury to the public.

The "Competitive activity" provision involved in this case may be viewed as having three distinct purposes or interests. First, the provision protects Nestle's allegedly "confidential" and "proprietary" information. By prohibiting its salesmen from working for a competitor firm for the period of one year, its salesmen are less likely to utilize Nestle's confidential customer-related information for the benefit of the competitor firms because they simply would not have that employment opportunity. Second, the provision protects the "goodwill" or "special relationship" which the departing salesman developed with the customer on behalf of Nestle. It allows the replacement salesman time to renew the relationship with the customer without competition from the former Nestle salesman. In the words of Mr. Weinstein, the one-year limitation gives the new sales associates "a fair chance to maintain [Nestle's] current customer base." Third, the provision protects Nestle from unfair and predatory competition by its competitors. By preventing its most experienced and productive salesmen from freely joining a competitor firm for one year, it reduces its competitors' ability to attract these salesmen to their employ, and thereby limiting its competitors' ability to unfairly increase sales.

In order for the Court to provide protection for any one of these interests, Nestle must first show that they are "legitimate." The first interest. Nestle's protection of customer-related information must be supported by a showing that the information is "confidential" and "proprietary" under the standard set forth in Home Gas. Under the standard set forth in that case, whether or not information is "confidential" depends upon how readily ascertainable the information is to a person conducting an independent investigation. Information has been held to be confidential where it is not readily ascertainable through ordinary business channels.

The evidence in this case clearly establishes that the customer-related information is not readily ascertainable through ordinary business channels, and therefore Nestle has a legitimate interest in protecting this information. Nestle has expended significant effort over many years to sift through a universe of some 2500 potential purchasers to create a database of the names of organizations that would have regular fund-raising needs. The database also contains names and addresses of "contact persons," the time of year when the group would be expected to purchase, and the amount that the group would be expected to purchase. Often the salesman must talk to a number of people before locating the "contact person." As Miller admitted, the information may sometimes be difficult to obtain.

Although Nestle has proven that protecting its confidential information qualifies as a "legitimate interest," it should also be noted that the trial testimony established that Nestle's customer information is not critical to a company wanting to build up its own "customer base" (such as Hebert). In the Rhode Island market, there are approximately 2500 potential customers in the fund-raising market. The most important initial information about these organizations is simply the organizations' name and phone number, which is generally obtainable through town directories, yellow pages and other publications. From that initial information, a company could invest a reasonable amount of time and effort to obtain information about the identity of the "contact person" and the buying preferences of the organization.

Nor is the "confidential" or "proprietary" nature of the information as valuable to Nestle as Nestle would like this Court to believe. The testimony established that Nestle's competitors probably have much of the same information about the "traditional" fundraising purchasers, and these competitors call on many of these same customers in competition with Nestle each year. Other information which Nestle lays claim to—the names and addresses of contact persons, the buying times, and the types of candy which the organization usually purchases—changes from year to year; and therefore quickly becomes obsolete. Finally, Nestle's commitment to protecting its "confidential information" is belied by the fact that other Nestle employees had access to this information—such as Mr. Taylor—but were not required to sign a competitive activity agreement.

All these factors seem to indicate that Nestle has a less important interest in protecting its confidential information than it does in protecting its "goodwill"—or the special relationship that its salesmen have developed with customers on behalf of Nestle. Indeed, the testimony established that the most important factors in making sales are simply the salesman's telephone call to the contact person each year and the advantage of utilizing the "special relationship" developed in previous years to close the sale. There is no doubt that this "goodwill" with the Rhode Island customers, built up by Miller over the years on behalf of Nestle, is a legitimate interest; but for the purposes of this decision, it must be further identified as the most crucial interest so that a proper remedy can be narrowly tailored. Protection of confidential information and goodwill are the only legitimate interests established by the evidence.

In order for the Court to enforce the "Competitive activity" provision, Nestle must establish that the provision is narrowly tailored to protect the legitimate interests of safeguarding either confidential information or goodwill, and it is not simply a restriction of the sales activity of one salesman in a competitor's employ. Nestle must also show that the restraint is reasonably limited in activity, geographic area and time. Whether the restriction is reasonable and therefore enforceable must be decided on the facts of the case within the framework of these limitations. Finally, Nestle must also show that the promisee's interests are not outweighed by the hardship to the promisor, and the restriction is not likely to injure the public.

Under applicable case law, the restriction in this case is clearly reasonable because the time period is limited to one year and the territory covered is no broader than the territory covered by the salesman when he worked for Nestle. There is, however, a fundamental problem with this provision. There has been no showing by Nestle that, in order to protect its legitimate interests, it is necessary to go to the extreme of prohibiting former employees from working for a competitor in their former territory for a period of one year. This provision imposes a severe hardship on the departing salesmen, who will have to change either their specific field of expertise or move to another location. Nestle has not established any real need to impose this burden; I have determined that Nestle's legitimate interests can be adequately protected by less draconian means.

Enforcement of a restrictive covenant should be narrowly tailored to precisely protect specifically defined interests of the former employer. Nestle surely has a right to prohibit the use of its "confidential information" for the benefit of another company and a right to protect the "goodwill" or "special relationship" that exists with its customers. But instead of going to the extreme of prohibiting its salesmen from working for a competitor for one year, a more effective, practical and fair way for Nestle to protect this customer base is to prohibit its former salesman from: 1) ever revealing or using any "confidential information" learned while at Nestle, and 2) soliciting the salesman's former customers for the period of one year. This modified provision gives Nestle's new salesman a fair chance to maintain his predecessor's "customer base" by preventing the former salesman from taking advantage of the special relationship the former salesman shares with Nestle customers, it protects Nestle's confidential information, and it gives the former Nestle salesman a chance to start fresh in a new company.

Even under this lesser standard however Miller clearly is in breach. Nestle, therefore, is entitled to both injunctive relief and damages.

2.   Confidential Information Provision

The "Confidential Information" provision defines confidential information as "customer-related information . . . received . . . from the Company, including . . . names and addresses of customers, key contacts at customers, customers expressions of interest in purchasing Company or other fund-raising products, information regarding customer buying habits and preferences . . . whether or not such information (i) is received in written or oral form or (ii) marked with any restrictive legend." This covenant basically prevents Miller from ever using any written or oral information he gained as a salesman for Nestle. As with the "Competitive activity" provision, the Court must first consider whether the provision has been breached, and then whether it is enforceable.

The testimony and evidence presented clearly show that Miller used Nestle's sales information for the benefit of his new employer, Hebert. During his first year at Hebert. Miller made a mass mailing to approximately one hundred accounts which he formerly serviced as a salesman for Nestle. He also initiated customer contact for approximately one half of the customers on a list of 25 Hebert current customers which were customers of Nestle during July 1991 through June of 1992. Miller is clearly in breach of this provision of his employment agreement because he used specific "customer-related" information, including specific customer names, addresses, and buying-times (lodged in his memory) for the benefit of Hebert.

Under the standard set forth in the Restatement (second) of Contracts, this Confidential Information provision, subject to a reasonable construction with regard to other provisions in the employment agreement and the factual context of the case, is reasonable and therefore enforceable. First, as discussed supra, Nestle has a legitimate interest in protection of confidential information. Second, the restraint goes no further than is needed to protect the confidential information—it simply prevents Miller from ever revealing it or using it for the benefit of a direct competitor. Finally, Nestle's interest is not outweighed by the hardship to Miller or the likely injury to the public because this provision puts no significant burden on Miller and none on the public. Nestle is entitled to damages for Miller's breach of this provision and to injunctive relief.

3.   Defenses

Two issues have been raised by Miller in an attempt to defeat the breach of contract claims. He first argues that the covenants in issue do not survive upon termination. Specifically, he maintains that because the termination section provides that "certain provisions of this Agreement will survive its termination as set forth below," anything that is not "set forth below" does not survive. This is contrary to the express language of the agreement and to the normal rules of contract construction. The

"Competitive activity" covenant expressly provides that Miller was not to engage in competitive activity "during your employment and for a period of one year thereafter. . . ." (emphasis added). Similarly, the "Confidential Information" covenant survives after termination as Miller was prohibited from using the information "for any purpose other than in furtherance of your responsibilities set forth above." Any other reading of these provisions would render them nullities.

Miller also argues that there was no consideration for the covenants in the employment agreement. Even if there was no consideration other than allowing Miller to continue as an employee with all of the associated benefits associated therewith, such continuation of employment constitutes adequate consideration.

4.   Counterclaim [Omitted]

5.   Damages

Nestle requests that this Court award damages based upon its computation of the profits lost for approximately 25 customers who switched from Nestle to Hebert in Miller's first year as a salesman for Hebert. The Court in Home Gas ruled that plaintiff may recover as damages the loss of profits resulting from the wrongful solicitations to date. However, the Court in Home Gas, emphasized the enduring rule that damages must be established by a reasonable certainty and may not be recovered if purely speculative. Plaintiff has failed to present any reasonable basis for determining that damages were suffered by Nestle as a result of Miller's wrongful solicitation of Nestle accounts, rather than some other factor.

The testimony presented at trial established that 25 out of approximately 300 former Nestle customers switched to Hebert. These customers could have switched to Hebert for any number of reasons, however. Miller stated that he only actively called on approximately one half of the 25 customers, while at least 120 Nestle customers were statistically expected not to return to Nestle in any case. Many of these customers are recognized in the industry as customers who traditionally purchase candy each year, and are frequently called on by other companies besides Nestle. Many times the deciding factor about whom to purchase from is based simply on the talent of the salesman. The customers could have chosen Hebert simply because Miller's replacement at Nestle, Robert Clarke, was ineffective at making the sale. Further, there was no Nestle salesman at all in Rhode Island for approximately one month during July and August of 1992—the Nestle customers could have chosen Hebert by default. In sum, Nestle's suggested computation of damages is entirely speculative. Accordingly, I award nominal damages in the amount of one dollar.

6.   Injunction

The Rhode Island Supreme Court, in Durapin, Inc. v. American Products, Inc., adopted the so-called "rule of partial enforcement." This rule allows the court to exercise its inherent equity powers to modify and enforce a covenant regardless of whether the unreasonable provision is severable from the other provisions in the agreement. Under this rule, unless the circumstances indicate bad faith or deliberate overreaching on the part of the promisee, a court will attempt to modify an unreasonable covenant and enforce it to the extent that it is reasonably necessary to protect the promisee's legitimate interests, if that can be done without imposing undue hardship on the promisor or adversely affecting the public interest.

As discussed above, I believe that Nestle does have a legitimate interest in protecting confidential information about current customers in its customer base, but more importantly it has an interest in protecting the "goodwill" or "special relationship" that its salesmen have built up with these customers. Therefore, the following injunction will enter against Stephen Miller:

1.   Defendant Stephen Miller is enjoined, for the period of September 1, 1993, through August 31, 1994, from soliciting any customers who purchased Nestle fund-raising products in the one-year period prior to Miller's resignation from Nestle, in the territory he serviced at the time of resignation. "Soliciting" includes any type of contact initiated by defendant, including direct mail, telephone and personal contact, direct specifically at the former Nestle customer. If there is any question in defendant's mind whether a certain customer was a customer of Nestle during that period, he may request this information in writing from an appropriate individual at Nestle, who shall respond within a reasonable time (not longer than three work days) after receipt of the inquiry.
2.   Defendant is further permanently enjoined from using or revealing any confidential information (as defined in the January 1, 1992 employment agreement) retained by memory or otherwise which:
a.   was obtained solely by virtue of defendants' position with Nestle; and
b.   is not readily accessible through normal business channels (yellow pages, printed municipal publications and the like).

Conclusion

For all of the foregoing reasons, the clerk is hereby directed to enter judgment as follows:

1.   Nestle's claim for damages is granted in the amount of one dollar.
2.   Nestle's claim for injunctive relief is granted as provided in this decision and order.
3.   Miller's counterclaim is denied and dismissed with prejudice.

Questions

1.   What elements does the court examine to determine whether the restrictive provision is reasonable?
2.   Is the restrictive provision of the contract a condition or a covenant?

Loyal Erectors, Inc. v. Hamilton & Son, Inc.
312 A.2d 748 (Me. 1973)

On July 7, 1971 the plaintiff, Loyal Erectors, Inc., initiated proceedings against the principal defendant, Hamilton & Son, Inc. (Hamilton), for the recovery of $40,301.58, plus interest, which the plaintiff asserts Hamilton owes it by virtue of certain contractual obligations. In the prosecution of its claim, the plaintiff, pursuant to Rule 4B, M.R.C.P., on July 15, 1971 served a trustee summons on Robert C. Ford, Inc. (Ford), requiring the latter to show cause through verified disclosure why execution issued upon such judgment as the plaintiff may recover against Hamilton, if any, should not issue against the credits, which, on the date of service, Hamilton had with Ford and which Ford had in its possession as trustee of Hamilton, to the value of the plaintiff's claim, together with a reasonable allowance for interest and costs. 14 M.R.S.A. §2601.

In the Court below, the principal defendant (Hamilton), by motion properly served on the plaintiff, sought the discharge of Ford as trustee, on the ground that the principal defendant's credits with Ford at the time of service of the trustee process were contingent claims only and not absolute liabilities. 14 M.R.S.A. §2602(4). Ford's discharge as trustee is the basis for plaintiff's appeal. We deny the appeal. . . .

Ford had entered into two contracts with Hamilton. Under the contract of April 21, 1969 Hamilton agreed to install a complete ventilation and duct work system in the high school building at Cape Elizabeth, Maine, in accordance with specifications and drawings prepared by a named architectural firm. The price which Ford promised to pay Hamilton for the complete job was $104,500.00. Payment of this money was to be made as the work progressed "in the amount of ninety percent (90%) of the satisfactorily completed work." The contract further provided that "[t]he retained percentage shall be paid within ninety-two (92) days of the final approval and acceptance of the building by the Architect." The second contract executed November 24, 1969 called for the installation of a complete ventilation system in accordance with specifications and drawings prepared by another firm of architects. It was designed for the Waterville Osteopathic Hospital in Waterville, Maine. This contract carried the price of $36,061.00 with a similar progress payment clause, the retained percentage, however, to be paid within 90 days "of the final approval and acceptance of the building by the Architect."

Ford maintains that, at the time of service of the trustee summons on July 15, 1971, it had not in its hands and possession any goods, effects or credits of Hamilton subject to trustee process, even though Hamilton's requisition for payment of the sum of $2,174.85 under the first contract and the sum of $3,334.90 under the second contract for alleged completion of the work had not been paid and the retained amount by the prime contractor, Fred I. Merrill, Inc. (Merrill) under terms similar to those provided in the contracts between Hamilton and Ford was in excess of Hamilton's requests for payment.

The trustee's sworn assertions further disclose that neither building at the time of service of the trustee process had been finally approved and accepted by the architect. . . .

Did the principal defendant, Hamilton, have a noncontingent claim against the trustee, Ford, at the time of service upon the trustee? In order to answer this ultimate question, we must determine whether the principal defendant's failure to secure "the final approval and acceptance of the building by the Architect," which the contract between the parties required, caused the retained percentage moneys to come within the statutory exception precluding trustee process, on the ground that, prior to the approval and acceptance of the building by the architect, there is no money or other thing "due absolutely and not on any contingency" within the meaning of 14 M.R.S.A. §2602(4).

This determination must be made as of the time the trustee process was served, since the validity of the trustee process depends upon the state of facts as they existed at that moment. Holmes v. Hilliard, 1931, 130 Me. 392, 394, 156 A. 692; Hussey v. Titcomb, 1929, 127 Me. 423, 427, 144 A. 218; Williams v. Androscoggin and Kennebec Rail Road Co., 1853, 36 Me. 201, 210.

It should be further noted that the statutory reference to money or other thing due absolutely and not on any contingency does not mean that the amount of the debt must be certain, but rather, that the monetary obligation itself is absolute and not contingent. The mere fact that the amount due under an absolute indebtment may be unascertained or in dispute will not defeat a trustee process.

As stated in Davis v. Davis, 1862, 49 Me. 282:

> The contingency under this section [of the statute, as settled in Dwinel v. Stone, 30 Maine, 384], "is not a mere uncertainty as to how the balance may stand between the principal and the supposed trustee; but it is such a contingency as may preclude the principal from any right to call the supposed trustee to settle or account."

See also, Wilson v. Wood, 1852, 34 Me. 123; Cutter v. Perkins, 1859, 47 Me. 557; Hussey v. Titcomb, supra.

We must have in mind, additionally, the provisions of 14 M.R.S.A. §2628 to the effect that "[a]ny money or other thing due absolutely to the principal defendant may be attached before it has become payable, but the trustee is not required to pay or deliver it before the time appointed therefor by the contract."

In *Davis*, supra, this Court ruled that the preliminary proof of loss required by a fire insurance policy was a condition precedent to the right of the insured to recover, and, as such, within the exclusionary clause of the trustee process statute, since the liability of the insurer does not become absolute, unless the preliminary proof of loss, as provided in the conditions of the policy, is furnished.

In *Wilson*, supra, it was held that, where the contract called for the payment of a commission when a particular note was collected, there existed no absolute indebtedness under the trustee process statute until after the note had been collected. Until that fact had taken place, there was only a contingent liability.

In Jordan v. Jordan, 1883, 75 Me. 100, this Court decided that a contract to pay commissions on the sale of goods "as the goods should be paid for" did not create an absolute, but only a contingent, debt prior to payment, the Court stating: "This is not a debt due in the present and payable in the future, for there may never be a debt."

In Holmes v. Hilliard, supra, the contract provided for the purchase and sale of so much of the principal defendant's crop of sweet corn as should be approved as to quality by the supposed trustee, with payment for all the corn so received within sixty days from the close of the canning season. There, the Court said: "Where money was to be paid on the contingency that work be well performed, trustee process was premature until the work had been duly performed."

When, by the terms of the contract, the price was payable upon the completion of the work and there was no acceptance of the work by the trustee, the use of trustee process prior to the completion of the contract was premature, as there was nothing due, and "non constat that there ever would be." Otis v. Ford, 1866, 54 Me. 104.

A widow's allowance, resting as it does in the sound discretion of the Judge of Probate, is not subject to trustee process prior to its actual adjudication, because, prior thereto, it is a mere contingent right. Hussey v. Titcomb, supra.

From a consideration of these cases, it appears that the potential debt to accrue out of a special contract may be characterized as contingent and not absolute, if the condition upon which the price is payable is deemed to be a condition precedent.

Whether the condition attached to the payment of the price be a condition precedent or subsequent depends upon the intention of the parties to the contract, to be determined by considering not only the words of the particular clause, but also the language of the whole contract as well as the nature of the act required and the subject matter to which it relates. Bucksport & Bangor Railroad Company v. Inhabitants of Brewer, 1877, 67 Me. 295, 299; Robbins v. Gleason, 1859, 47 Me. 259, 273.

In Bucksport & Bangor Railroad Company, supra, the condition in a subscription contract, which required that the road to be built "shall be located through the town of Brewer, satisfactory to the selectmen of said town," was viewed by the Court as intended and understood by the parties as a condition precedent and failure strictly to perform the same precluded any right of action by the plaintiffs.

In all cases where some person is agreed upon by the parties, in the contract, to examine and determine the character, quality, or quantity of the work done, *such examination and decision are conditions precedent to any right of payment*, and must be alleged and proved in order to maintain an action upon the contract. Veazie v. City of Bangor, 1863, 51 Me. 509, 514. Recovery was also denied in quantum meruit. Veazie v. City of Bangor, 1865, 53 Me. 50.

In Lynch v. Stebbins, 1928, 127 Me. 203, 142 A. 735, this Court, by way of illustration of conditions precedent, referred to construction contracts where recovery may be made dependent upon the production of an architect's certificate and cited Smith v. Brady, 1858, 17 N.Y. 173, in support thereof. The New York Court stated:

> Assuming that the contracts had been so far performed as to justify the plaintiff in treating them as substantially executed, as I am inclined to think they were, yet the final payment for the work was to be made when it was completed and a certificate of the architects to that effect obtained. The parties have seen fit to make the production of such a certificate a condition precedent to the payment. The plaintiff is as much bound by this part of his contract as any other. It is not enough for him to bring his action and say that he has completed the work which he undertook to do. He has agreed that the architects named should decide whether the work is completed or not. He cannot now withdraw the decision of this question from them and refer to it to the determination of a legal tribunal.

In Daily v. Jordan & Trustee, 1848, Mass., 2 Cush. 390, the construction contract provided for progress payments of three fourths of the amount due for labor, and this had been paid. The one fourth retainage money had not been paid. At the time of the service of the trustee process, the whole of the work contracted for had not been accepted agreeably to the clause in the contract which stated: "when the whole of the work contracted for is accepted, agreeably to contract, the balance due shall be paid to the contractor." Because the principal defendant had not obtained the engineer's certificate, the Massachusetts Court ruled that the trustees were properly discharged under a statute similar to ours.

In Hanley v. Walker, 1890, 79 Mich. 607, 45 N.W. 57, where, in a construction contract, the balance or retained percentage of 10% of the contract price was to be paid on the architect's certificate after the expiration of 30 days after acceptance and approval of the work by the architects and owner, the Michigan Court denied recovery on the contract or in quantum meruit, ruling that the parties had made the architect's certificate of approval a condition precedent to payment.

Where progress payments were payable under a construction contract to the extent of ninety percent of the amount of work done in accordance with schedule prices to be fixed by the engineer and upon the estimate and certificate of the engineer, our Court, in Ware v. Gowen, 1876, 65 Me. 534, characterized the monetary value of the ninety percent of the work performed as due absolutely and not on any contingency. It held, in effect, that the procurement of the certificate to establish the specific amount of work done and the value thereof was merely a condition subsequent, and that the debt arising out of the work performed was an absolute and not a contingent debt and was subject to trustee process, notwithstanding the fact the engineer's certificate of computation followed the service of the trustee process. It cited in support of its ruling, Ricker v. Fairbanks, 1855, 40 Me. 43, a case similar on its facts. In *Ricker*, this Court, construing a comparable progress payment clause, stated:

[I]t is obvious from the situation of the parties, as well as from the whole scope of the contract itself, that it was intended that the 90 per cent stipulated to be paid monthly, *should be so applied as to enable the contractor to prosecute and complete the work for which he had contracted.* (Emphasis supplied.)

The Court further said:

That amount [earned in each month] becomes due, absolutely, on the first day of each month. The sum then due, is determined, specifically, by the engineer's certificate.

But the Court in *Ricker*, quoting from Williams v. Androscoggin & Kennebec R. R. Co., 1853, 36 Me. 201, restated the fact that the rule applicable to the monthly progress payment clause would not necessarily be the same as that applicable to the reservation clause respecting the payment of the retainage money, reciting as it did: "whether the one fourth which was reserved, should ever become payable, depended upon the contingency of the contract being fully performed;. . . ."

The parties to the instant building contract had dissimilar purposes in mind when they conditioned, upon the architect's certificate of approval, the right to receive both 1) progress payments at periodic intervals of performance and 2) the final payment of the retainage fund at the end of the construction. Progress payment clauses are inserted in building contracts mostly for the protection of the contractor who is assured of periodic instalments of cash moneys with which he can continue performance of his contract and save himself from the embarrassment of extended credit and the costs thereof. True, the other party may be benefited incidentally by reason of the timely performance of the work, the avoidance of any breaches and the consequential inconveniences arising therefrom. On the other hand, the conditioning of the final payment of the retainage money upon the architect's certificate of approval is solely for the protection of the builder or owner; it is a substantial leverage to assure strict performance of the contract in accordance with the agreement, drawings and specifications and to compel correction for material deviations therefrom. The trustee, whether he be the owner or, as in this case, the primary subcontractor responsible to the prime contractor who in turn owes full compliance with the terms of the contract to the owner (the Cape Elizabeth authorities and the Waterville Osteopathic Hospital), has a paramount interest in not releasing the retained funds until he is assured by the experts, upon whom the parties have agreed, that the contract has been completely performed in conformance with the plans and specifications. The retainage clause conditioning the final payment upon the architect's certificate of approval serves a vital interest, in that it induces the contractor to render a performance that conforms in fact to plans and specifications, spurs him to stay with the job and, upon completion, furnishes the main incentive to make conforming corrections.

For such reasons, we hold that the architect's certificate of approval was a condition precedent to the right of the principal defendant to receive the retainage moneys, and since, at the time of the service of the trustee process, such certificate had not yet been obtained, the unpaid retained moneys under the contract were not a debt due absolutely, but only contingently, and the decision of the Court below discharging the trustee was correct. . . .

We do recognize that the strict rules of the common law which required, as a condition precedent to the right of recovery, full performance of all the material terms of a contract, and especially building contracts, where the defendant, usually the owner, was practically forced to accept the result of the work, have been relaxed. Relief has been granted on equitable principles, when services have been rendered or materials furnished in an honest endeavor to perform the special contract, but the performance has fallen short of fulfilling the express terms of the agreement, and the other party has received a windfall of some value. See, Skowhegan Water Company v. Skowhegan Village Corporation, 1906, 102 Me. 323, 66 A. 714; Norris v. School District No. 1, in Windsor, 1835, 12 Me. 293, 296; Hayward v. Leonard, 1828, Mass., 7 Pick 181. . . .

The entry will be appeal denied.

Questions

1. Do you agree with the decision of the court? Why, or why not?
2. Do you think the defendant was unjustly enriched?
3. Under what circumstances would the condition be considered a condition subsequent?

Suggested Case References

1. A man is home recuperating from an illness when he is approached by a contractor about installing aluminum siding. The salesperson is very persuasive, but because of his health, the customer is able to insert a clause stating that the contract for the siding will be null and void if he cannot obtain disability insurance. The contractor starts the work, but the customer cannot get the insurance because his health is so poor. The customer tells the contractor that he could not get the insurance. The customer shortly thereafter dies. Is his estate liable for the siding? If not, why not? Read Cambria Savings & Loan Association v. Estate of Gross, 294 Pa. Super. 351 (1982).

2. For a discussion of time of the essence clauses, read Carter v. Sherburne Corp., 132 Vt. 88 (1974).

3. If a person fails to meet a condition of her contract, does she thereby lose all rights due to her under the agreement? Read Brauer v. Freccia, 159 Conn. 289 (1970).

8 The Uniform Commercial Code

CHAPTER OVERVIEW

The Uniform Commercial Code (UCC) is the major statutory basis of several important areas of contract law. Although it is not a universally applied federal statute, every state, plus the District of Columbia, has enacted some version of all or part of the Code. To fully understand American contract law, it is necessary to discuss several sections of the UCC.

Three of the Code's articles are directly concerned with contract law: Article I, General Provisions; Article II, Sales; and Article IX, Secured Transactions.

Article I establishes the general outline, purpose, and objectives of the Code. Primarily, the UCC was created to promote commerce and to establish certain basic guidelines for those parties involved in commercial transactions. The UCC requires every party whose actions it governs to act in good faith, to perform in a timely manner, and to heed the dictates of the custom and usage prevalent in the industry.

Article II forms the primary modern statutory basis for contracts involving the sale of goods. This article regulates the sale of goods valued at over $500 and sales between merchants. It imposes certain warranties, or guarantees, that are passed by the manufacturer and/or seller of the goods to the ultimate consumer of those products. Additionally, this article provides certain remedies that differ from the general contractual remedies usually available to injured parties in a contractual dispute. (See Chapter 11, Remedies.)

Article IX creates the basis for creditors to secure their debtors' obligations with specific items of property that may be attached by the creditors in case the debtors default. Article IX sets out the specific procedures that a creditor must follow to create and establish a security interest against all other creditors of the debtor.

Before detailing each of the specifics of the articles, it would be helpful to understand some of the history and general background of the Code.

General Background

In 1952, after many years of work, The American Law Institute and the National Conference of Commissioners on Uniform State Laws promulgated a model act known as the Uniform Commercial Code (UCC). The objective of the codification was to clarify and modernize laws governing commercial transactions and to attempt to make mercantile law uniform among all of the states. This model statute represented the first major attempt to codify general contract law; unlike many other areas of law, contract law still rested firmly on its common law base.

Being a model (or proposed) act, the UCC had to be adopted by each state individually; it is not a federal law. Eventually, every jurisdiction adopted some version of the UCC, either in whole or in part (some states have only adopted a few of the provisions of the Code). It is necessary to research each jurisdiction specifically to determine whether its version differs from that of any other state that is involved in the transaction.

The UCC is important to all mercantile practices and transactions. The purpose of the Code is to promote interstate commerce and to facilitate the furthering of business interests. Consequently, the UCC forms a basic part of almost all business law and operations. However, it is important to bear in mind that, except where specifically noted, the Code generally only codifies the common law of contracts. The UCC was not intended or designed to create a radically new concept of contractual arrangements. Rather, it was intended to unify conflicting common law doctrines and to regularize existing commercial practices.

The Code is divided into thirteen articles, the articles are subdivided into parts, and the parts are further divided into sections and subsections. The UCC covers a wide spectrum of law, from sales to banking, to letters of credit and bulk transfers. For the purpose of contract law, three of the articles assume primary importance: Article I, General Provisions; Article II, Sales; and Article IX, Secured Transactions. Each of these articles will be discussed individually, emphasizing concepts not otherwise covered in previous and succeeding chapters.

Article I, General Provisions

Article I of the UCC establishes the form and operation of the entire statute. Not only does it affirmatively state the purpose and intent of the conference members in promulgating the Code, but it also establishes several basic guidelines for applying and interpreting the provisions of the Code. It imposes certain obligations on all parties to transactions that fall within the Code's province.

Basic Guidelines

Article I establishes three basic guidelines to be used in applying the provisions of the Code:

1. The law of the state applies unless otherwise superseded by the UCC.
2. The parties to a contract may, by their agreement, vary the provisions of the Code.
3. The UCC is to be liberally construed.

Law of the State Applies

Unless expressly superseded by the state's adopted version of the UCC, under §1-103 the general law of the site where the transaction occurs applies.

When the states' legislatures adopted their own versions of the Code, if they intended the UCC to be the prevailing law in a given subject, that intent was specifically stated in the statute. For example, in New York, when the UCC Article on Commercial Paper was adopted, it was affirmatively stated that this article was to revise the preexisting New York Negotiable Instrument Law, thereby superseding preexisting state law. Hence, when drafting a commercial agreement, you must determine exactly what the law of a given state is and whether the UCC supercedes it. You cannot assume that a UCC provision of one state is applicable in another state.

Parties May Agree to Vary UCC Provisions

The UCC was intended to help facilitate commerce; its rules were not intended, by their application, to hinder business. Therefore, §1-102 permits parties whose transaction comes within the UCC to vary the UCC terms by their own agreement in order to further their commercial interests. However, there must be evidence of the parties' agreement on the matter; if the parties are silent on a particular subject, the UCC provisions will prevail. Article I permits and encourages freedom of contract between the parties but supplies the legal standard should the parties be silent with respect to a given provision.

EXAMPLE:

Delta, Inc., a Michigan corporation, is contracting with TGI, Inc., a New York corporation, for the purchase of cement, bricks, and other building materials for the construction of a Delta warehouse in New Jersey. Although the contract is signed in New York, and delivery is to be made in New Jersey, Delta wants the law of Michigan to apply because it is a Michigan corporation and is more familiar with that state's law. Although this would be contrary to general UCC provisions, Article I §1-105 permits the parties to agree that the law of Michigan determines the interpretation of the contract.

UCC Provisions Are to Be Liberally Construed

Most importantly, §1-102 of the UCC states that its provisions are to be liberally construed. It may seem a simple statement, but it is fairly unique for statutory law. Most statutes and codes are created as regulatory devices to be strictly complied with. The UCC is different. Because it is meant to promote, not hinder, commerce, the UCC is to be applied in a manner that helps business along, which may mean a liberal interpretation. Of course, this liberal construction must be reasonably formed; the interpretation must still be consistent with the Code as a whole.

Obligations Imposed by Article I

Article I §1-102 imposes three obligations on all parties who come within the purview of its provisions. These obligations are

1. to perform in "good faith"—honesty in fact;
2. to perform in a "reasonable time," "reasonableness" to be determined by the facts and circumstances of each situation; and
3. to perform according to past business dealings and practices (custom and usage).

EXAMPLES:

1. Hiram agrees to sell 10,000 cardboard boxes to the Bon Ton Department Store, delivery to be within two weeks. Hiram knows that he cannot possibly meet that time limit but is willing to pay some damages for delays in delivery. Hiram is violating the UCC by not acting in good faith. He is contracting for promises he *knows* he cannot meet. Even though he may be willing to pay for the delay, he is knowingly injuring Bon Ton, which violates the intent of the Code to promote commerce.

2. Sylvester agrees to sell and deliver 10,000 nuts and bolts to the Mitchell Construction Company for a specific building project. Delivery is delayed, and Mitchell Construction must find a substitute supplier. Mitchell claims that Sylvester has failed to make delivery in a reasonable time. Sylvester's promise to deliver was conditioned, however, upon receipt of Mitchell's check, which was delayed in the mail. Under these facts, Sylvester's delivery was made within a reasonable time, and he is not in breach of contract or in violation of the UCC.

The most intriguing of these obligations is the codification of the concept of custom and usage. By establishing as law the past practices of the parties, the Code, in effect, is customizing the law to each particular industry and businessperson. In contracting under the UCC, it is necessary to determine the practices and terms peculiar to each industry and between the particular merchants, and make these customs a part of the contract itself. Consequently, contracts will vary with respect to the definitions of particular terms, dependent upon how each industry and the parties define those terms. There will be no one standard contract that can be used for all categories of business situations. Questions of proof also arise, i.e., what is the custom between these parties?

 EXAMPLES:

1. Azar manufactures men's topcoats and regularly buys fabric from Maria. For the past five years, Maria has billed Azar for payment 90 days after delivery. Suddenly, without any prior arrangement, Maria bills Azar for payment within 10 days of delivery. Azar still has 90 days in which to pay. Because the parties have not specifically agreed to payment within 10 days of delivery, they are still bound by their past practices and dealings. If Maria wants to change the payment date, she must make that a specific part of her agreement with Azar.

2. Hazel orders "standard" copper piping from Daniel. Hazel and Daniel have dealt with each other for years, and Daniel always sells Hazel piping 3½ inches wide; the standard pipe in the industry is 4 inches. If Daniel sends Hazel 4-inch piping for this order, Hazel can complain of breach of contract. Because of the past practices of the parties, "standard" for them means 3½-inch piping, not the industry "standard" of 4 inches.

The general provisions of Article I of the Code discussed above permeate all of the other provisions of the statute.

Article II, Sales

General Background

Article II §2-102 of the UCC states that contracts for the sale of goods must be in writing. This provision restates the Statute of Frauds (see Chapter 7) with respect to the sale of goods. In addition, this article reiterates the parol evidence rule and the rules of construction (see Chapter 7).

For the purposes of this chapter, Article II emphasizes three broad areas:

1. the type of contracts that are governed by the UCC;
2. specific contractual provisions regulated by the Code covering warranties and risk of loss; and
3. certain remedies that the contracting parties may be entitled to that differ from the general contractual remedies discussed in Chapter 11, Remedies.

The UCC both codifies the existing common law of contracts already discussed as well as makes some significant changes; all of those contract law concepts still apply unless otherwise stated.

Types of Contracts Covered by Article II

Generally, three types of contracts are regulated by UCC Article II:

1. contracts for the sale of goods;
2. contracts for the lease of goods; and
3. contracts between merchants.

Goods

As indicated above, Article II takes the place of the Statute of Frauds with respect to contracts for the sale of goods valued at over $500. **Goods** are defined by §2-105 as things that are existing and moveable. They may include such items as electricity, food or drink, or anything that can be removed from the land, such as minerals, oil, or crops.

In contracts for the sale of goods, the UCC holds the parties to a standard of **strict liability** with respect to the subject goods. Strict liability means that, regardless of how careful the manufacturer/seller may have been with respect to the making of the product, if the product proves defective, the seller is automatically liable to the injured party. Care, quality control, and like safeguards do not relieve the seller of its liability.

 EXAMPLE:

Piedmont Pipes, Inc., sells 50,000 feet of copper pipes to Carl's Construction Company for the purpose of building several condominium units. After installation, the pipes disintegrate with the first use. Piedmont is automatically liable to Carl's because the contract, under the UCC, imposes strict liability on the manufacturer. It doesn't matter how careful Piedmont was in making the pipes; because the pipes failed to function properly, the maker is liable.

It is important to keep in mind that the UCC only covers transactions in goods; any contract for the sale of services is not governed by Article II (unless the provisions are specifically extended to contracts for mixed goods and services, which is addressed below).

 EXAMPLE:

The law firm of Black & White, P.C., enters into an agreement with Elsie to represent her in pending litigation against her former employer. This contract is not covered by the UCC because the contract concerns services (legal representation), not goods.

If the contract is for the provision of services, the provider of the services will only be liable for injury to the other contracting party if the injured party can prove negligence, that is, that the provider failed to meet the standard of due care that exists for the particular service in question.

 EXAMPLE:

Return to the example with Elsie and the law firm. After Elsie contracts with Black & White, the firm procrastinates and only files Elsie's suit after the Statute of Limitations has run. The case is thrown out, and Elsie sues the firm for negligence. In maintaining her action, Elsie must show that the firm failed to meet its standard of care.

What if the contract in question involves both goods and services? Is the standard one of strict liability or of negligence? According to Article

II, if the contract cannot be determined to be one either strictly of goods or strictly of services, the court will determine the predominant category of the contract. Whatever the predominant category is determined to be will control the standard for the entire contract.

 EXAMPLES:

1. Faye contracts with Ilona to have Ilona make Faye's wedding dress for $750. As Faye walks down the aisle, the dress starts coming apart at the seams and the embroidery falls off. Ilona is strictly liable. Why? Because, although services are involved in the contract (the sewing of the gown), the predominant object of the contract was to provide Faye with a wedding dress (a good). Consequently, the contract is deemed to be a contract for the sale of goods carrying strict liability.

2. Arnold is in a car accident and is rushed to City General Hospital, where he receives a nutrient solution intravenously. Later it is discovered that the solution was tainted, and Arnold develops hepatitis. Arnold sues the hospital. In this instance, the contract is for the providing of services (medical care), and the standard is one of negligence. If Arnold could sue the person who sold the solution to the hospital, that would be a suit for the sale of goods.

Article II of the UCC concerns itself with contracts for the sale of goods, not with contracts for the providing of services. Contracts for the sale of goods impose strict liability for the seller, and, as will be discussed below, the seller's liability can extend not only to the purchaser of the good, but to the ultimate user of the good as well. Contracts for the providing of services carry a standard of due care, and in order to be found liable, the service provider must be shown to have failed to meet the standard of care that exists for the particular service in question. Obviously, for the injured party, it is an easier burden to have the contract considered to be one for the sale of goods.

Leases

Several jurisdictions have added a new section to the UCC concerning the long-term lease of goods. Because this provision is fairly new and has not been universally adopted, each jurisdiction's version must be checked to determine whether the lease of goods is covered by the UCC or is found under general contract principles. For an example of a contract for the lease of goods, see Chapter 12.

Contracts for the Sale of Goods Between Merchants

As discussed in Chapter 2, Offer, Article II makes several modifications to the general contract requirements if the contract is between merchants. The modifications exist so as to advance the Code's purpose to promote commerce, and it is assumed that merchants are the best judges of their own contractual needs. However, two problems may arise in these types of contracts.

The first problem arises from Article II's definition of **merchant** (§204). Because the UCC is to be liberally construed (Article I), Article II of the Code defines merchant as any person who regularly deals in the kind of goods covered by the contract, *or*, any person who, by his occupation, holds himself out as having knowledge or skill peculiar to the practice of dealing with the goods in question. What this means is that not only will a businessperson be deemed a merchant, but a hobbyist is considered a merchant for the purpose of Article II as well.

 EXAMPLE:

Lola has been collecting stamps as a hobby for the past 12 years. When she contracts with Aldo, a vendor of rare stamps, it is a contract for the sale of goods between merchants.

The second problem regarding merchants arises as an exception to the mirror image rule of contract formation (see Chapter 2). Merchants may meet the requirements of a writing by using purchase order forms, billing receipts, and the like. However, because businesses usually use preprinted forms, and each form is designed to protect the interests of the preparer, the writings that act as the memoranda of the verbal agreement may conflict. This is known as the **battle of the forms.** In this instance, the UCC indicates that the contract will be enforced according to the most reasonable expectations of the parties based on their past practices and their actual actions. Furthermore, as discussed in Chapter 3, merchant traders may vary the terms of the offer without that variance being deemed a rejection or counter-offer, unless the offer is "iron clad." Under the common law such negotiation would cause a significantly different result.

 EXAMPLE:

Helen operates a business selling seeds to nurseries throughout the country. Helen sends her catalog to Randy, who sends Helen his printed purchase order form mandating a specific method of delivery. Helen acknowledges the order with her own preprinted form indicating a different method of delivery. Whose form created the contract? Under the common law, the catalog is an invitation to bid, the purchase order is an offer, and the acknowledgment would be a counteroffer (see Chapter 3, Acceptance); therefore, there is no contract. However, under the UCC, the parties would have a contract because a commercial understanding has been achieved. It would be necessary to determine whether the difference in method of delivery is a material change. If the difference is material, involving greater expense or time, it will not be considered part of the contract, and the parties' past practices and actions will determine the delivery provision.

Therefore, when the contract in question is between merchants, the UCC is particularly liberal and provides many exceptions to general contract principles in order to facilitate commercial transactions.

Contractual Provisions

Warranties

As stated above, when the contract involves a sale of goods, the manufacturer/seller may not only be liable to the buyer. He may also be strictly liable to the ultimate consumer of the good as well because goods, unlike services, have UCC **warranties** that attach to them.

A warranty is a guaranty with respect to the goods covered by the sale. The manufacturer of the goods warrants, or guarantees, that the product is exactly what has been ordered, that it is fit as sold for its intended use, and that the seller has title sufficient to pass the goods to the buyer. A warranty can be created either by the express representations of the seller or be implied by the operation of law.

Express Warranties.   Under §2-213, **express warranties** are created by the words or conduct of the seller. They can be created in three different ways:

1.   An express warranty can be created by the specific promise or affirmation appearing in the contract itself. Many contracts contain special warranty clauses, and the parties are specifically held to the words of the warranty to which they have agreed.

EXAMPLE:

In a sales contract, a clause states that the "Seller warrants that all items furnished hereunder will be in full conformity with Buyer's specification." In this manner, the seller is guaranteeing that she will provide goods exactly meeting the buyer's expressed description.

2.   An express warranty can be created by a description that the seller uses in a catalog.

EXAMPLE:

Dora's Dress Company sends out a catalog describing one of its dresses as having a 48-inch sweep. When Smart Shops orders 100 of the dresses, each one must have a 48-inch sweep, or the contract is breached.

3. Finally, an express warranty can be created by a sample or model used by the seller to induce the sale.

EXAMPLE:

A Fuller Brush salesperson comes to Myra's house to demonstrate a vacuum cleaner. Delighted with the results, Myra buys one; however, when the vacuum cleaner arrives it contains modifications that did not appear on the sample the salesperson used to demonstrate the product. The company has breached its express warranty.

Implied Warranties.   Implied warranties, §2-314, come about by operation of law. There are two types of implied warranties: a **warranty of merchantability**, and a **warranty of fitness for a particular use**.

Warranty of Merchantability. This warranty guarantees the buyer that the goods as sold are in a fit condition for the ordinary purpose for which they were intended. In other words, if a retailer buys 500 pairs of shoes from a shoe manufacturer, the manufacturer implicitly guarantees that the shoes can be used as they are without defect. A warranty of merchantability applies only to goods sold by merchants.

Warranty of Fitness for a Particular Use. This warranty goes beyond that of a warranty of merchantability in that not only must the goods be capable of being used for their ordinary purposes, but the goods must be capable of performing any particular function the buyer has indicated. A warranty of fitness for a particular use applies both to merchants and nonmerchants.

EXAMPLE:

Hikers, Unlimited, is a chain of retail stores that sells hiking equipment. In a contract, Hikers buys 500 pairs of shoes from Seth Shoes after having indicated that the shoes are meant for mountain hikers. The shoes sold, although perfectly good shoes, do not have soles appropriate to mountain hiking. Seth Shoes has breached an implied warranty. Even though the shoes meet the description in Seth's catalog and are capable of being used, they do not meet the hiker's specific needs, of which Seth Shoes had been informed.

For there to be a warranty of fitness for a particular use, the particular use must be made known to the seller, and the buyer must be relying on the seller's expertise in purchasing the appropriate goods. The specific use could be made an express warranty if the parties include it as a part of the contract itself.

Warranty of Title.   Finally, §2-312 states that the seller must have **warranty of title:** title sufficient to sell the object to the buyer. The law does not intend buyers to purchase lawsuits along with the goods. The warranty of title means that the seller must own and have the right to pass ownership of the goods to the buyer free and clear of the interests of any other party to the goods, such as secured creditors. (Secured transactions are discussed later in this chapter.)

An important aspect of all warranties is that they extend not only to the contracting buyer, but to all subsequent purchasers as well, down to the ultimate consumer of the product. For example, any woman who purchased a dress from Smart Shops hoping for a 48-inch sweep could sue Doris, and any hiker who had her shoes fall apart while on a hike could sue Seth. These situations are most usually encountered in suits for defects in children's clothing, products, and toys. Parents, on behalf of the child, sue the manufacturer for breach of warranty, even though no direct contract exists between them. As the ultimate consumer, the child can maintain a suit against the manufacturer.

Risk of Loss

Another important provision of Article II of the UCC concerns the question of who bears the risk of the goods being destroyed after the contract has been signed. As a general rule, the risk of loss of the goods falls on the person who has control over the goods; however, the parties may specifically contract to determine at what point the risk passes from the seller to the buyer. Note that the risk of loss is a different concept than title.

It is imperative to understand the liabilities involved. Whoever bears the risk of loss has the right to maintain an action for the damages caused by the goods' destruction and has the responsibility to insure the goods. If the goods are destroyed when the seller bears the risk, the seller must replace the goods at his own expense. If the goods are destroyed when the buyer bears the risk, the buyer is still obligated to pay the seller for the goods. Careful drafting is always needed in these types of contracts.

In a general mercantile agreement, many of these contractual provisions are indicated merely by abbreviations of the terms. These abbreviations appear in the contracts without any words of explanation, because they are generally known. These provisions are extremely important in determining which party should insure the goods and who may maintain a suit should the goods be destroyed. A brief discussion of the most important of these clauses is in order and is given below.

Conditional Contracts.   With conditional contracts, the sale is predicated upon certain conditions being met at the time of transferring the goods. There are four types of conditional contracts under Article II.

1. *Cost on Delivery (§2-310).* A **cost on delivery**, or **COD**, provision indicates that the risk of loss of the goods remains with the seller until the goods have been delivered to *and paid for* by the buyer. The contract itself will indicate the place of delivery (for example, COD Buyer's Warehouse, 1000 Main Street, Garden City), and the buyer has no right of inspection unless specifically agreed to by the parties.

2. *Sale on approval (§2-326).* In a **sale on approval** contract, the seller retains the risk of loss until the goods have been delivered to the buyer and the buyer has indicated his approval of the goods. Even if the goods meet the specifications, the buyer may choose to return the goods. In this type of arrangement, the buyer, who must be the ultimate consumer, has a right to inspect the goods, so the risk is retained by the seller for a longer period than with a COD contract.

3. *Sale or return (§2-326).* With a **sale or return** provision, the risk passes to the buyer on delivery. If the buyer does not approve of the goods or chooses to return them, it is he who bears the risk and cost of returning the goods to the seller.

4. *Consignment (§2-326).* In a **consignment** contract, the risk of loss remains with the seller until the buyer resells the goods; in other words, the buyer never has a risk of loss. Many small retail stores carry goods on consignment, in which the manufacturer leaves goods with the retailer/buyer in the hopes that the buyer can resell the items. If the goods are not sold by the buyer within a stated period of time, they are returned to the seller, who has borne all the risk of loss.

Note that with all of the preceding types of contracts, the buyer may return the goods even if they conform to the contract specifications. These arrangements are only concerned with the risk of loss of the goods, not with other contractual rights of the parties.

Shipment Contracts. If the goods are transferred to the buyer by means of an independent carrier (the U.S. Postal Service, Federal Express, UPS, and so forth), a new element is added to the relationship: the third party. In a general **shipment contract**, the contract merely requires the seller to send the goods to the buyer. Therefore, once the goods are shipped, the risk passes to the buyer. However, the parties may make special contractual arrangements whereby the seller retains the risk for a slightly longer period, but still not to the point of delivery. There are three types of these special shipment arrangements.

1. *FOB (place of shipment) (§2-314).* FOB stands for *free on board*, and the risk stays with the seller until he places the goods in the hands of the carrier—for example, FOB Kennedy Airport, Air Express. In this instance, the seller bears the risk until the goods are given to the Air Express office at Kennedy Airport.

2. *FAS (vessel) (§2-319).* FAS *stands for free alongside*, and the vessel is the actual name of the mode of transportation—for example, FAS American Airlines Flight #100, Air Express, Kennedy Airport. In this in-

stance, the seller retains the risk until the goods are actually taken along-side the plane ready for loading, at which point the risk of loss passes to the buyer. FAS (vessel) keeps the risk of loss with the seller for a longer period than with FOB (place of shipment).

3.   *FOB (carrier) (§2-319).* With *FOB (carrier)*, the seller bears the risk of loss until the goods are actually loaded onto the means of transportation. This arrangement keeps the risk of loss with the seller for a longer period than any of the preceding types of shipment contracts.

Regardless of the type of shipment arrangement employed, the seller may agree to pay for insuring the goods during transportation, even though the risk of loss has passed to the buyer who would normally pay to insure the goods. This arrangement is indicated as **CIF** (*cost of insurance and freight*). Even though the seller has paid for the insurance, if the goods are lost, it is the buyer who bears the risk and who receives the insurance proceeds.

Shipment contracts are most commonly used when the seller is in a better bargaining position than the buyer; the seller has desirable goods that are in limited supply. As can be seen, with these arrangements it is the buyer who has the greater risk. However, most commonly the buyer has the better bargaining position—all sellers need customers—and so instead of shipment contracts the parties use destination contracts.

Destination Contracts.   With destination contracts, the seller retains the risk of loss of the goods until the goods arrive at a specified destination point. There are three types of destination contracts.

1.   *FOB (place of destination) (§2-319).* As with *FOB* (place of shipment), in *FOB (place of destination)* the risk passes when the carrier delivers the goods to a general destination point—FOB Port of San Diego.

2.   *Ex (ship) (§2-322).* With **Ex (ship)**, the risk only passes to the buyer when the goods are off-loaded from the mode of transportation. In the example above, if the contract read Ex American Airlines Flight #100, the risk would only pass to the buyer once the goods were unloaded from the plane.

3.   *No Arrival, No Sale (§2-324).* With **no arrival, no sale**, the risk only transfers to the buyer when the goods have arrived at the destination point and have been tendered to the buyer by the seller.

In each of these destination contracts, the risk remains with the seller for a slightly longer period of time than with a shipping contract.

These provisions are important in the drafting and interpreting of contracts for the sale of goods when transportation of the goods is involved. Typically, shipment provisions are simply indicated by the abbreviations given above and are not spelled out in further detail.

Remedies

For the most part, the remedies specified in Article II for the buyer and seller in a sales contract are the same remedies, both legal and equitable, permitted for all injured parties under general contract law. Chapter 11, Remedies, discusses these general remedies in detail.

Article II of the UCC grants certain additional remedies that are unique to the Code, which deserve some mention at this point.

Remedies Available to Seller

If the seller is the injured party to the contract, Article II, Part 7, permits three additional methods of rectifying the situation.

1. *Withhold delivery.* The seller may withhold delivery of the goods to the buyer if any one of the following circumstances arises:

   a. The buyer wrongfully rejects the goods.
   b. The buyer fails to pay for the goods as required by the contract.
   c. The buyer does not cooperate with the seller.
   d. The buyer repudiates the contract.
   e. The buyer becomes insolvent before delivery.

 EXAMPLE:

Under their contractual agreement, Rosie is obligated to send goods by a carrier that John is to name. John is prevaricating and won't specify a carrier. Rosie does not have to ship the goods because John is failing to cooperate according to the terms of the contract. Rosie has the right to resell the goods to another buyer.

2. *Stop delivery.* The seller may stop delivery of the goods in transit and resell them if one of the following circumstances arises:

   a. The buyer does not pay for the goods as required by the contract.
   b. The buyer repudiates the contract.
   c. The buyer becomes insolvent before delivery.

 EXAMPLE:

John finally specifies a carrier to Rosie, who then ships the goods. Shipment will take two weeks. After one week elapses, John files for protection under the bankruptcy law. Under Article II, Rosie is permitted to stop delivery of the goods, provided John has not yet paid for them. The UCC does not require sellers to become creditors in the bankruptcy of insolvent buyers. Note, however, that if John had already paid for the goods, Rosie would be required to deliver them. If the goods are nonconforming, John still has the right to reject them.

3.   *Reclaim goods from insolvent buyer.* The seller has the right to re-claim the goods from the buyer after delivery, but only if the goods are sold on credit, the buyer is insolvent, and the seller makes her demand within ten days of the buyer's receipt of the goods.

EXAMPLE:

Assume that Rosie sells the goods to John on credit but is unaware that John has filed for bankruptcy. Ten days after John receives the goods, Rosie discovers that John is insolvent; she immediately de-mands that John return the goods. Under the UCC, Rosie can reclaim the goods and thus avoid becoming one of John's creditors.

Remedies Available to Buyer

If the buyer is the injured party, in addition to general contractual remedies, UCC Article II offers him four specific remedies. Note that un-der the UCC a buyer is entitled to perfect performance and may reject nonconforming goods. The concept of substantial performance does not apply to merchant buyers unless the merchant buyer so wishes. This con-cept is known as **perfect tender**.

1.   *Cover.* The buyer is entitled to **cover** if the seller breaches the contract. Cover is the purchase of goods that substitute for those that are the subject of the breached contract. The buyer can sue the seller for damages if the substituted goods cost more than what the buyer expected to pay under the original sales contract.

EXAMPLE:

Buymore Supermarkets has a contract to buy 1000 bushels of plums from Farmer Jones. When the plums arrive, they do not meet Buy-more's specifications, and so it rejects the plums. Buymore purchases plums from Farmer Hicks as cover. The contract with Hicks costs Buymore $1000 more than the contract with Farmer Jones; Buymore can sue Jones for the extra $1000.

2.   *Replevin.* If cover is not available, the buyer may *replevy* the goods he had previously rejected from the seller. **Replevin** is an equitable remedy that means retaking, or recovering, the goods identified in the contract. The buyer may believe that nonconforming goods are better than none.

EXAMPLE:

If in the above situation, Buymore could not find plums anywhere else, it could replevy the plums it has already rejected from Farmer Jones.

3.   *Revocation*. If the goods do not conform to the contract specifications, the buyer can **revoke** his acceptance. This means that no contract exists.

EXAMPLE:

Assume the above situation. Because the plums did not conform to Buymore's specifications, Buymore could revoke its acceptance. No contract is ever formed.

4.   *Claim goods from insolvent seller*. If the seller becomes insolvent, the buyer can claim the goods from him, provided that the goods have been paid for. Just as the UCC will not require a seller to become a creditor of an insolvent buyer, neither will it require a buyer who has paid for goods to become a creditor of an insolvent seller. At this point, the goods are in fact the property of the buyer; the seller's creditors have the purchase price the buyer has already given to divide up among themselves.

Written Assurances

In addition to the foregoing, both parties to a contract under Article II have the right to demand assurances in writing that performance will occur. This can arise if either party becomes concerned about the other party's ability to perform. Note that this is different from a situation in which one party affirmatively states that she will not perform (See Chapter 10). Written assurances also have no applicability to situations in which a party has been judicially deemed bankrupt. If the assurances are not given within 30 days of the request, the requesting party can act as if the other party has breached the contract.

Summary

Article II is one of the most important provisions of the Uniform Commercial Code with respect to contract law. This article covers three main categories of contracts: contracts for the sale of goods valued at over $500; contracts between merchants; and contracts for the lease of property. Article II imposes warranties, or guarantees, with respect to the quality and usefulness of the subject goods. Additionally, it indicates special types of arrangements apportioning the risk of having the goods lost or destroyed while in transit between the seller and the buyer. Lastly, Article II details certain remedies for the injured party in a breach of one of the aforementioned contracts unique to the UCC.

Article IX, Secured Transactions

Secured Transaction Defined

Article IX of the UCC defines a **secured transaction** as any transaction, regardless of form, that is intended to create a security interest in personal property or fixtures, including *tangible goods, intangibles*, and *documents*. A *tangible good* (§9-105) is any good that can be touched and whose value is incorporated into the item itself. Examples of tangible goods are furniture, clothing, and automobiles. An intangible (§9-106) is a right to property, rather than a physical object. Examples of intangibles are stock certificates, bank savings account books, bonds, patents, and copyrights. Documents are such items as bills of lading and dock receipts.

A **security interest** represents the right of the holder of the interest to attach specific property in case of a default. In terms of contract law, this means that if the promissor defaults on his contractual obligation, and the promissee has a security interest, the promissee can attach the promissor's property that is subject to that interest to satisfy the default. It affords the innocent party greater protection in case of breach of contract because she knows that there will at least be the value of the secured property to lessen her injury.

 EXAMPLE:

Heather goes to the state bank to take out a personal loan. Before the bank loans Heather the money, it asks her to put up some property as security. Heather gives the bank a pearl ring she owns. The bank retains this ring as **collateral** (property to secure payment of the debt) until Heather repays the loan. Should Heather default, the bank can sell the ring to satisfy Heather's debt. Physical possession is one method of creating a security interest.

Nearly all security interests in personal property and fixtures are covered under Article IX of the UCC. There are only six categories of property that are not subject to this article—enumerated in §9-104.

1. *Real estate.* As indicated by the definition of a secured transaction in Article IX, real property is automatically excluded from this UCC provision, except for *fixtures.* A fixture is property that has been attached to real property but is capable of being removed without destroying or disturbing the real estate. Examples of fixtures would be door knobs, chandeliers, and light switches.

2. *Interests perfected under federal statutes.* Certain types of property, such as patents and copyrights, are created by federal statutes that also provide methods for establishing security interests in that property.

3. *Wage assignments. Wage assignments,* or *garnishments,* are covered by separate laws that protect the wage earner from having all of her wages taken from her to satisfy debts.

4. *Mechanic's liens.* A **mechanic's lien** is the right of any person who works on a piece of property to attach that property if the owner does not pay for the work performed. Mechanic's liens have been in existence for hundreds of years, are part of the common law, and automatically afford protection to workers.

5. *Claims arising out of judicial proceedings.* If a court of competent jurisdiction grants the specific right to a piece of property, the court's authority supersedes that of the UCC, and these claims are excluded from Article IX.

6. *Consumer sales agreements regulated by state laws.* Many states have enacted laws to protect consumers from having property reclaimed by stores if the consumer fails to make a payment years after the purchase, and these sales are exempted from Article IX where such statutes exist.

A security interest gives the holder of the interest the right to attach specific property subject to the interest in the case of default. This type of creditor has greater rights to the specific property of the debtor than other creditors. Whenever payment for merchandise is not concurrent with delivery of the goods, contracts usually specify that the party who conveys the goods shall have a security interest in the goods until payment. This protects the person who has already given his consideration in case the other party defaults. However, merely having a clause in the contract may be insufficient to create a valid and enforceable security interest pursuant to Article IX.

Requirements to Create a Security Interest

To create a valid and enforceable security interest, the parties must intend to create a security interest and evidence such interest by meeting three requirements under Part Two of Article IX:

1. There must be a security agreement.
2. There must be attachment.
3. There must be perfection.

1. *Security agreement*. A **security agreement** is a writing signed by both parties. It describes the property that is subject to the security interest and states that a security interest is being created in that property. The property is generally referred to as the collateral. Usually, the contract between the parties for the sale of the goods satisfies this requirement, provided that it contains a statement creating the security interest. For an example of such a statement, see the sample clauses given below.

2. *Attachment*. **Attachment** is the timing element of the security interest; it indicates the moment when the creditor gives consideration for the security interest. Typically, this occurs when the agreement is signed, or the security holder conveys his consideration to the other party, or the debtor takes possession of the collateral. At this moment the security holder has an inchoate right to the collateral.

What happens if the contract is for a loan, and the debtor is using the borrowed money to purchase the property that will become the collateral? The creditor's rights may not attach for several weeks. The reason that the attachment is delayed is because the property that is the subject of the security interest is not yet owned by the debtor. The debtor is using the borrowed money to purchase the collateral. During this time the debtor may default. Under these circumstances, the creditor has a **purchase money security interest** in the property the debtor buys with the creditor's funds. This interest is implied by law, and the debtor holds the property in trust for the creditor.

 EXAMPLE:

Leonard loans his brother-in-law Zack $50,000 to start a bottling company, and the loan states that Leonard will have a security interest in the bottling equipment. Zack orders the bottling equipment on credit and uses Leonard's money to buy office furniture and supplies. If Zack defaults prior to the equipment being delivered, Leonard has a purchase money security interest in the furniture and supplies because it was his money that paid for the items.

Another problem that can arise with respect to attachment occurs if the collateral is the inventory of the debtor. Many times, if money is loaned to a manufacturer, the creditor will take a security interest in the debtor's inventory. However, inventory is always being sold, so the specific items included in inventory one week are not the same items the following week. In this situation, the creditor is deemed to have a **floating lien**, giving her the right to attach any item that is included in inventory at the moment of default. The actual collateral is always being changed.

EXAMPLE:

Assume that in the above example, instead of taking a security interest in Zack's equipment, Leonard takes a security interest in Zack's inventory. On the day the loan agreement is signed, Zack has 100,000 bottles in inventory; on the day Zack defaults, his inventory contains 200,000 bottles. Leonard has a right to claim the 200,000 bottles, even though these specific bottles were acquired by Zack after the agreement. The floating lien gives Leonard the right to all existing inventory on the day of default up to the value of the debt.

3. *Perfection.* The third requirement to create a valid and enforceable security interest is **perfection**. Perfection is the process of protecting a creditor's rights to the collateral from all other claimants and can be effectuated in three ways:

First, in certain circumstances, the attachment itself is sufficient to perfect the interest, as in the case of a purchase money security interest.

Second, perfection can come about by the creditor having physical possession of the collateral. An example would be the state bank in the earlier instance with Heather and the loan. Because the bank is actually holding Heather's pearl ring, no one else can get control of it.

Third, and most typically, perfection can be accomplished by filing a **financing statement**. A financing statement is a document, signed by the parties, that contains their names and addresses and describes the collateral. (See sample financing statement on the next page.) A security agreement can be used as a financing statement, but the reverse is not true. The financing statement does not create the security interest. However, it is very rare that anyone uses the security agreement as the financing statement, because once the document is filed, it becomes publicly available. Most people do not want all the terms of their contractual arrangements to be public knowledge. Usually creditors file financing statements. These forms can be purchased from legal stationery stores and only indicate the minimum information required by Article IX.

Filing is mandatory for perfecting security interests in intangibles, inventory goods, and equipment, but is permissive for all other property. Filing is effective for a period of five years. If the debt is not satisfied within this period, the financing statement must be refiled. Where the financing statements are filed depends on the nature of the collateral: either the County Filing Office where the property is located, the County Recorder's Office (typically for timber, minerals, and crops), or the Secretary of State's Office. Part 4 of Article IX specifies the appropriate office, and therefore the version of the Code adopted by the state in question must be checked.

Not only does filing afford the creditor some protection against other claimants, but because filing is public, prior to agreeing to accept a security interest in a particular piece of property, a potential creditor must check the appropriate office to make sure that no one else already has a

FORM UCC-1

STATE OF MICHIGAN
UNIFORM COMMERCIAL CODE FINANCING STATEMENT
(Approved by the Secretary of State and Michigan Association of Registers of Deeds)

INSTRUCTIONS:

1. TYPE OR PRINT All information required on this Form.
2. If filing is made with the Secretary of State, send the WHITE copies to the Secretary of State, Lansing, Michigan. If filing is made with the Register of Deeds, send the YELLOW copies to the Local Register of Deeds. Retain the PINK copies for files of secured party and debtor.
3. Enclose filing fee.
4. IF ADDITIONAL SPACE IS NEEDED for any items on this Form, continue the items on separate sheets of paper (5" x 8"). One copy of these additional sheets should accompany the WHITE Forms, and one copy should accompany the YELLOW Forms. USE PAPER CLIPS to attach these sheets to the Forms (DO NOT USE STAPLES, GLUE, TAPE, ETC.) and indicate in Item 1 the number of additional sheets attached.
5. At the time of filing, the filing officer will return acknowledgement. At a later time, the secured party may date and sign the termination legend and use acknowledgement copy as a termination statement.
6. Both the WHITE and YELLOW Filing Officer copies must have original signatures. Only the debtor must sign the financing statement, and the signature of the secured party is not necessary, except that the secured party alone may sign the financing statement in the following 4 instances: Please specify action in Item 7 below.
   (1) Where the collateral which is subject to the security interest in another state is brought into Michigan or the location of the debtor is changed to Michigan.
   (2) "For proceeds if the security interest in the original collateral was perfected."
   (3) The previous filing has lapsed.
   (4) For collateral acquired after a change of debtor name etc., and a filing is required under MCLA 440.9402 (2) and (7); MSA 19.9402 (2) and (7).

1. No. of additional sheets			For Filing Officer (Date, Time, Number, and Filing Office)
	Liber	Page	
2. Debtor(s) (Last Name First) and address(es)	3. Secured Party(ies) and address(es)		
4. Name and address(es) of assignee(s) (if any)	CHECK ☒ if applicable 5. ☐ Products of collateral are also covered. 6. ☐ Collateral was brought into this state subject to a security interest in another jurisdiction.		

7. This financing statement covers the following types (or items) of property:

_____   _____

_____   _____

_____   by: _____
Signature(s) of Debtor(s)   (Signature of Secured Party or Assignee of Record)

SECRETARY OF STATE COPY

Order by Form 8411 Rev. 1/80 From Doubleday Bros. & Co., Kalamazoo, Mich. 49002 FINANCIAL PRINTERS

security interest in the collateral. This is crucial for the formation of an enforceable security interest.

But what happens if there are conflicting claims to the same property? Which creditor prevails? Part 3 of Article IX has established an order of priorities in such situations to determine which creditor has superior rights to the collateral.

Priorities

Article IX has established an order of priorities for creditors in case of the debtor's default. Should there be conflicting claims for the same property, the claimant with the highest priority will prevail. The general rule is that secured creditors have greater priorities than unsecured creditors. Among secured creditors, priorities date from the time of filing *or* perfection of the security interest. The order of the priorities is:

1. creditors with a purchase money security interest;
2. creditors with a floating lien;
3. among creditors who perfect on the same day: creditors who filed first (this is the actual date of filing the financing statement, not the date the agreement was signed), then creditors with interests perfected other than by filing (attachment or possession); and
4. creditors whose interests attached first among nonperfected creditors.

 EXAMPLE:

Julia loans $10,000 to Ariel, taking a security interest in Ariel's receivables. The loan agreement is signed and the money given on Monday. On Friday, Julia files her financing statement. In the interim, Ariel borrows $5000 from Mark, signing a security agreement for the receivables on Wednesday. Mark also files his financing statement on Wednesday. When Ariel defaults, Mark prevails because he filed before Julia (Wednesday versus Friday).

If the debtor defaults, the creditor with a valid security interest may either retain the collateral in satisfaction of the debt, sell the collateral to satisfy the debt (any amount above the debt acquired by the sale of the collateral belongs to the debtor), or may simply sue the debtor in an action for debt.

Generally, paralegals who work with contracts subject to Article IX of the UCC have very specific functions to perform. First, they must draft a legally accurate description of the property that will be subject to the security interest. If the property is inaccurately or incompletely described, the client will not have an effective security interest. Second, the legal assistant must check the appropriate government office to determine that no other security interest is attached to the subject property. Finally, the paralegal must file the financing statement in a timely manner in the appropriate office.

SAMPLE CLAUSES

| 1 |

MANUFACTURER HEREBY WARRANTS THAT THE MERCHANDISE WILL NOT FADE OR SHRINK.

This is an example of an express warranty made by a manufacturer. Any person who purchases these goods or who is the ultimate consumer (user) of these goods may sue the manufacturer if the goods do in fact fade or shrink. The warranty is a covenant of the seller.

2

We hereby grant to you a security interest in all receivables, as defined above, all present and future instruments, documents, chattel paper, and general intangibles (as defined by the Uniform Commercial Code), and all reserves, balances and deposits, and property at any time to our credit. All of the foregoing shall secure payment and performance of all of our obligations at any time owing to you, fixed or contingent, whether arising out of this or any other agreement, or by operation of law or otherwise.

The above is a contract clause intended to create a security agreement in documents and intangibles. Taken in conjunction with the entire agreement, which would indicate the parties' names, addresses, and signatures, this would constitute a valid security agreement, the first requirement to create an enforceable security interest under Article IX of the UCC.

3

You want waterproof? Breathable? Look at our clothing on page 20, all 100% waterproof and windproof, yet so breathable that overheating is a thing of the past.

The above catalog description constitutes an express warranty by the seller. Even though the word "warranty" is not used, because the description of the clothing appears in its sales literature, the manufacturer is held to guarantee that the clothes are 100 percent waterproof and breathable so that the customer will not get wet or overheated.

CHAPTER SUMMARY

The Uniform Commercial Code was created to promote and facilitate commerce among the states and to provide some uniformity in state laws with respect to commercial transactions. The UCC is a state law, and versions of the model UCC have been adopted in every jurisdiction, including the District of Columbia. Three UCC articles have a direct impact on the law of contracts.

Article I, General Provisions, establishes the general guidelines for interpretation of the entire Code. This article restates the purpose of the Code and indicates that the Code is to be liberally, not literally, construed, within the bounds of reasonable interpretation. Additionally, the state law will always prevail unless specifically superseded by the Code.

Article I also establishes three obligations for all persons whose transactions are covered by the UCC: (1) they are obligated to act in good faith; (2) they are obligated to perform within a reasonable time; and (3) they are expected to perform according to the custom, usage, and past practices of the parties and industry involved.

Article II, Sales, concerns itself with contracts for the sale of goods. It is the modern interpretation of the Statute of Frauds with respect to these types of contracts. The UCC does not cover contracts for the performance of services.

The UCC provisions on sales regulate the concept of warranties, or guarantees, with respect to contracts for the sale of goods. In this manner, Article II makes the manufacturer/seller of goods contractually bound not only to his direct purchaser, but to anyone who ultimately uses or consumes the goods. These warranties may be either express (created by words or conduct) or implied (created by operation of law).

Article II further establishes contractual methods of determining when the risk of loss of the goods transfers from the seller to the buyer. The Code specifies several different clauses or agreements that the parties may insert in their contract to make this determination.

Additionally, the article on sales provides specific remedies in case of breach of contract for both the seller and the buyer. These Article II remedies go beyond those generally afforded under contract law.

Finally, Article IX, Secured Transactions, indicates how a creditor may contractually provide for a security interest in specific property, property that he may then attach and sell to satisfy the debt in the case of the debtor's default. By meeting the UCC requirements for creating a security agreement and for attachment and perfection, a creditor is given greater protection for recovery in the case of breach of contract. Commerce is thus promoted by making credit and loans less risky for the creditor.

SYNOPSIS

UCC purpose: Modernizing, clarifying, and unifying state commercial law
Article I, General Provisions
    Obligations
      1.   Good faith
      2.   Reasonable time
      3.   Custom and usage
Article II, Sales
      1.   Contracts covered

     a. Sale of goods (not services)
     b. Lease of goods
     c. Contracts between merchants
  2. Contract provisions
     a. Warranties
        i. Express
           (1) Affirmation or promise
           (2) Description
           (3) Sample or model
        ii. Implied
           (1) Merchantability
           (2) Fitness for a particular use
        iii. Title
     b. Risk of loss
        i. Conditional
        ii. Shipment
        iii. Destination
  3. Remedies
     a. Seller
        i. Withhold delivery
        ii. Stop delivery in transit
        iii. Redeem goods from insolvent buyer
     b. Buyer
        i. Cover
        ii. Replevin
        iii. Revoke acceptance
        iv. Reclaim goods from insolvent seller
Article IX, Secured Transactions
  1. Exceptions
  2. Requirements
     a. Security agreement
     b. Attachment
     c. Perfection (filing)
  3. Priorities

Key Terms

Attachment: time at which security interest becomes an inchoate right
Battle of the forms: difference in forms used by merchants for sales
    agreements
CIF: cost of insurance and freight paid for by seller, even though risk
    of loss has passed to the buyer
COD: cost on delivery; conditional contract in which the risk of loss
    passes to buyer only after goods have been delivered and paid for
Collateral: property pledged to secure a security interest
Consignment contract: conditional contract in which risk of loss remains with seller until buyer resells the goods

Cover: remedy whereby buyer can purchase goods in substitution for breached contract

Express warranty: guarantee created by words or conduct of the seller

Ex ship: destination contract in which risk of loss passes to buyer when goods are off-loaded from the mode of transportation

FAS: free alongside; a shipping contract in which risk of loss passes to buyer when goods are placed alongside vessel used for transportation

Financing statement: document filed in government office to protect a security interest

Floating lien: security interest in after-acquired property

FOB (carrier): shipment contract in which risk of loss passes when goods are loaded onto third-party carrier

FOB (place of shipment): free on board; shipment contract in which risk of loss passes when goods are given to third-party carrier

Implied warranty: guarantee created by operation of law

Mechanic's lien: security interest given under common law to persons who repair property

Merchant: person who regularly trades in goods or who holds himself out as having knowledge peculiar to a specific good

No arrival, no sale: destination contract in which risk of loss risk passes to buyer when goods are tendered to the buyer

Perfect tender: buyers right to complete performance

Perfection: method of creating and protecting a security interest under Article IX of the UCC

Purchase money security interest: security interest created in the creditor whose money is used to buy the collateral

Replevin: equitable remedy in which buyer reclaims property previously rejected

Revocation: to recall an offer

Sale on approval: conditional contract in which risk of loss passes to buyer when buyer receives and approves goods

Sale or return: conditional contract in which risk of loss passes when buyer receives goods; buyer bears the cost of returning goods of which he does not approve

Secured transaction: any transaction, regardless of form, that creates a security interest in personal property or fixtures

Security agreement: document signed by debtor and creditor, that names the collateral, and creates a security interest in said collateral

Security interest: right acquired by a creditor to attach collateral in case of default by the debtor

Shipment contract: agreement whereby risk passes from seller to buyer when goods are transported by a third person

Strict liability: no standard of care; automatic liability if properly used goods do not meet the warranty

Warranty: guarantee made by manufacturer or seller with respect to quality, quantity, and type of good being sold

Warranty of fitness for a particular use: guarantee that goods can be used for a specified purpose

Warranty of merchantability: guarantee that goods can be used in their current condition

Warranty of title: guarantee that seller has a title sufficient to transfer goods to buyer

EXERCISES

1. Find two advertisements in your local newspaper that indicate warranties.
2. Discuss several methods of protecting a person's security interest.
3. Does the UCC in fact promote commerce? Explain.
4. Obtain and analyze a mortgage and chattel mortgage agreement.
5. Obtain the addresses of the appropriate government offices in your state for filing financing statements.
6. Check your own state statute for its version of the UCC.

Cases for Analysis

The concept of warranties under UCC Article II is discussed in Hong v. Marriott Corp. with respect to fast food, and the method of perfecting a security interest under UCC Article IX is discussed in In re Peregrine Entertainment, Ltd.

Hong v. Marriott Corp.
656 F. Supp. 445 (D. Md. 1987)

SMALKIN, District Judge.

The plaintiff, Yong Cha Hong, commenced this case in a Maryland court with a complaint alleging counts of negligence and breach of warranty against defendants, the proprietor of a chain of fast food restaurants called Roy Rogers Family Restaurants (Marriott) and the supplier of raw frying chicken to the chain (Gold Kist). The case was removed to this Court on diversity grounds. It seems that the plaintiff was contentedly munching away one day on a piece of Roy Rogers take-out fried chicken[1] (a wing) when she bit into something in the chicken that she perceived to a be a worm. She suffered, it is alleged, great physical and emotional

---

1. The court takes judicial notice (because it is so well-known in this jurisdiction) that Roy Rogers specializes in fried chicken, to eat in or take out. Fed. R. Evid. 201.

upset from her encounter with this item, including permanent injuries, in consequence of which she prays damages in the amount of $500,000.00.

The defendants moved for summary judgment on plaintiff's warranty count, and also, later, as to the entire complaint, on the ground that there is no genuine dispute of material fact and that, as a matter of law, there was no breach of warranty or negligence. If they are right, they are entitled to summary judgment. Fed. R. Civ. P. 56(c); Anderson v. Liberty Lobby, Inc., 106 S. Ct. 2505 (1986).

It appears that the item encountered by plaintiff in the chicken wing was probably not a worm or other parasite, although plaintiff, in her deposition, steadfastly maintains that it was a worm, notwithstanding the expert analysis. If it was not in fact a worm, i.e., if the expert analysis is correct, it was either one of the chicken's major blood vessels (the aorta) or its trachea, both of which (the Court can judicially notice) would appear worm-like (although not meaty like a worm, but hollow) to a person unschooled in chicken anatomy. The Court must presume plaintiff to be inexpert as to chickens, even though she admits some acquaintance with fresh-slaughtered chickens. See Ross v. Communications Satellite Corp., 759 F.2d 355, 364 (4th Cir. 1985). For the purposes of analyzing the plaintiff's warranty claim, the Court will assume that the item was not a worm. Precisely how the aorta or trachea wound up in this hapless chicken's wing is a fascinating, but as yet unanswered (and presently immaterial), question.

Thus, the warranty issue squarely framed is, does Maryland law[2] provide a breach of warranty[3] remedy for personal injury flowing from an unexpected encounter with an inedible[4] part of the chicken's anatomy in a piece of fast food fried chicken? Defendants contend that there can be no warranty recovery unless the offending item was a "foreign object," i.e., not a part of the chicken itself.

In Webster v. Blue Ship Tea Room, Inc., 347 Mass. 421, 198 N.E.2d 309 (1964), a favorite of commercial law teachers,[5] the plaintiff was injured when a fish bone she encountered in a bowl of New England fish chowder, served in a "quaint" Boston restaurant, became stuck in her throat. She was denied warranty recovery (on a theory of implied warranty of merchantability) on grounds that are not altogether clear from the court's opinion. The opinion can be read in several ways: (1) There was no breach because the bone was not extraneous, but a natural substance; (2) There was no breach because New England fish chowder always has bones as an unavoidable contaminant; or (3) The plaintiff, an

2. Of course, Maryland law applies in this diversity case. Erie Railroad v. Tompkins, 304 U.S. 64 (1938).

3. The relevant warranty is found in Md. Comm. Law Code Ann. [UCC] §2-314(2) (1975). The Maryland UCC warranty of merchantability applies to sales of food in restaurants, including take-out sales. UCC §2-1314(1).

4. Although perhaps digestible, the aorta and the trachea of a chicken would appear indisputably to belong to the realm of the inedible in that fowl's anatomy.

5. Of which this Judge is one (part-time).

undoubted Yankee, should have expected to find a bone in her chowder and should have slurped it more gingerly.

In their respected hornbook, UCC, §9-7 (2d Ed. 1979) at 351, Professors White and Summers classify *Webster* in a category of warranty cases involving "the presence of unexpected objects," along with several other cases illustrative of that genre. Id. at n.96. In DeGraff v. Myers Foods, 19 Pa. D&C2d 19, 1 UCC Rep. 110 (C.P. 1958), the unexpected object was a chicken bone in a chicken pot pie. (The plaintiff won.) In Flippo v. Mode O'Day Frock Shops, 248 Ark. 1, 449 S.W.2d 692 (1970), the unexpected object was a poisonous spider lurking in a newly bought pair of trousers. (It bit plaintiff. Plaintiff lost.)

Unlike New England Fish Chowder, a well-known regional specialty, fried chicken (though of Southern origin) is a ubiquitous American dish. Chicken, generically, has a special place in the American poultry pantheon:

> The dream of the good life in America is embodied in the promise of "a chicken in every pot." Domestic and wild fowl have always been abundant and popular, and each wave of immigrants has brought along favorite dishes—such as paella and chicken cacciatori—which have soon become naturalized citizens.

The Fannie Farmer Cookbook (Knopf: 1980) at 228.

Indeed, as to fried chicken, Fannie Farmer lists recipes for three varieties of fried chicken alone—pan-fried, batter-fried, and Maryland Fried chicken.[6] Id. at 238-239. As best this Judge can determine (and he is no culinary expert) the fast-food chicken served in Roy Rogers most resembles Fannie Farmer's batter-fried chicken. That is, it is covered with a thick, crusty (often highly spiced) batter, that usually conceals from inspection whatever lurks beneath. There is deposition testimony from plaintiff establishing that she saw the offending item before she bit into it, having torn the wing asunder before eating it. A question of fact is raised as to just what she saw, or how carefully she might reasonably be expected to have examined what she saw before eating. It is common knowledge that chicken parts often harbor minor blood vessels. But, this Judge, born and raised south of the Mason-Dixon Line (where fried chicken has been around longer than in any other part of America), knows of no special heightened awareness chargeable to fried chicken eaters that ought to caution them to be on the alert for tracheas or aortas in the middle of their wings.[7]

Certainly, in *Webster* and many other cases that have denied war-

---

6. Oddly enough, Maryland Fried Chicken is seldom encountered in Maryland restaurants, though this Judge has seen it on restaurant menus in Ireland and England.

7. Of course, if as a matter of fact and law plaintiff abandoned her reliance on defendants' warranty by eating the wing with "contributory negligence," the defendants would have a good warranty defense, as well as a good negligence defense, under Maryland law. Erdman v. Johnson Bros. Radio & Television, 260 Md. 190, 271 A.2d 744 (1970). But this is quintessentially a question of fact for the jury. Id. at 303-304, 271 A.2d at 751.

ranty recovery as a matter of law, the injurious substance was, as in this case, a natural (though inedible) part of the edible item consumed. Thus, in Shapiro v. Hotel Statler Corp., 132 F. Supp. 891 (S.D. Cal. 1955), recovery was denied for a fish bone in "Hot Barquette of Seafood Mornay." And in Allen v. Grafton, 170 Ohio St. 249, 164 N.E.2d 167 (1960), recovery was denied for oyster shell in fried oysters.[8] But in all these cases, the natural item was, beyond dispute, reasonably to be expected in the dish by its very nature, under the prevailing expectation of any reasonable consumer. Indeed, precisely this "reasonable expectation" test has been adopted in a number of cases. See, e.g., Morrison's Cafeteria of Montgomery, Inc. v. Haddox, 431 So. 2d 975, 35 UCC 1074 (Ala. 1983); Battiste v. St. Thomas Diving Club, 26 UCC 324 (D.V.I. 1979); Jeffries v. Clark's Restaurant Enterprises, Inc., 20 Wash. App. 428, 580 P.2d 1103, 24 UCC 587 (1978); Williams v. Braum Ice Cream Stores, Inc., 534 P.2d 700, 15 UCC 1019 (Okla. App. 1974); Stark v. Chock Full O'Nuts, 77 Misc. 2d 553, 356 N.Y.S.2d 403, 14 UCC 51 (1974). The "reasonable expectation" test has largely displaced the natural/foreign test adverted to by defendants. In the circumstances of this case and many others, it is the only one that makes sense. In the absence of any Maryland decisional law, and in view of the expense and impracticality of certification of the question to the Court of Appeals of, Maryland in this case, this court must decide the issue by applying the rule that that Court would likely adopt some time in the future. See, e.g., Wilson v. Ford Motor Co., 656 F.2d 960 (4th Cir. 1981). This court is confident that Maryland would apply the "reasonable expectation" rule to this warranty case, especially in view of the Court of Appeals' holding in Bryer v. Rath Packing Co., 221 Md. 105, 156 A.2d 442 (1959), recognizing a negligence claim for the presence in a prepared food item of "something that should not be there" which renders the food unfit. Id. at 112, 156 A.2d at 447.

Applying the reasonable expectation test to this case, the court cannot conclude that the presence of a trachea or an aorta in a fast food fried chicken wing is so reasonably to be expected as to render it merchantable, as a matter of law, within the bounds of UCC §2-314(2). This is not like the situation involving a 1 cm. bone in a piece of fried fish in *Morrison's Cafeteria*. Everyone but a fool knows that tiny bones may remain in even the best filets of fish. This case is more like *Williams*, where the court held that the issue was for the trier of fact, on a claim arising from a cherry pit in cherry ice cream. Thus, a question of fact is presented that precludes the grant of summary judgment. See Celotex Corp. v. Catrett, 106 S.Ct. 2548 (1986). The jury must determine whether a piece of fast food fried chicken is merchantable if it contains an inedible item of the chicken's anatomy. Of course, the jury will be instructed that the consumer's reasonable expectations form a part of the merchantability concept (under

---

8. Although the item encountered by plaintiff in this case does not carry the same potential for physical harm as do fish bones and oyster shells, plaintiff alleges compensable personal injury damage under UCC §2-715(2)(b).

the theory of ordinary fitness, UCC §2-314(2)(c)), as do trade quality standards (under UCC §2-214(2)(a)).

In short, summary judgment cannot be awarded defendants on plaintiff's warranty count, and their motion for partial summary judgment is, accordingly, denied.

Defendants' motion for summary judgment as to the entire complaint is mainly predicated upon plaintiff's insistence at her deposition that the offending item was in fact a worm, notwithstanding the independent analysis showing it not to be a worm. It is true that a party having the burden of proof cannot carry that burden by "evidence which points in both directions," see N.L.R.B. v. Patrick Plaza Dodge, Inc., 522 F.2d 804, 809 (4th Cir. 1975), but it is also the undoubted common law of all American jurisdictions that a plaintiff can advance alternative legal theories of recovery. Here, the negligence and breach of warranty counts (as interpreted by this court's preceding discussion of the scope of the warranty) would permit recovery whether the item was worm or non-worm. Of course, plaintiff's credibility may be severely damaged by her insistence (on deposition and perhaps even at trial) that the item was a worm, despite the contrary expert analysis, which stands unimpugned by contrary expert evidence. This, however, is a risk that plaintiff must assume as part of her right to have the issues of fact tried by a jury under the Seventh Amendment, and summary judgment cannot be used to foreclose that right under the state of this record.

Finally, the court perceives genuine, material disputes of fact and law on plaintiff's negligence count, precluding summary judgment thereon. Fed. R. Civ. P. 56(c). Neither expert testimony nor other direct evidence of any sort is needed (except in professional malpractice cases) to prove negligence under Maryland law; negligence can be inferred. Western Md. R. Co. v. Shivers, 101 Md. 391, 393, 61 A. 618, 619 (1905). Although perhaps weak, all inferences, including inferences establishing negligence, must be taken in plaintiff's favor at this stage of the proceedings. Ross v. Communications Satellite Corp., 759 F.2d at 364.

For these reasons, the defendant's motion for summary judgment *in toto* is also denied.

Questions

1. Why did the plaintiff attempt to bring the action as a breach of warranty?
2. Why does the court discuss various chicken recipes?
3. What do you think of the reasonable expectation theory?

In re Peregrine Entertainment, Ltd.
116 Bankr. 194 (C.D. Cal. 1990)

This appeal from a decision of the bankruptcy court raises an issue never before confronted by a federal court in a published opinion: Is a security interest in a copyright perfected by an appropriate filing with the United States Copyright Office or by a UCC-1 financing statement filed with the relevant secretary of state?

I

National Peregrine, Inc. (NPI) is a Chapter 11 debtor in possession whose principal assets are a library of copyrights, distribution rights and licenses to approximately 145 films, and accounts receivable arising from the licensing of these films to various programmers. NPI claims to have an outright assignment of some of the copyrights; as for the others, NPI claims it has an exclusive license to distribute in a certain territory, or for a certain period of time.

In June 1985, Capitol Federal Savings and Loan Association of Denver (Cap Fed) extended to American National Enterprises, Inc., NPI's predecessor by merger, a six million dollar line of credit secured by what is now NPI's film library. Both the security agreement and the UCC-1 financing statements filed by Cap Fed describe the collateral as "[a]ll inventory consisting of films and all accounts, contract rights, chattel paper, general intangibles, instruments, equipment, and documents related to such inventory, now owned or hereafter acquired by the Debtor." Although Cap Fed filed its UCC-1 financing statements in California, Colorado and Utah, it did not record its security interest in the United States Copyright Office.

NPI filed a voluntary petition for bankruptcy on January 30, 1989. On April 6, 1989, NPI filed an amended complaint against Cap Fed, contending that the bank's security interest in the copyrights to the films in NPI's library and in the accounts receivable generated by their distribution were unperfected because Cap Fed failed to record its security interest with the Copyright Office. NPI claimed that, as a debtor in possession, it had a judicial lien on all assets in the bankruptcy estate, including the copyrights and receivables. Armed with this lien, it sought to avoid, recover and preserve Cap Fed's supposedly unperfected security interest for the benefit of the estate.

The parties filed cross-motions for partial summary judgment on the question of whether Cap Fed had a valid security interest in the NPI film library. The bankruptcy court held for Cap Fed. See Memorandum of Decision re Motion for Partial Summary Adjudication (Nov. 14, 1989) [hereinafter "Memorandum of Decision"] and Order re Summary Adjudication of Issues (Dec. 18, 1989). NPI appeals.

II

A. *Where to File*

The Copyright Act provides that "[a]ny transfer of copyright ownership or other document pertaining to a copyright" may be recorded in the United States Copyright Office. 17 U.S.C. §205(a); see Copyright Office Circular 12: Recordation of Transfers and Other Documents (reprinted in 1 Copyright L. Rep. (CCH) ¶15,015) [hereinafter "Circular 12"]. A "transfer" under the Act includes any "mortgage" or "hypothecation of a copyright," whether "in whole or in part" and "by any means of conveyance or by operation of law." 17 U.S.C. §§101, 201(d)(1); see 3 Nimmer on Copyright §10.05[A], at 10-43–10-45 (1989). The terms "mortgage" and "hypothecation" include a pledge of property as security or collateral for a debt. See Black's Law Dictionary 669 (5th ed. 1979). In addition, the Copyright Office has defined a "document pertaining to a copyright" as one that

> has a direct or indirect relationship to the existence, scope, duration, or identification of a copyright, or to the ownership, division, allocation, licensing, transfer, or exercise of rights under a copyright. That relationship may be past, present, future, or potential.

37 C.F.R. §201.4(a)(2); see also Compendium of Copyright Office Practices II ¶¶1602–1603 (identifying which documents the Copyright Office will accept for filing).

It is clear from the preceding that an agreement granting a creditor a security interest in a copyright may be recorded in the Copyright Office. See G. Gilmore, Security Interests in Personal Property §17.3, at 545 (1965). Likewise, because a copyright entitles the holder to receive all income derived from the display of the creative work, see 17 U.S.C. §106, an agreement creating a security interest in the receivables generated by a copyright may also be recorded in the Copyright Office. Thus, Cap Fed's security interest *could* have been recorded in the Copyright Office; the parties seem to agree on this much. The question is, does the UCC provide a parallel method of perfecting a security interest in a copyright? One can answer this question by reference to either federal or state law; both inquiries lead to the same conclusion.

1

Even in the absence of express language, federal regulation will preempt state law if it is so pervasive as to indicate that "Congress left no room for supplementary state regulation," or if "the federal interest is so dominant that the federal system will be assumed to preclude enforcement of state laws on the same subject," Hillsborough County v. Automated Medical Laboratories, Inc., 471 U.S. 707, 713, 105 S. Ct. 2371, 2375, 85 L. Ed. 2d 714 (1985) (internal quotations omitted). Here, the comprehensive scope of the federal Copyright Act's recording provisions, along with the unique federal interests they implicate, support the view that federal law preempts state methods of perfecting security interests in copyrights and related accounts receivable.

The federal copyright laws ensure "predictability and certainty of copyright ownership," "promote national uniformity" and "avoid the practical difficulties of determining and enforcing an author's rights un-

der the differing laws and in the separate courts of the various States."
Community for Creative Non-Violence v. Reid, — U.S. — , 109 S. Ct. 2166,
2177, 104 L. Ed. 2d 811 (1989); H.R. Rep. No. 1476, 94th Cong., 2d Sess.
129 (1976), U.S. Code Cong. & Admin. News 1976, p. 5659. As discussed
above, section 205(a) of the Copyright Act establishes a uniform method
for recording security interests in copyrights. A secured creditor need
only file in the Copyright Office in order to give "all persons constructive
notice of the facts stated in the recorded document." 17 U.S.C. §205(c).
Likewise, an interested third party need only search the indices maintained by the Copyright Office to determine whether a particular copyright is encumbered. See Northern Songs, Ltd. v. Distinguished
Productions, Inc., 581 F. Supp. 638, 640-641 (S.D.N.Y. 1984); Circular 12,
at 8035-4.

A recording system works by virtue of the fact that interested parties
have a specific place to look in order to discover with certainty whether
a particular interest has been transferred or encumbered. To the extent
there are competing recordation schemes, this lessens the utility of each;
when records are scattered in several filing units, potential creditors must
conduct several searches before they can be sure that the property is not
encumbered. See Danning v. Pacific Propeller, Inc., (In re Holiday Airlines
Corp.), 620 F.2d 731 (9th Cir.), *cert. denied*, 449 U.S. 900, 101 S. Ct. 269, 66
L. Ed. 2d 130 (1980); Red Carpet Homes of Johnstown, Inc. v. Gerling (In
re Knapp), 575 F.2d 341, 343 (2d Cir. 1978); UCC §9401, Official Comment
¶1. It is for that reason that parallel recordation schemes for the same
types of property are scarce as hens' teeth; the court is aware of no others,
and the parties have cited none. No useful purposes would be served—
indeed, much confusion would result—if creditors were permitted to perfect security interests by filing with either the Copyright Office or state
offices. See G. Gilmore, Security Interests in Personal Property §17.3, at
545 (1965); see also 3 Nimmer on Copyright §10.05[A] at 10-44 (1989) ("a
persuasive argument . . . can be made to the effect that by reasons of Sections 201(d)(1), 204(a), 205(c) and 205(d) of the current Act . . . Congress
has preempted the field with respect to the form and recordation requirements applicable to copyright mortgages").

If state methods of perfection were valid, a third party (such as a
potential purchaser of the copyright) who wanted to learn of any encumbrances thereon would have to check not merely the indices of the U.S.
Copyright Office, but also the indices of any relevant secretary of state.
Because copyrights are incorporeal—they have no fixed situs—a number
of state authorities could be relevant. See, e.g., note 4 supra. Thus, interested third parties could never be entirely sure that all relevant jurisdictions have been searched. This possibility, together with the expense and
delay of conducting searches in a variety of jurisdictions, could hinder
the purchase and sale of copyrights, frustrating Congress's policy that
copyrights be readily transferable in commerce.

This is the reasoning adopted by the Ninth Circuit in Danning v.
Pacific Propeller. *Danning* held that 49 U.S.C. App. §1403(a), the Federal
Aviation Act's provision for recording conveyances and the creation of

liens and security interests in civil aircraft, preempts state filing provisions. 620 F.2d at 735-736. According to *Danning*,

> [t]he predominant purpose of the statute was to provide one central place for the filing of [liens on aircraft] and thus eliminate the need, given the highly mobile nature of aircraft and their appurtenances, for the examination of State and County records.

620 F.2d at 735-736. Copyrights, even more than aircraft, lack a clear situs; tangible, movable goods such as airplanes must always exist at some physical location; they may have a home base from which they operate or where they receive regular maintenance. The same cannot be said of intangibles. As noted above, this lack of an identifiable situs militates against individual state filings and in favor of a single, national registration scheme.

Moreover, as discussed at greater length below, see pp. 205–207 infra, the Copyright Act establishes its own scheme for determining priority between conflicting transferees, one that differs in certain respects from that of Article Nine. Under Article Nine, priority between holders of conflicting security interests in intangibles is generally determined by who perfected his interest first. UCC §9312(5). By contrast, section 205(d) of the Copyright Act provides:

> As between two conflicting transfers, the one executed first prevails if it is recorded, in the manner required to give constructive notice under subsection (c), *within one month after its execution in the United States or within two months after its execution outside the United States*, or at any time before recordation in such manner of the later transfer . . .

17 U.S.C. §205(d) (emphasis added). Thus, unlike Article Nine, the Copyright Act permits the effect of recording with the Copyright Office to relate back as far as two months.

Because the Copyright Act and Article Nine create different priority schemes, there will be occasions when different results will be reached depending on which scheme was employed. The availability of filing under the UCC would thus undermine the priority scheme established by Congress with respect to copyrights. This type of direct interference with the operation of federal law weighs heavily in favor of preemption. See generally Bonito Boats, Inc. v. Thunder Craft Boats, Inc., 489 U.S. 141, 109 S. Ct. 971, 103 L. Ed. 2d 118 (1989).

The bankruptcy court below nevertheless concluded that security interests in copyrights could be perfected by filing either with the copyright office or with the secretary of state under the UCC, making a tongue-in-cheek analogy to the use of a belt and suspenders to hold up a pair of pants. According to the bankruptcy court, because either device is equally useful, one should be free to choose which one to wear. With all due respect, this court finds the analogy inapt. There is no legitimate reason why pants should be held up in only one particular manner: Individuals and public modesty are equally served by either device, or even by a safety pin or a piece of rope; all that really matters is that the job gets done. Registration schemes are different in that the *way* notice is given is precisely what matters. To the extent interested parties are confused as to which system is being employed, this increases the level of uncertainty and multiplies the risk of error, exposing creditors to the possibility that they might get caught with their pants down.

A recordation scheme best serves its purpose where interested parties can obtain notice of all encumbrances by referring to a single, precisely defined recordation system. The availability of parallel state recordation systems that could put parties on constructive notice as to encumbrances on copyrights would surely interfere with the effectiveness of the federal recordation scheme. Given the virtual absence of dual recordation schemes in our legal system, Congress cannot be presumed to have contemplated such a result. The court therefore concludes that any state recordation system pertaining to interests in copyrights would be preempted by the Copyright Act.

2

State law leads to the same conclusion. Article Nine of the Uniform Commercial Code establishes a comprehensive scheme for the regulation of security interests in personal property and fixtures. By superseding a multitude of pre-Code security devices, it provides "a simple and unified structure within which the immense variety of present-day secured financing transactions can go forward with less cost and greater certainty." UCC §9101, Official Comment. However, Article Nine is not all encompassing; under the "step back" provision of UCC §9104, Article Nine does not apply "[t]o a security interest subject to any statute of the United States to the extent that such statute governs the rights of parties to and third parties affected by transactions in particular types of property."

For most items of personal property, Article Nine provides that security interests must be perfected by filing with the office of the secretary of state in which the debtor is located. See UCC §§9302(1), 9401(1)(c). Such filing, however, is not "necessary or effective to perfect a security interest in property subject to . . . [a] statute or treaty of the United States which provides for a national or international registration . . . or which specifies a place of filing different from that specified in [Article Nine] for filing of the security interest." UCC §9302(3)(a). When a national system for recording security interests exists, the Code treats compliance with that system as "equivalent to the filing of a financing statement under [Article Nine,] and a security interest in property subject to the statute or treaty can be perfected only by compliance therewith. . . ." UCC §9302(4).

As discussed above, section 205(a) of the Copyright Act clearly does establish a national system for recording transfers of copyright interests, and it specifies a place of filing different from that provided in Article Nine. Recording in the Copyright Office gives nationwide, constructive notice to third parties of the recorded encumbrance. Except for the fact that the Copyright Office's indices are organized on the basis of the title and registration number, rather than by reference to the identity of the debtor, this system is nearly identical to that which Article Nine generally provides on a statewide basis. And, lest there be any doubt, the drafters of the UCC specifically identified the Copyright Act as establishing the type of national registration system that would trigger the §9302(3) and (4) step back provisions:

> Examples of the type of federal statute referred to in [UCC §9302(3)(a)] are the provisions of [Title 17] (copyrights). . . .

UCC §9302, Official Comment ¶8; see G. Gilmore, Security Interests in Personal Property §17.3, at 545 (1965) ("[t]here can be no doubt that [the Copyright Act was] meant to be within the description of §9-302(3)(a)").

The court therefore concludes that the Copyright Act provides for national registration and "specifies a place of filing different from that specified in [Article Nine] for filing of the security interest." UCC §9302(3)(a). Recording in the U.S. Copyright Office, rather than filing a financing statement under Article Nine, is the proper method for perfecting a security interest in a copyright.

In reaching this conclusion, the court rejects City Bank & Trust Co. v. Otto Fabric, Inc., 83 B.R. 780 (D. Kan. 1988), and In re Transportation Design & Technology Inc., 48 B.R. 635 (Bankr. S.D. Cal. 1985), insofar as they are germane to the issues presented here. Both cases held that, under the UCC, security interests in patents need not be recorded in the U.S. Patent and Trademark Office to be perfected as against lien creditors because the federal statute governing patent assignments does not specifically provide for liens:

> Applications for patent, patents, or any interest therein, shall be assignable in law by an instrument in writing. The applicant, patentee, or his assigns or legal representatives may in like manner grant and convey an exclusive right under his application for patent, or patents, to the whole or any specified part of the United States. . . .
>
> An assignment, grant or conveyance shall be void as against *any subsequent purchaser or mortgagee* for a valuable consideration, without notice, unless it is recorded in the Patent and Trademark Office within three months from its date or prior to the date of such subsequent purchase or mortgage.

35 U.S.C. §261 (emphasis added).

According to *In re Transportation*, because section 261's priority scheme only provides for a "subsequent purchaser or mortgagee for valuable consideration," it does not require recording in the Patent and Trademark Office to perfect against lien creditors. See 48 B.R. at 639. Likewise, *City Bank* held that "the failure of the statute to mention protection against lien creditors suggests that it is unnecessary to record an assignment or other conveyance with the Patent Office to protect the appellant's security interest against the trustee." 83 B.R. at 782.

These cases misconstrue the plain language of UCC section 9104, which provides for the voluntary step back of Article Nine's provisions "*to the extent* [federal law] governs the rights of [the] parties." UCC §9104(a) (emphasis added). Thus, when a federal statute provides for a national system of recordation or specifies a place of filing different from that in Article Nine, the methods of perfection specified in Article Nine are supplanted by that national system; compliance with a national system of recordation is equivalent to the filing of a financing statement under Article Nine. UCC §9302(4). Whether the federal statute also provides a priority scheme different from that in Article Nine is a separate issue, addressed below. Compliance with a national registration scheme is necessary for perfection regardless of whether federal law governs priorities. Cap Fed's security interest in the copyrights of the films in NPI's library and the receivables they have generated therefore is unperfected.

B. Effect of Failing to Record with the Copyright Office

Having concluded that Cap Fed should have, but did not, record its security interest with the Copyright Office, the court must next determine whether NPI as a debtor in possession can subordinate Cap Fed's interest and recover it for the benefit of the bankruptcy estate. As a debtor in possession, NPI has nearly all of the powers of a bankruptcy trustee, see 11 U.S.C. §1107(a), including the authority to set aside preferential or fraudulent transfers, as well as transfers otherwise voidable under applicable state or federal law. See 11 U.S.C. §§544, 547, 548.

Particularly relevant is the "strong arm clause" of 11 U.S.C. §544(a)(1), which, in respect to personal property in the bankruptcy estate, gives the debtor in possession every right and power state law confers upon one who has acquired a lien by legal or equitable proceedings. If, under the applicable law, a judicial lien creditor would prevail over an adverse claimant, the debtor in possession prevails; if not, not. Wind Power Systems, Inc. v. Cannon Financial Group, Inc. (In re Wind Power Systems, Inc.), 841 F.2d 288, 293 (9th Cir. 1988); Angeles Real Estate Co. v. Kerxton (In re Construction General Inc.), 737 F.2d 416, 418 (4th Cir. 1984). A lien creditor generally takes priority over unperfected security interests in estate property because, under Article Nine, "an unperfected security interest is subordinate to the rights of . . . [a] person who becomes a lien creditor before the security interest is perfected." UCC §9301(1)(b). But, as discussed previously, the UCC does not apply to the extent a federal statute "governs the rights of parties to and third parties affected by transactions in particular types of property." UCC §9104. Section 205(d) of the Copyright Act is such a statute, establishing a priority scheme between conflicting transfers of interests in a copyright:

> As between two conflicting *transfers*, the one executed first prevails if it is recorded, in the manner required to give constructive notice under subsection (c), within one month after its execution in the United States or within two months after its execution outside the United States, or at any time before recordation in such manner of the later transfer. Otherwise, the later *transfer* prevails if recorded first in such manner, and if taken in good

faith, for valuable consideration or on the basis of a binding promise to pay royalties, and without notice of the earlier *transfer*.

17 U.S.C. §205(d) (emphasis added). The federal priority scheme pre-empts the state priority scheme.

Section 205(d) does not expressly address the rights of lien creditors, speaking only in terms of competing transfers of copyright interests. To determine whether NPI, as a hypothetical lien creditor, may avoid Cap Fed's unperfected security interest, the court must therefore consider whether a judicial lien is a transfer as that term is used in the Copyright Act.

As noted above, the Copyright Act recognizes transfers of copyright ownership "in whole or in part by any means of conveyance or by op-eration of law." 17 U.S.C. §201(d)(1). Transfer is defined broadly to in-clude any "assignment, mortgage, exclusive license, or any other conveyance, alienation, or hypothecation of a copyright . . . whether or not it is limited in time or place of effect." 17 U.S.C. §101. A judicial lien creditor is a creditor who has obtained a lien "by judgment, levy, se-questration, or other legal or equitable process or proceeding." 11 U.S.C. §101(32). Such a creditor typically has the power to seize and sell property held by the debtor at the time of the creation of the lien in order to satisfy the judgment or, in the case of general intangibles such as copyrights, to collect the revenues generated by the intangible as they come due. See, e.g., Cal. Civ. P. Code §§701.510, 701.520, 701.640. . . . Thus, while the cre-ation of a lien on a copyright may not give a creditor an immediate right to control the copyright, it amounts to a sufficient transfer of rights to come within the broad definition of transfer under the Copyright Act. See Phoenix Bond & Indemnity Co. v. Shamblin (In re Shamblin), 890 F.2d 123, 127 n.7 (9th Cir. 1989) (under the Bankruptcy Code, "[t]his court has consistently treated the creation of liens on the debtor's property as a transfer").

Cap Fed contends that, in order to prevail under 17 U.S.C. §205(d), NPI must have the status of a bona fide purchaser, rather than that of a judicial lien creditor. See Pistole v. Mellor (In re Mellor), 734 F.2d 1396, 1401 n.4 (9th Cir. 1984) (judicial lien creditor does not have the same rights as a bona fide purchaser); cf. 11 U.S.C. §544(a)(3) (for real estate in the bankruptcy estate, debtor in possession has the rights of a bona fide purchaser). Cap Fed, in essence, is arguing that the term transfer in sec-tion 205(d) refers only to consensual transfers. For the reasons expressed above, the court rejects this argument. The Copyright Act's definition of transfer is very broad and specifically includes transfers by operation of law. 17 U.S.C. §201(d)(1). The term is broad enough to encompass not merely purchasers, but lien creditors as well. NPI therefore is entitled to priority if it meets the statutory good faith, notice, consideration and re-cording requirements of section 205(a). As the hypothetical lien creditor, NPI is deemed to have taken in good faith and without notice. See 11 U.S.C. §544(a). The only remaining issues are whether NPI could have recorded its interest in the Copyright Office and whether it obtained its lien for valuable consideration.

In order to obtain a lien on a particular piece of property, a creditor who has received a money judgment in the form of a writ of execution must prepare a notice of levy that specifically identifies the property to be encumbered and the consequences of that action. See Cal. Civ. P. Code §699.540. If such a notice identifies a federal copyright or the receivables generated by such a copyright, it and the underlying writ of execution, constitute "document[s] pertaining to a copyright" and, therefore, are capable of recordation in the Copyright Office. See 17 U.S.C. §205(a); Compendium of Copyright Office Practices II ¶¶1602–1603 (identifying which documents the Copyright Office will accept for filing). Because these documents could be recorded in the Copyright Office, NPI as debtor in possession will be deemed to have done so.

Finally, contrary to Cap Fed's assertion, a trustee or debtor in possession is deemed to have given valuable consideration for its judicial lien. Section 544(a)(1) provides:

> The trustee [or debtor in possession] shall have, as of the commencement of the case . . . the rights and powers of, or may avoid any transfer of property of the debtor or any obligation incurred by the debtor that is voidable by . . . a creditor *that extends credit to the debtor at the time of the commencement of the case*, and that obtains, at such time and with respect to such credit, a judicial lien on all property on which a creditor on a simple contract could have obtained such a judicial lien. . . .

11 U.S.C. §544(a)(1) (emphasis added). The act of extending credit, of course, constitutes the giving of valuable consideration. See First Maryland Leasecorp v. M/V Golden Egret, 764 F.2d 749, 753 (11th Cir. 1985); United States v. Cahall Bros., 674 F.2d 578, 581 (6th Cir. 1982). In addition, the trustee's lien—like that of any other judgment creditor—is deemed to be in exchange for the claim that formed the basis of the underlying judgment, a claim that is extinguished by the entry of the judgment.

Because NPI meets all of the requirements for subsequent transferees to prevail under 17 U.S.C. §205(d)—a transferee who took in good faith, for valuable consideration and without notice of the earlier transfer—Cap Fed's unperfected security interest in NPI's copyrights and the receivables they generated is trumped by NPI's hypothetical judicial lien. NPI may therefore avoid Cap Fed's interest and preserve it for the benefit of the bankruptcy estate.

Conclusion

The judgment of the bankruptcy court is reversed. The case is ordered remanded for a determination of which movies in NPI's library are the subject of valid copyrights.

Questions

1.   What are the facts of this case (in your own words)?
2.   Do you agree with the court's analysis? Why, or why not?
3.   Why would the outcome be different if the security interest involved a patent instead of a copyright?
4.   Based on this case, how would you protect a client's security interest?

Suggested Case References

1.   For a discussion of the difference between an implied warranty of merchantability and an implied warranty of fitness for a particular use, read Crysco Oilfield Services Inc. v. Hutchison-Hayes International Inc., 913 F.2d 850 (10th Cir. 1990).

2.   A security agreement specified that the debtor's collateral could be his inventory of hogs, but it did not specifically state that it would include after-acquired property. Does this failure to specify after-acquired property destroy the creditor's ability to have a floating lien? Coats State Bank v. Grey, 902 F.2d 1479 (10th Cir. 1990).

9 Third Party Contracts

CHAPTER OVERVIEW

Typically, when a person enters into a contractual agreement, she expects to perform or deliver the consideration she has promised and to receive the consideration the other contracting party has promised her. Although this is the most usual contractual arrangement, there are situations in which the person who actually entered into the contract does not receive the promised consideration or does not perform her contractual promises herself.

One form of contract in which the promisee does not receive or expect to receive the bargained-for consideration is known as a third party beneficiary contract. In this contractual arrangement, the parties do not intend to contract to benefit themselves but intend to benefit some outside third person. All of the general contract rules and provisions still apply. The only difference between this and what would be considered the more usual contractual situation is that one of the parties to the contract agrees to convey the consideration not to the other contracting party, but to someone the other contracting party has designated when the contract was formed. In other words, the promissor conveys the consideration not to the promisee, but to a third party who, as a consequence, is benefiting from the contractual agreement.

If, in a similar situation, one party to the contract wishes, after the contract was formed, to have the consideration given not to her but to some third person, she may do so under certain circumstances. In this situation, known as an *assignment*, the promisor agrees, after formation of the contract, to convey the consideration not to the promisee but to the promisee's designee. Because this changes the promisor's contractual obligations, this type of arrangement may only be effectuated if the promisor agrees.

Finally, there are times when the promisor needs or desires assistance in fulfilling his contractual promise. Although a person may not relinquish his contractual obligation without being in default, in most instances a promisor may have some third person assist him in completing his promise. This situation is known as a *delegation*. Unlike the first two situations indicated above, this third person, the promisor's helper, receives no benefit from the contract itself.

When drafting and interpreting contract provisions, it is important to keep the above in mind. There are special contractual clauses that create or permit these arrangements, and these clauses become determinative of the contracting parties' rights and obligations under the contract. In each type of situation, the outside party may be entitled to some equitable relief for enforcement of the contract, even though he is not a contracting party himself.

Third Party Beneficiary Contracts: Generally

Third party beneficiary contracts are agreements in which the original intent of one of the contracting parties, when entering into the contractual arrangement, is to have the promised-for consideration pass not to her, but to some outside person. Generally, there are two reasons why a contracting party would desire this type of arrangement, and consequently, third party beneficiary contracts are divided into two categories.

The first category is a **third party creditor beneficiary** contract. In this type of third party contract, the purpose of the promisee's agreement is to extinguish a debt or obligation owed to some third person. In other words, the promisee was already obligated to the third person, his creditor, and the purpose for which he entered into the contract was to receive some consideration that would terminate his debt to the creditor.

 EXAMPLE:

Last month Peter had extraordinary expenses and didn't have enough money to pay his rent. Wendy loaned Peter $500 to help him meet his expenses, and he promised to repay the loan this month with interest. Now, Peter has met all his regular expenses but doesn't have the money to repay the loan. To repay Wendy, Peter agrees to sell his CD player to Ralph, and Peter asks Ralph to give the money for the CD player to Wendy. Wendy agrees. This is a third party creditor beneficiary contract. The reason Peter entered into the sales contract with Ralph was to repay his debt to Wendy. Wendy was the person Peter intended to benefit from his contract with Ralph.

The second category of third party beneficiary contracts is a **third party donee beneficiary** contract. As the name might indicate, the purpose of this contract is to confer a gift on a third person. The promisee of the contract is under no preexisting obligation to the third person but wishes to give the third person a present. Under current legal terminology both the creditor and donee beneficiaries are called **intended beneficiaries.**

 EXAMPLE:

Peter suddenly comes into some money. He is still grateful to Wendy for helping him out when he had financial difficulties. Even though his debt to Wendy is now extinguished, he feels that he would like to do something nice for her. While watching a shopping channel on television, Peter sees a bracelet he thinks Wendy would like. He calls the station and orders the bracelet, telling the vendor that the bracelet is a gift. He directs the vendor to send the bracelet to Wendy and to bill him. This is a third party donee beneficiary contract. The reason Peter entered into the contract with the television vendor was to convey a gift to Wendy. He owed no debt, and he never intended the bracelet for himself.

The most important aspect of a third party beneficiary contract is the intent of the parties when the contract is formed. For the contract to be considered a third party beneficiary contract, it must be evidenced that the purpose of the contract is to benefit a person not a party to the contractual agreement. If the desire to benefit some outside person comes about after the contract already exists, it is not a third party beneficiary contract (but an assignment, which will be discussed later).

Bear in mind the specific terminology that is being used in a third party beneficiary contract. In every contractual situation, there must be a mutuality of consideration; in all bilateral contracts each party to the contract is both a promisor and a promisee. He is a promisor for the consideration he promises to convey, and a promisee for the consideration the other party promises to give him. When describing third party beneficiary contracts, the term **promisee** designates the person who entered the contract intending to benefit the third person. He is expecting to have the consideration he was promised conveyed to the outsider. **Promisor** describes the party conveying the consideration to the third person, because of the promisee's wishes and intent when contracting. This transfer to the third person is part of the promise the promisor makes when entering into the contract.

EXAMPLE:

In the examples discussed above with Peter, Wendy, Ralph, and the shopping channel, in both instances the contract was between Peter and either Ralph or the vendor. In the first instance, Peter promised to convey his CD player to Ralph, and Ralph promised to convey the purchase price of the CD player to Wendy. Peter is the promisee for the receipt of the money, and Ralph is the promisor who has agreed to convey the cash to Wendy as part of his contractual promise to Peter. In the second instance, Peter promised to pay for the bracelet that the vendor promised to convey to Wendy. Peter is the promisor for payment, and the promisee for the receipt of the merchandise. The shopping channel is the promisee of Peter's payment, and the promisor for sending the jewelry. In each instance, Wendy, the third party, is receiving the consideration from Peter's promisors.

In a third party beneficiary contract, the third party, although not a contracting party, is given certain rights with respect to the contract. Legally, the beneficiary may be able to bring the contracting parties into court to have the contract enforced in his favor. This is true even though the beneficiary is neither a party to the agreement nor has any enforceable obligation with respect to the agreement. To understand the rights and obligations that attach to the two categories of third party beneficiary contracts, each will be discussed separately.

When analyzing the enforceable rights of a third party beneficiary, it is important to note that enforceable rights attach only to third persons intended primarily to benefit from the contract. Should a third person benefit secondarily from the contract, i.e., his benefit was not the intent of the contract, that person is known as an **incidental beneficiary** and has no enforceable rights. For example, in the situation given above, the shipper the shopping channel uses to send its merchandise benefits from the channel's sales contract, but this benefit is totally incidental to the contract itself.

Third Party Creditor Beneficiary Contracts

The starting point for any discussion of a third party creditor beneficiary contract is the determination that the promisee owes some debt to a third person. The debt must be in existence prior to the third party contract being formed. Remember, the purpose of a third party creditor beneficiary contract is to extinguish a debt owed to a third person, so that debt must in fact exist.

Because the contract is formed to benefit this creditor, the creditor is considered to be a **real party in interest.** He becomes the focal point of the central contract between the debtor and the promisor. As a real party in interest, he may be entitled to enforce the contract if the promisor does not fulfill his contractual obligation.

To have enforceable rights, it must first be demonstrated that those rights exist. This means that the creditor must show that his rights have **vested** (become enforceable in a court of law). For a third party creditor beneficiary, the rights in the contract vest as soon as he detrimentally relies on the contract's existence.

What constitutes "detrimental reliance"? As discussed previously, detrimental reliance usually means some economic loss suffered in reliance on the promise. For creditor beneficiaries, this detrimental reliance is simply assumed to be his willingness to accept payment from the promisor. Because the debt must exist as a prerequisite to the formation of a third party creditor beneficiary contract, the creditor can always go to court to enforce the debt against the debtor/promisee. Because the creditor is forestalling taking that action in reliance on the contract between the debtor and the promisor, just as with an accord and satisfaction, it is deemed sufficient to vest his rights in the third party contract. Also, as soon as the intended beneficiary is aware of the contract, or institutes a suit to enforce it, the beneficiary's rights are deemed vested.

 ### EXAMPLE:

Pedro enrolls in his city's Paralegal Institute. Pedro doesn't have the money for the tuition but arranges for a student loan from a local bank at the school's suggestion. The loan contract is a third party creditor beneficiary contract, entered into between Pedro and the bank for the purpose of paying Pedro's debt to the Institute. The Institute's willingness to take payment from the bank on Pedro's behalf constitutes its reliance on the contract, and its rights have vested.

Once the third party creditor beneficiary's rights have vested, she has enforceable rights. This means that she may sue the promisor of the contract if the promisor fails to convey the consideration. Because the creditor is the real party in interest, and the promisor has agreed to convey the consideration to her, failure to fulfill this promise is a breach of contract that the real party in interest can sue to have remedied.

 ### EXAMPLE:

In the example given above with Peter, Wendy, and Ralph, if Ralph does not give Wendy the money he promised in his contract with Peter, Wendy can take Ralph to court. Because Ralph's promise is to convey the money to Wendy, his failure to do so is a breach. As the real party in interest, Wendy is the one whom the breach injures.

Consequently, she has the right to enforce the contract against Ralph.

Should, for whatever reason, the creditor fail to get satisfaction from the promisor, he can always sue the promisee. Why? Because the promisee is still the debtor of the third party, and until that debt is extinguished he remains liable on the original obligation.

EXAMPLE:

Wendy discovers that Ralph is insolvent. Because Peter still owes her $500 plus interest, she can enforce her claim directly against Peter because the third party contract has not extinguished his debt.

Of course, the creditor is limited to just one recovery. She cannot sue both the debtor and the promisor and recover from both. Recovery from one excuses the other.

If the creditor attempts to enforce his rights under the contract, the promisor can defend himself by asserting any defense he might have against the debtor/promisee. Because it is the contract between the debtor/promisee and the promisor that is in question, any defense that would render the contract unenforceable relieves the promisor of any obligation to the creditor.

EXAMPLES:

1. When Wendy sues Ralph for the purchase price of the CD player, Ralph can defend by asserting that Peter never gave him the CD player, or that the CD player delivered was not the one promised. In each instance, Ralph is claiming that Peter is in default, and Peter's default relieves Ralph of his contractual obligations to Peter. Because this obligation was to convey money to Wendy, if Ralph prevails, he is under no obligation to Wendy.

2. Pedro starts classes, but the Institute has not received the tuition from the bank. The Institute attempts to enforce the loan contract between Pedro and the bank. The bank defends by proving that its obligation was conditioned on Pedro's submitting proof of attendance, which he has failed to do. Consequently, the bank is not obligated under its loan agreement, and the Institute must look to Pedro directly for the tuition.

In addition to the third party creditor beneficiary having enforceable rights, the contracting parties themselves always have enforceable rights against each other. The promisee and the promisor of the contract can sue each other to have the contract enforced.

 EXAMPLE:

When Wendy attempts to collect from Peter, Peter discovers that Ralph has not lived up to his obligation. Provided that Peter did in fact convey to Ralph the CD player he promised, Peter can sue Ralph to have the contract enforced because he, Peter, is a contracting party.

To summarize, in a third party creditor beneficiary contract, the third party creditor beneficiary has vested, enforceable rights in the contract once he has detrimentally relied on the contract. This detrimental reliance can simply take the form of agreeing to accept payment from the promisor rather than suing the debtor for payment. Once these rights have vested, the creditor beneficiary can sue the promisor of the contract to have these rights enforced. The promisor can defend by asserting any claim he may have against the promisee. The creditor may also sue the debtor on the original obligation if he receives no satisfaction from the promisor. Finally, the promisor and promisee of the contract can sue each other to have the contract provisions enforced.

Third Party Donee Beneficiary Contracts

The major difference between third party creditor beneficiary and third party donee beneficiary contracts is the element of the underlying debt. To have a creditor beneficiary contract, it must be shown that a debt exists between the promisee and the creditor. To have a donee beneficiary contract, it must be shown that the promisee intended to confer a gift on the donee (she is not repaying a debt).

Because the purpose of the contract is to convey a gift to the donee, the donee beneficiary is considered to be the real party in interest to the contract. As the real party in interest, she may have enforceable rights with respect to the contract once it is established that those rights have vested. For a third party donee beneficiary, the rights in the contract vest once she learns of the existence of the contract. No detrimental reliance is necessary.

 EXAMPLE:

In the example given above with Wendy, Peter, and the shopping channel, when Peter calls Wendy to tell her that she should expect a bracelet that he has bought for her, her rights have vested. When two weeks pass without the bracelet arriving, Wendy can call the vendor to complain and to find out when the bracelet will arrive.

Once the donee beneficiary's rights have vested, she can sue the promisor of the contract to have the promise enforced. Just as with third party creditor beneficiary contracts, the promisor can defend against claims of the third party donee by asserting any defenses he would have against the promisee of the contract.

EXAMPLES:

1. Several weeks pass, and Wendy still hasn't received the bracelet. She sues the shopping channel to have the contract enforced. The vendor can defend by proving that Peter attempted to pay for the bracelet with a check that bounced. Because Peter breached his promise to the shopping channel, the vendor is relieved of its contractual obligations.

2. Babs takes out a life insurance policy on her life with Connecticut Life, Inc., and names her best friend, Abdul, as the beneficiary. Babs is lost at sea, and Abdul claims the insurance. The company can defend by saying that Babs failed to make the premium payments, or that there is no proof that Babs is actually dead.

Unlike a third party creditor beneficiary, because there is no obligation between the donee and the promisee, the donee beneficiary, under contract law, cannot sue the donor/promisee for enforcement of the contract. A promise to give a gift, unless a charitable donation, is not enforceable under contract law. However, if the donee can show that she detrimentally relied on the promised gift, under property law concepts, she may be able to recover against the donor.

EXAMPLE:

When Peter tells Wendy about the bracelet, Wendy, in expectation of its arrival, buys a dress especially designed to show off the jewelry. When the bracelet doesn't arrive, Wendy may be able to recover the cost of the dress from Peter if she can prove that she only purchased it in expectation of the bracelet, and without the bracelet she has no use for the dress. Remember, the claim is based on property law concepts, and recovery may be permitted under the court's equitable jurisdiction to prevent injustice. It is not a contract case.

Of course, just as with creditor beneficiary contracts, the promisor and promisee of the contract can always sue each other for enforcement of the contract provisions.

 EXAMPLE:

When Peter finds out the shopping channel failed to send the bracelet to Wendy, he can sue the vendor directly. If Peter can show a cancelled check for payment, the vendor's original defense would fail, and it would have to ship out the bracelet.

In summary, a third party donee beneficiary contract is created for the purpose of conveying a gift to the third party. The donee has vested rights in the contract once she learns of its existence. Once the rights have vested, the donee can sue the promisor to have the contract enforced. Under contract law, the donee has no enforceable rights against the promisee (there is no consideration for a gift). The promisor and promisee of the contract can sue each other to have the contract enforced.

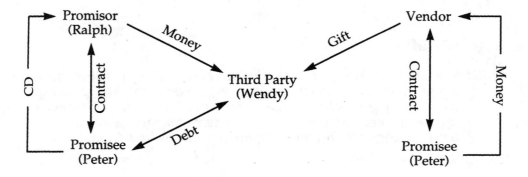

Third Party Beneficiary Contracts

Creditor Beneficiary	*Donee Beneficiary*
Created to extinguish debt	Created to confer gift
Rights vest with detrimental reliance*	Rights vest on knowledge*
Can sue promisor or promisee	Can sue promisor only
Promisor/promisee can defend by asserting any claim he has against the other contracting party	Promisor can defend by asserting any claim he has against promisee

*With respect to the vesting of third party beneficiary rights, some courts have adopted the approach that a third party beneficiary's rights vest, regardless of whether he is a creditor or donee beneficiary, only if he assents to the contract, sues to have it

Assignment

An **assignment** is the transfer of a promisee's rights under an existing contract. At first blush, it appears to be very similar to third party beneficiary contracts. Although they are similar, there are two important differences between assignments and third party beneficiary contracts:

1. Assignments come into existence *after* the original contract is created. The benefit to the third party is not the reason the contract was formed; it is an afterthought.
2. Because assignments are created *after* the original contract, a promisee may not assign his rights without the consent, express or implied, of the promisor.

Creating the Assignment

An assignment may be oral or written, subject to the requirements of the Statute of Frauds. If the basic contract must be in writing, so must the assignment.

 EXAMPLE:

Sharona and Vince enter into a written contract for the sale of Vince's house. After the contract is signed, Vince wants to transfer his right to receive the purchase price to his son. The contract permits assignments. Because the contract concerns an interest in real estate, both the contract and the assignment must be in writing.

A person may assign her rights to a contract either gratuitously or for consideration. In other words, the promisee may use the assignment to confer a gift or to fulfill an obligation under a separate contract.

 EXAMPLES:

1. In the example given above, Sharona decides to give the house as an anniversary gift to her parents. In writing, she assigns her right to receive the house's title to her parents. This is a gratuitous assignment.

---

enforced, or shows detrimental reliance. The standard followed by each jurisdiction should be specifically checked.

2. Sharona decides that she really doesn't want Vince's house, but her friend Wilma thinks that the house is "perfect." In writing, Sharona agrees to assign to Wilma her right to the title to Vince's house in consideration of Wilma giving Sharona $1000. This is an example of an assignment for consideration. Sharona is transferring her rights under her contract with Vince to fulfill her promise under her contract with Wilma.

The **assignor**, the person who is transferring the contract right, may also make a partial assignment of rights to the **assignee** (the transferee of the rights). An assignment need not be an all-or-nothing situation.

 EXAMPLE:

Fabio sold his tape deck to Tom for $30. Before he receives payment, Fabio assigns $15 to Leon to extinguish a debt he owes to Leon. The assignment is valid, even though it transferred only part of Fabio's rights.

However, not all contracts are capable of being assigned. There can be no assignment if the rights assigned consist of personal services or are dependent on the personal confidence or circumstances of the recipient.

 EXAMPLES:

1. Pavarotti has signed a contract with the New York Metropolitan Opera to perform *Pagliacci*. The Met cannot transfer its rights to the Omaha Civic Opera Company to have Pavarotti sing. Although Pavarotti may want to sing for the Met, he may not want to travel to Omaha. A person cannot be forced to perform for someone for whom he does not want to perform.

2. Sid purchases a health insurance policy from Connecticut Insurance, Inc. He cannot assign his contract's rights to Paul. The insurance company sold Sid the policy based on Sid's health and personal history; the same policy and premiums may not apply to someone with Paul's health and history. Because the insurance company's performance is dependent on the confidence it has in Sid's health, Sid cannot assign.

As with third party beneficiary contracts, if the assignment is valid, the assignee becomes the real party in interest and has enforceable rights against the promisor.

EXAMPLE:

In the situation given above, when Wilma gives Sharona $1000 for Sharona's rights to receive title to Vince's house, should Vince fail to transfer the title after payment of the purchase price, Wilma can take Vince to court to have the right enforced. Wilma is the real party in interest, the person who is entitled to receive the property.

Consent of the Promisor

Because the assignment comes into existence after the contract is formed, it is usually necessary to get the consent of the promisor because conveying the consideration to a third person was not what he agreed to under the contract. The assignment has the effect of changing the promisor's contractual obligation, and this can only be done with his consent.

Under the law, most contracts are assignable, subject to the exceptions noted above. However, if the effect of the assignment would be to *materially* change the promisor's obligation or duty, the promisor's consent must be specifically given. The consent may take the form of a clause in the contract in which the promisor agrees to an assignment. This clause can also specify the terms on which the promisor's consent is given.

EXAMPLE:

Rhoda leases an apartment from Brenda. In the lease, Brenda agrees that Rhoda may assign her rights to occupy the apartment, provided that written notice be given to Brenda at least 30 days prior to the assignee taking occupancy, and further provided that Brenda meets the assignee prior to the assignment taking effect. This clause gives Brenda's consent prospectively, provided certain conditions precedent are met. (See Chapter 7.)

What is considered a "material" change in the promisor's duty? The term is not specifically defined but is determined on a case-by-case basis. As long as the assignment does not create an unnecessary burden on the promisor, it most probably will not be considered material.

EXAMPLE:

In the earlier example, when Peter purchased a bracelet from a television shopping channel as a gift for Wendy, suppose Peter and Wendy have a falling out before the bracelet is mailed and before Wendy is told about the gift. Peter calls the vendor and tells the vendor to send the bracelet to Peter's mother instead of to Wendy. This is an assignment of Peter's right to receive the bracelet. Because the cost of shipping was already paid for, it makes no difference to the vendor who the recipient is, and so this would not materially affect its obligations. However, if Peter's mother lived in a foreign country that had stringent requirements regarding importing jewelry, and in order to ship the bracelet the vendor would have to fill out many custom forms, shipping documents, and pay extra mailing fees, Peter could not make the assignment without the vendor's consent. This assignment to Mom creates a wholly different obligation on the part of the seller.

Under general contract law principles, most contracts are assignable if they are silent on the point. However, the contract may state affirmatively that its rights may not be assigned. Such a "nonassignment clause" is a common provision in many contracts. This clause is usually inserted to protect the contracting parties. With this clause, each party to the contract knows exactly to whom he must perform his promise. There are no late surprises.

Effect of Assignment

The effect of an assignment is to transfer the assignor's rights to the assignee. The assignee thereby becomes a real party in interest with enforceable rights against the promisor.

If the assignor makes the assignment for consideration, as in the example of Sharona assigning her rights to Vince's house to Wilma for $1000, the assignment is irrevocable. When the promisor conveys the consideration to the assignee, he is relieved of all of his obligations under the original contract. However, if he conveys the consideration to anyone other than the assignee, he does so at his own risk.

 EXAMPLE:

After Sharona assigns her rights to Wilma, she informs Vince of the assignment. When Vince transfers the title to Wilma, he has fulfilled his contractual obligation to Sharona. Should Vince, however, transfer title to Sharona instead of Wilma, Wilma can take him into court. His obligation, after the assignment to which he has agreed, is to convey title to Wilma and to no one else.

On the other hand, if the assignment is gratuitous, the assignor may revoke, thereby cancelling the assignee's rights. Nevertheless, there are five situations in which a gratuitous assignment may become irrevocable:

1. delivery of a token chose;
2. writing;
3. estoppel;
4. performance; and
5. novation.

1. Delivery of a Token Chose. A **token chose** is merely some thing symbolic of the assignment. Although it may not have much monetary value, its existence is considered sufficient to make a gratuitous assignment irrevocable.

 EXAMPLE:

When Peter's mother hears about the bracelet Peter is having sent to her, she sends him a rose to commemorate the occasion. The rose is a token chose, and the assignment is irrevocable.

2. Writing. Simply putting the assignment in writing, for historical legal reasons, makes the gratuitous assignment irrevocable.

 EXAMPLE:

Peter writes to his mother telling her of the bracelet. The writing makes the assignment irrevocable.

3. Estoppel. If the assignee is attempting to assert a claim of **estoppel** because the assignment is a gift, the donee/assignee must show detrimental reliance on the promise to make it irrevocable.

EXAMPLE:

When Peter's mother hears about the bracelet, she buys a dress to show off the jewelry. This may create detrimental reliance that would bar, or estop, Peter from changing his mind.

4. Performance. It should be obvious that if the promisor has already performed and conveyed the consideration to the assignee before the assignor revokes, the assignment becomes irrevocable.

5. Novation. A **novation** is a substitution of parties in a contract; it is an interesting subset of assignments. Generally, assignments only transfer rights; they never transfer contractual obligations. In a novation, the original party to the contract is substituted by a third person, and the third person not only receives the benefits of the transferor but also assumes all of the transferor's obligations. The contract, after the novation, reads as though the original contracting party never existed.

EXAMPLE:

When Sharona decides that she does not want to purchase Vince's house, she asks to novate her contract to Wilma. Vince agrees, and now the contract reads as though it always was a contract for the sale of Vince's house to Wilma. Sharona's rights and obligations are totally transferred to Wilma.

Novations are very rare because the other party to the contract must agree to the novation. Whereas a person may be willing to contract with one person, she may not have the same reliance with someone else. With few exceptions, a person cannot be forced to enter into a contractual agreement with someone with whom she does not want to contract. Therefore, there must be a clause in the contract specifying the novation. Typically, these clauses indicate specific conditions that must be met before the other contracting party's assent to the substitution will be given.

Multiple Assignees

If an assignor assigns his rights to more than one assignee, a problem arises with respect to which assignee is entitled to the transferred rights. The general rule is that, with successive assignees, the first in time prevails, unless a later assignee has stronger equities (a greater equitable claim to the consideration).

EXAMPLE:

Lynn sells her car to Edward for $900. On Monday, Lynn assigns her right to receive the money to her mother as a birthday gift. The next day, Lynn buys Joan's pearl necklace and, instead of giving Joan a check, Lynn assigns to Joan her right to receive the $900 from Edward. When Mom and Joan both claim the money, the money will go to Joan. Even though Joan is a later assignee, because she gave consideration for the assignment she has the greater equity. Also, because the first assignment is gratuitous it may be revoked. Making the second assignment acts as a revocation of the first, revocable, assignment.

Take note that under the Uniform Commercial Code (UCC), assignees of certain types of contracts, specifically those involving a security interest, are required to file a notice of their claims with various county and state offices. This filing constitutes notice to all subsequent assignees that the property in question has been previously assigned and cuts off the rights of later assignees. For a complete discussion of UCC filing requirements, see Chapter 8, The Uniform Commercial Code, and Chapter 12, Drafting Simple Contracts.

An assignment is only a transference of the assignor's contractual rights. The assignor is still liable for her performance as promised under the contract. A person cannot assign obligations; she may only assign rights.

Delegation

Unlike third party beneficiary contracts and assignments, a **delegation** does not involve a transfer of rights. In a delegation, the promisor of a contract authorizes another person to perform some duty owed by the promisor under the contract. In other words, the promisor delegates someone to assist him in fulfilling his contractual obligations. The delegated person has absolutely no rights under the contract, unlike third party beneficiaries or assignees, nor does she have any obligations under the contract. The delegate's only obligation is to the promisor, and the promisor remains totally liable under the contract.

EXAMPLE:

Rosario is a paralegal working for attorney Janet. Janet's firm has accepted a case from a client, and to assist her Janet has given Rosario several tasks to perform. The firm is the promisor under the contract with the client, and Rosario and Janet are delegates. The firm remains liable to the client, and Rosario is responsible to Janet.

Generally, all nonpersonal duties owed under a contract may be delegated. If the duty does not involve the personal services of the promisor, unless otherwise denied under the contract, the promisor may delegate. However, it is important to remember that the promisor *always* remains liable under the contract if the delegate fails to perform.

EXAMPLES:

1. Mel has a contract with Warner Brothers to play a leading role in a new film. After the contract is signed, Mel realizes that he has another commitment. He delegates his responsibilities to Paul. This is invalid. The contract between Mel and Warner Brothers involves personal services and consequently may not be delegated.

2. In the situation with Rosario and Janet, Janet tells Rosario to complete a summons and complaint and to file them with the appropriate court. Rosario forgets, and the statute of limitations runs, barring the action. The firm is the one responsible to the client, and it may be charged with malfeasance. As the promisor, the firm remains personally liable for the promised performance under the contract. (This is not a contract for personal services because these types of agreements assume the firm will act by delegation, unless otherwise specified in the contract.)

In summary, only rights can be assigned, and only duties can be delegated. The only obligations under a contract that may be assigned are those that do not involve personal services or confidence, and the promisor always remains liable under the contract. The delegate has no rights or obligations under the contract. Finally, a delegation may be gratuitous, as in asking a friend for assistance, or may be contractual, as with a lawyer and a paralegal.

SAMPLE CLAUSES

1

Notwithstanding anything to the contrary contained herein, X may not assign any right, or delegate any duty hereunder without the prior written consent of Y. Y may assign any right, or delegate any duty hereunder to any person or entity controlled, directly or indirectly, by it or any of its shareholders.

The above clause is an example of a contractual provision in which both parties have some rights to assign or delegate, but the contractual provision to do so is unequal. X must first obtain written approval from Y, and should X not obtain such approval, the contract with respect to X is nonassignable and nondelegable. On the other hand, Y, in the clause itself, has the automatic right to assign or delegate, but the assignee and/or delegate is limited to certain described persons or entities. Therefore, as long as the assignee or delegate meets the definitional requirements of this provision, Y may assign or delegate without reference to X, and X must accept such action.

2   **Proxy**

The undersigned hereby constitutes and appoints X as his, her, or their proxy to cast the votes of the undersigned at all general, special, and adjourned meetings of the shareholders of Acme, Inc., from time to time and from year to year, when the undersigned is not present at any such meeting. This proxy shall be effective for one (1) year from the date hereof unless sooner revoked by written notice to the Secretary of the corporation.

Dated: /ss/_____

The above is an example of a general proxy used by a corporation shareholder. The contract in question is the contract the shareholder has with the corporation for the purchase of the shares; voting is a right incident to the stock ownership. The shareholder is assigning his right to vote to the proxy holder. Although not specified above, the proxy may be gratuitous or may be subject to its own contractual relation between the shareholder and the proxy holder (the proxy holder paying the share holder for the right to cast the vote). Remember, an assignment indicates a legal effect and is not necessarily determined by the words used. A proxy is an assignment, not a delegation, because it is a right of a shareholder, not a duty.

| 3 | **Life Insurance Policy**

The _____ Life Insurance Company agrees, subject to the terms and conditions of this policy, to pay the Amount shown on page ____ to the beneficiary upon receipt at its home office of proof of the death of the insured.

The above is a clause from a whole-life insurance policy. A life insurance policy is an example of the third party donee beneficiary contract. The insured contracts with the insurance company (the promisor); the insured promises to pay the stated premiums; and the insurer, conditioned upon proof of the insured's death, promises to pay the policy amount to the beneficiary. After the insured's death, the beneficiary has enforceable rights against the insurer should the insurer fail to pay. The insurer can always defend by proving the insured failed to meet the premiums or lied about his age or physical condition, by showing that proof of death was not given, or by using any other defense against the insured's meeting the contract provisions.

CHAPTER SUMMARY

Not every party to a contract is the person who will receive the contract rights or who will perform the contractual obligations. There are several situations in which some outside individual will either reap the benefit of the contract or will perform the obligation imposed by the agreement.

A third party beneficiary contract is formed for the express purpose of benefiting some noncontracting party. This noncontracting party is intended to receive the contract right as the repayment of a debt owed to him by the promisee or as a gift to him from the promisee. In the first instance, this noncontracting party is known as a third party creditor beneficiary; in the second instance, the noncontracting party is a third party donee beneficiary. Once the contract right vests in this third person, he becomes the real party in interest and has enforceable rights against the promisor. The promisor can defend against suits instituted by the third party by asserting any defense he may have against the promisee. If the underlying contract is unenforceable, the third party beneficiary's rights are likewise incapable of enforcement. The creditor beneficiary may proceed against the promisee to enforce the original debt the promisee owed to him. Donee beneficiaries may proceed against the promisee only if the donee can prove detrimental reliance based on the third party beneficiary contract.

If the contract is already in existence when one of the parties wishes to transfer rights under the agreement, such transference of rights is known as an assignment. In an assignment, the assignee becomes the recipient of rights to a contract to which she was not an original party. Assignments can be distinguished from third party beneficiary contracts by determining the underlying purpose behind the contract's formation. If the contract was formed to benefit a third person, it is a third party beneficiary contract; if the intent to benefit a third person arose after the contract existed, it is an assignment.

Just as with a third party beneficiary, an assignee becomes a real party in interest and has enforceable rights against the promisor of the original contract. The promisor can defend by asserting any claim he may have against the assignor. The assignee's ability to proceed against the assignor is dependent on the nature of the assignment itself, gratuitous or for consideration.

If instead of assigning rights, the promisor is attempting to have a third person assist him in fulfilling his contractual obligations, then he is making a delegation. Rights may be assigned; duties may be delegated. However, unlike third party beneficiaries and assignees, the delegate never becomes a real party in interest to the contract, and the promisor remains fully liable for her own performance under the contract.

SYNOPSIS

Third party beneficiary contracts
    1. Third party creditor beneficiary contracts

       a.   To extinguish existing debt
       b.   Rights vest on detrimental reliance
       c.   Creditor can sue promisor or promisee
       d.   Promisor can defend by asserting any defense he has against promisee
   2. Third party donee beneficiary contracts
       a.   To confer a gift
       b.   Rights vest on knowledge of contract
       c.   Donee can sue promisor
       d.   Promisor can defend by asserting any defense she has against promisee

Assignment
   1. Transfer of contract right
   2. Assignee becomes real party in interest
   3. Can be gratuitous or for consideration
   4. Gratuitous assignments can be revoked unless certain situations exist
   5. Assignments for consideration are irrevocable
   6. UCC filing requirements

Delegation
   1. Having a third party assist in fulfilling contractual obligation
   2. Cannot delegate contracts based on personal services or confidence
   3. Promisor remains liable for contractual obligations

Key Terms

Assignee: transferee of contractual right
Assignment: transference of contractual right by the promisee to a third person
Assignor: transferor of contractual right
Delegation: promisor having assistance in fulfilling contractual duties
Estoppel: equitable term; barring certain actions in the interest of fairness
Incidental beneficiary: person who benefits tangentially from a contract
Intended Beneficiary: third party donee or creditor beneficiary
Novation: substitution of a party to a contract; novated person takes over all rights and obligations under the contract
Promisee: one who receives consideration in a bilateral contract
Promisor: one who gives consideration in a bilateral contract
Real party in interest: person with enforceable contractual rights
Third party beneficiary contract: contract entered into for the purpose of benefiting someone not a party to the contract
Third party creditor beneficiary: person who receives the benefit of a contract in order to extinguish a debt owed him by the promisee

Third party donee beneficiary: person who receives the benefit of a
  contract in order to receive a gift from the promisee
Token chose: item of symbolic, rather than monetary, significance that
  makes a gratuitous assignment irrevocable
Vested: having a legally enforceable right

EXERCISES

1. How does an assignment differ from a delegation?
2. Give two examples of students being third party beneficiaries.
   Draft the clauses.
3. What factors would influence a third party beneficiary to sue the
   promisee rather than the promisor? Give examples.
4. How can you distinguish between a third party beneficiary and
   an incidental beneficiary?
5. Can a unilateral contract be a third party beneficiary contract?
   Explain.

Cases for Analysis

Not all contracts that benefit third persons are third party beneficiary
contracts. To exemplify the problems of interpreting such agreements, the
following case summaries are presented. Artist Management Office, Inc.
v. Worldvision Enterprises, Inc., discusses the rights of third party beneficiaries, and Matter of Gosmire Estate highlights a situation in which
familial relationships determine third party beneficiary status.

Artist Management Office, Inc. v.
Worldvision Enterprises, Inc.
1997 U.S. Dist. LEXIS 5144 (S.D. N.Y. 1997)

On October 15, 1996, five days before trial, defendants Worldvision
Enterprises, Inc. ("Worldvision"), Cecco Films, Ltd. ("Cecco") and Ales-
sandro Cecconi ("Cecconi") (collectively "movants") moved by Order to
Show Cause for judgment on the pleadings pursuant to Federal Rule of
Civil Procedure ("Fed. R. Civ. P.") 12(c) dismissing plaintiff Artist Management Office, Inc.'s ("AMO") claim for breach of contract, the fifth
claim in plaintiff's October 31, 1995 complaint. Plaintiff's opposition to
defendants' motion was to file a cross-motion on October 18, 1996, to
amend the complaint under Fed. R. Civ. P. 15(a) to add causes of action
against defendant Worldvision alleging a violation of plaintiff's rights as
a third-party beneficiary and alleging claims in quantum meruit and constructive trust.

Background

The complaint arises out of a contract ("Director's Agreement," Complaint Ex. A) between AMO, a Japanese corporation that is the managing agent of film director Nobuhiko Ohbayashi ("Ohbayashi"), and nonmoving defendant Momentous Events, Inc. ("MEI"), to provide Ohbayashi's services as a director for one segment of a six-hour made-for-television documentary series on Russia entitled "Momentous Events: Russia In the 90's." (Complaint p. 7.) Plaintiff alleges that MEI made unauthorized alterations which materially changed Ohbayashi's film prior to distribution. (Id. pp. 11-18.) The complaint also alleges that the final installment of $50,000 which was to be paid "within seven (7) days after delivery of all the Delivery Items of the Film to MEI" (Director's Agreement p. 5(E)) has not been paid. (Complaint p. 48.) Cecconi is President of Cecco Films which together with MEI contracted to give World-vision Enterprises, Inc. exclusive distribution rights to the documentary series (see "Distribution Agreement," Affirmation of Steven C. Beer, "Beer Aff." Ex. B).

Claiming that the defendants had improperly changed Ohbayashi's film so as to dilute his creative contribution, the complaint sought injunctive and monetary relief (1) for injury to plaintiff's business reputation since the "high quality and distinctive nature of its client's work has been diluted in the eyes of the public" in violation of New York General Business Law ("NY GBL") §368-d (first claim) (id. pp. 19-24); (2) for a violation of §43(a) of the Lanham Act, 15 U.S.C. §1125(a) by using Ohbayashi's name in connection with the distribution of the film and thus representing that the film was produced under Ohbayashi's creative control, "in that such misrepresentations are misleading and are likely to confuse the public" (second claim) (id. pp. 25-31); (3) for deceptive trade practices pursuant to NY GBL §349, by falsely advertising the film as Ohbayashi's unique creative product, which "deceived the film industry and the public" (third claim) (id. pp. 32-38); (4) for false advertising pursuant to NY GBL §350 by "representing to the film industry and public . . . that the Film reflects Ohbayashi's unique artistic talents" constituting a materially false misrepresentation causing injury to plaintiff's business reputation (fourth claim) (id. pp. 38-43); and (5) for breach of contract by refusing to make the final payment owed to AMO for delivery of the film (fifth claim) (id. pp. 44-51).

The Court consolidated the hearing on plaintiff's motion for a preliminary injunction on November 27-28, 1995 ("November 27-28, 1995 Hearing") with a trial on the merits as to AMO's claims for permanent injunctive relief on the first four claims. In an order dated December 4, 1995, the Court held that AMO was not entitled to any injunctive relief. (Declaration of Bruce R. Kelly, "Kelly Decl." Ex. D.)

Discussion

1. *Motion for Judgment on the Pleadings [Deleted]*

2. *Motion to Amend the Complaint [Deleted]*

a.   Third-Party Beneficiary

Under New York law, one who is not a party to a contract may bring an action for breach of contract if he or she is an intended beneficiary, and not merely an incidental beneficiary, of the contract. See, e.g., Banque Arabe et Internationale D'Investissement v. Bulk Oil (U.S.A.), Inc., 726 F. Supp. 1411, 1415 (S.D.N.Y. 1989). An "intended beneficiary" is one whose right to performance is "appropriate to effectuate the intention of the parties" to the contract and either the performance will satisfy a money debt obligation of the promisee to the beneficiary or "the circumstances indicate that the promisee intends to give the beneficiary the benefit of the promised performance."

Lake Placid Club Attached Lodges v. Elizabethtown Builders, Inc., 131 A.D.2d 159, 521 N.Y.S.2d 165, 166 (3d Dep't 1987) (quoting Restatement (Second) of Contracts §§301(1)(a) & 301(1)(b)). The putative third-party beneficiary must be "the real promisee," that is, "it must appear that the parties intended to recognize [the third party] as the primary party in interest and as privy to the promise." Worldwide Sugar Co. v. Royal Bank of Canada, 609 F. Supp. 19, 24 (S.D.N.Y.) aff'd, 751 F.2d 373 (2d Cir. 1984). The intention to benefit the third party need not be expressly stated in the contract. See Vista Co. v. Columbia Pictures Industries, Inc., 725 F. Supp. 1286, 1296 (S.D.N.Y. 1989).

Plaintiff asserts rights as a third-party beneficiary of Worldvision's Distribution Agreement with MEI/Cecco Films arising under the following clause: "The exploitation of the Program will be in accordance with [MEI's] obligations and obligations to third parties, including any obligation that [MEI] may have to the directors of each of the Episodes." (Distribution Agreement p. 13.) AMO argues that Worldvision violated this clause by distributing advertising which claimed Ohbayashi's segment of the series was his unique creation and also by licensing the documentary in at least 22 different countries despite knowledge that "MEI had not fulfilled its obligation to pay AMO." (Beer Aff. pp. 2, 5; Pl. Mem. in Opp. at 9.)

Defendant cites the paragraph in the Distribution Agreement that precedes the above-quoted clause as a more accurate description of Worldvision's obligations under the Distribution Agreement:

> Subject to the terms of this agreement . . . [Worldvision] . . . shall have the right to . . . disseminate, reproduce, print or publish the name, likeness, pictures, portraits and biographical materials of each person appearing in the material to be distributed, the producer, the director and title of the material to be distributed and excerpts from the material to be distributed. . . .

> Without in any way limiting the foregoing, the exploitation of the Program will be in accordance with [MEI's] obligations and obligations to third parties, including any obligation that you may have to the directors of each of the Episodes. . . .

(Distribution Agreement p. 13.) Worldvision also refers to Exhibit II of the Distribution Agreement entitled "Obligations to the Directors" which includes paragraphs entitled "Director Consultation Rights," "Musical Score," "Ownership Rights Acquired," and "Individual Directors." The director's right to payment by MEI is not mentioned on this list of "Obligations," nor is there any reference to any specific obligations by Worldvision to Ohbayashi.

The above clauses of the Distribution Agreement do not show that plaintiff was "the real promisee" and the intended beneficiary of payments made pursuant to the Distribution Agreement between MEI/Cecco Films and Worldvision. Worldvision is not alleged to have failed to carry out any of its obligations to MEI/Cecco Films under the Distribution Agreement. Plaintiff has not shown that either Worldvision or MEI intended to make a promise in the Distribution Agreement that guaranteed MEI's obligation to pay the directors, especially since "a promise to 'answer for the debt . . . of another person' must be in writing to be enforceable by a creditor," Van Brunt v. Rauschenberg, 799 F. Supp. 1467, 1472 (S.D.N.Y. 1992) (quoting NY GBL §5-701(a)(2) (McKinney 1989)), and there is no such written promise by Worldvision. Nowhere does the Distribution Agreement state that Worldvision may not promote the mini-series if MEI has not paid the directors. The clause plaintiff cites is insufficient to support a claim that Worldvision has an obligation to make payments to plaintiff that MEI has failed to make. Plaintiff has shown at best that it would be an "incidental beneficiary" of the obligation of Worldvision to exploit the mini-series in accordance with MEI's obligations to the directors.

As leave to amend would be futile, the motion to amend to add a third-party beneficiary claim is denied.

b.   *Quantum Meruit*

Plaintiff next seeks to assert a claim against Worldvision based on quantum meruit, which is not a contract, but rather "an obligation which the law creates, in the absence of any agreement, when and because the acts of the parties or others have placed in the possession of one person money, or its equivalent, under such circumstances that in equity and good conscience he ought not to retain it." Bradkin v. Leverton, 26 N.Y.2d 192, 309 N.Y.S.2d 192, 196, 257 N.E.2d 643 (1970) (citing Miller v. Schloss, 218 N.Y. 400, 407, 113 N.E. 337 (1916)). The legal obligation arising under quantum meruit is imposed in the absence of a valid enforceable written contract governing the particular subject matter in order to prevent unjust enrichment. See Clark-Fitzpatrick, Inc. v. Long Island Rail Road Co., 70 N.Y.2d 382, 521 N.Y.S.2d 653, 656, 516 N.E.2d 190 (1987).

Here, plaintiff has not alleged facts sufficient to state a cause of action in quantum meruit against Worldvision. In particular, plaintiff has failed to state a claim for unjust enrichment, which requires a showing that "a) the defendant has been enriched; b) the enrichment was at the plaintiff's expense; and c) defendant's retention of the benefit would be unjust." Hutton v. Klabal, 726 F. Supp. 67, 72 (S.D.N.Y. 1989); see also Mayer v. Bishop, 158 A.D.2d 878, 551 N.Y.S.2d 673, 675 (3d Dep't 1990) (to show unjust enrichment, "more is required than simply showing that one party received a benefit"); Paramount Film Distributing Corp. v. New York, 30 N.Y.2d 415, 334 N.Y.S.2d 388, 392, 285 N.E.2d 695 mod. on other grounds 336 N.Y.S.2d 911 (1972) ("The essential inquiry . . . for unjust enrichment . . . is whether it is against equity and good conscience to permit the defendant to retain what is sought to be recovered.")

Plaintiff essentially alleges that Worldvision had knowledge of MEI's contract to pay Ohbayashi and AMO but proceeded to market and distribute the film knowing that the director had not been fully paid. (Pl. Mem. in Opp. at 7.) On these facts, it cannot be said that Worldvision's marketing and distribution of the film, in accordance with its own contract with MEI/Cecco Films, was "against equity and good conscience," absent showing some basis for responsibility on the part of Worldvision to pay plaintiff. Cf. U.S. East Telecommunications, Inc. v. U.S. West Communications Servs., 38 F.3d 1289, 1298 (2d Cir. 1994) ("A party . . . may incur quasi-contractual obligations to a third party with whom it has not contracted by virtue of its direct representations to that party."); Van Brunt v. Rauschenberg, supra, (unjust enrichment found where defendant retained benefits of plaintiff's direct services to defendant without just compensation). Plaintiff does not allege any direct representations or other relationship between Worldvision and either AMO or the director. Thus, plaintiff's motion to amend its complaint to allege a claim in quantum meruit is denied.

c.   Constructive Trust [Deleted]

Conclusion

Defendants Worldvision, Cecconi and Cecco Films' motion for judgment on the pleadings is granted in part and denied in part. Plaintiff's cross-motion to amend its complaint to allege additional causes of action against defendant Worldvision is denied. All five claims for damages remain. The parties are to be ready for trial on April 28, 1997.

IT IS SO ORDERED.

Questions

1.   How does the court differentiate between intended beneficiaries and incidental beneficiaries?

2.   Why did the court deem the contract provision insufficient to require the defendant to make payments?

3.   Why does the court discuss *quantum meruit* in a contract claim?

Matter of Gosmire Estate
331 N.W.2d 562 (S.D. 1983)

. . . Facts

This is a South Dakota farm story of long, hard hours of work towards a dream with inadequate legal planning culminating in family litigation. The years of work were accomplished by Donald Gosmire and his sons, Ricky and Gerald. Norman Gosmire, Donald's brother and uncle of Ricky and Gerald, failed to properly plan and effectuate written legal instruments.

Donald and decedent lived together and farmed together on decedent's farm near Winfred, South Dakota. In 1956, Donald married and later had two sons, Gerald and Ricky. When briefs were filed herein, Ricky was twenty years of age and Gerald was twenty-three. During 1962, decedent made a cattle investment that financially devastated him. Decedent contemplated bankruptcy. Donald's family gave generously of their money, milk, eggs, and labor to help reestablish decedent. In fact, decedent told his neighboring farmer: "If it hadn't been for Don's cows and eggs, I would have been under." Silage cut on Donald's farm was hauled to decedent's farm. Such generosity also included the following: decedent approached Donald and told him that if Donald would give him his dairy calves from Donald's dairy herd, upon decedent's retirement or death, decedent's land and machinery would belong to Donald or his boys. From 1962 to 1972, Donald gave decedent his dairy calves, and sales of those calves, when fed out, established receipts of approximately $100,000. Some of these calves were contributed by Gerald.

Donald testified that decedent told him in 1962 that as a result of his family's efforts, the land and machinery would be for Donald or his two boys upon his retirement or death. The trial court found: "The decedent was the type of person who felt that a man's word was his bond and did not see the necessity of putting things in writing. Believing a person's word was his bond, he did business orally and with a handshake." Therefore, we do not have the nicety of a writing to examine. Shortly after decedent's statement, Donald acquired his own nearby dairy farmstead and moved his family. Decedent never married. Donald's family continued to dedicate the bulk of their time to helping decedent with his farming.

Numerous witnesses testified that Donald's sons, Gerald and Ricky, operated decedent's tractors when they were as young as seven years old. Gerald and Ricky plowed, raked hay, mowed, cultivated, baled, and ground feed. Donald and his sons worked long hours on decedent's farm without remuneration. As a general rule, the only free time Gerald and

Ricky had was on Sunday afternoons. When school started, the boys worked for their uncle both before and after school. High school sports had to be neglected because decedent's chores were first. When Gerald told decedent that he wanted to go to college, decedent told him to stay on the farm as the farm would be his and Ricky's when decedent retired or died. Decedent told others how close he was to the boys and how his farm would be theirs. Donald and his sons worked decedent's farm until decedent passed on. Decedent had planned on retiring at age sixty-five.

Donald, Gerald, and Ricky were never paid any wages for their years of hard work for decedent. Decedent was survived by three brothers, Donald, Harold, and Edgar, as well as several nieces and nephews who are issue of two deceased brothers. Witnesses testified that decedent was not fond of, and did not associate with, his brothers Harold and Edgar. Harold and Edgar asserted decedent was close to them. The facts do not bear this out. Decedent's life insurance policy named Ricky as the only beneficiary.

Substantial disputes occurred regarding statements made by decedent during the fall of 1980. Gerald testified that in the fall of 1980 his uncle told him that he and Ricky should remove his farm machinery telling them to remove it to Donald's farm because he was not going to be able to farm again. Gerald testified that his uncle told him "It's yours and Rick's, you can do whatever you want, you can take it to town, trade it off or fix it up to be ready to go next spring." Two witnesses testified that they saw decedent's machinery at Donald's farm prior to decedent's death. Appellants counter that after decedent's death, Gerald and Ricky prepared a list with Ted Gosmire, a son of appellant Harold Gosmire, which set forth forty-three items of decedent's machinery.

Strongly disputed is an offer decedent apparently made to Gerald just six days before his death. Gerald testified that decedent offered to sell his farmstead and machinery to Ricky and him for $150,000. Gerald said he accepted the offer. In their brief, Gerald and Ricky contend that their uncle's offer was only the final fruitation of the ongoing agreement between decedent and Donald with Gerald and Ricky as third-party beneficiaries. Such a contention goes to the very crux of this case. For support, Gerald and Ricky point out that decedent still owed $150,000 on his real estate mortgage and decedent could not convey unto them more than what he owned, i.e., his equity. Appellants assert that Gerald did not accept decedent's offer. Mary Jo Faber, a daughter of appellant Harold Gosmire testified that decedent told her Gerald had rejected his offer as too high. Appellant Edgar Gosmire testified that decedent told him that Gerald had rejected his offer as too high. The trial court responded by granting Gerald and Ricky's claims and ordering specific performance of the oral contract to transfer all of the decedent's property both real and personal to them. Appellants set forth five issues in their briefs. However, the record reflects that only three issues need be treated and they are separately set forth and examined [on the following page].

Issues

I.   [Omitted]

II.   Did Decedent Have a Valid and Binding Agreement to Convey His Property on Retirement or Death to Appellees?

III.   Were Appellees Entitled to a Decree of Specific Performance?

Decision . . .

II

Appellants assert that a valid, oral agreement did not exist between decedent, Donald, Gerald, and Ricky. Donald testified at trial, as did appellees, that decedent agreed to transfer his real and personal property to appellees on his retirement or death. Several friends, neighbors, and business acquaintances of decedent testified affirming decedent's intention to convey his farm to Gerald and Ricky. The trial court found that an enforceable oral contract existed.

Generally, where relatives reside together as one family, the services rendered by one member to another are presumed to be gratuitous. Mahan v. Mahan, 80 S.D. 211, 121 N.W.2d 367 (1963). Although Gerald and Ricky did not reside together with their uncle after 1963, the trial court in its memorandum opinion took full cognizance of the *Mahan* rule:

> The general rule is that where near relatives reside together as one family the services rendered by one member to another are presumed to be gratuitous. Herein, though farming together, Donald using mostly Norman's machinery, each maintained his seperate [sic] income and made seperate [sic] decisions as to their farming operations. Evidence showed the work performed for Norman far exceeded the value of the machinery used. Norman even collected the payment for custom work done by the boys. Performance by the claimants on their parts was more than substantially just and fair to constitute an adequate consideration. The presumption has been overcome.

This memorandum opinion was fully incorporated by reference in the findings of fact.

The trial court's findings of fact shall not be set aside unless clearly erroneous. A finding is clearly erroneous when upon reviewing the entire evidence, we are left with a definite and firm conviction that the trial court has erred. Estate of Nelson, 330 N.W.2d 151 (S.D. 1983); Matter of Estate of Pierce, 299 N.W.2d 816 (S.D. 1980). Due regard is afforded to the trial court's opportunity to judge the credibility of witnesses. People in Interest of P.M., 299 N.W.2d 803 (S.D. 1980).

After reviewing the extensive record herein, we are convinced that a valid, binding oral agreement existed between decedent, Donald, Gerald, and Ricky. Oral contracts affecting real estate do not fail merely because one of the parties becomes a decedent. Lass v. Erickson, 74 S.D. 503, 54 N.W.2d 741 (1952). SDCL 53-8-2, our statute of frauds, provides:

> The following contracts shall not be enforceable by action unless the same or some memorandum thereof be in writing and subscribed by the party to be charged or his agent, thereunto authorized in writing:
> (1) An agreement that by its terms is not to be performed within a year from the making thereof;
> (2) An agreement made upon consideration of marriage, other than a mutual promise to marry;
> (3) An agreement for the sale of real estate or an interest therein or lease of the same for a period longer than one year, but this does not abridge the power of any court to compel specific performance of any agreement for sale of real estate in case *of part performance thereof.* (Emphasis added.)

An oral promise to convey real property is enforceable by specific performance where the grantee has partially performed or has acted in reliance upon the promise of the grantor in such a manner that it would invoke a fraud or prejudice against the grantee not to grant specific performance thereon. Bentz v. Esterling, 76 S.D. 331, 78 N.W.2d 73 (1956). Donald, Gerald, and Ricky performed their obligation thereby taking the contract out of the ambit of the statute of frauds. Lampert Lumber Co. v. Pexa, 44 S.D. 382, 184 N.W. 207 (1921). See also, Dunmire v. Cool, 195 Neb. 247, 237 N.W.2d 636 (1976).

During the fall of 1980, decedent, in anticipation of retirement, began to fulfill his ongoing agreement by first delivering his farm machinery to Gerald and Ricky, and later by proposing the terms of conveying the equity in his farm unto Gerald and Ricky. Although some of the evidence is conflicting, we adopt the trial court's resolution as we are not left with a definite and firm conviction that a mistake has been made.

III

Appellants contend that the trial court erred in granting specific performance of the oral contract to convey decedent's property. Specific performance is an equitable remedy which is denied or granted based upon the facts and circumstances of each case within the sound discretion of the trial court. A decision to grant or deny specific performance will not be disturbed unless the trial court has abused its discretion. Stugelmayer v. Ulmer, 260 N.W.2d 236 (S.D. 1977); Skjoldal v. Myren, 86 S.D. 111, 191 N.W.2d 809 (1971); Dolan v. Hudson, 83 S.D. 144, 156 N.W.2d 78 (1968), *aff'd on rehearing*, 83 S.D. 331, 159 N.W.2d 128 (1968); Renner v. Crisman, 80 S.D. 532, 127 N.W.2d 717 (1964).

The trial court's memorandum opinion set forth the standard it held Gerald and Ricky's claim to:

Claimants, to prevail, must prove the terms of the contract (1) by clear and convincing evidence, (2) for an adequate consideration, (3) without inducement by fraud, misrepresentation or unfair practice, (4) enforcement of which will not cause unreasonable or disporportionate [sic] hardship or loss to others, and (5) the value of services rendered are not susceptible of measurement in dollars and cents or failure to grant such relief would operate as fraud upon claimants.

Applying the standards to the evidence, the trial court concluded:

No evidence was presented that Norman was incompetent. During the later years of his life, he was crippled to some extent, but this in no way affected his mental capacity. Neither has their [sic] been any evidence of fraud, misrepresentation, undue influence or other unfair practice.

In reliance of the oral agreement, Donald, Gerald, Ricky and Jeffery assisted their uncle to their detriment in a manner that at this time cannot be measured in dollars and cents. No accurate records have been kept and none could be reconstructed. Further, by granting specific performance, no other parties will suffer a hardship or loss.

A person may enter into a contract to devise property or make a will which is enforceable in equity by a third-party beneficiary. Kuhn v. Kuhn, 281 N.W.2d 230 (N.D. 1979). Being an equitable remedy, specific performance does not lie where an adequate remedy exists at law. Crawford v. Carter, 74 S.D. 316, 52 N.W.2d 302 (1952). As was held in Peterson v. Cussons, 63 S.D. 357, 361, 258 N.W. 810, 812 (1935):

That a court of equity will decree specific performance of oral contracts to convey real property or to make a devise of real property where the claimant has performed the services specified in the contract is too well settled to warrant the citation of authorities in support of the rule; but another rule that is just as well settled is that where the value of the services rendered is susceptible of measurement in dollars and cents, specific performance will not be decreed.

Here, legal remedies for Gerald and Ricky's years of hard work and dedication to their Uncle Norman are inadequate because it is impossible to quantify the dollar value the boys bestowed unto their uncle. Donald, Gerald, and Ricky provided decedent with far more than farm labor: they were his family bond, shared in his hardships, and perhaps more importantly, they embraced his work ethic and farming lifestyle. If Gerald and Ricky's labor could be valued, SDCL 15-2-15(5) forecloses recovery of wages two years after the cause of action occurs. These two young men devoted their lives to a farm and an uncle. It is right and just that equity enforce the bargain.

Therefore, we hold that specific performance was properly allowed on the facts of this case.

Affirmed.

Questions

1.   How does the court deal with the fact that the contract for real estate was oral?

2.   Do you believe that all contracts between family members are gratuitous? Why?

3.   Why was specific performance found to be the appropriate remedy?

Suggested Case References

1.   A municipality enters into a contract with a private company to construct sewers and make street repairs. The company agrees to be liable for any property damage resulting from its work. Are the citizens third party beneficiaries of this contract with enforceable rights against the company? Read Lundt v. Parsons Construction Co., 181 Neb. 609 (1967), and Anderson v. Rexroad, 182 Kan. 676 (1954).

2.   Is a mortgagor a third party beneficiary to a contract between the mortgagee and a contractor for the construction of the house? Schwinghammer v. Alexander, 21 Utah 2d 418 (1968).

3.   To be a third party beneficiary to a contract, must a person be specifically named in the contract? Read what the New Mexico court said in Stotlar v. Hester, 582 P.2d 403 (N.M. App. 1978).

4.   For a discussion of third party beneficiary contracts under Wyoming law, read Peter's Grazing Association v. Legerski, 544 P.2d 449, *reh'g denied*, 546 P.2d 189 (Wyo. 1975).

5.   Is any particular form needed to create a valid assignment? Stoller v. Exchange National Bank of Chicago, 199 Ill. App. 2d 674, 557 N.E.2d 438 (1990).

6.   Is an insurer's right of subrogation the same as an assignment of rights by the insured to the insurer? The Missouri court discusses this question in Farmer's Insurance Co., Inc. v. Effertz, 795 S.W.2d 424 (Mo. App. 1990).

7.   Are union members third party beneficiaries in a reorganization agreement between a corporation and its creditors? Read what the Iowa court said in Bailey v. Iowa Beef Processors, Inc., 213 N.W.2d 642 (Iowa 1973).

10 Discharge of Obligations

CHAPTER OVERVIEW

The contract is now complete. Every clause has been analyzed and discussed, and the contract meets all of the legal requirements to be an enforceable agreement. Does this mean that the parties to the contract are required to fulfill their promised performances? The answer is a resounding "Not necessarily."

In several situations a contracting party's performance is discharged, or excused, without his actually having fulfilled his contractual obligations. The circumstances that create these situations generally involve occasions when either the other party or external situations negate the necessity of performance.

Suppose that one of the conditions specified or implied in the contract fails to occur. Because the condition is a timing element for performance, if the condition giving rise to that performance does not come to pass, no performance is expected under the terms of the contract.

A contracting party's performance is excused if the other contracting party breaches. Because a valid contract requires mutuality of consideration, when one side fails to deliver the promised-for consideration, the other side is excused from performance as well.

The parties to the contract, for one reason or another, may agree that the contract is not worth completing. In these circumstances the parties are perfectly free to rescind or modify their existing obligations. As a consequence of this new "meeting of the minds," the obligations imposed under the original contract are no longer applicable. The parties agree to be bound to a new contractual arrangement instead.

Finally, situations that occur through no fault of either side may discharge the parties' contractual obligations. These are cases where outside forces have made fulfillment of the contract impossible, such as a change in the law or the unforeseen destruction of the subject matter of the contract. The law does not require the parties to perform the impossible or the illegal simply because a contract is in existence. Changed circumstances can change contractual obligations.

In summary, once the contract itself is determined to be valid and enforceable, it is necessary to see what happens after the agreement has been entered into. Dependent upon what the parties themselves, or what external factors, do, a party to a contract may not be legally bound to fulfill his contractual promises. The specifics of these methods of discharging contractual obligations are discussed below.

Methods of Discharge

A party to a contract may be discharged, or excused, from her contractual obligation in the following eight circumstances:

1. excuse of conditions;
2. performance;
3. breach of contract;
4. agreement of the parties;
5. impossibility of performance;
6. supervening illegality;
7. death or destruction of the subject matter or parties; and
8. frustration of purpose.

Each of these eight methods of discharge will be discussed individually.

Excuse of Conditions

As discussed in a previous chapter, a **condition** is a timing element of a contractual agreement. The condition either creates or extinguishes a party's duty to perform. Consequently, if the condition fails to occur, the performance does not come into play; conversely, a condition subsequent can terminate the obligation to perform.

EXAMPLES:

1. Abdul contracts to purchase Mamet's house. The contract is conditioned on Abdul finding financing for the purchase within 30 days. If Abdul is unable to find a mortgage within the 30 days, the contractual promises are excused. The condition precedent has not taken place, and so Abdul does not have to purchase Mamet's house. Mamet is free to sell the house to someone else.

2. Under their divorce settlement, Max has agreed to pay Fanny a set amount of alimony each month until one of them dies or Fanny remarries. When Fanny does remarry, Max is excused from his contractual obligation. The condition subsequent, Fanny's remarriage, discharges Max from his alimony obligations.

In each of the two examples above, the condition itself discharged the contractual obligation. In addition, because contractual conditions usually involve some element of time (either short, long, or indefinite), there exists the possibility that during the contractual time frame one of the parties will do something that will prevent or excuse the other side's performance. While such circumstances occur during the *time period* of the condition they are not situations in which *the condition itself* discharges the contractual obligation, as in the examples given above. Generally, there are four circumstances that fall into this category.

1. Performance Prevented. In this situation, one side, during the period of the condition, engages in some act that makes it impossible for the promisor to fulfill her obligation. The promisor will be excused from performing. The person who prevents the performance only excuses the counter performance of the other side; the wrongdoer is still contractually bound.

 EXAMPLE:

Jessie agrees to paint Fred's house on Thursday. When Jessie arrives at Fred's, Fred has bolted and locked the gate, making entrance to the house impossible. Fred's conduct excuses Jessie's performance, but Fred will still be liable for Jessie's costs and expenses.

If the party who must perform *after* the condition occurs is the one who prevents the condition happening, he will not be excused and must perform. A person cannot benefit from his own wrongdoing.

 EXAMPLE:

Ted hires Irene to remodel his house for a set sum and requires that after completion Irene give Ted an architect's certificate stating the remodeling meets all current standards. Ted prevents the architect from giving the certificate. Ted must pay Irene. Because Ted is the one who prevented the condition from occurring, it does not excuse his contractual obligation.

2.   Voluntary Disablement. Voluntary disablement means that one party to a contract voluntarily engages in some conduct that makes it virtually impossible for him to fulfill his obligation. It is not absolutely impossible, but the circumstances are such that it would be more than extremely unlikely that he will be able to perform. In these circumstances, the other side is excused from her obligations. The law will not force one side to perform if it is unlikely or impossible for the other side to perform. For contracts covered by the Uniform Commerical Code (UCC), voluntary disablement would give rise to the other party's right to seek written assurances of performance. (See Chapter 8.) If such assurances were not given within 30 days, the party seeking such assurances could consider the voluntary disablement a breach of contract.

 EXAMPLE:

Becky agrees to purchase Patti's antique vase. Payment and delivery are to take place in two weeks. One week after their contract is entered into, Patti sells the vase to Rose. Because there still is one week left until Patti has to convey the vase to Becky, it is conceivable that she could repurchase the vase from Rose so as to be able to give it to Becky, but the likelihood is negligible. This is an example of voluntary disablement. Patti has voluntarily engaged in an action that makes it unlikely that she will be able to fulfill her contractual obligation to Becky. Consequently, Becky's obligation to Patti is discharged.

The majority of states considers that voluntary disablement constitutes a full breach of contract, entitling the injured party to sue immediately for contractual relief in the courts. In those jurisdictions where it is not considered a breach of contract, the promisee must wait until the time element has passed to ascertain whether the other party will perform before being able to seek judicial relief.

3.   Insolvency. If one party to the contract becomes judicially insolvent, the other side is excused from performing. The law does not require that a person become a judicial creditor of a bankrupt, nor will it permit someone to attempt to fulfill a contract with a bankrupt resulting in increased debts for the insolvent party.

 EXAMPLE:

Farmer White has a contract to deliver 1000 bushels of sweet potatoes to Eatwell Supermarkets, Inc., at the end of the month. Three weeks prior to delivery, Eatwell files for protection under the bankruptcy laws. Neither Eatwell nor Farmer White is required to fulfill their contractual obligations to each other.

4. Anticipatory Breach. Anticipatory breach occurs when one party to the contract, during the time of the condition, states that she has decided not to fulfill her contractual obligations. In other words, one party tells the other that she has no intention of conveying the promised-for consideration. In this situation, the innocent party does not have to perform.

For the contracting party's conduct to be considered anticipatory breach, the words indicating her intentions must be positive, unconditional, and unequivocal. A person cannot merely suggest that her performance will not be forthcoming; she must state that in no uncertain terms. In anticipatory breach, both sides must have executory duties to perform. If the innocent party has already performed, with no other duty to fulfill, there is no "anticipatory" breach; the other side is in total breach.

 EXAMPLES:

1. Maura agrees to sell her used Property book to Wallace. Before payment and delivery, Maura tells Wallace that she has changed her mind, and that she is going to keep the book rather than sell it. This is anticipatory breach.

2. Maura agrees to sell her used Property book to Wallace. Wallace pays her and agrees to pick up the book the following week. Before the book is picked up, Maura tells Wallace that she has changed her mind, and that she is going to keep the book. This is not anticipatory breach; it is a breach of contract because Wallace has already performed, and his duties are executed.

In all of the situations discussed above, the injured, innocent party to the contract cannot simply sit back and sue the other person. The law imposes a duty on the injured party to a failed contract to attempt to minimize her injury. This is known as **mitigation of damages**. The injured party must make a reasonable attempt to find a replacement for the failed party's contractual performance. For example, in the situations given above, Jessie would have to find someone else's house to paint on Thursday, Farmer White would have to look for a new sweet potato purchaser, and Wallace would have to seek someone else's used book. In this fashion, the injured party will minimize the damages the injuring party will have to pay.

The injured party only need make "reasonable" attempts to mitigate. Extremely hard or expensive measures are not called for. What is "reasonable" is determined on a case-by-case basis. Also, should the innocent party make a better deal in attempting to mitigate than he originally had, the breaching party is totally excused from the contract.

One word about the antique vase and mitigation of damages. Because an antique vase is a unique piece of property, it is unlikely that the innocent party would be able to mitigate. This does not mean that she is not required to try, but the likelihood of success is reduced in these circumstances.

Performance

The simplest method of being excused from contractual obligations is to perform these obligations. Once performed, the duties are executed, and there is nothing more for the promisor to do. Fortunately, most contractual obligations are fulfilled in this fashion. The overwhelming majority of contractual duties are satisfied by the parties' actual performances.

Must a party perform completely to be excused from his obligations under the contract? The answer is no. Obviously, once a party has fully and completely performed nothing else could reasonably be expected. However, a party may be ready, willing, and able to perform, and the other side refuses the performance. The promisor in this instance is said to have **tendered complete performance,** which is legally sufficient to discharge him from his obligations. Remember the example above when Jessie arrived to paint Fred's house, only to find the entrance barred. In this instance, Jessie tendered complete performance. He arrived, ready, willing, and able to perform. His actual performance was forestalled by Fred's actions, and so Jessie was relieved of further obligations.

What happens if, instead of completely performing or tendering complete performance, a party only partially performs? Will she still be relieved of her contractual obligations? The answer depends on the nature of the promised performance and the extent of the performance actually given. Recall the case of Jimmy the Human Fly. In that instance, the court held that Jimmy climbing almost to the very top of the Washington Monument constituted "substantial" performance, satisfying his contractual obligation. If the performance is substantial, the performing party will be discharged, although she may have to compensate the promisee for the difference between the full performance and the substantial performance given.

 EXAMPLE:

Lonnie agrees to sell 25 CDs to Bruce for $100. In fact, Lonnie only delivers 23 CDs. Lonnie did not breach her obligation; her performance is substantial. However, she is not entitled to the full $100.

Bruce may deduct the price of two CDs from the total payment to Lonnie.

If, on the other hand, the performance delivered is insubstantial, the promisor is not relieved of his contractual obligation. Insubstantial performance never discharges a promisor's contractual obligation *unless* the promisee accepts that performance. Regardless of the performance actually given, if the promisee accepts the performance in complete satisfaction of the promisor's contractual obligation—be that performance complete, substantial, or insubstantial—that acceptance relieves the promisor of any further contractual responsibility.

As discussed in Chapter 8, part performance for merchant traders is unacceptable. A merchant buyer is entitled to perfect tender, and if the goods delivered do not completely conform to the contract specifications, the merchant buyer may reject the entire shipment or accept only conforming goods. The option is with the buyer. However, the UCC demands that the buyer give the seller the opportunity to remedy the defect within a reasonable time.

 EXAMPLE:

Sally is a collector of old books. Bruce agrees to sell to Sally a 1902 edition of the Book of Knowledge, a set containing 20 volumes, for a certain price. On delivery day Bruce conveys only 3 volumes, all he actually has. Sally still thinks the sale is a good buy, and accepts the 3 volumes. Even though the performance is rather insubstantial, Sally's acceptance discharges Bruce from further performance.

Breach of Contract

To **breach** a contract means to break one's obligation made under the agreement. If a party to a contract breaches, the other side, the innocent party, has an immediate cause of action. A breach means the promisor has not lived up to what he has promised, and the injured party may sue to recover what she expected to receive under the contractual agreement.

 EXAMPLE:

Harry agrees to buy Minnie's pearl necklace as a gift for his wife. Harry pays Minnie, but Minnie fails to deliver the necklace. Minnie has breached her promise, and Harry can sue her, either to get his money back or to have her convey the necklace.

Not all breaches give rise to an immediate cause of action. A **material breach** of contract always gives rise to an immediate cause of action for breach of the entire contract because it goes to the heart of the contract itself. A **minor breach** of contract, on the other hand, only gives rise to a cause of action for that minor, or insignificant, breach; the contract itself is still in force and effect.

EXAMPLES:

1. Corrinne agrees to sell Gary her car for $1500. When Gary takes possession, he discovers that the car is totally broken down and does not meet the contract specifications. This is a breach of the entire contract, giving Gary an immediate cause of action for the full purchase price.

2. When Gary takes possession of the car, he discovers that the spark plugs are worn out. Although the contract specified that the car was in perfect working order, this is only a minor breach, because replacing spark plugs is basically insignificant. Gary has a cause of action against Corrinne for the cost of replacing the spark plugs, but the contract is still valid and enforceable.

What factors determine whether a breach is material or minor? There is no set standard, but generally the courts look at the intent of the parties, the words used in the contract, the degree of hardship the breach imposes, and the extent to which the injured party can be compensated. As a general rule, if any portion of a contract is deemed to be of special importance to one of the parties, it should be identified in the contract as a "material" clause. One such example would be a time of the essence clause discussed in Chapter 2.

The distinction between material and minor breaches gives rise to another legal concept, that of the **divisible contract.** As discussed in Chapter 7, one of the contractual rules of construction used by the courts is to attempt to uphold contracts if at all possible. As a consequence of this doctrine, the courts have created the concept of divisible contracts. A divisible contract is one that can be divided into several separate, but equal, portions. The contract can either expressly state that it is divisible (or that it is not divisible, if the parties so wish), or its divisibility can be implied from the contract terms themselves. If the contract is deemed divisible, then a breach would only affect that one small divided contract; the rest of the contract relationships would remain intact. In this method, even if the breach were material, the materiality may only go to one portion of the contract, and the remaining portions would still be in effect.

EXAMPLE:

Mitzi rents an apartment from Louise for a 2-year period, with a monthly rent of $300. Mitzi pays her rent for the first 6 months, but in the seventh month her rent check bounces. Although Mitzi is in breach, the contract can be considered a divisible contract. The lease is for 24 months, with a monthly rent of $300, which could be looked at as 24 separate leases. In this context, Mitzi's breach is only a breach of one of those 24 contracts; all the remaining contracts are still deemed in effect.

The court will find a contract to be divisible only if it can be evenly and easily divided, and the parties themselves have not specified that the contract is nondivisible. Under the UCC, all contracts in which delivery is to be made in installments are deemed divisible unless such assumption would cause an undue hardship on the buyer merchant.

Agreement of the Parties

The parties to a contract are always free to rearrange their contractual agreements by mutual assent. As long as *both* parties agree to a change in the performances, the parties may be discharged from their original obligation without any negative consequences.

This mutual reagreement of the parties can come about in two ways. First, the original contract may contain a provision providing for the dissolution of the agreement. An example would be a lease providing for a tenancy at will where either party is free to terminate the relationship by providing notice to the other party. Or, a contract could contain a time period escape clause, meaning that during a specified period of time the parties could dissolve the contract without damage. An example of this type of arrangement would be a contract for schooling. From registration until the beginning of class, any student can change her mind and get a full tuition refund. Each contract must be individually analyzed to determine whether it contains some provision for the parties' termination of the contract without damage.

The second situation in which the parties can change their mutual obligations comes about not by the original contract, but by the parties forming a new contractual arrangement. There are six types of new agreements that have the effect of discharging the parties from their former contractual obligations.

1. Mutual Recission. A **mutual recission** occurs when both parties to the contract agree that they do not want to proceed any further under the agreement. Both sides agree to rescind, or take back, the original obligation. The consideration supporting this agreement is the detriment incurred by each party of not receiving the promised-for consideration of the original contract. For recission to be applicable the contract must be executory.

 EXAMPLE:

Barry and Lynette agree to be partners in a retail store. The partnership is evidenced by a written partnership agreement. Prior to establishing the business they have a falling out and decide to rescind the contract. Because the provisions are executory, this is valid.

   2.   **Release.**   A **release** is a contract in which one side relieves the other of any obligation existing under a previous contract. Many times people hear the term "release" in the context of tort claims, but the concept is contractual as well. Usually, the releasing party receives some consideration for her agreement to release the other side from his original obligation.

 EXAMPLE:

Tina has a contract with Melinda in which Melinda has agreed to supply Tina with 20 dresses each week for Tina's clothing store for a 2-year period. After several problems arise, Tina agrees to release Melinda from the contract in consideration of a certain sum of money. The release is very much like a private settlement between parties to a contractual dispute.

   3.   **Accord and Satisfaction.**   An **accord and satisfaction** is a special contractual situation in which the parties to a disputed contract agree to settle their dispute by changing the obligations of the contract itself with the new agreement. Accord and satisfactions are discussed in Chapter 4, Consideration, and can be reviewed in that section.

   4.   **Substituted Agreement.**   A **substituted agreement** is a new contract that incorporates the original contract in the new provisions. Because the original obligations are now absorbed by the new agreement, the original contractual duties are deemed discharged.

 EXAMPLE:

Judy is having a yard sale. Rise sees a shawl she likes, and the two women agree on a price. Before paying for the shawl, Rise spots a hat and a serving tray she would like to purchase. After some haggling, Judy agrees on one price for all three items. The original contract for the sale of the shawl is now absorbed into this substituted agreement, which covers three items instead of just one.

5.   Novation.   As discussed in Chapter 9, Third Party Contracts, a **novation** is a substitution of parties into an existing contractual agreement. When the novation is effectuated, the original party no longer has any rights or obligations under the contract. That person's contractual duties are discharged; they are now the responsibility of the novated party.

6.   Modification.   As discussed previously, if the contract is for the sale of goods between merchants, the merchants may make good faith modifications to their contractual obligations.

Impossibility of Performance

Under certain circumstances a contracting party's performance may become impossible to fulfill through no fault of his own. The law feels it would be unfair and unjust to hold the person responsible to a contractual obligation that could not possibly be met.

What constitutes **impossibility of performance** depends on the facts and circumstances of each individual case. It also must be ascertained whether the performance is totally incapable of being performed or whether the impossibility is of a temporary nature. If the impossibility is only temporary, the promisor is not discharged from her obligation, but her performance is temporarily suspended until the situation rectifies itself; at that point the promisor must fulfill her original obligation. Take careful note that circumstances that merely make the performances more difficult or expensive than originally believed, but not impossible to perform, do not relieve the promisor of her obligations. This is the risk of contract. However, for contracts covered by the UCC, if performance becomes unduly expensive due to events that could not be foreseen or assumed when the contract was formed, the party *may* be discharged.

EXAMPLES:

1. Buycheap Markets has a contract with Australian Produce, Ltd. to purchase various food products from the latter. One contract concerns the purchase of 5000 bushels of Tasmanian oranges that Australian Produce has agreed to ship to the port of San Diego. As the ship pulls into the harbor, the longshoremen go on a national strike, and the oranges cannot be off-loaded anywhere in the United States. The oranges begin to perish. Australian Produce is relieved of its obligation by the impossibility of performance.

2. In a second contract, Buycheap has agreed to buy tinned lamb from Australian Produce, shipment to be to the port of Los Angeles. This ship arrives the same day as the one in the previous example, and the goods cannot be off-loaded. Australian Produce is not permanently relieved of its obligation. Because canned goods have an indefinite life, and time is not of the essence, Australian Produce's obligation is merely suspended until the strike is over.

Supervening Illegality

A **supervening illegality** will discharge contractual obligations because, since the inception of the contractual arrangement, the purpose for which the contract was created has become illegal. The law will not permit persons to engage in illegal activities, and therefore the parties are deemed discharged from their contractual duties.

 EXAMPLE:

Jan and Dean enter into a contract to open and manage a gambling casino in Atlantic City, New Jersey. Six months after the casino opens, the town officials of Atlantic City rescind the ordinance permitting gambling in the town. Jan and Dean are now discharged from their contractual promises by a supervening illegality. The law will not allow them to break the law just to fulfill a contract.

Death of the Parties or Destruction of the Subject Matter

If the subject matter of the contract is destroyed, obviously the contract cannot be fulfilled. This is true provided that the object in question is unique and is not destroyed by an act of one of the parties. If the object is capable of near exact replacement, the promisor is expected to find a substitute product and fulfill his obligation. The fact that it might be more expensive for him is of no concern to the law. That is a risk of contract.

Death is self-evident; a person cannot be expected to perform from the grave. Note that a person's estate may be liable for contracts entered into by the deceased prior to death. If the decedent merely had to convey property she had sold or pay for property she had purchased, the estate is capable and expected to fulfill these obligations.

EXAMPLES:

1. Ian has agreed to buy Peg's house. Before closing, the house is destroyed by fire. Ian is discharged from his obligation by the destruction of the subject matter of the contract.

2. Willie has agreed to let his prize race horse stud with Liz's fillie for a fee. Before consummation of the contract, Willie's horse dies. Willie and Liz are relieved of their contractual obligations.

Frustration of Purpose

Probably the least common method of discharge, but the most interesting, is **frustration of purpose**. Frustration of purpose occurs when the contract, on its face, is both valid and apparently capable of performance, but the underlying reason for the agreement no longer exists. This reason is not specified in the contract itself but is discernible by the circumstances surrounding the contract's creation.

EXAMPLE:

The most famous of the cases regarding frustration of purpose are known as the Coronation Cases, dealing with the coronation of Edward VII of England. At the turn of the century, after Queen Victoria's death, her son and heir, Edward, was to be crowned king after a 60-year wait. The procession route was announced months in advance, and people with homes and offices overlooking the route found themselves in possession of desirable real estate. One-day leases were entered into for the day of the coronation, so that the "tenants" could have a view of the parade. Two days before the ceremony, Edward developed appendicitis, and the coronation was postponed for several months. The one-day landlords brought the tenants into court for rent when the tenants refused to pay. The court held that, while the contracts, on their faces, were valid and enforceable, the purpose of the contracts—to view the coronation procession—no longer existed. Consequently, the tenants were discharged from their rental obligations because of frustration of purpose.

SAMPLE CLAUSES

1

If, during the term of the lease, the described premises shall be destroyed by fire, the elements, or any other cause, or if they be so injured that they cannot be repaired with reasonable diligence within six (6) months, then this lease shall cease and become null and void from the date of such damage or destruction, and the lessee shall immediately surrender the premises to the lessor and shall pay rent only to the time of such surrender.

Here, the parties to the contract indicate a discharge caused by the loss or destruction of the subject matter. By having this clause in the original instrument specifying the grounds for discharge, the parties have hopefully avoided a lawsuit to have their obligations excused.

> 2

In the event bankruptcy or state proceedings should be filed against the lessee, his heirs or assigns, in any federal or state court, it shall give the right to said lessee, his heirs or assigns, immediately to declare this contract null and void.

This provision, as the preceding one, would appear in the original contract and specifies insolvency as a ground for discharging the contractual obligation.

> 3

If Subscriber within five (5) days after the execution of the Agreement notifies Seller in writing that Subscriber wishes to withdraw from the Agreement, the amount theretofore paid by him under the Agreement will be returned to him and thereafter all rights and liabilities of Subscriber hereunder shall cease and terminate.

This clause in the original sales contract provides a conditional time period during which the subscriber can withdraw from the contract without any negative effect. In this manner, the parties have agreed to a method of discharge in the original agreement.

> 4

If any obstacle or difficulty shall arise in respect to the title, the completion of the purchase, or otherwise, the vendor shall be at full liberty, at any time, to abandon this contract on returning the deposit money to the purchaser.

In this instance the parties in a contract for the sale of real estate have specified an excuse of conditions in the original contract. Of course, the specific obstacle or difficulty has not been definitely defined or described, which could create questions of interpretation later on. In drafting contracts, it is always a matter of judgment with respect to specificity. The more precise the clauses, the less leeway later on; the less precise the clauses, the more potential for a lawsuit.

CHAPTER SUMMARY

A party to a contract does not necessarily have to perform what he has promised under the agreement itself. There are several situations and circumstances that act to discharge a promisor from his duties without any negative consequences to the party himself. Generally, there are eight situations that have the effect of discharging the promisor's obligations. They are:

1. having the performance excused by a contractual condition not being met;
2. performing, either fully or partially, and having that performance accepted by the promisee;
3. by the other side's breach of contract;
4. by having the parties mutually agree to a new or different performance;
5. by impossibility of performance;
6. by having the law change so as to make the contract illegal;
7. by the death or destruction of the subject matter or parties; or
8. by frustration of purpose.

When any of these preceding situations occur, the promisor is excused from any further obligation under the contract.

SYNOPSIS

Methods of discharging or excusing performance
1. Excuse of conditions
    a. Condition fails to create or extinguishes duties
    b. Other side prevents performance during time of condition
        i. Prevention
        ii. Voluntary disablement
        iii. Insolvency
        iv. Anticipatory breach
2. Performance

        a.   Full
        b.   Tendered full performance
        c.   Substantial v. insubstantial
   3. Breach
        a.   Material or minor
        b.   Divisible contracts
   4. Agreement
        a.   In original contract
        b.   New agreement
            i.   Mutual Recission
           ii.   Release
          iii.   Accord and satisfaction
          iv.   Substituted agreement
           v.   Novation
   5. Impossibility of performance
        a.   Permanent
        b.   Temporary
   6. Supervening illegality
   7. Death or destruction
   8. Frustration of purpose: Coronation cases

Key Terms

Accord and satisfaction: new contract based on parties' agreement to settle dispute existing under a contract

Anticipatory breach: positive, unconditional, and unequivocal words that a party intends to breach his contractual obligations

Breach: breaking one's contractual promise

Conditions: a fact or event, the happening or nonhappening of which creates or extinguishes an absolute duty to perform

Divisible contract: contract capable of being broken down into several equal agreements

Frustration of purpose: purpose for which the contract was formed no longer exists

Impossibility of performance: promisor's performance is incapable of being fulfilled due to outside forces

Material breach: breach of contract that goes to the heart of the agreement

Minor breach: breach of contract that goes to an insignificant aspect of the contract

Mitigation of damages: duty imposed on injured party to lessen, by reasonable means, the breaching party's liability

Mutual recission: agreement by both contracting parties to do away with the contract

Novation: substitution of contracting parties

Release: contract relieving promisor from an obligation under an existing contract

Substituted agreement: a new contract that incorporates the original contract in the new provisions.

Supervening illegality: change in law that makes the performance of the contract illegal

Tender complete performance: being ready, willing, and able to perform

Voluntary disablement: volitional act by a promisor that makes her obligation virtually incapable of being performed

EXERCISES

1. Give two examples of impossibility of performance.
2. What factors determine whether a contract is divisible? Draft a divisible contract.
3. What would be the result of an injured party failing to mitigate damages? Why?
4. Give an example of frustration of purpose other than the Coronation Cases?
5. What factors determine whether performance is substantial or insubstantial? Draft a contract clause that would help in this determination.

Cases for Analysis

The following case summaries are included to demonstrate how contracts may or may not be discharged by the contracting parties. In Dunaj v. Glassmayer, the court discusses whether a party may be discharged from a contract because the contract has become overly expensive to perform, and in Broome Construction Co. v. Beaver Lake Recreation Center, Inc., the court is called on to determine whether a written contract may be rescinded orally.

Dunaj v. Glassmayer
61 Ohio Misc. 2d 493, 580 N.E.2d 98 (1990)

. . . This case arises from the termination of a management agreement between plaintiff Luxbury Hotels and two limited partnerships, Ad Ventures I limited partnership and Ad Ventures II limited partnership, each of which owns a hotel that was managed by Luxbury Hotels. Besides reinstatement of Luxbury Hotels as manager, this suit seeks reinstatement of Matthew Dunaj as the general partner of both of these limited partnerships. Matthew Dunaj is president of Luxbury Hotels, Inc. Ad Ventures claims that the termination of the managers under the management agreements was appropriate because the agreements specified certain objective performance standards for Luxbury Hotels. . . .

The management agreements negotiated here between the parties set forth termination rights to the limited partners. They provide that the partnerships have the right to terminate Luxbury Hotels as manager of the hotels when the actual cash flow from the hotels is seventy percent or less of the named consultants' market feasibility study cash flow projections for a consecutive twelve-month period. Section 15.03 of the management agreements between Luxbury Hotels and the partnerships provides as follows:

Section 15.03—Option to Terminate

The owner shall have the option to terminate this agreement upon the occurrence of either of the following circumstances: . . .

(b)   Excepting events or occurrences as contemplated in Article 21, cash flow for debt service on the hotel is insufficient to the extent that only 70% or less of the Market Feasibility Study Consultant's cash flow projections (and subsequent projections prepared on the same basis each year by the General Partners, which are subject to independent outside third-party consultant review and verification if Owner desires such) is realized for a consecutive twelve-month period. . . .

The test was not to be applied during the first year of the hotel's operation. This effectively gave Luxbury Hotels a two-year grace period before any termination despite the level of performance.

It is clear that Luxbury Hotel's performance did not fulfill the seventy percent requirements specified above. However, plaintiff Dunaj asserts this is not dispositive. Rather, he contends that the income must be insufficient, the definition of "insufficient" turning on whether "cash flow for debt service on the hotel is insufficient." Since here apparently the cash flow was not insufficient to pay the mortgages, Dunaj asserts that this performance standard of the agreement has not been breached. While his may be a commonsense interpretation had the definition of "insufficient" not been specified in the agreement, such is not the case here. Clearly "insufficient" is defined in the agreement as being "only 70% or less of the Market Feasibility Study Consultant's cash flow projections."

Plaintiff Dunaj also contends that projections other than the market feasibility study projections should be the standard. This position is also without merit. The agreements note that the standard should be according to either the market feasibility study projections or "subsequent projections prepared on the same basis each year by the General Partners, which are subject to independent outside third-party consultant review and verification if Owner desires such. . . ." However, no such projections were prepared here, as Dunaj admitted in his deposition.

Plaintiffs also contend that performance here is excused by the following "force majeure" language in the management agreement:

When prevented by any "force majeure" cause beyond the reasonable control of such party (except financial inability of such party) such as strike, lockout, breakdown, accident, compliance with an order or regulation of any governmental authority, failure of supply or inability, by the exercise of reasonable diligence, to obtain supplies, parts or employees necessary to perform such obligation, or war or other emergency.

Plaintiffs assert that surrounding economic conditions such as the development of competing hotels, and incorrect projections concerning expenses and supporting businesses constitute such a "force majeure" so as to excuse the failure to meet seventy percent of cash flow projections.

The "force majeure" clause of the management agreement spells out several specific events of "force majeure" such as fire, war, strikes, and acts of God. These are dramatic unforeseen events which could cause the hotel or hotels to be partially or completely shut down and actually prevent performance. No such catastrophic events have occurred here. Rather, plaintiffs have simply failed to meet the income requirements of the management agreement.

It was well known to all parties involved in the agreement that the performance standards were based on projections, that a grace period was allowed, and that various factors were and are at work in the hotel business that could affect income. These factors include a late startup, varying expenses and the existence or nonexistence of surrounding businesses to support the hotel trade. When a party assumes the risk of certain contingencies in entering a contract, as is the case here, such contingencies cannot later constitute a "force majeure." Austin Co. v. United States (1963), 314 F.2d 518, 520, 161 Ct. Cl. 76, 80–81. Mistaken assumptions about future events or bad economic conditions do not qualify as a "force majeure." See, e.g., Gulf Oil Corp. v. Fed. Energy Regulatory Comm. (C.A.3, 1983) 706 F.2d 444, 449; Buono Sales, Inc. v. Chrysler Motors Corp. (C.A.3, 1966), 363 F.2d 43, 47. For all the above stated reasons, the failure of the plaintiffs to meet the performance standards set out in the agreement constitutes a failure to perform which justified the termination of Luxbury Hotels as the manager of the hotels.

Plaintiffs Dunaj and Luxbury Hotels also claim that there was no valid action to terminate the management agreement or to replace Dunaj as the general partner. They claim that a meeting was required to be held for such a vote to terminate. Section 20.02 of each partnership agreement, however, expressly provides that the "limited partners" and the "special limited partner" have the right to vote on the termination of the hotel manager. There is no requirement that such a vote be conducted at a formal meeting. This contention is therefore without merit.

Finally, the defendants move for summary judgment on the issue of whether the "general partner" was properly removed. They base the validity of their action on the assumption that the termination of the management agreement results in the general partner's removal, permitting the "special limited partner" and "limited partners" to elect a "successor general partner." This, however is not provided for in the partnership agreements. The facts brought to this court do not support the contingencies outlined in the agreement for termination of general partner, to wit, death, or "no general partner remains." Section 13.02. The motion for summary judgment with respect to this issue is therefore not well taken and is denied.

Accordingly, the court concludes that the motion for summary judgment with regard to the termination of the hotel manager is well taken and is granted in favor of the defendants. The motion for summary judgment on the issue of termination of the general partner, however, is not well taken and is denied.

Judgment accordingly.

Questions

1.   Do you agree with the court's decision? Why, or why not?
2.   Could the contract have been worded so as to avoid the lawsuit? How?

Broome Construction Co. v. Beaver Lake Recreation Center, Inc.
29 So. 2d 545 (Miss. 1969)

The issues in this suit on a construction contract involve the admissibility of parol evidence to show that a proffered instrument was not the complete contract, and mutual rescission or abandonment of a contract. Broome Construction Company, Inc., appellant, brought this action in the Chancery Court of Lamar County against Beaver Lake Recreational Center, Inc., for damages and specific performance on a contract under which Broome was to clear, dig, and construct a lake for the defendant. After a lengthy hearing, the chancery court, by necessary implication, found that the contract as executed required approval by the Farmers' Home Administration, which never approved it; and further held that Broome had "voluntarily relinquished" or rescinded the contract with the consent of Beaver Lake. However, the court awarded damages of $4,261.17 to Broome for work which it had already done in clearing 19.5 acres, and for certain plans and cost of bonds. Broome appeals, asserting that the court erred in both respects and that it should be awarded a decree for specific performance and more adequate damages. We conclude that the decree should be affirmed.

Beaver Lake is a non-profit corporation which owns a recreation center in Lamar County near Purvis. It was organized and is operated by local people, apparently as a country club, with a club house, swimming pool, and golf course. The controversy stems from Beaver Lake's efforts to add a man-made lake to its physical plant. Broome is a contractor specializing in heavy construction.

Negotiations between Broome and Beaver Lake apparently commenced in January 1966, when Broome contacted Beaver Lake's directors and volunteered to construct the lake at a price within the corporation's budget on the basis of plans and specifications which he had prepared by R. L. Morrison, an engineer. Although interested in the offer, Beaver Lake was unable to accept, because the federal Farmers' Home Administration, which was the guarantor of the loan, preferred competitive bidding. Broome therefore agreed to release its plans and specifications to other contractors and to bid competitively against them, with the understanding that if it did not secure the contract, Beaver Lake would reimburse it for the cost of the plans.

Beaver Lake invited bids, and on January 17 opened them and accepted Broome's. On January 19, 1966, Beaver Lake, by its president and secretary, executed the contract. Beaver Lake's officers signed it in a local F.H.A. office; Broome, in a local bank. The executed contract and the attached plans and specifications were then forwarded to Jackson for approval by the FHA. Pursuant to stipulations in the contract, Broome obtained a performance bond, and on April 22 Beaver Lake instructed him to commence work under the contract. Shortly thereafter, Broome's subcontractor began clearing the lake bed and dam site, and continued with this work for several months.

While this work was in progress, the specifications upon which Broome's contract was based were disapproved by the FHA, and Morrison was requested by Beaver Lake to draw plans satisfactory to FHA. The revised plans were substantially more demanding than the original, and FHA approved them. Beaver Lake invited Broome to revise its original bid of $48,000 in light of the revisions, and Broome entered a new bid of $75,000. Other contractors were invited to bid, with H. R. Morgan Contracting Company entering a bid of $58,000. In a letter dated August 17, 1966, Broome wrote Beaver Lake reaffirming its "willingness to work with you on the matter. We would not object to giving up our contract with you on all items except the clearing." On August 25, when, according to Beaver Lake, it became apparent that Broome's new bid would not bring him the contract, Beaver Lake by letter formally directed Broome to cease the clearing work.

On September 3 Beaver Lake awarded the contract for construction of the lake to Morgan on its bid of $58,000, and on December 9, offered Broome $1,665 in compensation for work done. Broome refused the tender and brought this action. Broome contends that the contract with Beaver Lake executed on January 9 was complete unto itself, that it required no precedent approval by FHA, and argues that its negotiations with Beaver Lake concerning the revised specifications were undertaken with an eye to mere modification of the existing contract under an adjustment clause, not a new contract. On the other hand, Beaver Lake denies that an enforceable contract ever existed. It contends that an express, written provision of Broome's contract required approval of plans and specifications by the FHA as a prerequisite to enforceability, and that this provision had either been lost or removed from the copy of the contract offered in evidence by Broome.

First: On conflicting evidence the trial court was justified in concluding that the construction contract contained a provision on a separate sheet requiring approval of it by FHA, and there is no dispute that it never was approved by FHA. The copy of the contract between Broome and Beaver Lake which was in the possession of Broome and was introduced in evidence did not contain the approval clause, and Broome said that it never was in the executed contract. On the other hand, the president and secretary of Beaver Lake, who executed the document, said that it definitely was in the contract. Moreover, Broome was well aware that the construction funds were to come from a loan insured by the FHA. He appeared at several meetings of the board of directors of Beaver Lake for discussions of the proposed contract. There was a direct conflict of evidence on the existence of the FHA approval clause in the contract. The chancery court was warranted in finding that it was in the instrument when executed.

Appellant argues that the trial court erred in overruling its objections to the introduction of evidence by Beaver Lake to "vary the written terms" of a contract. The parol evidence rule does not apply, unless both parties to a contract have consented to it as a complete and accurate integration of that contract. The particular writing asserted by Broome to constitute the contract is claimed by Beaver Lake not to be a complete and accurate integration of that instrument, because it omits the FHA approval clause. The testimony for appellee, admitted in evidence, contested the completeness of the document offered by appellant. This was an issue of fact. 3 Corbin on Contracts §573 (1960). In short, the parol evidence rule does not become applicable unless there is an integration of the agreement, that is, unless the parties have assented to a certain writing as a statement of the agreement between them. Accordingly, it may be shown by parol evidence not only that the contract was never executed or delivered as a contract, but also that the proffered instrument was not the complete contract, or that its validity was impaired by fraud, illegality, duress, mistake, lack of or failure of consideration rendering the agreement voidable or void. Jones v. Index Drilling Co., 251 Miss. 578, 170 So. 2d 564 (1965); 4 Jaeger, Williston on Contracts §§631–634 (3d ed. 1961); 32A C.J.S. Evidence §933 (1964).

Second, assuming the contract between the parties to be valid without FHA approval, the chancery court found that the contract was "voluntarily relinquished by the complainant in all respects except the 'cleanup' portion thereof. . . ." There was ample evidence to support this finding of a mutual and voluntary rescission or abandonment of the contract.

Rights acquired under a contract may be abandoned or relinquished by agreement or conduct clearly indicating such purpose. Intent to abandon or rescind may be inferred from conduct of the parties which is inconsistent with the continued existence of the agreement. Mutual assent to rescind or abandon a contract may be manifested in other ways than by words. 2 Restatement of Contracts §406 (1932); 17 Am. Jur. 2d, Contracts §494 (1964); 17A C.J.S. Contracts §412 (1963).

Affirmed.

Questions

1. Why was parol evidence admitted in this case?
2. How did the parties rescind the contract?
3. Do you believe this decision was well reasoned? Why, or why not?

Suggested Case References

1. In a contract the parties have agreed to settle disputes by arbitration. A conflict arises regarding price, but the parties failed to set the arbitration process in motion. Is the action of not establishing the arbitration called for in the contract an example of mutual rescission by act of the parties? Read what the Louisiana court said in Shell Oil Co. v. Texas Gas Transmission Corp., 210 So. 2d 554 (La. App. 1968).

2. Does a new agreement between the parties that covers the matters in a disputed contract absorb the original contract into the new agreement? Is this new agreement a separate contract or an accord and satisfaction? Read what the North Dakota court held in First National Bank, Bismarck v. O'Callaghan, 143 N.W.2d 104 (N.D. 1966).

3. If a party to a contract refuses to complete performance without additional consideration and continues to delay performance for a month, does that conduct constitute anticipatory breach? Amberg Granite Co. v. Marinette County, 247 Wis. 36 (1945).

4. May a written contract be verbally rescinded without any additional consideration? Read the decision in Cowin v. Salmon, 244 Ala. 285, 13 So. 2d 190 (1943).

11 Remedies

CHAPTER OVERVIEW

The time has finally come to answer the question everyone usually wants to start with: "What can I get?" The contract itself is complete, it has met every requirement of the law, all of the parties with vested interests in the agreement have been properly identified, and all conditions have been met. At this point, the promiser does not perform. The promisee is now injured; he has not received his promised-for consideration. What remedies are available to the injured party in a contractual relationship?

Historically, the judicial system was divided into **law** and **equity.** Law and the law courts were based on statutes and judicial precedents, and their purpose was to see that all citizens were treated equally and fairly. Equity and the equity courts were established from the concept of the sovereign's mercy and dealt with situations in which the legal outcomes might be just but were not merciful. These are situations in which, under legal principles, one party could "get away with something." To rectify this potentially unjust situation, equity was established. Equity prevents unjust enrichment that might result from a pure application of legal principles. Although today both these systems are merged into one, the theories proposed by the litigants follow the ancient concepts and precedents of law and equity, and the remedies are different depending on which theory, the legal or the equitable argument, prevails.

With respect to contract law, the concepts of legal and equitable remedies come into play whenever one party breaches her contractual obligations. A breach of contract is a broken promise. The promiser has failed to deliver what she had promised under the contract. When this occurs, the nonbreaching or innocent party to the contract is permitted to seek judicial relief to remedy the situation.

The injured party may seek *legal remedies* if her injury can be corrected simply by money. Legal remedies are known as *damages*, which denotes monetary relief. The type of damages available depends on the specific nature of the contract, the breach, and the injury incurred.

Equitable remedies are nonmonetary relief. They are awarded in those limited situations in which a monetary award would not compensate the innocent party for the injury occasioned by the breach. Equitable remedies are less frequently awarded than damages, and the circumstances must clearly meet all of the requirements of equitable doctrines.

Because the legal and equitable systems are now merged into one judicial process, an injured party may seek both legal and equitable remedies in the same action, and the court will determine which would be the most appropriate for the particular injury involved.

Legal Remedies

Legal remedies, or **damages,** are monetary awards granted to an injured party in a contractual dispute whenever money would be an appropriate method of rectifying the injury. The court awards four types of damages:

1. compensatory damages;
2. punitive damages;
3. consequential damages; and
4. liquidated damages.

Compensatory Damages

Compensatory damages are monetary awards designed to put the injured party in the same position he would have been in had the contract been completed as originally planned. The court determines the amount of the monetary loss the injured party suffered because of the breach.

The formula the courts use to determine the exact amount of compensatory damages was outlined in a judicial case decided many decades ago. The events of the case occurred in a rural community. A farmer's son was injured in a fire, and the palm of his hand was severely burned. In a nearby community, a doctor had been experimenting with skin grafts on farm animals, and when he heard about the farm boy, he offered to try a skin graft on the child for a specified sum of money. The doctor promised that the boy would have a "perfectly good hand."

The farmer agreed, and the operation took place. The doctor grafted skin from the boy's thigh onto the hand. After surgery, the hand healed, and the farmer was delighted. Unfortunately, a few years later the boy entered puberty, and hair started growing on the palm of his hand. The skin the doctor used for the graft was from a hair-producing part of the body. The farmer sued for breach of contract.

In determining that the boy was entitled to compensatory damages, the court arrived at the following formula for making the dollar determination: Take the value of what the injured party started with, add to it the value of what he was promised, and then subtract or add what he was left with to determine whether there was an injury, and the amount of the damage. Compensatory damages are used to put the party in the position he would have been in if the contract had not been breached. If he ends up with more than he was promised, there are no damages. In the case of the farm boy, he started with a burned hand, was promised a perfectly good hand, and was left with a hand with a hairy palm. The amount of his damage is the difference between a "perfectly good hand" and a hand with a hairy palm.

 EXAMPLES:

1. Alice purchases a pearl ring from Jean for $200. After the sale is complete, Alice discovers that the ring is phony and is only worth $2. The amount of Alice's compensatory damage would be $198, the difference between what she was promised (a genuine pearl ring worth $200) and what she actually received (a phony pearl ring worth $2).

2. Eatwell contracts to buy 100 bushels of Grade A plums from Farmer Grey at $10 per bushel. Farmer Grey delivers plums that are Grade B, worth $8 per bushel. Eatwell's compensatory damages are $2 per bushel, the difference between what it was promised and what it received.

To determine the amount of the compensatory damages, the courts have established certain guidelines depending on the type of contract in question. For instance, if the contract is for the sale of goods, compensatory damages are generally the difference between the market price and the contract price. If the buyer is the innocent party, she can recover the difference between the contract price and what she paid for substituted goods in mitigation. If the seller is the injured party, she can resell the goods and recover the difference from the buyer, or, if the goods cannot be resold, she is entitled to the full contract price.

For employment contracts, if the employer breaches, the employee gets the contract price; if the employee breaches, the employer can recover the cost of replacing the worker. Generally, in computing compensatory damages the court simply uses common sense under the given circumstances.

Compensatory damages are the most common remedy for breach of contract.

Punitive Damages

Punitive, or **exemplary, damages** are monetary awards granted by a court for a breach of contract that involves very unusual circumstances. Exemplary damages are intended not only to compensate the injured party but to punish the breaching party. Punishment is not a usual aspect of contract law. As a consequence, for a party to be entitled to punitive damages, there must be some statutory basis for the award under the state's law. Generally, punitive damages are only awarded by statute where the breach of contract is accompanied by some other violation of a breach of trust, such as fraud or antitrust. If a party is seeking punitive damages, he must be able to show the existence of a breach of contract as well as a statutory violation. The innocent party is awarded not only compensatory damages, but punitive damages as well.

EXAMPLE:

Ira is induced to buy a table from Harry for $500. Harry is an antique dealer, and although he claims that it *is* an antique, he knows that the table is not. Because a fraud is involved as well as a breach of contract, Ira may be entitled to punitive as well as compensatory damages if the state statute permits.

Consequential Damages

Consequential damages are monetary awards beyond the standard measure (compensatory damages) due to the special circumstances and expenses incurred because of the injury. For the innocent party to be entitled to consequential damages, when entering into the contractual relationship, she must make the other party aware of special losses that might result from a breach of contract. In this manner, the promisor can decide whether or not to enter into the contractual relationship.

In a famous case, a mill owner had contracted with several farmers in the area to mill their grain during a bumper season. Unfortunately, the mill shaft broke right before the harvest. The miller brought the shaft to a repairman who promised to repair the shaft in a week. The miller made no mention of any special need for the shaft. After the repair, the shaft broke during the first day of use, and the miller sued the repairman, not only for the value of the shaft, but for all his lost profit as well. It seems that because the shaft was the only one the miller had, when it broke he had to cancel his contract with the farmers. The court held that the miller was not entitled to lost profits. This was a loss that could not be foreseen by the repairman when the contract was entered into, and so he could not be responsible for those types of losses. The repairman did have to return to the miller the price of the repairs as compensatory damages.

Therefore, to be entitled to consequential damages, the promisee must make the promisor aware of any unusual or unforeseen consequences that could result from a potential breach at the time the contract is entered into; otherwise the breaching part will only be liable for compensatory damages.

Consequential and punitive damages must be distinguished from the concept of **speculative damages.** Speculative damages are monetary injuries the injured party believes she suffered because of the breach, but they are not readily ascertainable, provable, or quantifiable. An example of speculative damages would be profit the injured party had hoped to make as a result of the contract. Speculative damages cannot be recovered under any circumstances.

 EXAMPLE:

Leane hires a limousine to take her to an important business meeting where she is to sign a million dollar contract. The limousine fails to appear, Leane cannot get to the meeting, and she loses the deal. She sues the limousine company for her lost profit of $300,000. Leane will not prevail. She would be entitled to the cost of the limousine, if she had paid for it, but her loss of a million dollar contract is not a foreseeable result of a car service failing to perform. Under these circumstances Leane would not be entitled to consequential damages. Also, her loss may be speculative; more information is needed to determine how realistic that contract was.

Liquidated Damages

Liquidated damages are reasonable damages that the parties themselves have agreed to in the contract itself. Normally, parties to a contract would specify liquidated damages if it would be difficult or impossible to compute compensatory damages because of the uncertain nature of the contract or the subject matter. When liquidated damages are specified, the court will usually award those damages, and the parties are generally precluded from arguing that the amount is too high or too low. Because liquidated damages are determined at the outset of the contract, in order to avoid lengthy litigation later on, the court will simply abide by the parties' agreement under the concept of freedom of contract. The parties never had to agree in the first place, so if they did, their agreement prevails.

However, for the liquidated damages provision of a contract to be enforced, it must be clear that the provision is in fact meant to ease recovery of hard-to-determine losses; if the liquidated damages clause is in fact meant as a punishment for the breaching party or to compensate for speculative damages, the court will not honor the provision.

EXAMPLE:

Gene and Elga have a contract to develop and patent an inexpensive process for creating a clotting agent. Because they don't know whether the idea is patentable or will be successful, they contract with a liquidated damages provision in the amount of $100,000. The contract is breached by Gene, and Elga sues. Regardless of the actual dollar amount of the loss, if Elga can show the existence of a valid contract and a breach by Gene, she will be awarded $100,000.

Liquidated damages should be distinguished from **limitation of damages,** another type of provision that can appear in contractual agreements. With a limitation of damages, the parties agree when entering into the contract that, in case of breach, the breaching party will be liable for no more than the amount established as the ceiling, or limitation, in the contract. Unlike liquidated damages, with a limitation of damages provision the injured party must not only prove the contract and the breach, but must prove the actual damages as well. The financial award is limited to the amount contractually specified, but if the actual loss is less than that amount, the smaller sum is awarded. Liquidated damages set the amount of the recovery, regardless of actual loss, whereas a limitation of damages caps liability of actual loss to be no higher than the amount specified.

EXAMPLE:

Assume that instead of a liquidated damages provision, Gene and Elga insert a limitation of damages clause, setting the amount at $100,000. When Gene breaches, Elga now has to prove her actual loss. If she can only show a loss of $75,000, that is all she will recover. If she can show a loss of $250,000, she will only get $100,000, because she has contracted to limit her recovery to that amount.

As discussed in the previous chapter, whenever the court is computing the value of the damages suffered by the injured party, the court also looks to see whether the injured party attempted to **mitigate damages**. It is the duty of every innocent party in a breach of contract to attempt to lessen the damages the breaching party may have to pay, provided that such attempts are not unreasonable or unduly burdensome for the innocent person. The promisee does not have to go out of his way to mitigate but must make some attempt, if possible, to remedy the situation himself. The ultimate award will thereby be reduced by the amount of the mitigation.

 EXAMPLES:

1. Ace Supermarkets has a contract to purchase 1000 bushels of oranges from Farmer Jones at $10 per bushel. Farmer Jones fails to deliver, and Ace is able to find another farmer to sell it the oranges at $11 per bushel. Ace has mitigated its damages, and now is only entitled to $1000 from Farmer Jones instead of $10,000 (the difference between the $10 per bushel it was to pay farmer Jones and the $11 per bushel it actually had to pay).

2. In the same situation as above, Ace can find a farmer to sell it oranges at $9 per bushel. In this instance, Farmer Jones' breach has put Ace in a better position than it would have been in had the contract gone through, and so Ace is not entitled to any award from Farmer Jones.

3. Tiffany's contracts with a Thai mine to purchase a 50-carat sapphire for one of its customers. When the mine fails to deliver the jewel, Tiffany's cannot find a replacement stone. Because it is impossible for Tiffany's to mitigate, it is entitled to full compensatory damages.

Equitable Remedies

Whenever the legal remedy of damages is insufficient to compensate the injured party to a breach of contract, the innocent party can look for some equitable relief. **Equitable remedies** are designed to prevent unfairness and unjust enrichment. These largely nonmonetary awards are divided into five categories:

1. injunctions;
2. specific performance;
3. rescission and restitution;
4. reformation; and
5. quasi-contractual.

Injunction

An **injunction** is a court order to stop someone from engaging in a specific action. The verb is *to enjoin*, and the court will only order this when the innocent party could not otherwise be compensated.

 EXAMPLES:

1. Salim has a contract to purchase Whiteacre from Faruk, closing to take place in one month. Two weeks before the closing date, Salim discovers that Faruk is attempting to sell the property to someone else. Salim could go to court to have the court enjoin Faruk from selling the house to anyone other than Salim, pursuant to the contract. Although the injunction would stop Faruk from selling the property to anyone other than Salim, it does not mean that he will actually convey the property to Salim; he can still breach the contract by some other action later on.

2. Joe leaves Acme, Inc., after working there for 20 years. Joe and Acme have a contract in which Joe agreed that, should he leave Acme, he would not go into competition against them for 2 years. One week after Joe leaves Acme, he goes to work for Acme's biggest competitor. Acme can enjoin Joe from working for the competitor, pursuant to their contract.

Injunctions are permanent or temporary orders of the court to stop a particular action or activity. Because the courts do not usually order injunctions easily or without a full hearing (and only on a showing that irreparable harm would result from a refusal to order the injunction), until a full hearing can be arranged a litigant may be entitled to a **temporary restraining order (TRO).** A TRO is only a temporary measure by the court until the hearing for full injunctive relief can take place. A TRO is for a short period of time; an injunction is more far reaching.

Specific Performance

Specific performance is a court order requiring the breaching party to perform exactly what she promised under the contract. Specific performance is only granted when the subject matter of the contract is considered unique and therefore not replaceable, or when no other remedy would rectify the injury to the innocent party. Unlike an injunction, in which the court orders a party to stop doing something, with specific performance the court is ordering a party to do something.

EXAMPLES:

1. In the situation above with Salim and Faruk, on closing day Faruk refuses to convey the property to Salim. Because real estate is generally considered unique, Salim could go to court to seek specific performance. The court would order Faruk to convey Whiteacre to Salim, pursuant to the contract.

2. In the example with Joe and Acme, Acme could also have the court order specific performance of the contract provision. Joe would then have to abide by the agreement and not compete with Acme for two years. The injunction only stopped Joe from working for a specific competitor.

Rescission and Restitution

If a party to a contract finds that fulfillment of the contract would be unduly burdensome, he can ask the court for **rescission and restitution,** whereby the court will rescind, or revoke, the contract in the interest of fairness. It will then have each party restore to the other what the other has expended on the contract to date. If the parties can agree to this procedure by themselves, it is a form of discharge of obligation by a new agreement, as discussed in Chapter 10. If the parties cannot agree to terminate the relationship themselves, the court may do it for them.

Unlike the equitable remedies discussed previously, it is the party who wants to breach who is seeking relief from the court in the form of rescission and restitution. To be entitled to rescission and restitution, the party seeking the remedy must be able to demonstrate that fulfillment of the contract would be so burdensome as to be unjust. Mere economic loss, unless very substantial, is insufficient; economic loss is a risk of contract. What is deemed burdensome is determined by the court on a case-by-case basis.

EXAMPLE:

Chad and Jeremy have entered into a partnership agreement to publish a magazine. Chad has an independent income; Jeremy does not. After two years of operation, the publication is still losing money with no change likely in the foreseeable future. Jeremy has gone through his money, and he needs to get a paying job. Chad wants to continue the magazine pursuant to the agreement. Under these circumstances, Jeremy could have the court rescind the contract because its fulfillment would be unduly burdensome.

Reformation

Reformation can be considered a court-ordered accord and satisfaction. When the parties to a disputed contract cannot resolve the conflict, the court may do so for them while still keeping the contractual relationship intact. Under the rule of construction that contracts are to be upheld if at all possible (Chapter 7), if the dispute merely involves one of quantity or quality of subject matter, the court can reform the contract to correspond to what was actually delivered. In this manner, the contractual relationship can go forward, and neither of the parties will be in breach.

 EXAMPLE:

In the example discussed earlier in which Eatwell received the plums from Farmer Grey, Eatwell claimed the plums were Grade B, whereas Farmer Grey claimed they were in fact Grade A. The parties themselves could not resolve the dispute, but this was the first installment of a year's worth of deliveries. In court, instead of awarding damages, because of the long-term nature of the contract and the difficulty of proving grades of plums, the court could reform the contract to delete mention of the grade of plums and to change the price to $8.50 a bushel. In this manner, the contract between Eatwell and Farmer Grey can be maintained.

Quasi-contractual Remedies

The **quasi-contractual remedies** are the only equitable remedies that involve a monetary award. Quasi-contractual remedies are available in situations in which no contract exists, but there has been unjust enrichment to one of the parties of the dispute. To rectify the unjust enrichment, the court will order the injured party to be awarded the value of what she has lost (the value of the unjust enrichment). There are two types of quasi-contractual remedies:

1. *Quantum meruit* and
2. *Quantum valebant.*

Quantum Meruit

Quantum meruit means the value of the service rendered. If the defendant is unjustly enriched by receiving uncompensated-for services, she must pay the injured party the value of those services. Remember the paralegal who worked for her aunt with the expectation of receiving the aunt's property on the aunt's death (Chapter 1): Although no contract did in fact exist, the paralegal was entitled to the value of the services she performed for the aunt. This is *quantum meruit.*

Quantum Valebant

Quantum valebant means the value of the property received. If the injured party conveys property that unjustly enriches the recipient, the recipient is required to pay the innocent party for the value of the property. An example would be the newspaper that was left on the doorstep in Chapter 1. The person who kept accepting the newspaper is liable for the value of the paper to the publisher, who never intended to give the paper as a gift.

Both *quantum meruit* and *quantum valebant* are applied in cases involving quasi-contracts in the interests of justice.

Waivers and Their Effect

A party cannot be sued for breaching his obligation under a contract if the innocent party waives that breach. A **waiver** is the forgiveness by a party to a contract of the other side's failure to meet a contractual obligation. The waiver can be for a contractual covenant or for any condition specified in the contract.

A party can waive a contractual provision either expressly or implicitly. An **express waiver** occurs when the promisee specifically manifests that she intends to forgive the other side's breach. An **implied waiver** occurs, not by the words or manifestations of the promisee, but by the promisee's actions. In both instances, when a contractual provision has been waived, the other side is relieved of that specific obligation.

 EXAMPLES:

1. Leo contracts with Bob for the construction of an addition to his house. The contract states that Leo will only pay for the work when it is complete, and Bob gets an architect's certificate that the work meets all structural specifications. The work is done, and Leo pays Bob without having the architect's certificate. Leo has waived this condition of the contract by his actions.

2. Leona rents an apartment from ABC Realty, and the lease specifies that the apartment cannot be sublet. Leona has to go out of town for a long period of time and asks ABC if they would permit a short-term sublet to help her out. ABC agrees in writing to waive the nonsublet provision of the lease. Leona is now free to sublet without being in breach.

As a general rule, any party to a contract is free to waive any provision she wishes. However, the promisor cannot always rely on the waiver to relieve him of all liabilities, especially if the waiver waives an obligation that is an ongoing obligation, such as monthly rent during a two-year lease. To protect the parties, many contracts include a waiver provision in which it is specifically stated that waiving one provision of the contract does not necessarily waive any other provision, nor is a waiver at one time to be considered a continuing waiver of that contractual provision during the full term of the contract. Therefore, if one party to a contract is going to be unable to fulfill a particular contractual provision, it would behoove him to seek a waiver for the provision to avoid being in breach. The effect of an obligation being specifically waived is that the obligation cannot be reinstated or made the subject of a suit for breach of contract. The party who waives the provision is estopped, or barred, from raising that provision as the grounds of a lawsuit.

Arbitration Provisions

Despite the foregoing, many contracts specify that disputes will be decided not by going to court, but by having the matter resolved by **arbitration.** Arbitration is a nonjudicial method of settling legal disputes in which both sides agree to submit the claim to an agreed-on arbitrator for relief. Arbitration is usually a faster and less expensive method of resolving disputes than litigation.

Arbitrators are not bound by evidenciary rules and are free to determine liabilities and relief as they see fit. In most instances, the decision of the arbitrator is final and binding, precluding the parties from seeking further judicial relief. Examples of arbitration clauses appear in Chapter 12, Drafting Simple Contracts.

Because arbitration is now so popular, it must be considered when determining appropriate remedies for a contractual disagreement.

SAMPLE CLAUSES

1

The failure of the lessor to insist upon the strict performance of the terms, covenants, agreements and conditions herein contained, or any of them, shall not constitute or be construed as a waiver or relinquishment of the lessor's right to thereafter enforce any such term, covenant, agreement or condition, but the same shall continue in full force and effect.

The above is an example of a waiver provision in a lease. By these words, the promisee is stating that he may, if he so desires, forgive enforcement of a contract promise, but that waiver is not to be considered a continuing waiver, or a waiver of all his rights. What he forgives once he may not forgive a second time, and the promisor is still contractually bound for all covenants and conditions not waived. Typically contracts will specify that waivers must be in writing; this protects both sides to the agreement. Remember, a promisor is not obligated to fulfill any promise that the promisee has waived. Failure to fulfill a waived obligation is *not* a breach of contract.

> 2

Should Seller breach any of the provisions of the agreement, Seller shall be liable for liquidated damages in the amount of $X.

The preceding is an example of a liquidated damages clause. The contracting parties, when entering into the agreement, have specified what the damages shall be in the case of breach. In this instance, the seller would be liable for $X, provided the buyer could prove the contract was breached. No evidence need be given with respect to the actual damages involved; damages have already been contractually determined.

> 3

In the event of breach of any of the provisions of this agreement, damages shall be limited to $X, exclusive of attorneys' fees and court costs.

In the above example, the parties have set a limitation to their potential liability. In this case, the injured party not only has to prove breach but must also prove the amount of damages. Regardless of what can be proven, damages will not exceed the amount stipulated by the parties in their contract.

CHAPTER SUMMARY

Remedies are the awards the injured party in a contractual dispute can receive from the party who has breached her obligation. The type and the amount of the award depends on the nature of the injury occasioned by the breach; the purpose is to put the injured party in the same position she would have been in had there been no breach.

Legal remedies, known as damages, are monetary awards based on the injury suffered. The standard measure of damages is compensatory damages, which attempts to put the innocent party in the same position he would have been in had the contract been fulfilled as planned. In unusual circumstances, the injured party may be entitled to a monetary award different from the standard measure. If the nonbreaching party makes the promisor aware of some special losses that would be occasioned by a breach, he may be entitled to consequential damages to compensate him for this extraordinary loss. If the breach is accompanied by some other wrongdoing (such as fraud), the court, under statutory authority, may punish the breaching party. In this case, punitive, or exemplary, damages are awarded in addition to the standard measure.

When negotiating the agreement, the parties to the contract are always free to agree on liquidated damages or a limitation of liability. With liquidated damages, the parties agree that, in case of breach, the amount recovered by the nonbreaching party will be an amount established in the contract itself. With a limitation of liability provision, damages must be proven but cannot exceed the amount stipulated in the agreement.

If monetary awards would be insufficient, or inappropriate, to compensate the injured party, under the court's equitable jurisdiction the innocent party may be entitled to some nonmonetary relief. Examples of these equitable remedies are injunctions, to stop the breaching party from engaging in a specific action; specific performance, ordering the breaching party to fulfill the specific obligations of the contract; rescission and restitution, in which the court will rescind the contract and put the parties in the same position they were in before the contract was entered into; and reformation, in which the court will alter the terms of the agreement to keep the total contract in effect. In addition to these nonmonetary awards, if the source of the dispute is a quasi-contractual relationship, the court may order some monetary relief for the value of the unjust enrichment.

A promisee may waive any provision of a contract that she wishes, and the waiver relieves the promisor of that contractual provision without being in breach of contract. However, the waiver of one provision is usually not considered to be a waiver of any other provision, and except for the specifically waived obligation, the promisor remains contractually bound.

In court, the injured party may ask for as many different types of remedies as seem appropriate to the action. The court will make the ultimate decision as to which remedies to award.

SYNOPSIS

Legal remedies
    Damages (money)
    1.   Compensatory
    2.   Punitive
    3.   Consequential
Equitable remedies (nonmonetary)
    1.   Injunction

2. Specific performance
3. Rescission and restitution
4. Reformation
5. Quasi-contractual

Contract clauses
1. Liquidated damages
2. Limitation of damages
3. Waivers
4. Arbitration

Key Terms

Arbitration: nonjudicial method of resolving legal disputes

Compensatory damages: standard measure of damages; puts injured party in the position he would have been in had the contract been fulfilled

Consequential damages: damages above the standard measure due to special losses occasioned by the breach

Damages: legal remedies; monetary awards

Equitable remedies: nonmonetary awards

Equity: area of law concerned with preventing unfairness and unjust enrichment

Exemplary damages: additional monetary award designed to punish the breaching party

Express waiver: a waiver occurring when the promisee specifically manifests an intention to forgive the other side's breach

Implied waiver: a waiver occurring when the promisee's actions imply an intention to forgive the other side's breach

Injunction: court order to stop engaging in a specific action

Law: division of law concerned with historical legal principles designed to provide equal treatment to all persons

Legal remedies: monetary awards

Limitation of damages: contractual provision placing a ceiling on the amount of potential liability for breach of the contract

Liquidated damages: contractual provision providing a specified dollar amount for breach of the contract

Mitigation of damages: duty imposed on innocent party to make reasonable attempts to lessen the liability of the breaching party

Punitive damages: exemplary damages

Quantum meruit: quasi-contractual award; value of the service performed

Quantum valebant: quasi-contractual award; value of the good given

Quasi-contractual remedy: an equitable remedy involving a monetary award

Reformation: a court-ordered accord and satisfaction

Rescission and restitution: a court order revoking a contract that would be unduly burdensome to fulfill

Specific performance: court order to perform contractual promise
Speculative damages: damages that are not specifically provable
Temporary restraining order (TRO):   preliminary step to an injunction
Waiver: forgiveness of a contract obligation

EXERCISES

1. Give an example of a situation in which punitive damages would be possible.
2. Your school decides to disband the paralegal program before you complete your studies. What damage would you claim, and how could you substantiate that claim?
3. What is the effect of a disclaimer on consequential damages?
4. Argue that a limitation of damages provision should not be considered valid.
5. Give two examples not discussed in the chapter in which quasi-contractual remedies would be appropriate.

Cases for Analysis

The following case summaries highlight the concepts of when specific performance may be granted, Guard v. P & R Enterprises, Inc., and when exemplary damages are appropriate, Edens v. Goodyear Tire & Rubber Co.

Guard v. P & R Enterprises, Inc.
631 P.2d 1068 (Alaska 1981)

This appeal is a sequel to the events described in Alaska Laborers Training Fund v. P & R Enterprises, Inc., 583 P.2d 825 (Alaska 1978). We are asked to decide whether the trial court properly denied relief from a judgment under Alaska Civil Rule 60(b) following our decision in Alaska Laborers and, if relief is warranted, to determine the proper measure of damages. We find that the trial court abused its discretion in denying relief from the judgment.

In 1975, the Guards signed an earnest money agreement with P & R Enterprises (P & R) to sell it property upon which a restaurant, lounge, and motel known as Edgewater Inn was located. However, Alaska Laborers Training Fund (Alaska Laborers) subsequently purchased the property in a trustee's sale in 1976. P & R sued the Guards and Alaska Laborers for damages and specific performance of the earnest money agreement. On March 9, 1977, the superior court entered summary judgment for P & R, directing Alaska Laborers to transfer the property to P & R. The superior court indicated in its judgment that the Guards were liable to P & R for damages, the amount of which would be determined at a later trial. On April 21, 1977, the superior court entered judgment against the Guards for $164,000 as of April 1, 1977, and for $10,000 per month until the property was transferred to P & R. Alaska Laborers appealed and in Alaska Laborers Training Fund v. P & R Enterprises, 583 P.2d at 827, we reversed the superior court decision of April 21, 1977, and remanded the case. Almost nine months later, the Guards petitioned for relief from the damage portion of the original judgment under Alaska Civil Rule 60(b)(4) and the superior court denied relief without an opinion.

Civil Rule 60(b) requires that motions for relief be made within a reasonable time. Because of the unique circumstances in this case, the Guards' petition for relief, filed almost nine months after our decision in Alaska Laborers and twenty-four months after the superior court judgment in April, 1977, was timely. Although in Alaska Laborers, we specifically stated that the Guards had not appealed the April, 1977, judgment, 583 P.2d at 826, the wording of the mandate issued in Alaska Laborers is confusing as to the parties affected by the decision. The mandate states that the judgment of April 21, 1977, is reversed. The April 21, 1977, judgment was entered against both the Guards and Alaska Laborers. Considering the interrelationship of the damage award and the order of specific performance, and that the mandate did not limit its application to only Alaska Laborers, it is understandable that the Guards assumed there was no valid judgment against them. That this was not the situation was brought to the Guards' attention when P & R attempted an execution of the April 21, 1977, judgment on their property in Idaho in May, 1979. The superior court denied a stay of execution on the property. When the execution proceedings began, the Guards filed a motion for relief from judgment. Thus, the Guards moved quickly after learning of their confusion regarding the Alaska Laborers decision and mandate. On these facts, their petition for relief was timely.

The superior court awarded a money judgment against the Guards as part of its decree of specific performance. The monetary relief awarded in association with an order of specific performance is not the same as damages awarded for breach of contract. Ellis v. Mihelis, 60 Cal. 2d 206, 384 P.2d 7, 15, 32 Cal. Rptr. 415 (1963). This principle was clearly set forth in Tri State Mall Associates v. A.A.R. Realty Corp., 298 A.2d 368, 371–372 (Del. Ch. 1972):

> "The compensation awarded to a purchaser incident to a decree of specific performance is not for breach of contract. By its very nature, a suit for specific performance affirms the contract and seeks that it be enforced. The purchaser is not due both specific performance of the contract and damages for its breach. . . . Rather, the Court in decreeing specific performance will adjust the equities of the parties in such a manner as to put them as nearly as possible in the same position as if the contract had been performed according to its terms." (emphasis omitted).

In adjusting the equities between the Guards and P & R, the trial court acted properly in considering the profits which were foregone because of the delay in conveying the land. Since the order of specific performance was improper, the judgment against the Guards for $164,000 and for $10,000 per month until the property is transferred to P & R by Laborers must be vacated. However, the Guards did breach their contract with P & R to convey the Edgewater Inn. On remand the superior court must determine what damages, if any, should be awarded to compensate P & R for that breach. We set out below the general rules which the superior court should utilize when determining the award of damages.

Alaska Civil Rule 60(b) provides that a "court may relieve a party . . . from a final judgment . . . [when] (5) . . . it is no longer equitable that the judgment should have prospective application. . . ." Generally, we will not disturb a superior court decision to deny a motion under Civil Rule 60(b) "except upon a showing of an abuse of discretion, which would be the case only if we were left with the definite and firm conviction on the whole record that the judge had made a mistake. . . ." (footnote omitted). Gravel v. Alaskan Village, Inc., 423 P.2d 273, 277 (Alaska 1967). In this case, the Guards have established the two requirements necessary for relief under Civil Rule 60(b)(5). First, the judgment clearly falls into the category of those judgments which, equitably, should no longer have application. In Alaska Laborers we held that the order requiring Alaska Laborers to transfer property to P & R was improper. 583 P.2d at 826–827. The damage award against the Guards for $164,000 and $10,000 a month from April 1, 1977, until the land was transferred, was based on the superior court's conclusion that the contract was breached and that P & R was entitled to the land and loss of profits. Since P & R is not entitled to the land, however, the continuing damage award has no proper application.

The purpose of awarding damages for a breach of contract is to put the injured party in as good a position as that party would have been had the contract been fully performed. McBain v. Pratt, 514 P.2d 823, 828 (Alaska 1973); Green v. Koslosky, 384 P.2d 951, 952 (Alaska 1963). In contracts for land sales, the award for the loss of the bargain is "the difference between the contract price and the market value, plus any payments which have been made." C. McCormick, Law of Damages §177 (1935). See 11 S. Williston, Law of Contracts §1399, at 527 (Jaeger 3d ed. 1968). Consequential losses which the seller could reasonably have anticipated when the contract was made are also recompensible. C. McCormick, Law of Damages §681 (1935). Thus, lost profits can be awarded, City of Whittier v. Whittier Fuel & Marine Corp., 577 P.2d 216, 222 (Alaska 1977), as consequential damages, if they were reasonably anticipated. C. McCormick, Law of Damages §681 (1935).

An award of lost profits is not proper if it is the result of speculation. Dowling Supply & Equipment, Inc. v. City of Anchorage, 490 P.2d 907, 909–910 (Alaska 1971). See State v. Hammer, 550 P.2d 820, 824–825 (Alaska 1976). This is based on the generally accepted principle of contract law that damages are not recoverable unless they are reasonably certain. 5 A. Corbin, Corbin on Contracts §§1021–1022 (1961); Restatement of Contracts §331 (1932).

Application of this principle has led courts to deny recovery for lost profits of an unestablished business, as an invariable rule. The more en-lightened approach, however, is to allow damages for lost profits to new businesses if the injured party can show damages with reasonable cer-tainty. Ferrell v. Elrod, 63 Tenn. App. 129, 469 S.W.2d 678, 686 (1971). In Ferrell, 469 S.W.2d at 686, the court noted that if profits could be shown with reasonable certainty, "there is no reason to penalize the enterprise of the founder of a new business by denying him his remedy for losses occasioned by the default of the defendant." In Vickers, the Kansas Su-preme Court noted that to preclude recovery "as a matter of law merely because a business is newly established would encourage those contract-ing with such a business to breach their contracts." 518 P.2d at 517. We agree, and thus do not apply an inflexible rule denying recovery of lost profits to a new business for breach of contract.

Nevertheless, the lost profits must be proven with reasonable cer-tainty. In cases involving an established business, courts have considered past profits a reasonably certain measure by which to calculate a damage award. See Buck v. Mueller, 221 Ore. 271, 351 P.2d 61, 67 (1960); Note, The Requirement of Certainty in the Proof of Lost Profits, 64 Harv. L. Rev. 317, 319–320 (1950). A new business, however, does not have its own history of profits. Thus, courts have considered both the profit history from the plaintiff's similar business at a different location, Standard Ma-chinery Co. v. Duncan Shaw Corp., 208 F.2d 61, 64–65 (1st Cir. 1953), and the profit history from the business in question if it was successfully run by someone else before the plaintiff, General Electric Supply Co. v. Mt. Wheeler Power, Inc., 94 Nev. 766, 587 P.2d 1312, 1313 (Nev. 1978), to be a measure of reasonable certainty for a damage award when a new busi-ness has been injured.

If P & R is to recover in this case, its profit history must come from a substantially similar business run by the P & R shareholders, because none of the previous owners of the Edgewater operated the facilities on the scale proposed by P & R. Ralph Kalenka, one of the P & R share-holders, profitably ran a restaurant in Mountain View. Peter Dalhausser, another shareholder, had managed a restaurant and nightclub in Fair-banks. Although Kalenka and Dalhausser each had extensive experience in the catering industry and general experience in managing restaurants, their previous businesses were not substantially similar to the planned "multi-million dollar restaurant," nightclub, and motel. Thus, their past profits cannot be used as a basis for awarding lost profits here.

If P & R were allowed to recover from the Guards without estab-lishing the certainty of profits, the Guards would become the guarantors of P & R's ability to make a profit in their new venture. At the time of the land sale agreement, P & R was in the better position to anticipate its profits than were the Guards. Because this was a contract between two parties, P & R could have negotiated a liquidated damages clause into the contract, thereby allocating the risk of lost profits in the event of the breach, and giving the Guards adequate information on which to value the risk of breach. Since P & R had the ability to negotiate the allocation of risk, the Guards should not be the guarantors of P & R's anticipated profits in the absence of more certain proof establishing that profits would have eventuated. Thus we conclude that the damage award must be revised.

Reversed and remanded to the superior court for further proceedings consistent with this opinion.

Questions

1. Why does the court say that a remedy for damages and specific performance are mutually exclusive?
2. Why was the plaintiff seeking specific performance?
3. What does the court say about awarding lost profits to the injured party?

Edens v. Goodyear Tire & Rubber Co.
858 F.2d 198 (4th Cir. 1988)

Goodyear Tire and Rubber Company appeals from a judgment for actual and punitive damages in favor of North Strand Investments for breach of contract accompanied by a fraudulent act. We affirm.

I

Since Goodyear appeals from a jury verdict and the denial of a motion for judgment notwithstanding the verdict, we consider the evidence in the light most favorable to North Strand Investments. Evington v. Forbes, 742 F.2d 834, 835 (4th Cir. 1984). North Strand is a South Carolina general partnership formed in 1979 for the purpose of purchasing the North Strand Shopping Center in North Myrtle Beach, South Carolina which it resold in 1983 to Wespac Investors Trust for approximately $2,000,000.00. North Strand retained title to a lot adjacent to the parking area for the purpose of building a Goodyear tire store on it. Wespac separately contracted to pay $497,500.00 for the lot, if within one year North Strand constructed a building on it and obtained a lease from Goodyear. In the event that a lease was not obtained, title to the lot would be transferred to Wespac without monetary consideration.

After several months of preliminary negotiations, in November 1983 Goodyear presented North Strand with a proposed lease agreement. North Strand signed the lease in December 1983 and returned it to Goodyear. Modification by mutual consent resulted in a final lease being executed in April 1984. The lease imposed on Goodyear the responsibility for providing final plans and specifications for the construction of a building by North Strand. The lease established a completion date of June 1, 1984, but allowed a 90-day extension for delay due to unavoidable contingencies.

Although Goodyear had provided preliminary plans for the building in December 1983 prior to the lease being finalized, final plans were not furnished until June 6, 1984. The plans were subject to North Strand's approval and Goodyear advised North Strand not to begin construction until they were so approved. Negotiations regarding changes continued into September 1984 and the parties never arrived at agreement on the final plans. As a result, construction never commenced.

The June 1 completion date was agreed upon in the early stages of negotiations, but when the finalization of the lease was delayed until April 1984, North Strand requested an extension of the completion date until October 1, 1984. Goodyear did not respond to this request and North Strand did not pursue it. After the final plans were delivered on June 6, North Strand requested an extension until March 1, 1985. Following its somewhat unusual, yet customary procedure, Goodyear drafted a "proposed Lease Amendment" requesting an extension on behalf of North Strand and forwarded it with instructions that all copies be signed by North Strand and returned to Goodyear. In its cover letter of September 5, 1984, Goodyear stated that the extension was "subject to approval and signature by Goodyear Management in Akron, Ohio." The proposed amendment specifically requested that "[i]f the foregoing change is acceptable to you, will you please so indicate by signing and returning to the undersigned the attached carbon copy of this letter." Lloyd Kapp signed the proposal on behalf of North Strand and returned the copies to Goodyear on September 10. Paul J. Smith, national director of real estate for Goodyear signed the proposal, but it was never returned to North Strand.

Meanwhile, Goodyear's region management became dissatisfied with the site "due to the lack of viability of the shopping center in which the facility [was] proposed." On or before October 12, 1984, R. W. Frederick, an administrative assistant in the real estate department, met with Dave Siladie of the architectural division and legal counsel Bill Runyan to discuss cancellation of the lease. Frederick documented this discussion in a memorandum as follows:[1]

> Runyan felt that if we cancelled using the fact that completion date had not been met we could have a problem with litigation in that an extension of said completion date was in the works.
>
> He suggested that our fieldman (Freed) converse with the Landlord and advise him that because of the delays on the finalization of plans we are no longer interested in this location. If that works we'll need a mutual cancellation agreement. If not we'll have to cancel using completion date and take our chances. . . .

---

1. At trial Goodyear opposed the admission of this document, asserting an attorney-client privilege. However, it had waived any arguable privilege by producing the memorandum during discovery without objection. United States v. Mierzwicki, 500 F. Supp. 1331, 1334 (D. Md. 1980); see also United States v. Martin, 773 F.2d 579, 584 (4th Cir. 1985).

On October 19, 1984, L. J. Thompson, manager of location development, advised Smith of region management's desire to cancel the lease and requested that he "pursue the Law Department for a determination if the lease can be cancelled."

During approximately this same time period, R. K. Freed, southern region real estate manager for Goodyear, informed Michael Edwards, North Strand's real estate agent, that Goodyear had "lost interest in the area and no longer wanted to put a Goodyear store there on [the] site." Edwards subsequently met with Freed in Atlanta, Georgia in late October. Although they discussed the request for the extension at that meeting, Freed did not inform Edwards that Smith had approved and signed the extension. Freed offered mutual cancellation which Edwards refused.

Edwards left the meeting with the impression that Goodyear was going to continue with the deal. However, on December 4, 1984 Thompson reiterated dissatisfaction with the site and directed Frederick to consult the legal department again, stating: "It is desired that every avenue of lease cancellation be pursued." Shortly thereafter on December 10, 1984, Smith notified North Strand of Goodyear's decision to cancel the lease. Goodyear gave as its justification North Strand's failure to complete construction by the June 1 deadline plus the 90-day extension provided for under the original terms of the lease.

North Strand subsequently brought suit, initially alleging breach of contract. After the Goodyear internal memoranda and signed extension were produced during discovery, North Strand amended its complaint to allege a claim for breach of contract accompanied by a fraudulent act, seeking punitive damages. At trial, except for a few documents introduced during cross-examination of witnesses for North Strand, Goodyear presented no evidence and offered no testimony. Consequently, much of the critical testimony given by North Strand's witnesses was uncontradicted. The jury returned a verdict for North Strand, awarding $277,517.00 in actual damages and $675,000.00 in punitive damages. The district court denied Goodyear's motions for judgment notwithstanding the verdict and for a new trial and awarded North Strand prejudgment interest.

Goodyear appeals the judgment on numerous assignments of error, primarily arguing that North Strand failed to establish a prima facie case of breach of contract accompanied by a fraudulent act. Goodyear also challenges certain jury instructions. We find that North Strand presented sufficient evidence to establish its prima facie case and that the district court properly instructed the jury.

II

The primary question presented is whether, under the law of the State of South Carolina, North Strand has established the essential elements of a claim for breach of contract accompanied by a fraudulent act sufficient to support the award of actual and punitive damages. Erie R. R. v. Tompkins, 304 U.S. 64, 58 S. Ct. 817, 82 L. Ed. 1188 (1938). Since the turn of the century, it has been well settled in South Carolina that punitive damages may be recovered for breach of contract accompanied by a fraudulent act.[2]

Over the years, the South Carolina appellate courts have found a wide variety of factual allegations sufficient to constitute a claim for fraudulent breach of contract. Welborn v. Dixon, 70 S.C. 108, 49 S.E. 232 (1904); Blackmon v. United Ins. Co., 233 S.C. 424, 105 S.E.2d 521 (1958); Harper v. Ethridge, 290 S.C. 112, 348 S.E.2d 374 (Ct. App. 1986). And they have repeatedly refused to limit the type of acts giving rise to liability for breach of contract accompanied by a fraudulent act, instead providing that:

> Fraud assumes so many hues and forms, that courts are compelled to content themselves with comparatively few general rules for its discovery and defeat, and allow the facts and circumstances peculiar to each case to bear heavily upon the conscience and judgment of the court or jury in determining its presence or absence.

Wright v. Public Savings Life Ins. Co., 262 S.C. 285, 289, 204 S.E.2d 57, 59 (1974). In most cases, the courts have affirmed submission of these claims to the jury and affirmed the resulting awards of punitive damages. The courts occasionally have sustained demurrers to complaints attempting to state a claim for breach of contract accompanied by a fraudulent act where plaintiffs failed to allege fraudulent intent or a fraudulent act. Patterson v. Capital Life & Health Ins. Co., 228 S.C. 297, 89 S.E.2d 723 (1955). And jury awards of punitive damages on such claims have been reversed only where there was a failure of proof of a requisite element. Ray v. Pilgrim Health & Life Ins. Co., 206 S.C. 344, 34 S.E.2d 218 (1945); Hardee v. Penn Mutual Ins. Co., 215 S.C. 1, 53 S.E.2d 861 (1949); Gavin v. North Carolina Mutual Ins. Co., 265 S.C. 206, 217 S.E.2d 591 (1975); Rutledge v. St. Paul Fire & Marine Ins. Co., 286 S.C. 360, 334 S.E.2d 131 (Ct. App. 1985).

From this body of South Carolina law, several basic principles have emerged. First, a claim for breach of contract accompanied by a fraudulent act is not a claim separate and apart from one for breach of contract. Smith v. Canal Ins. Co., 275 S.C. at 260, 269 S.E.2d at 350. Rather, proof

2. See Note, Punitive Damages for Breach of Contract in South Carolina, 10 S.C.L.Q. 444 (1958). In contrast, other states in this circuit do not allow punitive damages for breach of contract unless the conduct constitutes an independent and willful tort. McDaniel v. Bass-Smith Funeral Home, Inc., 80 N.C. App. 629, 343 S.E.2d 228 (1986); Hayseeds, Inc. v. State Farm Fire & Cas., 352 S.E.2d 73 (W. Va. 1986); Gasque v. Mooers Motor Car Co., 277 Va. 154, 313 S.E.2d 384 (1984); Brand Iron, Inc. v. Koehring Co., 595 F. Supp. 1037 (D. Md. 1984). In fact, it appears that South Carolina is the only state in the nation which permits punitive damages for conduct which does not give rise to an independent tort claim. See 22 Am. Jur. 2d Damages §245 (1965); J. Calamari & J. Perillo, The Law of Contracts §14-3 (2d ed. 1977). While New Mexico recognizes a claim for punitive damages for breach of contract accompanied by a fraudulent act, it further requires that the act be "wanton in character and maliciously intentional." Whitehead v. Allen, 63 N.M. 63, 66, 313 P.2d 335, 336 (1957).

that a breach of contract was accompanied by a fraudulent act is a predicate for recovery of punitive damages. Id. Further, a claim for breach of contract accompanied by a fraudulent act does not require proof of the same elements as a tort claim for fraud and deceit. Harper v. Ethridge, 290 S.C. at 118, 348 S.E.2d at 378. "However, mere breach of a contract, even if willful or with fraudulent purpose, is not sufficient to entitle a plaintiff to go to the jury on the issue of punitive damages." Floyd v. Country Squire Mobile Homes, Inc., 287 S.C. at 53, 336 S.E.2d at 503. To establish a breach of contract accompanied by a fraudulent act and recover punitive damages, a plaintiff must prove three elements: (1) breach of contract, (2) fraudulent intent relating to the breach, and (3) a fraudulent act accompanying the breach. Id.; Harper, 290 S.C. at 119, 348 S.E.2d at 378.

A

To establish a breach of contract, North Strand was first required to prove the existence of a contract. Goodyear contends that North Strand failed to establish this, asserting that the evidence did not show a meeting of the minds or a mutual manifestation of assent regarding the construction plans and specifications or the completion date. North Strand maintains that the completion date and final approval of the plans were conditions precedent to performance of the contract, not to its formation. While there was conflicting evidence on this issue, it was clearly one for resolution by a jury.

As the trial court correctly charged the jury, mutual assent to all essential terms of an agreement is necessary to formation of a contract. W. E. Gilbert & Associates v. South Carolina Nat'l Bank, 285 S.C. 421, 330 S.E.2d 307 (Ct. App. 1985). The lease executed by both parties clearly shows that they agreed to a completion date of June 1, 1984 and that Goodyear was responsible for providing construction plans and specifications for North Strand's approval. The question of whether approval of the plans and completion of the building were conditions precedent to the formation of the contract or to Goodyear's duty of performance depends on the intent of the parties. Champion v. Whaley, 280 S.C. 116, 122, 311 S.E.2d 404, 408 (Ct. App. 1984). In its answer, Goodyear admitted that it "entered into a lease agreement with [North Strand] contingent on certain terms and conditions being met prior to finalization of the lease." Goodyear also characterized the conditions as precedent to its performance under the contract.

Goodyear further contends that North Strand failed to present evidence that it breached the contract, and that it was North Strand who breached the contract by failing to timely construct the building. As the jury was properly charged, generally the party suing on a conditional contract has the burden of proving that the conditions to performance have been met. Id. at 120, 311 S.E.2d at 406. However, if one party prevents a condition from occurring, then the condition is excused and he cannot rely upon the other party's resulting nonperformance. Id. The uncontradicted evidence of Goodyear's failure to provide the required construction plans and specifications prior to the completion date was sufficient to support a finding by the jury that Goodyear breached the contract and prevented North Strand from fulfilling the conditions.

B

At trial North Strand sought to prove the remaining elements of fraudulent intent and a fraudulent act by presenting evidence that Goodyear offered a false excuse for cancelling the lease and withheld information that the extension had been granted. Goodyear argued that, even if proven, these contentions were insufficient to support a claim for punitive damages. We agree that offering a false excuse for cancellation of a contract, standing alone, would have been insufficient to establish breach of contract accompanied by a fraudulent act. However, if the jury found, as it obviously could have, that Goodyear granted an extension and then intentionally concealed that information, this would constitute a separate and distinct fraudulent act sufficient to support an award of punitive damages.

In an ordinary breach of contract case, the motive of the breaching party is irrelevant to a determination of damages. Holland v. Spartanburg Herald-Journal Co., 166 S.C. 454, 465, 165 S.E. 203, 207 (1932). However, in a claim for breach of contract accompanied by a fraudulent act, motive is relevant to the requisite element of fraudulent intent.[3] Normally this element is proven by circumstances surrounding the breach. Scott v. Mid Carolina Homes, Inc., 293 S.C. at 197, 359 S.E.2d at 295. Here Goodyear's internal memoranda clearly support a jury finding of fraudulent intent.

Proof of fraudulent intent alone does not justify an award of punitive damages because a fraudulent act accompanying the breach must also be established. Floyd v. Country Squire Mobile Homes, Inc., 287 S.C. at 54, 336 S.E.2d at 503, 504. "The fraudulent act is any act characterized by dishonesty in fact, unfair dealing, or the unlawful appropriation of another's property by design."[4] Harper v. Ethridge, 290 S.C. at 119, 348 S.E.2d at 378. The act must be separate and distinct from the breach itself, but still must be closely connected with it and "not be too remote in either time or character." Smith v. Canal Ins. Co., 275 S.C. at 260, 269 S.E.2d at 350; Floyd, 287 S.C. at 54, 336 S.E.2d at 504.

---

3. The trial court properly refused Goodyear's request to charge the jury that "whether the breach is willful or intentional or malicious has no bearing on the matter [of breach of contract accompanied by a fraudulent act] whatsoever."

4. In contrast, North Carolina requires proof of aggravated conduct such as fraud, malice or oppression. McDaniel v. Bass-Smith Funeral Home, Inc., 343 S.E.2d at 231. And Maryland requires proof of malice, consisting of "an evil or rancorous motive influenced by hate; the purpose being to deliberately and wilfully injure the plaintiff." Wiggins v. North American Equitable Life Assurance Co., 644 F.2d 1014, 1018 n.2 (4th Cir. 1981) (quoting Food Fair Stores, Inc. v. Hevey, 275 Md. 50, 55, 338 A.2d 43, 46 (1975)). Accord Hayseeds, Inc. v. State Farm Fire & Cas., 352 S.E.2d 73 (W. Va. 1986); Kamlar Corp. v. Haley, 224 Va. 699, 299 S.E.2d 514 (1983).

Goodyear's false excuse for cancelling the lease was not sufficiently separate and distinct from the breach to constitute an accompanying fraudulent act. However, proof that Goodyear granted an extension and intentionally concealed that information while claiming North Strand's failure to meet the initial completion date as justification for cancellation, would be a separate and distinct, but closely connected, dishonest act sufficient to support an award of punitive damages.

C

The question remaining is whether the extension was in fact granted. Goodyear argues that although Smith signed the extension, it was not effective because it was not returned to North Strand. North Strand maintains that it was effective upon signing by Smith. The uncontradicted evidence presented by North Strand provides more than a sufficient basis on which the jury could have found that by Goodyear's own terms the extension was effective when signed by Smith.

Generally, an offeror is entitled to notification of acceptance unless the offer reveals a contrary intention. Restatement (Second) of Contracts §56 comment a (1981). And under South Carolina law, "[a]ssent to an offer need not be expressed to constitute a contract, but may be inferred from acts and conduct." Scott v. Mid Carolina Homes, Inc., 293 S.C. at 197, 359 S.E.2d at 295. For example, where an offer provides that it "becomes a contract" or "shall take effect" when approved at the offeree's home office, such approval is an acceptance even though no steps are taken to notify the offeror. Restatement, supra, illustrations 1 & 2; see Int'l Filter Co. v. Conroe Gin, Ice & Light Co., 277 S.W. 631 (Tex. Comm. App. 1925); Field v. Missouri Life Ins. Co., 77 Utah 45, 290 P. 979 (1930). Dispensing with notice may present practical problems since the offeror may not promptly learn of its duty to perform, but this does not affect the creation of an agreement which is binding on the offeree.

Here, North Strand requested an extension of the completion date. Goodyear then prepared "a proposed Lease Amendment" on North Strand's behalf and sent four copies to North Strand on September 5, 1984 for signature, directing that all four copies be returned to the regional office in Atlanta. Lloyd Kapp signed the document on behalf of North Strand and returned the copies to Atlanta on September 10. The copies were forwarded to Akron where they were signed by Smith, although North Strand was never notified of this approval.

The document was drafted by Goodyear as a letter from North Strand to the attention of the real estate department at Goodyear's main office in Akron. It provided that: "If the foregoing change is acceptable to you, will you please so indicate by signing and returning to the undersigned the attached carbon copy of this letter." However, in its cover letter, Goodyear expressly stated that the amendment was "subject to approval and signature by Goodyear Management in Akron, Ohio." The cover letter and the amendment are facially inconsistent regarding the necessity of notification. North Strand partner Lloyd Kapp testified on cross-examination without objection that it was his understanding from the cover letter that the extension was final upon approval and signature in Akron. Although Goodyear drafted both documents and created the conflict, it failed to offer any evidence on this issue. The uncontradicted evidence of Kapp's understanding was sufficient to support the jury's determination that the extension was effective when approved and signed by Paul Smith in Akron.

III

In comparing the facts here to those in similar cases where South Carolina courts have found that claims of breach of contract accompanied by a fraudulent act were sufficiently pled and affirmed awards of punitive damages, it is clear that North Strand's claim was properly submitted to the jury. For example, recently in Harper v. Ethridge, the South Carolina Court of Appeals held that a claim was sufficiently pled where one partner of a real estate development partnership alleged that the other partners dishonestly refused to renew or extend a promissory note, consent to reasonable development offers or arbitrate third-party offers, and wrongfully appropriated partnership assets and opportunities. 290 S.C. 112, 348 S.E.2d 374.

Harper was a member of a partnership formed to develop a convention center on a parcel of land on which it had an option. When it was unable to obtain the necessary financing, Ethridge was invited to join the partnership to provide additional financial strength. Pursuant to the agreement, Harper assigned the option to Ethridge and another partner, Fann, who obtained a purchase money loan and bought the property in trust for the partnership. Harper was responsible for his proportionate share of the taxes, interest and the loan balance, and his partnership interest was forfeitable if he failed to meet those responsibilities.

The agreement provided that the partners would search for a developer to repurchase the land and the proceeds would be used to pay off the loan and pay expenses with any profit to be distributed among the partners. The agreement further provided that if a partner presented a reasonable development plan and Ethridge and Fann withheld approval to the jeopardy of the interests of the other partners, the default provision would be suspended pending arbitration.

Harper arranged a contract with foreign investors but Ethridge refused to approve the proposal and then refused to arbitrate. Instead, Ethridge and Fann entered into an option with a local developer which was never exercised. When the loan matured, Ethridge and Fann refused to renew or extend the note. Rather, they declared Harper in default and invoked the forfeiture provision. Subsequently Ethridge and Fann entered into a contract with the same foreign investors under conditions substantially similar to those of Harper's previously rejected proposal.

The court of appeals held that these factual allegations were clearly sufficient to state a claim for breach of contract accompanied by a fraud-

ulent act, finding that dishonest refusal to renew or extend the note evidenced fraudulent intent, and that wrongful appropriation of trust
property and a partnership opportunity constituted accompanying fraudulent acts. In comparison, while the facts here are different since Goodyear did not refuse an extension or misappropriate any North Strand
asset, the substance of the dishonest schemes are similar. Goodyear as
well as Ethridge and Fann dishonestly created the excuses for ending
their contractual relationships. And although Goodyear did not directly
profit from those actions as did Ethridge and Fann, it did not profit indirectly by avoiding anticipated losses on the lease.

In several cases, South Carolina courts have affirmed an award of
punitive damages where a party offered a false excuse for breaching a
contract and committed an accompanying fraudulent act. Recently in
Glover v. North Carolina Mutual Life Ins. Co., the South Carolina Court
of Appeals affirmed a punitive damages award against an insurance company for cancellation of a life insurance policy. 295 S.C. 251, 368 S.E.2d
68. Ms. Glover had purchased the policy in November 1973 and timely
paid her monthly premiums through August 1984. At the time she made
the August 1984 payment, she requested a copy of her policy. Instead of
providing a copy, North Carolina Mutual notified her that the policy had
been cancelled ten years previously for failure to pay premiums. The
court held that the jury could have found the insurance company's fraudulent intent was to induce Glover not to make further premium payments
which would then cause the policy to lapse and that the accompanying
fraudulent act was the collection of premiums after purportedly repudi-
ating the contract. Both Goodyear and North Carolina Mutual attempted
to avoid their contractual responsibilities by falsely claiming that North
Strand and Glover had breached the respective contracts and each committed a separate accompanying fraudulent act.

The South Carolina Court of Appeals affirmed a punitive damages
award against a mobile home dealer for breach of a sales contract in Scott
v. Mid Carolina Homes, Inc., 293 S.C. 191, 359 S.E.2d 291. After the Scotts
signed a contract for the purchase of a mobile home and made a deposit,
a Mid Carolina salesman informed them that he could not sell them the
home because the frame was bent. Although the Scotts offered to accept
the home and sign a release, the salesman stated that he was prohibited
by state law from selling the home with a bent frame. In fact there was
no such law and the same home was sold within the week to another
purchaser for almost double the price quoted to the Scotts. And, after
cancelling the contract, Mid Carolina cashed the Scotts' deposit check and
refused to return their money until they threatened legal action.

The court held that fraudulent intent was inferable from the salesman's false excuse for cancelling the sale and that the jury could have
viewed the false excuse in conjunction with the subsequent sale and the
cashing of the deposit check as accompanying fraudulent acts. Here,
fraudulent intent was inferable from Goodyear's internal memoranda and
the false excuse, and intentional concealment of the extension could have
been viewed by the jury as an accompanying fraudulent act.

In Corley v. Coastal States Life Ins. Co., a punitive damages award was affirmed where the defendant insurance company attempted to settle a beneficiary's claim for less than the amount owed. 244 S.C. 1, 135 S.E.2d 316. Mrs. Corley's husband had purchased a life insurance policy from Coastal States under which death benefits included the face value of the policy and also provided for return of all paid premiums. After the death of the insured a dispute arose about the amount of premiums to be returned. Coastal States informed Mrs. Corley through the state Insurance Commission of the total amount payable, but after she surrendered the policy, the company issued a check for substantially less. The company contended that the previous quotation was a good faith mistake in calculations arising from the unusual nature of the policy. However, the assistant secretary of the company who prepared the second set of calculations and issued the check, testified that he made a "deliberate decision" about the amount due. The court held that the jury could have inferred a breach of contract accompanied by a fraudulent act and that the issue was properly submitted to it. If those facts justified submission of a claim for punitive damages to the jury, the facts here similarly justify such submission, for in both situations the defendants offered "false" excuses in an effort to avoid their legal obligations.

If one party to a contract elects to breach it, he is responsible for the actual consequential damages resulting from the breach. Holland v. Spartanburg Herald-Journal Co., 166 S.C. at 469, 165 S.E. at 208. If Coastal States had simply refused to pay the initially quoted amount due and offered to settle for less, or Mid Carolina had flatly refused to complete the sale, or North Carolina Mutual had only cancelled the policy, there would not have been any issues of fraudulent breach. See Rutledge v. St. Paul Fire and Marine Ins. Co., 286 S.C. 360, 334 S.E.2d 131 (refusal to make payment on a fire insurance policy unless the insured agreed to take a polygraph test was not a fraudulent act); Vann v. Nationwide Ins. Co., 257 S.C. 217, 185 S.E.2d 363 (refusal to pay medical expenses due under an automobile insurance policy unless the insured settled the uninsured motorist claim was not a fraudulent act). Similarly, if as proposed in the October memorandum, Goodyear had simply cancelled using the missed completion date as an excuse and "taken its chances," North Strand could only have sought recovery for actual damages. Likewise, if Goodyear had notified North Strand that the extension had been approved and then cancelled the contract, it would only have been liable for actual damages.

Under South Carolina law, if a breach of contract is accomplished with fraudulent intent and accompanied by a fraudulent act punitive damages may also be awarded. Thus, by giving false excuses for breaching their contracts and otherwise dealing dishonestly and unfairly, Coastal States, Mid Carolina and North Carolina Mutual subjected themselves to liability for punitive damages. And here, evidence that Goodyear granted an extension of the completion date until March 1, 1985 but intentionally concealed that fact, and cancelled the lease in December 1984 using the excuse that North Strand failed to complete the building by the initial completion date was sufficient to support a jury finding of dishonesty or unfair dealing and an award of punitive damages.

IV

As the dissent correctly states, the South Carolina Supreme Court has held that when the fraudulent act accompanying a breach of contract is a misrepresentation, the plaintiff must prove reliance on the misrepresentation. Kelly v. Nationwide Mut. Ins. Co., 278 S.C. 488, 489, 298 S.E.2d 454, 455 (1982) (citing Vann v. Nationwide Ins. Co., 257 S.C. 217, 185 S.E.2d 363); Rutledge v. St. Paul Fire & Marine Ins. Co., 286 S.C. at 365, 334 S.E.2d at 135. The dissent would reverse the award of punitive damages on the basis that North Strand failed to prove detrimental reliance on Goodyear's misrepresentation. However, the actionable independent fraudulent act here was not Goodyear's misrepresentation of its reason for cancellation, but rather its affirmative concealment of the extension of the completion date. And, direct proof of reliance on the concealment was not required for it was practically impossible to prove, by direct evidence, reliance on that which had been intentionally concealed.

As the United States Supreme Court has recognized, "cases involving omissions create difficult problems of proof of reliance." Piper v. Chris-Craft Industries, Inc., 430 U.S. 1, 50, 97 S. Ct. 926, 954, 51 L. Ed. 2d 124 (1977) (Blackmun, J., concurring) (citing Affiliated Ute Citizens of Utah v. United States, 406 U.S. 128, 92 S. Ct. 1456, 31 L. Ed. 2d 741 (1972)). "Requiring a plaintiff to show a speculative state of facts, i.e., how he would have acted if omitted material information had been disclosed . . . would place an unnecessarily unrealistic evidentiary burden on the . . . plaintiff. . . ." Basic Inc. v. Levinson, 485 U.S.—,—, 108 S. Ct. 978, 990, 99 L. Ed. 2d 194, 217 (1988) (citing Ute, 406 U.S. at 153-154, 92 S. Ct. at 1472-72) (other citations omitted). Because of such problems, the Court in Ute held that where fraudulent conduct involves "primarily a failure to disclose, positive proof of reliance is not a prerequisite to recovery." Ute, 406 U.S. at 153, 92 S. Ct. at 1472.

Ute involved a securities fraud action for omission of material facts in connection with the purchase of stock. Securities Exchange Act of 1934, §10(b), 15 U.S.C.A. §78j(b) (West 1981); S.E.C. Rule 10b-5, 17 C.F.R. §240.10b-5 (1987). As is the case with a claim for fraudulent breach of contract, a securities fraud claim does not require proof of the traditional nine elements of a common law fraud claim, see Basic, 485 U.S. at—n.22, 108 S. Ct. at 990 n.22, 99 L. Ed. 2d at 216 n.22, and the basic fraud element of reliance need not always be proven to establish claims for either securities fraud or fraudulent breach of contract.

Reliance is generally a requisite element of a 10b-5 claim, id. at—, 108 S. Ct. at 989, 99 L. Ed. 2d at 215, and it is also required where a fraudulent breach of contract claim arises from a misrepresentation. However, in nondisclosure cases, a 10b-5 plaintiff is relieved of the difficult, if not impossible, burden of producing direct evidence of reliance. And applying the same reasoning of the Court in *Ute* to the circumstances here, North Strand was excused from directly proving reliance, since the unfair or dishonest act accompanying the breach of contract was Goodyear's intentional concealment of the extension.[5]

Goodyear tacitly conceded that reliance was not a requisite element of North Strand's claim, for it never contended that North Strand was required to prove reliance on the concealment. At trial, Goodyear apparently did not request a charge on reliance and did not object to the district court's decision not to charge the jury that North Strand was required to prove reliance on the concealment to establish its claim for breach of contract accompanied by a fraudulent act. Further, Goodyear has made no such assertion on appeal.

V

Goodyear also contends that the court erred in charging the jury on the measure of actual damages. Considering the charge as a whole, we find that the instructions "fairly and adequately state[d] the pertinent legal principles involved." Chavis v. Finnlines, Ltd., 576 F2d 1072, 1076 (4th Cir. 1978).

The district court instructed the jury that "the injured party in a contract dispute may recover as damages any profits which were prevented or lost because of the other party's breach." The contract price of the sale of the lot to Wespac with a building and Goodyear lease was $497,500.00 and the projected cost of development was $219,983.00. The jury awarded North Strand actual damages of $277,517.00, North Strand's lost net profit.

Goodyear contends that the court erred in refusing its request to charge the jury that "the allowance of compensatory damages is the difference between the real or market value of the property and the contract price, and not the profits that might have accrued to the lessor." However, the district court's instruction correctly stated South Carolina law, under which "[l]ost profits are well recognized as a species of consequential damages" in breach of contract actions. John D. Hollingsworth on Wheels, Inc. v. Arkon Corp., 279 S.C. 183, 186, 305 S.E.2d 71, 73 (1983).

Affirmed.

Questions

1. Under what circumstances can a court award punitive damages?
2. What was the "fraudulent act" in this case?

---

5. Despite the difficulty of direct proof, here reliance was clearly inferable from the fact that North Strand did not construct and tender a completed building by March 1, 1985, although the evidence showed it was ready, willing and able and would have done so had it known that Goodyear had granted the extension.

3. Did a contract in fact exist?
4. Do you agree with the outcome of the case? Why, or why not?

Suggested Case References

1. Read the requirements needed to be granted punitive damages in North Carolina. Process Components v. Baltimore Aircoil Co., Inc. 89 N.C. App. 649, 366 S.E.2d 907 (1988).
2. Who has the burden of proving mitigation of damages, the breaching party or the injured party? Cobb v. Osman, 83 Nev. 415 (1967).
3. What circumstances are necessary before a court may order specific performance? Mann v. Golub, 182 W. Va. 523, 389 S.E.2d 734 (1990); In re Estate of Hayhurst, 478 P.2d 343 (Okla. 1970).
4. Does a party's actual performance under a contract in which performance was subject to a condition precedent constitute a waiver of the condition? See what the Montana court said in Hein v. Fox, 126 Mont. 514, 254 P.2d 1076 (1954).

12 Drafting Simple Contracts

CHAPTER OBJECTIVE

This chapter incorporates all of the principles and ideas discussed in the previous chapters into one complete contract. Many people are daunted at the prospect of creating a contractual relationship, but in fact the process is quite interesting and challenging.

There are three keys to creating a contract that will truly reflect the parties' wishes: 1) start with a thorough understanding of the precise wishes of the contracting parties; 2) use a checklist of clauses, or topics, that should be covered; and 3) create the agreement by referring to existing contracts covering the same or similar subject matter. No lawyer or paralegal is expected to devise a contract out of whole cloth, and to this end there are many sources of sample contracts available to the drafter.

Before attempting to draft a contract, make sure that you have a clear idea of the precise nature of the relationship the parties intend. This must include all of the six major requirements of every valid contract (Chapter 1). Additionally, every industry has its own special terminology and relationships that must be included in an industry contract. To ascertain what those areas might be, use the library to read books about the particular area involved. Not only law libraries, but regular public libraries have innumerable volumes covering every conceivable industry, and this should always be a first reference before drafting a contract. These sources not only will indicate special areas of concern but usually will include sample agreements that can be used as models.

Always ask the parties themselves and the attorney whether they have old contracts that they wish to have used as a basis for the new agreement. This is usually the best source of a sample because the parties have already used, and presumably have been happy with, that format. Just bear in mind that these former contracts are usable only as samples; it is exceedingly rare that one contract will be perfect for several different parties. There is always going to be a need to make certain changes in the contractual provisions to reflect the current contractual relationship. And finally, always check the appropriate state law, both common and statutory, to insure compliance with any particular requirements.

The following section of this chapter will discuss many of the most typical types of clauses that appear in contracts. This section can be used as a checklist in preparing a draft contract. By going through the list, the paralegal will be able to determine that all of the important provisions have been discussed. Of course, the list is hardly exhaustive, but it does provide the basic guidelines for simple contract drafting. Additionally, sample contracts have been included that cover many different areas of law and that can be used as models by the novice drafter. After a while, attorneys and paralegals develop their own samples from the contracts they have drafted. To build an excellent resource for samples, paralegals should develop the habit of keeping copies of all legal documents that they come in contact with for future use, deleting the parties' names and identifying information. As long as a person has a sample format to follow, drafting contracts becomes an easy process.

Always bear in mind that each clause in a sample contract must be read to determine whether its wording is in the best interests of a given client; if not, simple changes in the language can be made. To this end, it is always a good idea to use more than one sample contract; by having multiple samples, clauses can be compared and contrasted, and sentences can be taken from different contracts to create a clause that would suit the given client.

Reviewing existing contracts and contract interpretation should also be mentioned here. There will be many instances in which the paralegal must analyze an existing contract to determine the rights and liabilities of a client. The process of interpretation is the exact reverse of drafting. Simply read the contract to determine what is said in each clause, and use the checklist to make sure no major areas have been deleted or ignored. Pretend that the contract to be analyzed is a sample and go through it the same way you would if you were drafting the contract.

Checklist of Clauses

The following clauses are presented in an order most often followed in drafting contracts, but, of course, changes in the order can always be made.

Description of the Parties

The first clause of every contract usually contains a description of the parties to the agreement. The term *description* means the legal names and aliases of the parties, type of entity each party is, and the manner in which the parties will be referred to throughout the remainder of the contract.

EXAMPLE:

This agreement is made this ＿＿＿ day of ＿＿＿＿＿, 20＿＿＿, between Acme Realty, Inc., a New York corporation (hereinafter "Corporation"), and Lyle Roberts, an individual resident in the State of Pennsylvania (hereinafter "Roberts").

It is necessary to note the exact legal names of the parties and the type of entity each party is—corporation, limited partnership, individual, and so forth—in case of a potential dispute with respect to the agreement. When commencing a lawsuit and serving process, it is necessary to know exactly how the parties are legally designated. To this end, the introductory clause may also include the parties' addresses. Addresses usually appear at the end of a contract below the parties' signatures or may appear in provisions providing for notice to the parties.

Indicating a nomenclature for the parties other than their legal names is for the purpose of achieving simplicity throughout the remainder of the agreement. Many times, especially if the contract is a form contract used by one of the parties, this designation may indicate the roles the parties play in the agreement, such as Buyer, Seller, or Landlord. Any designation agreed on is appropriate. Simply make sure that the same designation is used throughout the remainder of the agreement. Be consistent.

Description of the Consideration

For the purpose of contract law, this section of the agreement assumes primary importance. In this clause, the offer, acceptance, and consideration coalesce into a binding contract. As indicated in the first four chapters of this book, it is mandatory that the consideration be specifically described, indicating a mutuality of consideration. This means the description must specify what each party to the contract is giving and receiving. It must include such terms as price, quantity, quality, and time of performance. This clause is generally the first covenant of the contract.

In addition to the specifics of the consideration, any conditions the parties wish to attach to their performances should be included in this clause. Such conditions could include such items as provisions for installment purchases, if and how the agreement may be modified, and how payments may be accelerated. It is important to ascertain exactly what covenants and conditions the parties expect to have placed on their performances.

Also remember that whereas most contracts make payment of money the consideration for a good or service received, a contract is just as valid if the consideration is a good for a good, a service for a service, or a service for a good. The concept of barter is a legal one.

 EXAMPLE:

In consideration of Five Hundred Dollars ($500), Seller agrees to sell to Buyer the following: one used CD player.

Note that dollar amounts are usually written out as well as indicated numerically to avoid confusion and mistakes.

 EXAMPLE:

It is agreed that Vendor will sell and Purchaser will buy all of the oranges growing at the farm of Vendor located at _____ _____, during the year of _____, for the sum of Ten Thousand Dollars ($10,000.00), of which Four Thousand Dollars ($4,000.00) shall be paid upon the signing of this Agreement, Three Thousand Dollars ($3,000.00) shall be paid upon completion of the harvest, and Three Thousand Dollars ($3,000.00) shall be paid no later than one month after delivery of said oranges to Purchaser.

Purchaser shall, at his own expense, gather and harvest said fruit when it is sufficiently mature, and Purchaser and his employees shall have free access to the above-mentioned farm for the sole and exclusive purpose of harvesting said fruit.

In the above example, an output contract, the parties have agreed to an installment sale for the purchase of the oranges. All of the requisite terms and conditions have been specified.

 EXAMPLE:

Seller agrees to convey to Buyer, for the sum of Eight Thousand Dollars ($8,000.00), upon the conditions set forth below, the following personal property:

(Exact description of the property)

The Buyer hereby agrees to pay to the Seller the sum of Two Thousand Dollars ($2,000) upon delivery of the above mentioned goods to the Buyer's place of business, and the sum of One Thousand Dollars ($1,000) on the first day of each month following the date of this agreement until the full amount is paid. It is further agreed that, in the event of failure by the Buyer to make any installment as it becomes due, the whole of the sum then outstanding shall immediately become due and payable. If the Buyer so wishes, he may accelerate payments. No modification of this agreement shall be effective unless executed in writing and signed by both parties.

The above example indicates an installment sales contract that provides for remedies if an installment is not made on time, and further permits acceleration of the payment schedule as well as a method of modifying the agreement.

 EXAMPLE:

In consideration of Attorney drafting and executing the Last Will and Testament of Dentist, Dentist hereby agrees to perform root canal work on Attorney's number 18 tooth. All services shall be completed no later than two months from the date of this agreement.

This is an example of a contract clause in which each side performs services for the other, indicating exactly what services are to be performed and the timing of the performances.

In drafting the consideration clause, be sure to include the following:

1. A complete description of the consideration:
   a. for *money*, indicate the exact amount;
   b. for *real estate*, give a complete legal description or street address;
   c. for *personal property*, give as many identifying adjectives as are necessary to avoid confusion;
   d. for *services*, specify the service to be performed.
2. Indicate a mutuality of consideration.
3. Indicate the time of performance.
4. Specify any conditions or timing elements that attach to the performance.
5. Use words of present tense; don't use conditional words when indicating the covenants.
6. If the contract is covered by the UCC, determine whether a UCC

form exists by checking the state statute book or a legal stationery store.

Security Agreement

As discussed in Chapter 8, The Uniform Commercial Code, if a party to the agreement wishes to create a security interest in some property in the case of default, one of the requirements is to have a security agreement specifying that a secured interest is being created. Typically, the contract between the parties will satisfy this requirement of Article IX of the Code, provided that the contract indicates words to that effect. To this end, it becomes encumbent on the drafter to include such a clause in the contract.

 EXAMPLE:

We grant to you a security interest in, and the right of set-off with respect to, all receivables as defined above, all present and future instruments, documents, chattel paper, and general intangibles (as defined in the Uniform Commercial Code), and all proceeds thereof. All of the foregoing shall secure payment and performance of all our obligations at any time owing to you, fixed or contingent, whether arising out of this agreement or by operation of law.

The preceding example constitutes a security agreement for receivables and intangibles under the UCC. This clause would read the same regardless of the collateral specified.

Warranties

As discussed in Chapter 8, The Uniform Commercial Code, whenever the agreement involves the sale of goods, certain warranties attach. Obviously the implied warranties exist regardless of what the contract says, but the contract itself is one method of creating express warranties between the parties. If the parties intend specific guarantees with respect to the subject goods, it is recommended to include provisions concerning these express warranties. These clauses may be part of the Description of the Consideration or may follow those provisions as indicated by the order given here. All express warranties become covenants of the seller.

 EXAMPLE:

Seller hereby warrants that the (good) is in good and merchantable condition, and is free and clear of all liens, security interests and encumbrances. Seller further warrants that the (good) meets all of the following specifications: (specifications).

The preceding clause not only creates express warranties based on particular specifications of the parties but also makes express warranties of the implied warranty of merchantability and title.

Title

Title to the property indicates ownership, right of control, possession, and transfer, and the right to insure the property. As a consequence, it becomes important to indicate in a contract the moment at which title transfers from the seller to the buyer. In any transaction where the mutual consideration is exchanged at the same time, title is transferred simultaneously. Problems arise only when there is to be a delay in full payment for the property conveyed or a lag time due to delivery. Some examples of these situations would be installment sales or mortgaging real estate. In these instances, it is necessary to insert a clause in the contract indicating the condition that gives rise to the transfer of the title.

 EXAMPLES:

1. Seller hereby agrees to convey all his right, title, and interest in and to the aforementioned property upon receipt of a certified check from the Buyer in the amount of _____.

2. In an installment sale:
     When the full sum above mentioned is fully paid, title to said property shall vest in the vendee, but until then title shall remain in the vendor.

The parties themselves are always free to determine the exact moment title passes; however, there are three timing elements that are typically used: (1) when the contract is signed; (2) when the goods are fully paid for; or (3) for installment sales, at the moment an agreed-on percentage of the total selling price has been paid. Simply insert the timing element the parties have agreed on into the contract.

Risk of Loss

Risk of loss, as discussed in Chapter 8, The Uniform Commercial Code, comes into play whenever there is some delay in having the goods transferred from the seller to the buyer, either because of a conditional sales agreement or because of transportation of the items. As exemplified in Chapter 8, there are several standard clauses that can be inserted into the contract to cover this contingency; simply refer to that chapter to find and use the appropriate description.

Waivers

See Chapters 7 and 8 for a discussion of waivers and their effects on a contract. There are certain standard clauses with respect to waivers that are usually inserted into contracts, examples of which appear below.

 EXAMPLES:

1. This Agreement shall constitute the entire Agreement between the parties, and no variance or modification shall be valid except by a written agreement, executed in the same manner as this Agreement.

2. No delay or failure on the part of _____ to fulfill any of these provisions shall operate as a waiver of such or of any other right, and no waiver whatsoever shall be valid unless in writing and signed by the parties, and only to the extent therein set forth.

3. The waiver of any one provision of this Agreement shall not constitute a continuing waiver.

Assignments

Most contracts are assignable (see Chapter 9, Third Party Contracts), but usually parties insert clauses into contracts specifically covering this topic, either by stating that the contract may not be assigned or, if assignable, by indicating the method of effectuating the transfer of rights. It is generally a good idea to have such a clause in every contract to avoid problems later on.

 EXAMPLES:

1. The rights herein permitted to _____ may be assigned, and upon such assignment, such Assignee shall have all of _____'s rights with respect thereto.

2. This contract is not transferable or assignable.

3. No assignment of this contract shall be effective unless executed in writing and signed by all parties.

In addition to specific assignment clauses, if a contract refers to assignees, that reference is sufficient to indicate that the contract is assignable. An example would be the phrase "the Agreement shall be binding on _____, his heirs, executors, assigns, etc." Also be aware that many states have specific case and statutory law with respect to the assignability of commercial leases, and for such contracts each jurisdiction's law must be specifically checked.

Delegation

Just as with assignments discussed above, many contracts may be delegated, unless performance depends on personal services or confidence. (See Chapter 9.) Once again, a provision may be inserted into the agreement specifically covering this point.

EXAMPLES:

1. The obligations specified in this Agreement may not be delegated by the parties.

2. _____ may delegate his obligation to _____.

Terminology

Unless otherwise indicated, all contractual terms are construed in their ordinary meaning. Consequently, if the contracting parties expect specific words, terms, or designations to be defined in a particular manner, it is necessary to indicate that definition in the contract itself. Because many terms are peculiar to particular industries, it becomes imperative that the meaning the parties want to attach to those terms be stated. Also, because "custom and usage" is the standard under the UCC for interpreting sales contracts, it would best serve the parties to have the custom and usage delineated in the agreement so that it does not become a problem of interpretation later on.

It is impossible to give a detailed list of terms because terms are particular to each contracting party; however, some of the sample contracts that follow will have a terminology section that can be used as a model. Simply remember to define any important term in the agreement itself.

Special Provisions and Clauses

In the same way that terminology will be peculiar to particular industries, so will special contractual covenants and conditions. There are certain matters that must be contractually agreed on by the parties, but these clauses are dependent on the nature of the contract and the industry involved. Following is merely a sample of the types of special provisions that may appear in various agreements.

Covenant Not to Compete

"Employee hereby covenants and agrees that in the event of the termination of this Agreement for any reason, with or without cause, that Employee will not compete directly or indirectly with Employer on his own account or as an employee of any other person or entity in _____ for a period of _____ years."

Duties

In an employment or personal services contract, every one of the duties of the employee should be specified, including details of the authority of the employee, any limitations on her authority, and any special accounting methods that may be used to determine compensation. In addition, all other employee benefits to which the employee will be entitled should either be specified, or, if part of a general employee benefit and compensation package, should be incorporated by reference in the main body of the agreement.

Pronouns

"Any masculine personal pronoun as set forth in this Agreement shall be considered to mean the corresponding feminine or neuter personal pronoun, as the case may be."

Severability

"If, for any reason, any provision hereof shall be inoperative, the validity and effect of all other provisions shall not be affected thereby."

Successors

"This Agreement and all provisions hereunder shall inure to the benefit of and shall be binding upon the heirs, executors, legal representatives, next of kin, transferees, and assigns of the parties hereto."

Time of the Essence

Time in all respects is of the essence of this contract.

Trade Secrets

"_____ further covenants not to divulge, during the term of this Agreement, or at any time subsequently, any trade secrets, processes, procedures, or operations, including, but not limited to, the following: _____."

Work Product

"Employee hereby agrees that all inventions, improvements, ideas, and suggestions made by him and patents obtained by him severally or jointly with any other person or persons during the entire period of his employment, are and shall be the sole property of the Employer, free from any legal or equitable title of the Employee, and that all necessary documents for perfecting such title shall be executed by the Employee and delivered to the Employer."

It is usually a good idea to specify the type of property involved.

Duration and Termination

Every contract should specify the duration of its provisions. This is established in two ways: First, the contract should have a specific statement indicating the intended termination date. Second, the contract should specify grounds for terminating the agreement prior to the intended termination date without causing the parties to be in breach. The duration clause is usually as simple as a one-sentence statement indicating the number of years of duration from the date indicated in the contract, or indicating that the agreement shall terminate on a specified date or on the occurrence of a specified event.

Clauses involving grounds for termination are a bit more problematical. The usual grounds given for termination are

1. failure of a party to fulfill a covenant;
2. failure of a condition specified in the contract;
3. dissolution of one or more of the contracting entities;
4. bankruptcy;
5. death, illness, or disability of one or both of the parties;
6. destruction of the subject matter;
7. commission of a felony by one of the parties;
8. incarceration of one of the parties; or
9. change in circumstance (such changes must be delineated in the agreement).

All of the foregoing indicate grounds for terminating the agreement for cause. However, the parties may also provide that the contract may be terminated without cause by one or both of the parties by giving appropriate notice to the other party.

All properly drafted contracts should contain some provision with respect to duration and termination of the agreement; the specifics are dependent on the wishes of the parties to the contract.

Remedies

A contract should contain some provision with respect to remedies available to the innocent party in the case of a breach.

In contracts that include a provision for a security interest, the security holder, in addition to rights granted to her under the UCC, usually specifies the right to dispose of the collateral so as to satisfy the default. Any money the injured party receives from the disposition of the property above the amount owed belongs to the defaulting party.

 EXAMPLE:

Should the Buyer in any way default upon his obligation under this agreement, the Seller shall be at full liberty, at any time thereafter, to resell the _____(property)_____ , either by public auction or by private contract, and the expenses attending thereto shall be borne by the Buyer, but any excess in the price obtained shall belong to the Buyer.

As discussed and exemplified in Chapter 11, Remedies, the parties may specify liquidated damages, or include a limitation of damages clause. Any cost incurred in proceeding against the breaching party may be specified as being the breaching party's obligation.

 EXAMPLE:

All costs, including reasonable attorneys' fees, resulting from any dispute or controversy arising out of or under this Agreement shall be borne by _____.

Choice of Law

As a rule, contracts specify the state law that will govern its provisions and application.

EXAMPLE:

This Agreement shall be construed in accordance with and governed in all respects by the law of the State of _____.

Arbitration

Nowadays, to avoid the time and expense of judicial litigation for problems arising out of a contract, many parties include an arbitration clause by which the parties agree to submit disputes to an arbitrator instead of to the courts.

EXAMPLE:

All disputes, differences, and controversies arising under and in connection with this Agreement shall be settled and finally determined by arbitration according to the rules of the American Arbitration Association now in force or hereafter adopted.

Submission to Jurisdiction

Many contracts specify that the parties agree to submit to the jurisdiction of a particular court.

EXAMPLE:

The parties hereto agree that, in the case of any dispute or controversy arising under or out of this Agreement, to submit to the jurisdiction of the courts of the State of _____ for a settlement of said dispute or controversy.

Many contracts contain what is known as a *cognovit* provision, or a *confession of judgment*, whereby one party agrees to have the other party, in the case of a dispute, hire an attorney to represent and plead the alleged breaching party guilty. Many states do not favor these clauses, although they have been upheld by the U.S. Supreme Court, and so each jurisdiction should be researched to determine the appropriateness of such clauses.

Signatures

The final part of every contract is the signature of the parties. The signatures are usually introduced by the standard phrase: "IN WITNESS WHEREOF, the parties hereto, have hereunder signed this Agreement the day last above written." Following this introductory phrase, the parties sign above their typewritten names. If any of the parties is signing in a representative capacity, the full name of the organization should appear along with the signatory's name and title indicating the authority to sign the contract. If the party is a corporation, occasionally the corporate seal may be affixed as well.

CHAPTER SUMMARY

There are three preliminary rules to drafting a well-written contract:

1. Be conversant with the parties' wishes.
2. Use a checklist of clauses and topics incident to the subject matter involved.
3. Use several sample contracts to establish the format.

Most important in drafting a contractual agreement, be extremely precise in the choice of words. Do not be afraid to draft long clauses; precision requires words of limitation that may appear long-winded but that in fact create precision. For instance, the words "my house" are not nearly as precise as "my house located in Sunapee, New Hampshire," nor is that as precise as giving an exact street address or legal description. Laypersons confuse "lengthy" with "precise." Never be afraid of being wordy if the words create precision and avoid confusion. However, always scrutinize each clause you intend to use to make sure that it serves a useful purpose. Never insert a meaningless clause simply because it appears in a sample format.

After you have drafted a contract, go back over it to interpret what you have written, just as opposing counsel will do. Determine exactly what has been stated in each clause, whether anything has been left out, how each clause affects each party, whether the words are capable of multiple interpretations, and whether it truly reflects the parties' intent. If you are satisfied with what has been written, you now have a sample contract for your next assignment.

EXERCISES

1. Draft an employment contract for yourself as a paralegal working for the firm of Pratt & Chase, a partnership of 25 attorneys working in your town. The contract is for a two-year period.
2. Go to the library and find two more sales contracts. Compare them to the samples in the Appendix. How would you use these contracts to create a new model for your own use?
3. What clauses would you include in a complex Antenuptial Agreement? Why?
4. Analyze the following draft of a contract:

Marketing Agreement

This document will outline the agreed to understanding between ___(Credit Union)___ and ___(Group)___; or any client of associate relationships presented to Credit Union and accepted in the membership of said Credit Union.

The Group will present said Credit Union with individuals and employer institutions that may wish to become members of Credit Union and become eligible to participate in said Credit Union benefits. It is understood by the management of said Credit Union that the Group is a life and health organization.

It is the intention of the Group to offer its insurance products to these marketed organizations, and any individuals within these organizations on a voluntary basis. The Credit Union may not enter into an agreement with any competing organization as it pertains to any group marketed by the Group, its clients or any of its associate organizations. The Credit Union will not impose any administrative fees to be paid by the Group on this block of premium production. The Credit Union may not directly compete against the Group.

The Credit Union will remit premiums to the selected insurance carriers from the Credit Union accounts of any individual who chooses to participate in said life and health plans provided proper documentation is presented to said Credit Union in a timely manner.

It is also understood that the Group will be responsible to provide said Credit Union members with sales and service and be accountable to the Board of Directors of the Credit Union as it pertains to their practices. Should the Group not sufficiently provide service to, or engage in unethical practices, the Credit Union may require that the Group be presented to the Board of the Credit Union to state its case. Should said inquiry result in the desire not to have the Group represent the Credit Union, this agreement can be terminated within 90 days, providing that the following items are enacted at the point of said termination:

The Group will secure an agreement with a properly bonded "third party administrator" that will assume the responsibility of collecting insurance premiums marketed by the Group or any of its clients and/or associate organizations, from the Credit Union in the form of a list bill.

The Credit Union will be given the option of keeping said Group marketed individuals in its membership with written request during said 90-day transition period, and may continue to provide benefits to said members. However, the Credit Union may not introduce a competitive insurance organization to this block of members. Should the Board of the Credit Union impose this clause, the Group will not represent to any Credit Union member that we are being sponsored by, or have any involvement with, the Credit Union.

The Credit Union will remit said insurance premiums to the "third party administrator" of the Group's choice, and will impose no administrative charge to either the Group or the third party administrator for this fee. The Credit Union will continue to provide the Group with any documentation pertaining to policy service on this block of business.

This Agreement between the Credit Union and the Group governs that block of business that is marketed by the Group.

There will be another Agreement that will govern premiums that were not introduced to the Credit Union and the Group.

_____
The Credit Union

_____
The Group

Date: _____
Witness: _____
Witness: _____

APPENDIX A

Sample Contracts

Antenuptial Agreement (Simple Form)
Assignment
Bill of Sale (Simple Form)
Consulting Agreement
Employment Contract (Simple Form)
Employment Contract
Equipment Lease Agreement
General Partnership Agreement (Simple Form)
Limited Partnership Agreement
Promissory Note
Purchase Order
Real Estate Lease
Release
Shareholders Agreement
Subscription Agreement (Limited Partnership)

Antenuptial Agreement (Simple Form)

Agreement entered into this _____ day of _____, 20_____, by and between _____ and _____.

Whereas the parties agree to enter into the marriage relationship and hereafter live together as husband and wife,

NOW THEREFORE, in consideration of the marriage to be entered into by the parties they do hereby agree to the following:

1. That all manner of property hereafter acquired or accumulated by them, or either of them, shall be held in joint or equal ownership.

2. That each of the parties hereby grants, bargains, sells and conveys to the other an undivided one-half interest in all the property, real and personal, which he or she now owns, for the purpose and with the intent of vesting in both parties the joint ownership of all property at this date owned in severalty by either of them.

3. In case of the death of one of the above mentioned parties, all said property shall, subject to the claims of creditors, vest absolutely in the survivor.

4. That in the case of divorce of the above mentioned parties, all rights to property shall be equally divided between them pursuant to the terms of this Agreement.

IN WITNESS WHEREOF, the parties have executed this Agreement the day and year first above written.

_____

_____

Assignment

This Agreement made this ＿＿ day of ＿＿＿＿＿, 20＿＿, between
＿＿＿＿＿＿＿＿＿ (Vendor), and ＿＿＿＿＿＿＿＿＿ (Vendee), to wit:
In consideration of the sum of ＿＿＿＿＿ Dollars ($ ＿＿) now paid
to Vendor by Vendee, the receipt of which is hereby acknowledged, the
Vendor does hereby assign and convey to the Vendee, his executors, ad-
ministrators, and assigns, all right and title to ＿＿＿＿＿＿＿＿.

IN WITNESS WHEREOF, the parties hereto set their hands and seal
the day and year first above written.

＿＿＿＿＿＿＿＿＿＿＿＿＿＿

＿＿＿＿＿＿＿＿＿＿＿＿＿＿

Bill of Sale (Simple Form)

In consideration of the sum of _____ Dollars ($ ____) to be paid by _____, of _____, I _____, of _____ have bargained and sold to said _____ the following goods and chattels, to wit:

(Specify the goods sold)

IN WITNESS WHEREOF, I have set my hand and seal this _____ day of _____, 20 ____.

_____

Consulting Agreement

This Agreement is made this _____ day of _____, 20 ____, by and between _____ (X), an individual residing at _____, and _____ (Consultant), an individual doing business at _____.

Consultant agrees to act as a financial consultant to X with respect to the development, production, and promotion of _____. Consultant shall meet and consult with X as the need arises, and shall perform services consistent with the duties of a financial consultant.

As full compensation for the services to be performed by Consultant, X agrees to pay Consultant 10% (ten percent) of the gross profit derived from the sale and marketing of the _____. The determination of the amount of said profit shall be made by an independent accounting firm should the parties to this Agreement disagree as to the amount of said profit.

Reasonable expenses actually incurred by Consultant incidental to the services performed shall be paid by X once money is received from the sale and marketing of _____ upon submission of a voucher of expenses to X by Consultant.

Should X willfully fail to develop, produce, and promote the _____, X shall pay Consultant reasonable compensation for work actually performed by Consultant on X's behalf.

Consultant, with respect to the services performed under this Agreement, is acting as an independent contractor and is not an employee. Consultant may be employed by other persons, firms, associations, or corporations not in conflict of interest with the terms of this Agreement during the term of this Agreement. Any employee or other personnel engaged by Consultant not for the express and direct benefit of X shall be under the exclusive direction and control of Consultant.

This Agreement is effective from the date above written and shall terminate when X no longer has any rights or title, direct or indirect, in _____.

This Agreement constitutes the entire Agreement between the parties relating to the subject matter contained in it, and supersedes all prior and contemporaneous representations, agreements, or understandings between the parties. No amendment or supplement of this Agreement shall be binding unless executed in writing by the parties. No waiver of one provision of this Agreement shall constitute a waiver of any other provision, nor shall any one waiver constitute a continuing waiver. No waiver shall be binding unless executed in writing by the party against whom the waiver is asserted.

This Agreement shall be construed and interpreted in accordance with, and governed by, the laws of the State of _____.

This Agreement may not be assigned by either party without the written consent of the other party.

If any provision of this Agreement is held by a court of competent jurisdiction to be invalid or unenforceable, the remainder of this Agreement shall remain in full force and shall in no way be impaired.

Any controversy or claim arising out of or relating to this Agreement, or the breach thereof, shall be settled by arbitration in accordance with the Rules of the American Arbitration Association, and judgment upon the award rendered by the arbitrator(s) may be entered in any court having jurisdiction thereof.

IN WITNESS WHEREOF, the parties have executed this Agreement on the date first above written.

X _____

_____
Consultant

Employment Contract (Simple Form)

Agreement made this _____ day of _____, 20 ____, between X of _____ (X), and Y, Inc., a corporation with principle offices at _____ (Y).

WHEREAS X is a well-known _____; and

WHEREAS Y is a well-known _____; and

WHEREAS Y wishes to make use of X's expertise; and

WHEREAS X accepts such employment,

NOW THEREFORE, in consideration of the mutual covenants herein contained, and other good and valuable consideration, it is agreed between the parties as follows:

1. Services

X shall provide Y with (describe specific services).

2. Compensation

Y shall compensate X in the sum of _____ Dollars ($ _____), payable in equal weekly installments.

3. No Further Obligations

All obligations with respect to the services to be performed by X shall cease upon _____.

4. Arbitration

Any controversy or claim arising out of or relating to this Agreement shall be settled by arbitration in the City of _____ in accordance with the Rules of the American Arbitration Association, and judgment upon the award rendered in such arbitration may be entered in any court having jurisdiction thereof.

5. Controlling Law

This Agreement shall be governed by the laws of the State of
_____.

6. Entire Agreement

This Agreement expresses the whole Agreement between the parties hereto as of the date hereof. This Agreement shall not be changed, modified, terminated, or discharged except by a writing signed by the parties hereto.

7. Binding Effect

This Agreement shall be binding upon and enure to the benefit of each of the parties hereto, their heirs, executors, administrators, or assigns.

IN WITNESS WHEREOF, the parties have executed this Agreement on the day and year first above written.

_____
X

_____
Y

By: _____

Employment Contract

Agreement dated _____, 20_____, between X, Inc., a _____ corporation with principal offices at _____ (the Company), and Y, residing at _____ (Y).

WITNESSETH:

WHEREAS the Company is doing business as a _____ and wishes to avail itself of the services of Y; and

WHEREAS Y has substantial expertise and experience and is willing to perform services for the Company, all in accordance with the following terms and conditions;

NOW THEREFORE, it is agreed as follows:

1. Employment

The Company agrees to hire Y, and Y agrees to serve the Company as its _____, with overall responsibility for _____.

2. Term

The term of employment shall be for one (1) year, commencing on the _____ day of _____, 20_____, and ending as of the _____ day of _____, 20_____ (Termination Date). Sixty (60) days' written notice prior to the Termination Date must be given by either party if the intention of either party is not to negotiate a new Agreement.

3. Compensation

As compensation for the services hereunder, the Company shall pay Y a total of (i) _____ Dollars ($ _____), payable in equal semi-monthly installments; and (ii) a sum equal to one-half (½) percent of the gross sales volume accrued during the term of this Agreement, payable in one installment not later than thirty (30) days after the Termination Date.

4. Records

The Company shall cause to be made available to Y, at least monthly, whatever figures are necessary to ascertain accurate records as to the gross volume of the Company.

5. Expenses

Y shall be reimbursed for all reasonable and necessary expenses incurred hereunder, upon the presentation of paid vouchers, or, as the case may be, the Company shall pay directly such expenses as may be determined in advance.

6. Travel

The Company agrees that it will consent to send Y at least twice yearly to the _____ in connection with the furtherance of his employment, and it is further agreed that Y will make two trips to _____ on behalf of the Company to introduce the Company's line.

7. Incidental Services

The Company shall make available to Y the various incidental services he deems necessary to successfully carry out his employment.

8. Responsibility

The Company intends that Y assume full responsibility for _____, maintaining a climate of maximum creativity within the Company's _____. It therefore agrees that Y shall be given substantial decision-making power in hiring and firing of all personnel.

9. Benefits

Y shall be entitled to receive those benefits which the Company provides for its key executive employees, including, without limiting the foregoing, hospitalization, major medical insurance, and disability insurance.

10. Life Insurance

The Company shall provide Y with life insurance of at least _____ Dollars ($ _____) during the term of this Agreement. Said insurance shall be convertible upon termination.

11. Vacation

Y shall be entitled to at least three (3) weeks' paid vacation per year, it being understood that said vacation shall be taken at times which are mutually convenient for the parties and shall not be taken consecutively.

12. Representation and Warranty

Y represents and warrants that he is not bound by any covenant or agreement, oral or written, which prohibits him from entering into this employment and from being employed by the Company.

13. Restrictive Covenant

Y will, during the term of this Agreement, devote his entire time, attention, and energies to the performance of his duties hereunder, and he will not directly or indirectly, either as a shareholder, owner, partner, director, officer, employee, consultant, or otherwise, be engaged in or concerned with any other commercial duties or pursuits whatsoever.

It is expressly understood and agreed that:

(a) All inventions, patents, copyrights, developments, and ideas and concepts developed by Y during the course of his employment under this Agreement shall be the exclusive property of the Company.

(b) Y shall have no right, either during or after employment under this Agreement, to use, sell, copy, transfer, or otherwise make use of, either for himself or for any other person other than the Company, any of the confidential information and trade secrets of the Company.

14. Illness or Disability

If during the term of this Agreement, Y becomes disabled or incapacitated by reason of illness, physical or mental, as to be unable to perform all duties to be performed hereunder, he shall be paid by the Company his salary during the first three (3) months of such disability, less a sum equal to the amount received by him under a disability insurance policy. In addition, Y shall be entitled to a sum equal to one-half (½) percent of the gross volume of the sales during said disability. Said sum shall be paid at the end of the three (3) months.

15. Severability

If any one or more of the provisions hereof shall be held to be invalid, illegal or unenforceable, the validity and enforceability of its other provisions shall not be affected thereby.

16. Notice

Any notice required to be given pursuant to the provisions of this Agreement shall be in writing and mailed prepaid to the parties at the addresses given at the beginning of this Agreement, by certified or registered mail, return receipt requested.

17. Arbitration

Any controversy or claim arising out of or relating to this Agreement, or the breach thereof, shall be settled by arbitration in the city

_____ in accordance with the Rules of the American Arbitration Association, and the judgment upon the award rendered by the arbitrator(s) may be entered in any court having jurisdiction thereof.

18. Governing Law

This Agreement shall be governed by and construed according to the laws of the State of _____.

19. Modification

This Agreement contains the entire understanding of the parties and may not be amended, supplemented, or discharged except by an instrument in writing signed by the parties hereto.

20. Binding Effect

This Agreement shall enure to the benefit of and shall be binding upon the Company, its successors, and assigns.

IN WITNESS WHEREOF, the parties hereto have executed this Agreement as of the date and year first above written.

_____

Company

By: _____

_____

Y

Equipment Lease Agreement

Agreement made the _____ day of_____, 20_____, between _____, Inc., with a place of business at _____ (Lessor)and_____Inc.withaplaceobusinessat_____ (Lessee).

1. The Lessor hereby leases to the Lessee, and the Lessee hereby hires from the Lessor, subject to the terms and conditions hereinafter set forth, the following property consisting of _____ (Equipment).

2. The lease is for _____ months commencing on the _____ day of _____, 20_____, and ending on the _____ day of _____, 20_____. The total rent for said initial term is the sum of _____ Dollars ($ _____), plus sales tax payable as follows:

(a) _____ Dollars ($ _____) upon execution of the lease.

(b) The balance of the total rental of _____ Dollars ($ _____), i.e., $ _____, shall then be payable in equal monthly installments from and after payment of the initial $ _____ rental sum plus sales tax.

3. Lessee shall have the right and option to renew the said lease by the giving of ninety (90) days' advance written notice to the Lessor of its intention to do so. Lessee may renew the Lease for _____ terms (_____) of two (2) years each, with each term being renewed by the giving of the same ninety (90) days' advance written notice. Rent for each remaining term shall be as follows:

4. This Agreement creates a lease only of the Equipment and not a sale thereof or the creation of a security interest therein. The Lessor shall remain the sole owner of the Equipment, and nothing contained herein or the payment of rent hereunder shall enable the Lessee to acquire any right, title, or other interest in or to the Equipment.

5. Lessor agrees that neither it nor any principal or shareholder therein, nor any affiliate or entity in any way associated with Lessor, shall compete with the Lessee at any time during the term of this lease.

6. Upon delivery of the said Equipment by Lessor to Lessee, Lessor warrants that the same shall be in proper working order and fit for the purpose for which it was intended. The monthly rental payments by Lessee to Lessor specifically include consideration for Lessor's maintenance of the said Equipment, and during the term of the lease it shall be Lessor's responsibility to repair and maintain the same at Lessor's expense, provided that such repair and maintenance is for ordinary wear and tear.

7. (a) The Lessor shall pay all use taxes, personal property taxes, or other direct taxes imposed on the ownership, possession, use or operation

of the Equipment or levied against or based upon the amount of rent to be paid hereunder or assessed in connection with the execution, filing, or recording of this Agreement. The term "direct taxes" as used herein shall include all taxes (except income taxes), charges, and fees imposed by any federal, state, or local authority.

(b) The Lessee assumes all responsibility and the cost and expense as may be required for the lawful operation of the Equipment. All certificates of title or registration applicable to the Equipment shall be applied for, issued, and maintained in the name of the Lessor, as Owner.

(c) The Lessee shall observe all safety rules and other requirements of regulatory bodies having jurisdiction and shall pay all fines and similar charges that may be duly and lawfully imposed or assessed by reason of the Lessee's failure to comply with the rules, regulations, and orders of regulatory bodies having jurisdiction.

(d) If the taxes, fines, or other charges, with the exception of permit fees, that the Lessee is responsible for under this Paragraph are levied, assessed, charged, or imposed against the Lessor, it shall notify the Lessee in writing of such fact. The Lessor shall have the option, but not the obligation, to pay any such tax, fine, or other charge, whether levied, assessed, charged, or imposed against Lessor or Lessee. In the event such payment is made by the Lessor, the Lessee shall reimburse the Lessor within seven (7) days after receipt of an invoice therefor, and the failure to make such reimbursement when due shall be deemed a default within Paragraph 8 hereof.

8. The Equipment shall be delivered by the Lessor to the Lessee at the Lessee's place of business. The Lessor shall have the right to place and maintain conspicuously on the side of the Equipment during the term of this lease the inscription _____, indicating the name of the owner of the Equipment or words of similar import in the event the lease is assigned by the Lessor, and the Lessee shall not remove, obscure, deface, or obliterate such inscription or suffer any other person to do so. Lessor can only assign its rights in this lease subject to all of the terms and conditions and rights that vest in Lessee herein.

9. The Lessee shall pay all operating expenses. The Lessee shall at all times provide suitable storage facilities and appropriate services for the Equipment including washing, polishing, cleaning, inspection, and storage space, and at the end or other expiration of this lease shall return the Equipment to the Lessor at the address above set forth in operating order and in the same condition and state of repair as it was at the date of delivery, ordinary wear and tear excepted.

10. The Lessee hereby indemnifies and shall hold the Lessor harmless from all loss and damage the Lessor may sustain or suffer by reason of the death of or injury to the person or property of any third person as a result, in whole or in part, of the use or maintenance of the Equipment during the term of this lease; and the Lessee shall procure, at the Lessee's cost and expense, a policy or policies of insurance issued by a company satisfactory to the Lessor with premiums prepaid thereon, insuring the Lessee against the risks and hazards specified above to the extent of the

full value of the equipment and in the minimum amounts of _____ Dollars ($ ____) personal injury liability, together with fire and casualty loss. Such policy or policies shall name the Lessor as loss payee and not as co-insured. It shall be delivered to the Lessor simultaneously and prior to the delivery of the Equipment leased hereunder and shall carry an endorsement by the insurer either upon the policy or policies issued by it or by an independent instrument that the Lessor will receive thirty (30) days' written notice of the alteration or cancellation of such policy or policies. Failure by the Lessee to procure such insurance shall not affect the Lessee's obligations under the terms, covenants and conditions of this lease, and the loss, damage to, or destruction of the Equipment shall not terminate the lease nor, except to the extent that the Lessor is actually compensated by insurance paid for by the Lessee, as herein provided, relieve the Lessee from the Lessee's liability hereunder. Should the Lessee fail to procure or maintain the insurance provided for herein, the Lessor shall have the option, but not the obligation, to do so for the account of the Lessee. In the event payment for procuring or maintaining such insurance is made by the Lessor, the Lessee shall reimburse the Lessor within seven (7) days after receipt of an invoice therefor, and the failure to make such reimbursement when due shall be deemed a default hereof.

11. The Lessee shall employ and have absolute control and supervision over the operator or operators of the Equipment and will not permit any person to operate the equipment unless such person is licensed.

12. In the event the Lessee fails to perform any material term, condition, and covenant contained herein in the manner and at the time or times required hereunder, including, but not limited to, the payment in full of any rental payment or the reimbursement of the Lessor for a disbursement made hereunder, or if any proceedings in bankruptcy or insolvency are instituted by or against the Lessee, or if reorganization of the Lessee is sought under any statute, state or federal, or a receiver appointed for the goods and chattels of the Lessee, or the Lessee makes an assignment for the benefit of creditors or makes an attempt to sell, secrete, convert, or remove the Equipment, or if any distress, execution, or attachment be levied thereon, or the Equipment be encumbered in any way, or if, at any time, in the Lessor's judgment (reasonable standard is applicable), its rights in the Equipment shall be threatened or rendered insecure, the Lessee shall be deemed to be in default under this Agreement, and the Lessor shall have the right to exercise either of the following remedies:

(a) To declare the balance of the rental payable hereunder to be due and payable whereupon the same shall become immediately due and payable, but Lessor shall use due diligence to release all Equipment covered in this Agreement; or

(b) To retake and retain the Equipment with demand on five (5) days' notice or legal process free of all right of the Lessee, in which case the Lessee authorizes the Lessor or its agents to enter upon any premises where the Equipment may be found for the purpose of repossessing the same, and the Lessee specifically waives any right of action it might otherwise have arising out of such entry and repossession, whereupon all rights of the Lessee in the Equipment shall terminate immediately. If the Lessor retakes possession of the Equipment and at the time of such retaking there shall be in, upon, or attached to the Equipment any property, goods, or things of value belonging to the Lessee or in the custody or under the control of the Lessee, the Lessor is hereby authorized to take possession of such property, goods, or things of value and hold the same for the Lessee or place such property, goods, or things of value in public storage for the account of and at the expense of the Lessee.

13. Forbearance on the part of the Lessor to exercise any right or remedy available hereunder upon the Lessee's breach of the terms, conditions, and covenants of this Agreement, or the Lessor's failure to demand the punctual performance thereof, shall not be deemed a waiver:

(a) Of such right or remedy;

(b) Of the requirement of punctual performance; or

(c) Of any subsequent breach or default on the part of the Lessee.

14. Neither this lease nor the Lessee's rights hereunder shall be assignable by the Lessee without any prior written consent of the Lessor, which consent shall not unreasonably be withheld.

15. The Lessee shall make available to the Lessor the Equipment for inspection as required by any governmental agency. The Equipment shall be available on forty-eight (48) hours' notice to Lessee at Lessee's place of business. Failure to make the Equipment available for said inspection shall be a substantial breach of this Agreement, and the operator will surrender the Equipment immediately upon notice.

16. The Lessee shall be responsible for obeying all laws, rules, and regulation of the State of _____ and the City of _____, and any other governmental authority having jurisdiction. Further, any fines or penalties imposed because of the Lessee's failure to obey such laws, rules, and regulations shall be the sole responsibility of the Lessee, and paid for solely by him or her.

17. The Lessee acknowledges that he or she is not in the employ of the Lessor but is an independent contractor responsible for his or her own acts. Further, the Lessee shall maintain records and be responsible for the payment of any and all taxes and fees as previously mentioned. Any substantial violation by the Lessee to this Agreement shall render the entire Agreement in default, and the Lessee will be responsible to return the Lessor's Equipment within forty-eight (48) hours.

18. All notification from one party to the other as set forth in this Agreement must be in writing and forwarded by certified mail at the address specified on the first page of this lease.

19. Lessor represents that the permits and/or licenses it has in order to effectuate the said terms and conditions of this lease are in good standing and that the Lessor has the authority to enter into the within lease. Lessor further warrants that there are no assessments, taxes, levies, charges, encumbrances, liens, security interests, or other rights presently outstanding that would in any way interfere with or affect Lessee's intended operation.

20. The parties hereto specifically agree that Lessee has the right to cure any default provided the same occurred within ten (10) days' of written notification by Lessor to Lessee of the same.

21. This instrument contains the entire Agreement between the parties and shall be binding on their respective heirs, executors, administrators, legal representatives, successors, and assigns. This Agreement may not be amended or altered except by a writing signed by both parties.

22. This Agreement is subject to the laws of the State of _____ _____.

IN WITNESS WHEREOF, the parties hereto have executed this Agreement on the day and year first above written.

_____
Lessor

By: _____

_____
Lessee

By: _____

General Partnership Agreement (Simple Form)

This Agreement, made this ____ day of _____, 20____, by and between _____, First Party, _____, Second Party, and _____, Third Party, witnesses as follows:

That the said parties hereby agree to become partners in the business of _____ under the firm name of _____ for the term of ____years from the date hereof, upon the terms and conditions hereinafter stated:

1. That the business shall be carried on at _____ or at any other place that may hereinafter be mutually agreed upon by the parties.

2. That proper books of account shall be kept, and therein shall be duly entered, from time to time, all dealings, transactions, matters, and things whatsoever in or relating to the said business; and each party shall have full and free access thereto at all times, but shall not remove the same from the premises.

3. That the capital requirements for carrying on the said business shall be borne by said partners in equal parts, and the said capital, and all such stock, implements, and utensils in trade purchased out of the partnership funds as well as the gains and profits of the said business, shall belong to the said partners in equal parts.

4. That each partner shall be at full liberty to have _____ Dollars ($ ____) monthly for his own private use, on account, but not in excess of his presumptive share of the profits, so long as the said business shall be found profitable.

5. That an account of the stock, implements, and utensils belonging to the said business, and of the book debts and capital, shall be taken, and a statement of the affairs of the said partnership to be made yearly, to be computed from the date hereof, when the sums drawn by each partner during the preceding year shall be charged to his share of the profits of said business; but, if, at the end of any one year of the said partnership it shall be found to be unprofitable, the said partnership shall thereupon be dissolved, unless it shall be occasioned by some accidental circumstances.

6. That each party shall sign duplicate copies of each of such statement of affairs, and shall retain one of these for his own use, and another copy shall be written in one of the partnership books, and likewise signed by each of them.

7. That all partners of the same class shall have identical and equal rights except as herein otherwise provided: _____. Each partner shall devote his best efforts to the firm and its clients and customers, and each partner shall follow the rules and policies of the business that may from time to time be adopted by them.

8. That no partner may be added to the firm unless each additional partner be unanimously elected by all of the existing partners.

9. That the death of a partner shall terminate all his interest in the partnership, its property and assets. The continuing firm shall pay in cash to his estate, or to his nominee, the following amounts to be paid in installments at the times indicated: _____.

10. That any partner may voluntarily withdraw from the partnership at any time on notice of thirty (30) days to the other partners. At the expiration of the thirty (30) day period, or sooner if mutually agreed upon, the withdrawal shall become effective. The withdrawing partner's rights, title, and interests in the firm shall be extinguished in consideration of the payments to him by the continuing firm on the following basis: _____.

11. That any partner may be expelled from the firm for cause when it has been determined by a vote of the partners that any of the following reasons for his expulsion exist:

    (a)   Loss of professional license;
    (b)   Professional misconduct;
    (c)   Insolvency;
    (d)   Breach of any of the provisions of this Agreement;
    (e)   Any other reason that the other partners unanimously agree warrants expulsion.

Upon expulsion, the expelled partner shall have no further rights, duties, or interest in the firm or any of its assets, records, or affairs. He shall immediately remove himself and his personal effects from the firm's offices. A partner so expelled shall be entitled to the same rights, the same payments by, and be subject to the same duties to the continuing firm as if he were voluntarily withdrawing from the firm.

12. That all provisions of this Agreement shall be construed and shall be enforced according to the laws of the State of _____.

13. That any controversy or claim arising out of or relating to any provision of this Agreement or the breach thereof shall be settled by arbitration in accordance with the Rules then in effect of the American Arbitration Association, to the extent consistent with the laws of the State of _____.

14. That no partner may assign or in any way transfer his interest in the partnership, all such rights and interests being personal to him.

15. That the invalidity or unenforceability of any one provision of this Agreement shall not affect the validity or enforceability of the other provisions of this Agreement.

IN WITNESS WHEREOF, the parties hereto have executed this Agreement on the day and year first above written.

_____

First Party

_____

Second Party

_____

Third Party

Limited Partnership Agreement

Agreement of Limited Partnership (the Agreement) of _____
_____ (the Partnership), entered into this ____ day of _____,
20____, by and among _____, Inc. (the General Partner),
and each of the persons executing this Agreement (the Limited Partners).
Reference herein to "Partners" without designation to "General" or "Limited" includes the General Partner and the Limited Partners except as the
context otherwise requires.

PREAMBLE

The Partnership has been organized as a Limited Partnership under
the laws of the State of _____ for the purpose of
_____.

NOW THEREFORE, in consideration of the promises and mutual
covenants hereinafter set forth, the parties hereto do hereby agree and
certify as follows:

Article I

Definitions

1.0 Whenever used in this Agreement, the following terms shall have
the following meanings:

(a)"Affiliate" shall mean (i) any person directly or indirectly controlling, controlled by or under common control with another person, (ii)
a person owning or controlling ten percent (10%) or more of the outstanding voting securities of such other person, (iii) any officer, director, or
partner of such person, and (iv) if such other person is an officer, director,
or partner, any company for which such person acts in any such capacity.

(b) "Capital Account" means with respect to each partner his Capital
Contribution, to the extent contributed, *increased* by: (i) any additional
contributions and (ii) his distributive share of Partnership income and
gains, and *decreased* by (i) cash and the Partnership's adjusted basis of
property distributed to him and (ii) his distributive share of Partnership
losses.

(c)"Capital Contribution" means the capital contributed by the General Partner and Limited Partners as set forth in Article IV and as
hereinafter contributed to the Partnership by any Partner.

(d)"Cash Flow" means cash form revenues to the Partnership available for distribution after payment of Partnership expenses, advances

made by the General Partner and others, and after amounts reserved to meet future contingencies as determined in the sole discretion of the General Partner.

(e)"Closing Date" shall mean the date the offering of the Units is complete.

(f)"Code" shall mean the Internal Revenue Code of 1986, as amended.

(g)"General Partner's Contribution" shall mean the contribution of the General Partner pursuant to Section 4.2 hereof.

(h)"Interest" shall mean the individual interest of each Partner in the Partnership.

(i)"Limited Partners' Contributions" shall mean the aggregate cash contributions of the Limited Partners.

(j)"Original Limited Partner" shall mean the Limited Partner who executed the original Certificate of Limited Partnership of the Partnership.

(k)"P&L Percentage" shall mean the percent of Profits and Losses allocable to each Partner.

(l)"Partnership Property" or "Partnership Properties" shall mean all interest, properties and rights of any type owned or leased by the Partnership.

(m)"Permitted Transfer" shall mean a transfer by a Limited Partner of his Interest to: (i) his spouse, unless legally separated, child, parent, or grandparent; or (ii) a corporation, partnership, trust or other entity, fifty-one percent (51%) of the equity interest of which is owned by such Limited Partner individually or with any of the persons specified in subparagraph (i) hereof.

(n)"Profits and Losses" shall mean the Profits and Losses of the Partnership as reflected on its Federal Partnership Income Tax Return.

(o)"Unit" shall have the same meaning ascribed to such a term in a Private Placement Memorandum of the Partnership and any and all amendments thereto (the Memorandum).

Article II

ORGANIZATION

2.1 *Addition of Limited Partners*. Promptly following the execution hereof, the General Partner, on behalf of the Partnership, shall execute or cause to be executed an Amended Certificate of Limited Partnership reflecting the withdrawal of the Original Limited Partner and the addition of the Limited Partners to the Partnership and all such other certificates and documents conforming thereto and shall do all such filing, recording, publishing and other acts, as may be necessary or appropriate from time to time to comply with all requirements for the operation of a limited partnership in the State of _____ and all other jurisdictions where the Partnership shall desire to conduct business. The General Partner shall cause the Partnership to comply with all requirements for the qualification of the Partnership as a Limited Partnership (of a partnership in which the Limited Partners have limited liability) in any jurisdiction before the Partnership shall conduct any business in such jurisdiction.

2.2 *Withdrawal of Original Limited Partner.* Upon execution of this Agreement by the Limited Partners, the Original Limited Partner shall withdraw as a Limited Partner and acknowledge that he shall have no interest in the Partnership as a Limited Partner and no rights to any of the profits, losses, or other distributions of the Partnership from the inception of the Partnership.

2.3 *Partnership Name.* The name of the Partnership shall be _____.

2.4 *Purposes of the Partnership.* The purposes of the Partnership shall be to acquire, own and continue to acquire, own, lease, and deal in or with real and personal property, securities, and investments of every kind, nature and description consistent with the best interests of the Limited Partners.

2.5 *Principal Place of Business and Address.* The principal office of the Partnership shall be maintained as _____, or such other address or addresses as the General Partner may designate by notice to Limited Partners. The Partnership may maintain offices and other facilities from time to time at such locations, within or without the State of _____, as may be deemed necessary or advisable by the General Partner.

2.6 *Term.* The Partnership shall dissolve on December 31, 20____, unless sooner terminated or dissolved under the provisions of this Agreement.

Article III

Operation of the Partnership

3.1 *Powers and Duties of the General Partner.* Except as set forth in Section 3.2 below, the General Partner (if more than one, then such General Partners shall act by any one of the General Partners with the consent of the majority of the General Partners) shall have full, exclusive, and irrevocable authority to manage and control the Partnership and the Partnership Properties, and to do all reasonable and prudent things on behalf of the Partnership including, but not limited to, the following:

(a) To acquire any additional Partnership Property, including all property ancillary thereto and obtain rights to enable the Partnership to renovate, construct, alter, equip, staff, operate, manage, lease, maintain, and promote the Partnership Property, as well as all of the equipment and any other personal or mixed property connected therewith, including, but not limited to, the financial arrangements, development, improvement, maintenance, exchange, trade, or sale of such Property (including, but not limited to, all real or personal property connected therewith) at such price or amount for cash, securities, or other property, and upon such terms as it deems in its absolute discretion to be in the best interests of the Partnership;

(b) To sell or otherwise dispose of the Partnership Property and terminate the Partnership;

(c) To borrow or lend money for operation and/or for any other Partnership purpose, and, if security is required therefor, to mortgage or subject to any other security device any portion of the Partnership Property, to obtain replacements of any mortgage or other security device, and to prepay, in whole or in part, refinance, increase, modify, consolidate, or extend any mortgage or other security device, all of the foregoing at such terms and in such amounts as it deems, in its absolute discretion, to be in the best interest of the Partnership;

(d) To enter into contracts with various contractors and subcontractors for the maintenance of the Property;

(e) To enter into employment or other agreements to provide for the management and operation of the Partnership Property (including the right to contract with affiliates of the General Partner on behalf of the Partnership for such services);

(f) To place record title to, or the right to use, Partnership assets in the name or names of a nominee or nominees for any purpose convenient or beneficial to the Partnership;

(g) To acquire and enter into any contract of insurance that the General Partner deems necessary and proper for the protection of the Partnership, for the conservation of its assets, or for any other purpose, convenience, or benefit of the Partnership;

(h) To employ persons in the operation and management of the Partnership business, including, but not limited to, supervisory managing agents, consultants, insurance brokers, and loan brokers on such terms and for such compensation as the General Partner shall determine;

(i) To employ attorneys and accountants to represent the Partnership in connection with Partnership business;

(j) To pay or not pay rentals and other payments to lessors;

(k) To sell, trade, release, surrender, or abandon any or all of the Partnership Properties, or any portion thereof, or other assets of the Partnership;

(l) To settle claims, prosecute, defend, and settle and handle all matters with governmental agencies;

(m) To purchase, acquire, lease, construct, and/or operate equipment and any other type of tangible, real or personal property;

(n) To open bank accounts for the Partnership and to designate and change signatories on such accounts;

(o) To invest the funds of the Partnership in certificates of deposit or evidence of debt of the United States of America or any state, or commonwealth thereof, or any instrumentality of either;

(p) To enter into any other partnership agreement whether general or limited, or any joint venture or other similar agreement; and

(q) Without in any manner being limited by the foregoing, to execute any and all other agreements, conveyances, and other documents and to take any and all other action which the General Partner in its sole discretion deems to be necessary, useful, or convenient in connection with the Partnership Properties or business.

In accomplishing all of the foregoing, the General Partner may, in its sole discretion, but shall not be required to, use its own personnel, properties, and equipment, and may employ on a temporary or continuing basis outside accountants, attorneys, brokers, consultants, and others on such terms as he deems advisable. Any or all of the Partnership Properties, and any or all of the other Partnership assets, may be held from time to time, at the General Partner's sole discretion, in the name of the General Partner, the Partnership, or one or more nominees; and any and all of the powers of the General Partner may be exercised from time to time, at the General Partner's sole discretion, in the name of any one or more of the foregoing.

3.2 *Limitations of the Powers of the General Partner.* The General Partner may not act for or bind the Partnership without the prior consent of the holders of fifty-one percent (51%) of Limited Partnership Interests on the following matters:

(i) Amendment of the Partnership Agreement (except as set forth in Section 12.4); or

(ii) A change in the general character or nature of the Partnership's business.

3.3 *Powers and Liabilities of the Limited Partners.* No Limited Partner shall have any personal liability or obligation for any liability or obligation of the Partnership or be required to lend or advance funds to the Partnership for any purpose. No Limited Partner shall be responsible for the obligations of any other Limited Partner. No Limited Partner shall take part in the management of the business of the Partnership or transact any business for the Partnership, and no Limited Partner shall have power to sign for or bind the Partnership. No Limited Partner shall have a drawing account. No Limited Partner shall be entitled to the return of his capital contribution, except to the extent, if any, that distributions are made or deemed to be made to such Limited Partner otherwise than out of Profits pursuant to this Agreement. No Limited Partner shall receive any interest on his capital account. Upon the consent of fifty-one percent (51%) in interest of the Limited Partners, the Limited Partners shall have a right to call a meeting of the Partnership upon written notice to all of the Partners of the time, date, and place of such meeting. Upon the written request of twenty-five percent (25%) in interest of the nonaffiliated Limited Partners, the General Partner shall promptly call an informational meeting of the Partnership upon written notice to all of the Partners of the time, date, and place of such meeting.

3.4 *Exculpation and Indemnification of the General Partner.* (a) The Limited Partners recognize that there are substantial risks involved in the Partnership's business. The General Partner is willing to continue to serve as General Partner only because the Limited Partners hereby accept the speculative character of the Partnership business and the uncertainties and hazards which may be involved, and only because the Limited Partners hereby agree, that despite the broad authority granted to the General Partner by Section 3.1, the General Partner shall have no liability to the Partnership or to the Limited Partners because of the failure of the General Partner to act as a prudent operator, or based upon errors in judgment, negligence, or other fault of the General Partner in connection with its management of the Partnership, so long as the General Partner is acting in good faith. Accordingly, the Limited Partners, for themselves, their heirs, distributees, legal representatives, successors, and assigns, covenant not to assert or attempt to assert any claim or liability as against the General Partner for any reason whatsoever except for gross negligence, fraud, bad faith, or willful misconduct in connection with the operation of the Partnership. It shall be deemed conclusively established that the General Partner is acting in good faith with respect to action taken by him on the advice of the independent accountants, legal counsel, or independent consultants of the partnership.

(b) In the event of any action, suit, or other legal proceeding, including arbitration, instituted or threatened against the General Partner or in which he (or if more than one, any of them) may be a party, whether such suit, action, or proceeding is brought on behalf of third parties or Limited Partners, individually or as a class, or in a derivative or representative capacity, the General Partner shall have the right to obtain legal counsel and other expert counsel at the expense of the Partnership and to defend or participate in any such suit, action, or proceeding at the expense of the Partnership, and he shall be reimbursed, indemnified against, and saved harmless by the Partnership for and with respect to any liabilities, costs, and expenses incurred in connection therewith. It is understood and agreed that the reimbursement and indemnification herein provided for shall include and extend to any suit, action, or proceeding based upon a claim of misrepresentation or omission to reveal any act of substance in any document pursuant to which the Limited Partnership Interests have been offered. It is expressly agreed that any claim of the nature referred to in the preceding sentences is and shall be subject to the provisions of this Subsection 3.4(b), other provisions of this Section, and other provisions of this Agreement relating to the nonliability, reimbursement, and indemnification of the General Partner. This Agreement is part of the consideration inducing the General Partner to accept the Limited Partners as members of the Partnership. The foregoing provisions for the indemnification and reimbursement of the General Partner shall apply in every case except in which it is affirmative determined in any proceeding that the General Partner shall not be entitled to have indemnification or reimbursement by reason of his having been guilty of gross negligence, fraud, bad faith, or willful misconduct.

(c) Nothing herein shall be deemed to constitute a representation or warranty by the General Partner with respect to the title to or value of any Partnership Property or with respect to the existence or nonexistence of any contracts or other encumbrances with regard thereto, whether as against its own acts in the normal course of business or otherwise.

3.5 *Power of Attorney.* (a) Each Limited Partner by the execution of this Agreement does irrevocably constitute and appoint the General Partner or any one of them, if more than one, with full power of substitution, as his true and lawful attorney in his name, place, and stead to execute, acknowledge, deliver, file, and record all documents in connection with the Partnership, including but not limited to (i) the original Certificate of Limited Partnership and all amendments thereto required by law or the provisions of this Agreement, (ii) all certificates and other instruments necessary to qualify or continue the Partnership as a limited partnership or partnership wherein the Limited Partners have limited liability in the states or provinces where the partnership may be doing its business, (iii) all instruments necessary to effect a change or modification of the Partnership in accordance with this Agreement, (iv) all conveyances and other instruments necessary to effect the dissolution and termination of the Partnership, and (v) all election under the Internal Revenue Code governing the taxation of the Partnership. Each Limited Partner agrees to be bound by any representations of the attorney-in-fact under this power of attorney, and hereby ratifies and confirms all acts which the said attorney-in-fact may take as attorney-in-fact hereunder in all respects as though performed by the Limited Partner.

(b) The Power of attorney granted herein shall be deemed to be coupled with an interest and shall be irrevocable and survive the death of a Limited Partner. In the event of any conflict between this Agreement and any instruments filed by such attorney-in-fact pursuant to the power of attorney granted in this Section, this Agreement shall control, and no power granted herein shall be used to create any personal liabilities on the part of the Limited Partners.

(c) By virtue of the power of attorney granted herein, the General Partner, or any one of them, if more than one, shall execute the Certificate of Limited Partnership and any amendments thereto by listing all of the Limited Partners and executing any instrument with the signature of the General Partner(s) acting as attorney-in-fact for all of them. Each Limited Partner agrees to execute with acknowledgement of affidavit, if required, any further documents and writings which may be necessary to effectively grant the foregoing power of attorney to the General Partner(s).

Article IV

Capitalization and Capital Contribution

4.1 *Capitalization.* The total initial capital of the Partnership shall be a minimum of _____ ($ _____) and a maximum of _____ ($ _____), exclusive of any capital contribution by the General Partner.

4.2 *General Partner's Contribution.* The General Partner has contributed _____ ($ _____) in cash to the capital of the Partnership and will be reimbursed at Closing for amounts that he has expended on behalf of the Partnership prior to Closing.

4.3 *Limited Partner's Contribution.* Each Limited Partner has made the contribution of capital to the Partnership in the amount set forth on Schedule A annexed hereto. Subscription for a Unit shall be made upon the execution hereof by the payment of ($ _____) in cash on subscription.

4.4 *Capital Accounts.* A separate Capital Account shall be maintained for each Partner and shall be credited with his Capital Contribution and his allocable share of all revenues, income, or gain and shall be debited with his allocable share of costs, expenses, deductions, and losses of the Partnership and any distributions made to him.

Article V

Fees and Compensation

In consideration of various services to be rendered to the Partnership by the General Partner, the General Partner will receive the compensation and fees as described in the Memorandum.

In furtherance of the provisions of Article III hereof, the General Partner may contract with any person, firm, or corporation (whether or not affiliated with the General Partner) for fair value and at reasonable competitive rates of compensation, for the performance of any and all services which may at any time be necessary, proper, convenient, or advisable to carry on the business of the Partnership.

Article VI

Distribution of Proceeds from Operations and Profit and Loss Allocations

6.1 *Distribution of Cash Flow.* Subject to the right of the General Partner to retain all or any portion of the annual cash flow for the anticipated needs of the Partnership, the net annual cash flow of the Partnership available for distribution from operations will be allocated ninety-nine percent (99%) to the Limited Partners (pro rata among them in the proportion that each Unit owned by a Limited Partner bears to the total number of Units owned by all Limited Partners) and one percent (1%) to the General Partner, until such time as the Limited Partners shall have received their capital contributions (Payout) and thereafter, fifty percent (50%) to the Limited Partners, pro rata, and fifty percent (50%) to the General Partner.

6.2 *Allocation of Profits and Losses.* Profits and losses of the Partnership from operation will be allocated ninety-nine percent (99%) to the Limited Partners (pro rata among them in proportion that each Unit owned by a Limited Partner bears to the total number of Units owned by all Limited Partners) and one percent (1%) to the General Partner until Payout. After Payout, profits and losses will be allocated fifty percent (50%) to the Limited Partners, pro rata, and fifty percent (50%) to the General Partner.

6.3 *Allocation of Income for Certain Tax Purposes.* (a) Anything contained in this Agreement to the contrary notwithstanding, in the event an allocation of income in any calendar year pursuant to Section 6.2 above would cause the General Partner to have a positive Capital Account at the end of such year at a time when the Limited Partners have negative Capital Accounts, the amount of such income which would have been allocated to the General Partner pursuant to Section 6.2 in excess of the aggregate negative Capital Accounts of the Limited Partners shall instead be allocated to the Capital Accounts of the Limited Partners on a pro rata basis. For purposes of computing what a Partner's Capital Account would be at the end of a year, any cash available for distribution at such time which is intended to be distributed shall be deemed to have been distributed to such Partner on the last day of such year.

(b) Anything contained in this Agreement to the contrary notwithstanding, a Partner or Partners with deficit Capital Account balances resulting, in whole or in part, from an interest or other expense accrual, shall be allocated income resulting from the forgiveness of indebtedness of such deficit Capital Account balances no later than the time at which the accrual is reduced below the sum of such deficit Capital Account balances.

(c) If any Partner is, for income tax purposes, allocated additional income or denied a loss because of Section 6.3(b) above, a compensating allocation shall be made, for income tax purposes, at the first time such an allocation would be permissible thereunder.

Article VII

Allocation of Profits and Losses on a Sale or Other Taxable Disposition of Partnership Property

7.1 Any gain realized by the Partnership in connection with the sale or other taxable disposition of the Partnership Property shall be allocated to the Partners in the following order of priority:

(a) If any Partner has a negative Capital Account, any gain from the sale or other disposition of the Partnership Property shall be allocated to such Partners in the amount of their respective negative account balances, until the balance of each such Partner's Capital Account is equal to zero; and

(b) Any remaining gains shall be allocated ninety-nine percent (99%) to the Limited Partners, pro rata, and one percent (1%) to the General Partner until Payout, and thereafter fifty percent (50%) to the Limited Partners, pro rata, and fifty percent (50%) to the General Partner.

7.2 Any loss realized by the Partnership in connection with the sale or other taxable disposition of the Partnership Property shall be allocated to the Partners in the following order of priority:

(a) If any of the Partners has a positive Capital Account, any loss from the sale or other disposition of the Partnership Property shall be allocated to such Partners in the amount of their respective positive account balances, until the balance of each such Partner's Capital Account is equal to zero; and

(b) Any remaining losses shall be allocated to the Partners as set forth in Section 7.1(b) above.

7.3 It is the intention of the General Partner that the allocation set forth herein have "substantial economic effect" within the meaning of regulations promulgated under Internal Revenue Code Section 704. In the event such allocations are deemed by the Internal Revenue Service or the courts not to have substantial economic effect, the General Partner reserves the right to modify allocations of profits and losses, after consulting with counsel, to achieve substantial economic effect. Nothing herein shall be construed to require the General Partner to so modify the allocation as set forth herein.

Article VIII

Limited Partners' Covenants and Representation with Respect to Securities Act

8.1 *Investment Representations.* Each of the Limited Partners, by signing this Agreement, represents and warrants to the General Partner and to the Partnership that he (a) is acquiring his Interest in the Partnership for his own personal account for investment purposes only and without any intention of selling or distributing all or any part of the same; (b) has no reason to anticipate any change in personal circumstances, financial or otherwise, which would cause him to sell or distribute, or necessitate or require any sale or distribution of such Interest; (c) is familiar with the nature of and risks attending investments in securities and the particular financial, legal, and tax implications of the business to be conducted by the Partnership, and has determined on his own or on the basis of consultation with his own financial and tax advisors that the purchase of such Interest is consistent with his own investment objectives and income prospects; (d) has received a copy of the Private Placement Memorandum, to which a copy of this Agreement is attached as Exhibit A, and has had access to any and all information concerning the Partnership which he and his financial, tax, and legal advisors requested or considered necessary to make proper evaluation of this investment; (e) is aware that no trading market for Interests in the Partnership will exist at any time and that his Interest will at no time be freely transferable or be transferable with potential adverse tax consequences; and (f) is aware that there is a substantial risk that the federal partnership tax returns will be audited by the Internal Revenue Service and that, upon such audit, a part of the deductions allocated to the Limited Partners could be disallowed, thereby reducing the tax benefits of investing in the Partnership.

8.2 *Covenant Against Resale.* Each of the Limited Partners agrees hereby that he will, in no event, sell or distribute his Interest in the Partnership or any portion thereof unless, in the opinion of counsel to the Partnership, such Interest may be legally sold or distributed without registration under the Securities Act of 1933, as amended, or registration or qualification under then applicable state or federal statutes, or such Interest shall have been so registered or qualified and an appropriate prospectus shall then be in effect. *Notwithstanding the foregoing, no Limited Partner will be permitted to sell, distribute, or otherwise transfer his Interest in the Partnership or any portion thereof without the written consent of the General Partner (except as otherwise provided in Paragraph 9.1(b) below), the granting of which consent is in the absolute discretion of the General Partner.*

8.3 *Reliance on Private Offering Exemption.* Each of the Limited Partners represents and warrants hereby that he is fully aware that his Interest in the Partnership is being issued and sold to him by the Partnership in reliance upon the exemption provided for by Section 4(2) of the Securities Act of 1933, as amended, and Regulation D promulgated under such Act, and exemptions available under state securities laws, on the grounds that no public offering is involved, and upon the representations, warranties, and agreements set forth in this Article VIII.

Article IX

Transfer of Partnership Interests

9.1 *Limited Partnership Interest.* (a) No transfer of all or any part of a Limited Partner's Interest (including a transferee by death or operation of law and including a transferee in a Permitted Transfer) shall be admitted to the Partnership as a Limited Partner without the written consent of the General Partner, which consent may be withheld in the complete discretion of the General Partner. In no event shall the General Partner consent to the admission of the transferee as a Limited Partner unless the transferee executes this Agreement and such other instruments as may be required by law, or as the General Partner shall deem necessary or desirable to confirm the undertaking of such transferee to: (i) be bound by all the terms and provisions of this Agreement; and (ii) pay all reasonable expenses incurred by the Partnership in conjunction with the transfer, including, but not limited to, the cost of preparation, filing, and publishing such amendments to the Certificate as may be required by law of such other instruments as the General Partner may deem necessary and desirable.

A sale, assignment, or transfer of a Limited Partner's Interest will be recognized by the Partnership when it has received written notice of such sale or assignment, signed by both parties, containing the purchaser's or assignee's acceptance of the terms of the Partnership Agreement and a representation by the parties that the sale or assignment was lawful. Such sale or assignment will be recognized as of the date of such notice, except that if such date is more than thirty (30) days prior to the time of filing of such notice, such sale or assignment will be recognized as of the time the notice was filed with the Partnership. For purposes of allocating Profits and Losses, the assignee will be treated as having become a Limited Partner as of the date of which the sale, assignment, or transfer was recognized by the Partnership.

(b) Except for: (i) a Permitted Transfer and/or transfer by operation of law other than transfers in excess of the "forty" percent (40%) limitation" (see subsection (c) below); or (ii) a transfer by gift, bequest, or inheritance, no Limited Partner may transfer all or any part of his Interest without first giving written notice of the proposed transfer to the General Partner (setting forth the terms thereof and the name and address of the proposed transferee) and obtaining the written consent of the General Partner to such transfer. Such consent shall be within the complete discretion of the General Partner and subject to such conditions, if any, as it shall determine.

(c) Anything else to the contrary contained herein notwithstanding:

(i)   in any period of twelve (12) consecutive months, no transfer of an Interest may be made which would result in increasing the aggregate Profit and Loss Percentages of Partnership Interests previously transferred in such period above forty percent (40%). This limitation is herein referred to as the "forty percent (40%) limitation";

(ii)   a Permitted Transfer is fully subject to the forty percent (40%) limitation;

(iii)   subparagraph (i) hereof shall not apply to a transfer by gift, bequest, or inheritance, or a transfer to the Partnership, and for the purposes of the forty percent (40%) limitation, any such transfer shall not be treated as such;

(iv)   if, after the forty percent (40%) limitation is reached in any consecutive twelve- (12-) month period, a transfer of a Partnership In-

terest would otherwise take place by operation of law (but not including any transfer referred to in subparagraph (iii) hereof), then such
Partnership Interest shall be deemed sold by the transferor to the Partnership immediately prior to such transfer for a price equal to the fair
market value of such interest on such date of transfer. The price shall
be paid within ninety (90) days after the date of the sale out of the
assets of the Partnership and the General Partner. If the Partnership
and the transferor do not agree upon the fair market value of the Partnership Interest, then the purchase price shall be determined in accordance with Section 9.3. The purchase price shall be paid by the
Partnership out of its assets in cash within ten (10) days after such
determination.

9.2 *Events Requiring Sale of Partnership Interest.* (a) The Interest of a
Limited Partner shall be deemed offered for sale to a person designated
by the General Partner upon the happening of any of the following
events:

(i)   a petition in bankruptcy having been filed by or against a Limited Partner and not discharged within ninety (90) days from the date
of such filing; or

(ii)   a receiver or committee having been appointed to manage a
Limited Partner's property; or

(iii)   a creditor of a Limited Partner having attached his Interest and
such attachment not being discharged or vacated within ninety (90)
days from the date it became effective.

The General Partner shall have ninety (90) days after the occurrence
of any of the foregoing within which to accept such offer, designate such
a purchaser (including the General Partner), and transmit written notice
thereof to such Limited Partner. If the General Partner fails to make such
designation within ninety (90) days as aforesaid, the offer shall be deemed
withdrawn. The purchase price for such Interest shall be its appraised
value as determined in accordance with Section 9.3. The purchaser shall
pay over to the selling Limited Partner the purchase price in cash within
ten (10) days after such determination. Upon payment of the purchase
price to the selling Limited Partner, his Interest shall be deemed transferred to the aforesaid designated person.

(b) If any of the events described in Subsection 10.1(a)(v) should
occur to the General Partner, or any one of them if more than one, and
the Partnership shall not thereafter be dissolved but shall continue as a
successor Limited Partnership with a successor General Partner, then
upon the happening of any of such events the Interest of such General
Partner shall be deemed offered for sale to the successor General Partner
at its appraised value determined in accordance with Section 9.3 (except
in the case of a voluntary withdrawal by a General Partner, in which
event the value shall be determined by the withdrawing General Partner
and the proposed successor General Partner, as selected by the withdrawing General Partner). The successor General Partner shall not become a
General Partner of the Partnership until such former General Partner's
Interest has been paid for in full in cash.

9.3 *Appraisal*. For the purpose of this Agreement, the appraised value of an Interest shall be the average of the values determined by three appraisers who are experts in evaluating property similar to the Partnership Property selected at the request of the General Partner. The appraisal made by such appraisers shall be binding and conclusive as between the selling Partner or Partners and the persons purchasing such Interest. The cost of such appraisal shall be borne equally by the selling and purchasing parties, and by each set of parties, among themselves, in proportion to their respective shares.

9.4 *Death, Bankruptcy, Incompetence, or Dissolution of a Limited Partner*. (a) Upon the death, bankruptcy, or legal incompetency of an individual Limited Partner, his legally authorized personal representative shall have all of the rights of a Limited Partner for the purpose of settling or managing his estate, and shall have such power as the decedent, bankrupt, or incompetent possessed to make an assignment of his Interest in the Partnership in accordance with the terms hereof and to join with such assignee in making application to substitute such assignee as a Limited Partner.

(b) Upon bankruptcy, insolvency, dissolution, or other cessation to exist as a legal entity of any Limited Partner which is not an individual, the authorized representative of such entity shall have all of the rights of the Limited Partner for the purpose of effecting the orderly winding up and disposition of the business of such entity, and such power as such entity possessed to make an assignment of its Interest in the Partnership in accordance with the terms hereof and to join with such assignee in making application to substitute such assignee as a Limited Partner.

9.5 *Voluntary Withdrawal or Transfer by a General Partner*. (a) A General Partner may resign as General Partner at any time, but only upon compliance with the following procedures:

(i)   The General Partner shall give notification to all Limited Partners that he proposes to withdraw and that he proposes that there be substituted in his place a person designated and described in such notification.

(ii)   Enclosed with such notification shall be (a) an opinion of counsel to the Partnership that the proposed General Partner qualifies to serve as a General Partner under federal law, and (b) a certificate, duly executed by or on behalf of such proposed successor General Partner, to the effect that he is experienced in performing (or employs sufficient personnel who are experienced in performing) functions of the type then being performed by the resigning General Partner.

(iii)   The consent of the remaining General Partner and the holders of at least fifty-one percent (51%) in interest of the Limited Partner shall be required for the appointment of the proposed successor General Partner pursuant to this Section 9.5(a). If the proposed successor General Partner shall not receive such consent within sixty (60) days after the date of the withdrawing General Partner's notification, then, at the sole option of the General Partner seeking to withdraw, the Partnership may be terminated and dissolved and its assets liquidated in accordance with Article VIII of this Agreement.

(iv) The General Partner who has withdrawn pursuant to this Section shall cooperate fully with the successor General Partner so that the responsibilities of such withdrawn General Partner may be transferred to such successor General Partner with as little disruption of the Partnership's business and affairs as is practicable.

(b) Except as part of a transfer to a successor General Partner pursuant to Section 9.5(a), the General Partner shall not have the right to retire or to transfer or assign his General Partner's Interest.

9.6 *Removal of a General Partner.* (a) A General Partner may be removed as General Partner only without his consent or the consent of the other General Partners only for cause upon the consent of 51% in Interest of the Limited Partners, such removal to be effective upon the service of written notice upon the General Partner to be removed by posting said notice in the United States mails. Upon such removal, the Partnership shall continue and the remaining General Partners shall continue the Partnership. If all the General Partners are removed, then the Partnership shall be dissolved unless 51% in Interest of the Limited Partners vote to continue the Partnership as a successor limited partnership and appoint a successor General Partner who (i) in the opinion of counsel to the Partnership qualifies to serve as General Partner under federal law, and (ii) agrees to purchase the Interest of the other General Partners in accordance with Sections 9.2(b) and 9.3 hereof.

(b) Any successor General Partner appointed by the Limited Partners to replace the General Partner shall, beginning on the effective date of such replacement, have the same rights and obligations under this Agreement as the General Partner would have had subsequent to such date if the General Partner continued to act as General Partner.

9.7 *Death, Retirement, Bankruptcy, Legal Incapacity, etc. of a General Partner.* Upon the death, retirement, or legal incapacity of a General Partner, or the filing by or against a General Partner of a petition in bankruptcy, the adjudication of the General Partner as a bankrupt, or the making by the General Partner of an assignment for the benefit of creditors, the remaining General Partners shall continue the Partnership unless all of the General Partners are subject to the foregoing events, in which case the Partnership shall terminate unless fifty-one percent (51%) in Interest of the Limited Partners (or one hundred percent (100%) in the case of the death, retirement, or insanity of a General Partner) vote to continue the Partnership as a successor Limited Partnership and appoint a successor General Partner, who (i) in the opinion of counsel to the Partnership qualifies to serve as General Partner under federal law, and (ii) agrees to purchase the Interest of the General Partner in accordance with Sections 9.2(b) and 9.3 hereof.

9.8 *Admission of a Successor General Partner.* The admission of a successor General Partner shall be effective only if the Interests of the Limited Partners shall not be affected by the admission of such successor General Partner.

9.9 *Liability and Rights of Replaced General Partner.* Any General Partner who shall be replaced as General Partner shall remain liable for his portion of any obligation and liabilities incurred by him as General Partner prior to the time such replacement shall have become effective, but he shall be free of any obligation or liability incurred on account of the activities of the Partnership from and after such time. Such replacement shall not affect any rights of the General Partner which shall mature prior to the effective date of such replacement.

Article X

Dissolution, Liquidation, and Termination

10.1 *Dissolution.* (a) The Partnership shall be dissolved upon the earliest of:

    (i)   the expiration of its term as provided in this Agreement;

    (ii)   he sale of all or substantially all of the Partnership Property;

    (iii)   the occurrence of any event which causes the dissolution of a limited partnership under the laws of the State of _____;

    (iv)   the written election of Limited Partners owning eighty percent (80%) of the Limited Partnership Interests; or

    (v)   except as otherwise provided herein, the withdrawal or removal of, the death, retirement, or legal incapacity of, or the filing of a petition in bankruptcy, the adjudication as a bankrupt, or the making of an assignment for the benefit of creditors by the last remaining General Partner, unless fifty-one percent (51%) in Interest of the Limited Partners (or one hundred percent (100%) in the case of the death, retirement, or legal incapacity of the General Partner) appoint a successor General Partner and vote to continue the Partnership as a successor Limited Partnership.

(b) The Partnership shall not be dissolved upon the death of a Limited Partner.

(c) In the event of such dissolution, the assets of the Partnership shall be liquidated and the proceeds thereof distributed in accordance with Section 7.1 hereof.

10.2 *Liquidating Trustee.* Upon the dissolution of the Partnership, the liquidating trustee (which shall be those General Partners which are not subject to any of the events set forth in subparagraph 10.1(a)(v), or, in the event all General Partners are subject to such events, a trustee appointed by the Limited Partners representing a majority in interest of the profit and loss percentages of the Limited Partners), shall proceed diligently to wind up the affairs of the Partnership and distribute its assets in accordance with Section 7.1 hereof. All saleable assets of the Partnership may be sold in connection with any liquidation at public or private sale, at such price and upon such terms as the liquidating trustee in his sole discretion may deem advisable. Any Partner and any partnership, corporation, or other firm in which any Partner is in any way interested may purchase assets at such sale. Distributions of Partnership assets may be made in cash or in kind, in the sole and absolute discretion of the liquidating trustee. The liquidating trustee shall make a proper accounting to each Limited Partner of his Capital Account and of the net profit or loss of the Partnership from the date of the last previous accounting to the date of dissolution.

Article XI

Accounting, Records, Reports, and Taxes

11.1 *Fiscal Year and Reports.* The fiscal year of the Partnership for both accounting and federal income tax purposes shall be the calendar year. At all times during the continuance of the Partnership, the General Partner shall keep or cause to be kept full and faithful books of account in which shall be entered fully and accurately each transaction of the Partnership. All of the books of account shall be open to the inspection and examination of the Limited Partners or their duly authorized representatives upon reasonable notice during normal business hours. Annual financial statement of the Partnership shall be transmitted by the General Partner to each Limited Partner. The General Partner shall further transmit to each Limited Partner annually, within a reasonable time after the end of each calendar year (but in no event later than seventy-five (75) days after the end of the calendar year or as soon as practicable thereafter), a report setting forth the Limited Partner's share of the Partnership's Profits or Losses for each such year, and such Limited Partner's allocation of cash receipts. The reports and statements delivered in accordance herewith may be changed from time to time to cure errors or omission and to give effect to any retroactive costs or adjustments. All costs and expenses incurred in connection with such reports and statements shall constitute expenses of Partnership operation.

11.2 *Income Tax Elections.* (a) No elections shall be made by the Partnership, the General Partner or any Limited Partner to be excluded from the application of the provision of Subchapter K of Chapter I of Subtitle A of the Code or from the application of any similar provisions of state tax laws.

(b) All other elections required or permitted under the Code shall be made by the General Partner in such manner as will, in the opinion of the Partnership's accountants, be most advantageous to a majority in Interest of the Limited Partners.

11.3 *Tax Matters Partner*. The General Partner shall be designated the tax matters partner of the Partnership pursuant to Section 6231(7) of the Internal Revenue Code.

Article XII

General

12.1 *Notices*. Any notice, communication, or consent required or permitted to be given by any provision of this Agreement shall, except as otherwise expressly provided herein, be deemed to have been sufficiently given or served for any purpose only if in writing, delivered personally, or sent by registered mail, postage and charges prepaid, or by standard prepaid telegram.

12.2 *Further Assurances*. Each of the Partners agrees hereafter to execute, acknowledge, deliver, file, record, and publish such further certificates, instruments, agreements and other documents and to take all such further actions as may be required by law or deemed by the General Partner to be necessary or useful in furtherance of the Partnership's purposes and the objectives and intentions underlying this Agreement and not inconsistent with the terms hereof.

12.3 *Banking*. All funds shall be deposited in the Partnership's name in such checking accounts as shall be designated by the General Partner. All withdrawals therefrom shall be made upon checks signed by the General Partner.

12.4 *Amendment of Certificate of Limited Partnership*. The General Partner may amend the Certificate of Limited Partnership and the Agreement when any one of the following events occur: (a) there is a change in the name of the Partnership, or the amount of character of the contribution of any Limited Partner; (b) a person is substituted as a Limited Partner; or (c) an additional Limited Partner is admitted.

12.5 *Voting Rights of Limited Partners*. This Agreement may not be modified or amended in any manner whatsoever except with the written consent of the General Partner and the written consent of Limited Partners whose Profit and Loss percentages at that time are sixty-six and two-thirds percent (66⅔%) of the total Profit and Loss Percentages of all Limited Partners.

12.6 *Meetings*. Any vote of the Limited Partners on any matters upon which Limited Partners are entitled to vote hereunder may be accomplished at a meeting of Limited Partners called for such purposes by the General Partner or by the nonpromoted, nonaffiliated Limited Partners whose Profit and Loss Percentages at that time exceed fifty-one percent (51%) of the total Profit and Loss Percentages of all such Limited Partners, upon not less than ten (10) days' prior notice or, in lieu of a meeting, by the written consent of the required percentage of Limited Partners.

12.7 *Access to Records*. The Limited Partners and their designated representatives shall be permitted access to all records of the Partnership at the office of the Partnership during reasonable hours. The Partnership records shall include a list of the names and addresses of the Limited Partners.

12.8 *Miscellaneous*. (a) Except as otherwise expressly provided herein, the headings in this Agreement are inserted for convenience of reference only and are in no way intended to describe, interpret, define, or limit the scope, extent, or intent of this Agreement or any provision hereof.

(b) Every provision of this Agreement is intended to be severable. If any term or provision hereof is illegal or invalid for any reason whatsoever, such illegality or invalidity shall not affect the validity of the remainder of this Agreement.

(c) This Agreement, and the application and interpretation hereof, shall be governed exclusively by the terms hereof and by the laws of the State of _____.

(d) The rights and remedies provided by this Agreement are cumulative, and the use of any one right or remedy by any party shall not preclude or waive its right to pursue any or all other remedies. Such rights and remedies are given in addition to any other rights the parties may have by law, statute, ordinance, or otherwise.

(e) This Agreement may be executed in any number of counterparts with the same effect as if the parties had all signed the same instrument. All counterparts shall be construed together and shall constitute one Agreement. Limited Partners may become parties to this Agreement by executing and delivering to the General Partner a signature page hereto in the form approved by the General Partner.

(f) Time is of the essence hereof.

(g) Each and all of the covenants, terms, provisions and agreements therein contained shall be binding upon and inure to the benefit of each party and, to the extent permitted by this Agreement, the respective successors and assigns of the parties.

(h) No person, firm, or corporation dealing with the Partnership shall be required to inquire into the authority of the General Partner to take any action or to make any decision.

(i) This instrument incorporates the entire agreement between the parties hereto, regardless of anything to the contrary contained in any certificate of limited partnership or other instrument or notice purporting to summarize the terms hereof, whether or not the same shall be recorded or published.

(j) The General Partner shall prepare or cause to be prepared and shall file on or before the due date (or any extension thereof) any federal, state, or local tax returns required to be filed by the Partnership. The General Partner shall cause the Partnership to pay any taxes payable by the Partnership.

IN WITNESS WHEREOF, the undersigned have executed this Agreement as of the day and year first above written.

_____

General Partner

_____

Limited Partner

Promissory Note

In consideration of funds this day in hand received, I, _____
_____, of _____, do hereby promise to pay to
the order of _____ the sum of _____ Dollars ($ _____),
without defalcation, on the _____ day of _____, 20_____.

/s/ _____

Dated: _____

Purchase Order

Acme, Inc.
123 Front Street
City, State 00000

Purchaser:

Account Number:

Item Number:

Description:

Quantity:

Unit Price:
   Discount: 1% if ordering between 500 and 999 Units
            1.25% if ordering between 1000 and 2999 Units
            1.5% if ordering over 3000 Units

Merchandise Total Price:

Sales Tax (Tax Resale Number):

Delivery Charges:
   Express Delivery: Next Day Add:
                    One Week Add:
                    Special Shipper (Specify) Add:

Order Total:

Method of Payment:
   Discount: 2% for COD
            1.5% for 2-Week Payment
            1% for 30-Day Payment

Late Fee: 1% per month after 60 Days

Ship To:

Real Estate Lease

Agreement made this _____ day of _____, 20_____, between X, Inc., a _____ corporation (Lessor), and _____, an individual (Lessee).

The Lessor hereby devises and lets to the Lessee the premises known as _____ for the term of one year, commencing on the _____ day of _____, 20_____, and ending on the _____ day of _____, 20_____, for which the Lessee agrees to pay the Lessor, at his place of business, promptly on the first day of each month, in advance, a monthly rental of _____ Dollars ($ _____). On the failure of the Lessee to pay said rent when due, all further rent under this contract shall immediately become due and payable, and the Lessor has the right, at his option, to declare this lease void, cancel the same, enter and take possession of the premises.

It is further agreed that:

(Indicate all specific covenants the parties agree to, for example:
Allocation of cost of repairs
Maintenance of premises
Right of Lessor to enter
Subletting
Destruction of property due to fire or act of God
Alteration of premises
Payment of damages due to negligence
Notice to quit
Security deposit)

All of the aforementioned agreements, covenants, and conditions shall apply to and be binding upon the parties hereto, their heirs, executors, administrators, and assigns.

IN WITNESS WHEREOF, the parties hereto have set their hands and seals this _____ day of _____, 20_____

_____
Lessor

By: _____

_____
Lessee

Release

Know All Men By These Present:

That I, _____, of _____, in consideration of the sum of _____ Dollars ($ ____), do hereby remise, release, and forever discharge _____ of _____, his heirs, executors, and administrators of and from all manner of action and causes of action, suits, debts, claims, accounts, bonds, contracts, agreements, judgments, and demands whatsoever in law or equity, which I ever had, now have, or which my heirs, executors, administrators, or assigns, or any of them, hereafter can, shall, or may have, for or by reason of ____(Matter in Controversy)____ against said _____.

IN WITNESS WHEREOF, I have hereunto set my hand and seal this ____ day of _____, 20____.

_____

Shareholders Agreement

Agreement made this ___ day of _____, 20___, by and between _____, residing at _____ (hereinafter X), and _____, residing at _____ (hereinafter Y).

IN CONSIDERATION OF the mutual covenants and conditions contained herein, it is hereby agreed as follows:

1. Organization of the Corporation

1.1 The parties agree that upon the execution of this Agreement, they will cause a corporation to be formed under the laws of the State of _____ to be named _____ (hereinafter called the Corporation). The Corporation shall be authorized to issue ___ shares of common voting stock, all with(out) a par value (of $ ___).

1.2(a) Each party hereto agrees that he will subscribe for and purchase shares of the common stock of the Corporation as follows:

X—___ shares
Y—___ shares

(b) Each party agrees that in consideration of the shares of the Corporation's stock to be purchased by him he will pay to the Corporation the sum of $ _____.

1.3 The parties hereto shall vote (as shareholders or directors, as the case may be) as follows:

(a) To elect the following as Directors of the Corporation so long as they are stockholders thereof: X and Y.

(b) To elect the following as Officers of the Corporation so long as they are stockholders, directors, and/or employees thereof:

X—President
Y—Secretary-Treasurer

(c) To cause the Corporation to become a party to this Agreement by adopting same after the Corporation has been organized and to take all necessary action to carry out the terms of this Agreement.

2. Operation of the Corporation

2.1 The business of the Corporation shall be _____ _____.

2.2 X and Y each agrees to make available to the Corporation, as additional working capital, up to $ _____ each, upon such terms as they and the Corporation may from time to time agree.

2.3 It is agreed by the parties hereto that no action shall be taken with respect to any of the following matters except by a unanimous vote of all of the stockholders and directors:

(a) Sale of all or substantially all of the assets of the Corporation;

(b) The merger, consolidation, or reorganization of the Corporation;

(c) The issuance or sale, or the offer to sell, any additional shares of stock to existing shareholders or third parties;

(d) The commitment of the Corporation to any lease or distributorship;

(e) The creation of indebtedness on behalf of the Corporation to any one person or firm in excess of $ _____ .

The Bylaws of the Corporation shall set out and include a statement of the foregoing action requiring the unanimous consent of the directors and/or shareholders, as the case may be.

2.4 The Corporation shall select as its depository the _____ Bank. The resolution authorizing the opening and maintenance of such bank account shall provide that all checks, notes, drafts, and other evidence of indebtedness, etc., drawn on the account of the Corporation at such bank, shall be executed by the President and the Secretary-Treasurer.

2.5 The Corporation shall enter into an employment agreement with X in the form annexed hereto, which shall also contain the following terms:

(a) X shall be paid a salary of $ _____ per week during the first five (5) years of his employment or until its earlier termination, plus _____ % of the net profits of the Corporation.

(b) X agrees that he shall devote all of his business time to the Corporation and agrees that so long as he is an employee and a stockholder of the Corporation and for such further period of two (2) years thereafter, he will not directly or indirectly, engage as a principal, owner, stockholder, employee, officer, or director, or in any other capacity in any business venture or enterprise which deals directly or indirectly, or by association, in the business from time to time conducted by the Corporation or by any wholly owned subsidiary corporation or affiliate.

(c) The salary of X shall from time to time be increased as determined by the Board of Directors of the Corporation.

(d) The parties hereto shall each be entitled to receive as benefits under their respective employment with the Corporation, at the expense of the Corporation, health insurance coverage and such other benefits as the Corporation from time to time may determine.

3. Transfer for Shares

3.1 No share of stock of the Corporation, whether preferred or common, and whenever issued, shall be sold, assigned, transferred or otherwise disposed of, encumbered, pledged or hypothecated except as hereinafter provided. A stockholder desiring to sell all (and not a part) of his stock shall offer to sell all of his shares in the Corporation in writing, which offer shall be mailed to the Corporation and to each of the stockholders. The Corporation shall have the first option to accept or reject the offer. Such option must be exercised within thirty (30) days and no longer from the date of receipt of the offer, which acceptance must be in writing and mailed to the offeror. Failure on the part of the Corporation to respond to the offer shall constitute rejection as of the end of the thirtieth day following receipt of the offer. If the Corporation rejects the offer (and any partial acceptance or partial rejection shall constitute a total rejection), the other stockholders or stockholder, as the case may be, shall pro rata to their then shareholdings in the Corporation, have second option to accept or reject the offer. Such option must be exercised within fifteen (15) days (and no longer) from the date of the rejection and must be exercised in writing and mailed to the offeror. Failure to timely respond by such other stockholders (or any of the stockholders) shall likewise constitute a total rejection. Thereafter, for an additional fifteen (15) days (and no longer) the remaining stockholders who have not rejected the offer made to them, may, in proportion to their shareholdings, accept the entire offer of all such offered shareholdings. If all of the offered shares are not wholly accepted as provided above, all of the shares of the offeree stockholders shall, without further act, be automatically deemed counteroffered for sale to the original offeror, which counteroffer must be accepted by the original offeror within fifteen (15) days (and no longer) from the making of the counteroffer. Such counteroffer shall be deemed to have been made as of the date of the rejection by the remaining stockholders as provided above. Failure to timely respond to such original offeror shall likewise constitute a total rejection of such counteroffer. In all cases a partial acceptance or a partial rejection shall constitute a total rejection.

If all of the offered shares are not wholly accepted as provided above, the parties covenant to and shall take immediate steps thereafter to dissolve and liquidate the Corporation and its assets; and for such purposes, the offeror is hereby, without further act or document, constituted, appointed, and delegated as attorney-in-fact and as irrevocable agent (which agency shall be deemed to be "coupled with an interest") with all proxy rights in connection therewith, to dissolve and liquidate the Corporation on behalf and at the pro rata cost and expense of all of the then shareholders.

The price and terms of any offer shall be as a hereinafter set forth. Closing shall take place on the 15th business day following the receipt of the acceptance at the Corporation's then principal office at 10:00 A.M. of that day.

(a) The stockholders, simultaneously herewith, have executed a "Certificate of Agreed Value," setting forth the total net value of the Corporation as of this date. They agree to execute new such Certificates semiannually or more often. The term "total net value" as used herein shall be deemed to mean the agreed total value of all of the assets of the Corporation, after deducting therefrom any and all liabilities, howsoever characterized.

(b) The price for the offered shares in the Corporation shall be computed as follows:

The total number of common shares of stock then issued and outstanding in such Corporation shall be divided into the total net value set forth in such Certificate of Agreed Value, and the quotient shall be the price for each share of common stock of the Corporation sold, subject to no adjustments, except as hereinafter provided. The latest dated such Certificate of Agreed Value shall control, except that if any such Certificate, at the time of any total acceptance by any offeree is dated prior to one year from the date of such total acceptance, there shall be added to or subtracted from the total net value set forth in the last dated such Certificate of Agreed Value the difference between the "book value" of the Corporation (as hereinafter defined) as of the date of the last dated such Certificate and such "book value" as of the date of the total acceptance. In computing book value, if necessary, as hereinbefore provided, the established accounting practices, including, but not limited to, Reserves for Bad Debts, Contingent Liabilities, Depreciation, and Amortization, theretofore employed by the Corporation, shall be applied, subject to and in accordance with the following rules:

1. Goodwill, franchises, trademarks, and trade names shall in no way be considered assets for the purpose of determining the "book value";

2. The value of the fixed assets and merchandise inventory shall be fixed by agreement amongst the parties or, if the parties cannot agree, by arbitration, as hereinafter provided;

3. All other assets and liabilities shall be taken at the net figures at which they appear on the books of account;

4. Any life insurance policy owned by the Corporation shall be valued at its cash surrender value.

(c) The price, as hereinbefore determined, shall be adjusted as follows: (i) by subtracting therefrom all personal debts and interest thereon, if any, owed by the offeror to the Corporation, whether or not due; and (ii) by adding thereto all debts and interest thereon, if any, owed by the Corporation to the offeror, whether or not due. If the purchaser is another stockholder, and not the Corporation, an assignment without recourse shall be delivered to him at the closing by the offeror of such corporate debt due to the offeror; and likewise, such other stockholder-purchaser shall be liable (in such same percentage) for debts due to the Corporation from the offeror if an adjustment was made therefor in computing the price, as aforesaid, and the offeror and the Corporation shall execute and deliver unto the offeror a Release in connection with such obligation.

(d) If any offering stockholder shall be indebted to any other stock-holder of the Corporation, such selling-stockholder shall, at the closing hereinabove provided for, discharge any such indebtedness by payment thereof to such other stockholder, with all interest due thereon, whether or not such debt is then due. Furthermore, should any offering-stockholder have monies or other collateral deposited as security for any corporate indebtedness, such monies or collateral shall be returned in full at such closing. In addition, and at the same time, the Corporation and each purchasing-stockholder thereof shall indemnify the selling-stockholder and agree to hold him harmless against any and all claims, losses, demands, and expenses of every nature, arising out of or which may result from or be based upon any guarantee executed or given by the selling-stockholder with respect to any corporate obligation.

(e) The price, as adjusted, shall be paid as follows: 25% in cash or by good, certified check, at the closing, and the balance in twelve (12) equal monthly installments, with interest as set forth below. The install-ments shall be evidence by a series of twelve (12) negotiable promissory notes to be made by the offeree as "Maker" to the order of the offerer as "Payee," dated the date of the closing, the first note being due one month after the closing and monthly consecutively thereafter; each of the notes to bear interest at the rate of _____ percent (_____ %) per annum and contain a grace period of ten (10) days, and shall be payable at the bank of the Maker. The notes shall contain an acceleration clause, but failure to assert such right of acceleration shall not be deemed a waiver thereof. If the Corporation is the Maker, the other stockholders shall, jointly and severally, endorse each note and guarantors.

(f) The notes may be prepaid without penalty on any installment date, upon thirty (30) days' prior written notice, in inverse order, with all accrued interest on each note so prepaid; provided, however, that at the option of the offeror: (i) no prepayment shall be allowed in the same calendar year of the closing; and (ii) the payment of all or any part of the notes ordinarily due in such calendar year shall be deferred (and all in-terest thereon shall run) to January 2 of the next calendar year.

(g) Should the surplus and/or the net assets of the Corporation be insufficient to authorize the purchase of all of the stock so offered in accordance with the provisions of the ____(State corporation law)____ as the same is or may be from time to time amended, and should the Cor-poration exercise the option to purchase, then and in such event, the Corporation shall purchase so much as it is authorized by law and the other stockholders shall purchase (such obligation being mandatory upon such other stockholders) the balance of such offered shares, which obli-gation shall be joint and several.

3.2 In the event of the death of X or Y, his estate or his personal representative shall sell his stock to the Corporation. The Corporation shall purchase the same upon the following terms: the price per share shall be as determined in paragraph 3.1 and shall be payable as therein set forth, except as may be hereinafter provided. Should there be insurance on the life of such deceased stockholder (of which insurance the Corporation shall be the beneficiary in whole or in part), then, upon the death of X or Y, the Corporation shall proceed immediately to collect the proceeds of such insurance on his life and upon such collection of all such proceeds and the qualification of a legal representative of such deceased stockholder, the Corporation shall use such insurance proceeds by payment thereof in cash against the purchase price; provided, however, that if the insurance proceeds be greater than the purchase price, the entire price shall be paid in cash at the closing, and the Corporation may retain the balance of the proceeds for its own corporate purposes, but if the purchase price is greater than the insurance proceeds, the entire proceeds shall be applied as the cash deposit against the price and the balance of the price shall be paid in twelve (12) equal monthly installments, the first such installment to be due thirty (30) days after the closing and each installment to bear interest at the rate of _____ percent (_____ %) per annum and which said installments are to be evidenced by a series of promissory notes as hereinabove provided in paragraph 3.1, and the same provisions as therein set forth shall apply herein with respect to such notes, except that the said notes may be prepaid in inverse order in whole or in part at any time with all accrued interest on any notes so prepaid.

4. Escrow

At the option of the seller, all of the documents required to be delivered at the closing by the seller shall be retained in escrow with his attorneys, pending full payment of the "adjusted" price. Should the escrowee receive notice of a default, he shall forthwith deliver the documents to the seller of his representative, who shall, upon ten (10) days' written notice to the defaulting purchaser, by certified or registered mail, return receipt requested, sell the shareholdings at public or private sale, at which sale the seller or his representative may purchase. Any sales proceeds received in excess of the unpaid balance due and interest, and the expenses of the sale, shall forthwith be turned over to the defaulting purchaser, who shall be liable for any deficiency. There shall be included as a cost of sale legal fees calculated on the unpaid balance and interest, at _____ percent (_____ %), together with the costs and disbursements of the sale. Upon the escrowee receiving written notice from the seller of full payment, he shall forthwith deliver the escrowed documents to the purchaser or purchasers. At the closing, the seller and the purchasers shall execute general releases, excepting therefrom the provisions of this Agreement applicable to the purchaser and the provisions of all Agreements and notes executed at the closing provided for deferred payments and indemnification by the purchaser.

5. Endorsement of Stock Certificates

The Certificates of Stock of the Corporation shall be endorsed as follows:

"The shares of stock represented by this Certificate are subject to all the terms and conditions of an Agreement made on the _____ day of _____, 20____, a copy of which is on file in the office of the Corporation."

6. Voting

At any stockholders' meeting called by the Corporation, for the purpose of accepting or rejecting any offer made by a stockholder to sell his shares in accordance with this Agreement, such stockholder shall be deemed to have voted for the Corporation's purchasing or redeeming the offered shares.

7. Equity

The provisions of this Agreement may be enforced in a court of equity by injunction or specific performance. Such remedies shall be cumulative and not exclusive and shall be in addition to any other remedies which the parties may have. Should any part or parts of this Agreement be determined to be void by a court of competent jurisdiction, the remaining provisions hereof shall nevertheless be binding.

8. Notices

All notices, options, offers, and acceptances hereunder (unless deemed to have been made by the operation of the terms of this Agreement) shall be in writing and served by certified or registered mail, return receipt requested and, unless otherwise herein specified, shall be deemed to have been made as of the date of mailing.

9. Arbitration

Any question or controversy with respect to any question arising hereunder shall be resolved by arbitration in accordance with the laws of the State of _____ and pursuant to the Rules of the American Arbitration Association.

10. Entire Agreement

This Agreement constitutes the entire understanding of the parties concerning the subject matter herein contained. No modification of any provision of this Agreement shall be valid, and the same may not be terminated or abandoned except by a writing signed by the parties to this Agreement.

IN WITNESS WHEREOF, the parties have hereunto set their hands and seals the day and year first above written.

X _____

Y _____

Subscription Agreement (Limited Partnership)

1. The undersigned hereby subscribes for the number of Units of limited partnership interests set forth below in _____, a _____ limited partnership (the Partnership), each Unit of _____ Dollars ($ ____) payable in full on subscription.

2. The undersigned understands that the General Partner will notify him prior to _____, 20____, as to whether this subscription has been accepted or rejected. If rejected, the check tendered by him will be returned to him forthwith without interest or deduction. The undersigned understands that the payments made under this Subscription Agreement will be held in escrow by the Partnership for his benefit at a commercial bank in _____ with assets of at least $10,000,000. If accepted, the check tendered by the undersigned will be applied in accordance with the use of proceeds description set forth in the Private Placement Memorandum relating to the Partnership (the Memorandum).

3. The undersigned had been furnished with and has carefully read the Memorandum relating to the Partnership and the documents attached as Exhibits thereto, including the Partnership Agreement. The undersigned is aware that :

(i)   The Partnership has no financial or operating history;

(ii)   There are substantial risks incident to an investment in the Partnership, as summarized under "Risks" and "Tax Risks" in the Memorandum;

(iii)   No federal or state agency has passed upon the Units or made any finding or determination as to the fairness of the investment;

(iv)   The discussion of the tax consequences arising from investment in the Partnership set forth in the Memorandum is general in nature, and the tax consequences to the undersigned of an investment in the Partnership depend upon his particular circumstances;

(v)   There can be no assurance that the Internal Revenue Code or the regulations thereunder will not be amended in such manner as to deprive the Partnership and its Partners of some of the tax benefits they might now receive; and

(vi)   The books and records of the Partnership will be available for inspection of the undersigned at the Partnership's place of business.

4. The undersigned understands that investment in the Partnership is an illiquid investment. In particular, the undersigned recognizes that:

(i)   The undersigned must bear the economic risk of investment in the Units for an indefinite period of time since the Units have not been registered under the Securities Act of 1933, as amended, and, therefore, cannot be sold unless either they are subsequently registered under said Act or an exemption from such registration is available and a favorable opinion of counsel for the Partnership to such effect is obtained;

(ii)   There will be no established market for the Units and it is not likely that any public market for the Units will develop; and

(iii)   The undersigned's rights to transfer his Units will be restricted, as provided for in the Partnership Agreement.

5. The undersigned represents and warrants to the Partnership and to the General Partner that:

(i)   The undersigned has carefully reviewed and understands the risks of, and other considerations relating to, a purchase of Units, including the risks set forth under "Risk Factors" and "Tax Risks" in the Memorandum and the considerations described under "Federal Income Tax Consequences" in the Memorandum;

(ii)   The undersigned has been furnished with all materials relating to the Partnership and its proposed activities, the offering of Units, or anything set forth in the Memorandum which he has requested, and has been afforded the opportunity to obtain any additional information necessary to verify the accuracy of any representations or information set forth in the Memorandum;

(iii)   The General Partner has answered all inquiries of the undersigned concerning the Partnership and its proposed activities, the offering of Units, or any other matter relating to the business of the Partnership as set forth in the Memorandum;

(iv)   The undersigned has not been furnished any offering literature other than the Memorandum and the documents attached as Exhibits thereto, and the undersigned has relied only on the information contained in the Memorandum and such Exhibits and the information furnished or made available by the Partnership or the General Partner, as described in subparagraphs (ii) and (iii) above;

(v)   The undersigned is acquiring the Units for which he hereby subscribes for his own account, as principal, for investment and not with a view to the resale or distribution of all or any part of such Units;

(vi)   The undersigned, if a corporation, partnership, trust, or other form of business entity, is authorized and otherwise duly qualified to purchase and hold Units in the Partnership, such entity has its principal place of business as set forth on the signature page hereof and such entity has not been formed for the specific purchase of acquiring Units in the Partnership;

(vii)   The undersigned has adequate means of providing for his current needs and personal contingencies and has no need for liquidity in this investment;

(viii)   All the information which the undersigned has heretofore furnished the General Partner, or which is set forth in his Purchase Questionnaire and elsewhere with respect to his financial position and business experience, is correct and complete as of the date of this Agreement and, if there should be any material change in such information prior to the completion of the Offering, the undersigned will immediately furnish such revised or corrected information to the General Partner;

(ix)   The undersigned further agrees to be bound by all of the terms and conditions of the Offering made by the Memorandum and Exhibits thereto, and by all of the terms and conditions of the Partnership Agreement and to perform any obligations therein imposed upon a Limited Partner thereof.

6. In order to facilitate the admission of the undersigned and other subscribers into the Partnership, the undersigned hereby irrevocably constitutes and appoints the General Partner, or any one of them if more than one, as his agent and attorney-in-fact, in his name, place and stead, to make, execute, acknowledge, swear to, file, record, and deliver the Amended Certificate of Limited Partnership of the Partnership to admit the undersigned into the Partnership, and any and all other instruments which may be required to effect the admission of the undersigned into the Partnership as a Limited Partner thereof or otherwise comply with applicable law. It is expressly understood and intended by the undersigned that the grant of the foregoing power of attorney is coupled with an interest, and such grant shall be irrevocable. Said power of attorney shall survive the death, bankruptcy, or mental incapacitation of the undersigned, to the extent he may legally contract for such survival, or the assignment or transfer of all or any part of the undersigned's interest in the Partnership. Any person dealing with the Partnership may conclusively presume and rely upon the fact that any instrument referred to above, executed by such agents and attorneys-in-fact, is authorized, regular, and binding without further inquiry. If required, the undersigned shall execute and deliver to the General Partner, within five (5) days after the receipt of a request therefor, such further designations, powers of attorney, or other instruments as the General Partner shall reasonably deem necessary for the purpose of this provision.

7. This subscription is not transferable or assignable by the undersigned.

8. If the undersigned is more than one person, the obligations of the undersigned shall be joint and several and the representations and warranties herein contained shall be deemed to be made by and be binding upon each such person and his heirs, executors, administrators, successors, and assigns.

9. This subscription, upon acceptance by the Partnership, shall be binding upon the heirs, executors, administrators, successors, and assigns of the undersigned.

10. This Subscription Agreement shall be construed in accordance with and governed in all respects by the laws of the State of _____.

11. Any masculine personal pronoun as set forth in this Subscription Agreement shall be considered to mean the corresponding feminine or neuter personal pronoun, as the context requires.

12. The undersigned represents that the information furnished in the Purchaser Questionnaire is true and complete as of the date hereof, and the undersigned agrees to notify the Partnership of any changes in the information prior to completion of the Offering.

13. The undersigned is subscribing for the following number of Units:

Number of Units subscribed for: _____
Amount of check enclosed: $ _____

Dated: _____

/s/ _____

_____
Printed Name:

Address: _____

_____

APPENDIX B
Supplemental Cases

The following cases are presented to highlight certain material discussed in the text:

1. *K.D. v. Educational Testing Service:* discusses the contract that may exist between an applicant and the testing service that administers the law school admissions test (Chapter 1)
2. *Fiege v. Boehm:* discusses whether forebearing to sue in a bastardy proceeding may constitute the consideration for a contract (Chapter 4)
3. *Bartus v. Riccardi:* highlights the fact that the UCC merely codified the common law (Chapter 7)
4. *Schwinghammer v. Alexander:* interprets the concept of an incidental beneficiary in a contract to construct a home (Chapter 9)

1. K.D. v. Educational Testing Service
87 Misc. 2d 657, 386 N.Y.S.2d 747 (1976)

Opinion

This is a motion to dismiss the complaint, pursuant to CPLR 3211 (subd [a], pars 1, 7; subd [c]) on the grounds that there is a defense founded upon documentary evidence and that the complaint fails to state a cause of action.

Plaintiff is a 37-year-old college graduate, having entered college at the age of 32. Seeking to attend law school, he took the Law School Admission Test (LSAT) twice within a four-month period in 1973–1974. Defendant is a nonprofit corporation engaged in the business of preparing and administering various well-known educational tests, including the LSAT, for use by colleges and graduate schools throughout the nation. It has administered the LSAT since 1954. The LSAT is an objective test designed to measure general aptitude for the study of law of candidates seeking admission to law school. It consists of approximately 130 so-called multiple choice questions and it also has a section of about 70 questions of a similar nature designed to test writing ability. Defendant administers the LSAT for the Law School Admissions Council (LSAC), a nonprofit membership association of graduate schools of law. The LSAC sets policy for administration of the examinations and the reporting of scores.

Test scores play an important role in determining whether a candidate will be admitted to law school. To insure that they accurately reflect the candidate's own effort, the administration of the tests is carefully monitored, and after they are scored, individual scores are checked by computer against any previous scores by the same candidate. Where an increase of more than 150 points (out of a total of 800) is found, defendant conducts an investigation before the candidate's score is reported to the law schools.

Each candidate who applies to take the LSAT is sent a booklet entitled "Law School Admissions Bulletin" and a registration form. Upon receipt of the completed form, defendant sends the candidate an admission card to take the examination on a specified date at a designated testing center. The registration form requires the applicant to write out in longhand the following statement and to sign it: "I accept the conditions set forth in the Bulletin concerning the administration of the test and the reporting of information to law schools." Plaintiff took the examination in December, 1973 and again in April, 1974. Before each examination, he was sent a copy of the bulletin and completed in his own handwriting the statement above on his registration forms. The bulletins received by plaintiff each contained the following language under the heading "Scores Cancelled by ETS":

> We are concerned with reporting only valid scores. On rare occasions, misconduct or circumstances beyond the candidate's control may render scores invalid. If doubts are raised about your score because of these or other circumstances, we will expect you to cooperate in our investigation. We reserve the right to cancel any test score if, in our sole opinion, there is adequate reason to question its validity. Before exercising this right, we will offer you an opportunity to take the test again at no additional fee.
>
> If we cancel a score, we will notify the law schools that received, or were to receive, the scores as well as the schools receiving subsequent reports.

On his December, 1973 examination plaintiff received a score of 399 on the LSAT portion and 26 on the writing ability portion. His April, 1974 LSAT score was 637, or 238 points higher, and his writing ability score was 62. The 238-point discrepancy between the two LSAT scores prompted an investigation by defendant which disclosed striking similarities between plaintiff's answers and the answers of one "KL," the candidate seated adjacent to plaintiff. Plaintiff answered 39 of the 130 multiple choice questions on the LSAT portion of the test incorrectly. Of these, 27 were the same incorrect answers as those selected by KL. The significance of this correlation is made evident from an analysis by defendant of the answer sheets of 10 other candidates taking the same LSAT who obtained scores in the same range as plaintiff and KL. Comparing their incorrect answers with plaintiff's, discloses that, on average, there were only seven incorrect responses identical to plaintiff's. Of the 10 other answer sheets analyzed, the most incorrect responses on any one answer sheet which were identical to those of plaintiff was 11. A comparison and analysis of plaintiff's writing ability answer sheet with KL's and the 10 other candidates disclosed a similar result.

On the basis of the foregoing, defendant wrote to plaintiff requesting that he furnish any information which he believed was relevant to his questioned scores. In addition, he was offered an opportunity to take the examination again at a regularly scheduled time at no cost. If he elected to do so, and his retest score came within 50 points of the questioned score, defendant stated that the questioned score would be forwarded to the law schools. On the other hand, if the retest score failed to confirm the questioned score, or if plaintiff refused to take the retest, defendant indicated that it would cancel the questioned score and notify the law schools that plaintiff's score was canceled "due to serious doubt as to [its] authenticity."

In response to this letter, plaintiff submitted a sworn statement that he did not cheat on the examination. However, he refused to take a retest. He then commenced the instant action for a declaratory judgment and an injunction restraining defendant from canceling his April, 1974 test score; from notifying the law schools that this action was taken because of the score's doubtful authenticity; and compelling defendant to report the April, 1974 score to the law schools as a valid score.

In support of its motion to dismiss the complaint, defendant alleges that plaintiff is barred by the contract he entered into when he agreed on his registration forms to accept the conditions set forth in the bulletin concerning the administration of the test and the reporting of results to the law schools. Defendant contends that its actions are in full accord with the following provisions in the bulletin: "We reserve the right to cancel any test score if, in our sole opinion, there is adequate reason to question its validity. If we cancel a score, we will notify the law schools that were to receive the score."

As a further argument in support of its motion, defendant claims that so much of the injunctive relief sought by plaintiff as would restrain defendant from notifying the law schools that it was canceling plaintiff's test score because of its doubtful authenticity constitutes a prior restraint against publication of information, and would therefore be violative of the First Amendment to the United States Constitution.

Plaintiff, in opposition to the motion, contends that the agreement relied upon by defendant is void as a contract of adhesion. Further, he argues that defendant's actions are in violation of the due process clause of the Fourteenth Amendment.

With respect to that portion of the injunctive relief seeking to restrain defendant from notifying the schools of the reason it was canceling plaintiff's scores, the court is satisfied that the granting of such relief would not constitute a prior restraint in violation of the First Amendment. The guarantees of free speech and a free press provided for in the Constitution would in no way be impinged upon by an order of this court prohibiting defendant from sending such a notice, which would seriously reflect upon plaintiff's honesty and integrity and could conceivably affect his future livelihood. No useful purpose would be served by it. The failure of defendant to forward plaintiff's scores to the law schools with no further action on its part, or a simple notice to the schools that plaintiff had elected not to have his scores forwarded would have exactly the same result; the schools would deny plaintiff admission. Thus the possible harm to plaintiff from sending out of the notice contemplated by defendant far exceeds the possible useful purposes which would be served thereby, which so far as the court can determine are nil, either to society as a whole or to the law schools. In such context, the First Amendment has no relevancy. It "was fashioned to assure unfettered interchange of ideas for bringing about of political and social changes desired by the people." (Roth v. United States, 354 U.S. 476, 484.) It was not adopted to permit the commercial publication of a possibly libelous statement which might have serious consequences upon the future livelihood of the subject, where absolutely no useful social purpose is served thereby. Under such circumstances, it has been held that the First Amendment does not protect commercial speech. (Pittsburgh Press Co. v. Human Rel. Comm., 413 U.S. 376; Valentine v. Chrestensen, 316 U.S. 52; Grove v. Dun & Bradstreet, 438 F2d 433, 437.)

New York Times v. Sullivan (376 U.S. 254, 266), which held that the commercial publication there involved was protected by the First Amendment, is clearly distinguishable. The court so held because the communication in question, although commercial, "communicated information, expressed opinions, recited grievances, protested claimed abuses and sought financial support on behalf of a movement whose existence and objections are matters of the highest public interest and concern." The same cannot be said for the proposed publication here. In fact, none of the cases relied upon by defendant involved the prior restraint of a commercial publication such as that before the court in the instant case.

Nor did plaintiff ever agree that a notice in the form contemplated could be sent to the law schools in the event defendant canceled his scores. The bulletin provided merely that in such event, defendant would notify the law schools that were to receive the scores. Nothing was said about advising them of the reasons for the cancellation. Accordingly, defendant's motion to dismiss that part of plaintiff's complaint seeking to enjoin defendant from notifying the law schools that it has canceled plaintiff's test scores because of serious doubts as to their authenticity, is denied.

We turn now to a consideration of that portion of the injunctive relief sought by plaintiff wherein he seeks to restrain defendant from canceling his April, 1974 test scores and to compel it to forward the scores to the law schools. As noted above, the right to cancel any test score if in its opinion there was adequate reason to question its validity was expressly reserved to itself by defendant in the bulletin, and plaintiff accepted that as well as all other conditions set forth in the bulletin when he completed his registration form. Nevertheless, plaintiff contends that he is not bound by his agreement, because, he argues, his contract with defendant is a contract of adhesion, and therefore void. A contract of adhesion is one entered into between parties with unequal bargaining power. They are typically standard contracts which are offered by the party with strong bargaining power to the weaker party on a take it or leave it basis. The instant agreement would appear to fit this description. Almost every accredited law school in the United States requires a candidate for admission to take the LSAT. Thus, when plaintiff decided to attend law school he had no alternative but to accept the standard conditions fixed by defendant for all test takers. Plaintiff could neither contract with a party other than defendant to take a law school aptitude test, since no such entity exists, nor indicate to defendant that the terms contained in the bulletin were not acceptable to him. In the latter case it is clear that if he had done so he would not have been permitted to take the examination.

However, while plaintiff's description of the agreement herein as a contract of adhesion may be justified, his conclusion that it is therefore void, is not. Where the court finds that an agreement is a contract of adhesion, effort will frequently be made to protect the weaker party from the agreement's harsher terms by a variety of pretexts, while still keeping the elementary rules of the law of contracts intact. (Kessler, Contracts of Adhesion—Some Thoughts about Freedom of Contract, 43 Col. L. Rev. 629, 633.) The court may, for example, find the obnoxious clause "ambiguous," even where no ambiguity exists, and then construe it against its author; or it may find the clause to be against public policy and declare it unenforceable; or finally, the court may hold that although the offending clause prohibits a recovery by plaintiff ex contractu, it does not prohibit a recovery in tort.

Thus, the issue in the instant case is whether the clause reserving to defendant itself the right to cancel plaintiff's test score if there is a question about its validity, and requiring him to take a retest in such event, is so unfair and unreasonable that the court, having found it a part of a contract of adhesion, will disregard it by means of one or more of the pretexts above. The issue as thus stated must be answered in the negative. To the extent that defendant can accurately predict the aptitude of a candidate for law school by means of its test results, it performs a highly valuable service not only to the law schools but to the public as well. Moreover, the accuracy of its predictions is defendant's sole stock in trade. The less accurate as a forecaster its tests are, the less value they have to the law schools. Thus, if defendant reasonably believed that the test scores of plaintiff as scored on the April, 1974 test, did not accurately reflect his aptitude for law school, it acted within its right to protect its own image as well as its obligation to the schools who are its clients in canceling plaintiff's scores and requiring him to take a retest. Almost the identical issue was before the court in De Pina v. Educational Testing Serv. (31 A.D.2d 744). There the examination involved was the College Entrance Examination Board Test, also administered by this same defendant, to students seeking admission to college. In that case, after plaintiff's scores were forwarded to the school of his choice, and he was accepted for admission, a letter from plaintiff's high school guidance counsellor caused defendant to investigate plaintiff's mathematics score. The investigation disclosed circumstances indicating that plaintiff had achieved his math score by cheating. Accordingly, on the basis of a clause in its agreement with plaintiff similar to the one in the instant case, defendant requested that plaintiff take a retest, and indicated that if he refused to do so, it would notify the college to which he had been admitted that it was rescinding plaintiff's mathematics score because of doubts about its validity. Plaintiff sought to enjoin defendant from taking such action, and the Supreme Court granted his motion for a preliminary injunction. On appeal, the Appellate Division reversed the lower court's order and held that "defendant acted within its rights and indeed within its obligations and duties to the (college) and to the public in requesting the plaintiff take a re-examination." (At p. 745.)

In the instant case, the evidence that plaintiff did not achieve his scores on the April, 1974 LSAT unaided was sufficient to justify the action contemplated by defendant. Moreover, its offer of a free retest under normal testing conditions with the understanding that it would forward plaintiff's April, 1974 scores if the retest score came within 50 points of the earlier scores was eminently fair and reasonable under the circumstances. Finally, with respect to plaintiff's claim that defendant's actions violated the due process clause of the Constitution, it is sufficient to note that the Fourteenth Amendment is applicable only to State action and not private action and hence is not relevant here. Even if it were, the court finds no basis to conclude that plaintiff was not afforded due process.

For all the foregoing reasons, the motion to dismiss so much of the complaint as seeks to enjoin defendant from canceling plaintiff's April, 1974 test scores, and to compel it to forward those scores to the law schools is granted.

2.   Fiege v. Boehm
210 Md. 352, 123 A.2d 316 (1955)

Opinion

This suit was brought in the Superior Court of Baltimore City by Hilda Louise Boehm against Louis Gail Fiege to recover for breach of a contract to pay the expenses incident to the birth of his bastard child and to provide for its support upon condition that she would refrain from prosecuting him for bastardy.

Plaintiff alleged in her declaration substantially as follows: (1) that early in 1951 defendant had sexual intercourse with her although she was unmarried, and as a result thereof she became pregnant, and defendant acknowledged that he was responsible for her pregnancy; (2) that on September 29, 1951, she gave birth to a female child; that defendant is the father of the child; and that he acknowledged on many occasions that he is its father; (3) that before the child was born, defendant agreed to pay all her medical and miscellaneous expenses and to compensate her for the loss of her salary caused by the child's birth, and also to pay her ten dollars per week for its support until it reached the age of 21, upon condition that she would not institute bastardy proceedings against him as long as he made the payments in accordance with the agreement; (4) that she placed the child for adoption on July 13, 1954, and she claimed the following sums: Union Memorial Hospital, $110; Florence Crittenton Home, $100; Dr. George Merrill, her physician, $50; medicines, $70.35; miscellaneous expenses, $20.45; loss of earnings for 26 weeks, $1,105; support of the child, $1,440; total, $2,895.80; and (5) that defendant paid her only $480, and she demanded that he pay her the further sum of $2,415.80, the balance due under the agreement, but he failed and refused to pay the same.

Defendant demurred to the declaration on the ground that it failed to allege that in September, 1953, plaintiff instituted bastardy proceedings against him in the Criminal Court of Baltimore, but since it had been found from blood tests that he could not have been the father of the child, he was acquitted of bastardy. The Court sustained the demurrer with leave to amend.

Plaintiff then filed an amended declaration, which contained the additional allegation that, after the breach of the agreement by defendant, she filed a charge with the State's Attorney that defendant was the father of her bastard child; and that on October 8, 1953, the Criminal Court found defendant not guilty solely on a physician's testimony that "on the basis of certain blood tests made, the defendant can be excluded as the father of the said child, which testimony is not conclusive upon a jury in a trial court."

Defendant also demurred to the amended declaration, but the Court overruled that demurrer.

Plaintiff, a typist, now over 35 years old, who has been employed by the Government in Washington and Baltimore for over thirteen years, testified in the Court below that she had never been married, but that at about midnight on January 21, 1951, defendant, after taking her to a moving picture theater on York Road and then to a restaurant, had sexual intercourse with her in his automobile. She further testified that he agreed to pay all her medical and hospital expenses, to compensate her for loss of salary caused by the pregnancy and birth, and to pay her ten dollars per week for the support of the child upon condition that she would refrain from instituting bastardy proceedings against him. She further testified that between September 17, 1951, and May, 1953, defendant paid her a total of $480.

Defendant admitted that he had taken plaintiff to restaurants, had danced with her several times, had taken her to Washington, and had brought her home in the country; but he asserted that he had never had sexual intercourse with her. He also claimed that he did not enter into any agreement with her. He admitted, however, that he had paid her a total of $480. His father also testified that he stated "that he did not want his mother to know, and if it were just kept quiet, kept principally away from his mother and the public and the courts, that he would take care of it."

Defendant further testified that in May, 1953, he went to see plaintiff's physician to make inquiry about blood tests to show the paternity of the child; and that those tests were made and they indicated that it was not possible that he could have been the child's father. He then stopped making payments. Plaintiff thereupon filed a charge of bastardy with the State's Attorney.

The testimony which was given in the Criminal Court by Dr. Milton Sachs, hematologist at the University Hospital, was read to the jury in the Superior Court. In recent years the blood-grouping test has been employed in criminology, in the selection of donors for blood transfusions, and as evidence in paternity cases. The Landsteiner blood-grouping test is based on the medical theory that the red corpuscles in human blood contain two affirmative agglutinating substances, and that every individual's blood falls into one of the four classes and remains the same throughout life. According to Mendel's law of inheritance, this blood individuality is an hereditary characteristic which passes from parent to child, and no agglutinating substance can appear in the blood of a child which is not present in the blood of one of its parents. The four Landsteiner blood groups, designated as AB, A, B, and O, into which human blood is divided on the basis of the compatibility of the corpuscles and serum with the corpuscles and serum of other persons, are characterized by different combinations of two agglutinogens in the red blood cells and two agglutinins in the serum. Dr. Sachs reported that Fiege's blood group was Type O, Miss Boehm's was Type B, and the infant's was Type A. He further testified that on the basis of these tests, Fiege could not have been the father of the child, as it is impossible for a mating of Type O and Type B to result in a child of Type A.

Although defendant was acquitted by the Criminal Court, the Superior Court overruled his motion for a directed verdict. In the charge to the jury the Court instructed them that defendant's acquittal in the Criminal Court was not binding upon them. The jury found a verdict in favor of plaintiff for $2,415.80, the full amount of her claim.

Defendant filed a motion for judgment n.o.v. or a new trial. The Court overruled that motion also, and entered judgment on the verdict of the jury. Defendant appealed from that judgment.

Defendant contends that, even if he did enter into the contract as alleged, it was not enforceable, because plaintiff's forbearance to prosecute was not based on a valid claim, and hence the contract was without consideration. He, therefore, asserts that the Court erred in overruling (1) his demurrer to the amended declaration, (2) his motion for a directed verdict, and (3) his motion for judgment n.o.v. or a new trial.

It was originally held at common law that a child born out of wedlock is filius nullius, and a putative father is not under any legal liability to contribute to the support of his illegitimate child, and his promise to do so is unenforceable because it is based on purely a moral obligation. Some of the courts in this country have held that, in the absence of any statutory obligation on the father to aid in the support of his bastard child, his promise to the child's mother to pay her for its maintenance, resting solely on his natural affection for it and his moral obligation to provide for it, is a promise which the law cannot enforce because of lack of sufficient consideration. Mercer v. Mercer, 87 Ky. 30, 7 S.W. 401; Wiggins v. Keizer, 6 Ind. 252; Davis v. Herrington, 53 Ark. 5, 13 S.W. 215. On the contrary, a few courts have stated that the natural affection of a father for his child and the moral obligation upon him to support it and to aid the woman he has wronged furnish sufficient consideration for his promise to the mother to pay for the support of the child to make the agreement enforceable at law. Birdsall v. Edgerton, 25 Wend., N.Y., 619; Todd v. Weber, 95 N.Y. 181, 47 Am. Rep. 20; Trayer v. Setzer, 72 Neb. 845, 101 N.W. 989.

However, where statutes are in force to compel the father of a bastard to contribute to its support, the courts have invariably held that a contract by the putative father with the mother of his bastard child to provide for the support of the child upon the agreement of the mother to refrain from invoking the bastardy statute against the father, or to abandon proceedings already commenced, is supported by sufficient consideration. Jangraw v. Perkins, 77 Vt. 375, 60 A. 385; Beach v. Voegtlen, 68 N.J.L. 472, 53 A. 695; Thayer v. Thayer, 189 N.C. 502, 127 S.E. 553, 39 A.L.R. 428.

In Maryland it is now provided by statute that whenever a person is found guilty of bastardy, the court shall issue an order directing such person (1) to pay for the maintenance and support of the child until it reaches the age of eighteen years, such sum as may be agreed upon, if consent proceedings be had, or in the absence of agreement, such sum as the court may fix, with due regard to the circumstances of the accused person; and (2) to give bond to the State of Maryland in such penalty as the court may fix, with good and sufficient securities, conditioned on making the payments required by the court's order, or any amendments thereof. Failure to give such bond shall be punished by commitment to the jail or the House of Correction until bond is given but not exceeding two years. Code Supp. 1955, art. 12, sec. 8.

Prosecutions for bastardy are treated in Maryland as criminal proceedings, but they are actually civil in purpose. Kennard v. State, 177 Md. 549, 10 A.2d 710; Kisner v. State, 209 Md. 524, 122 A.2d 102. While the prime object of the Maryland Bastardy Act is to protect the public from the burden of maintaining illegitimate children, it is so distinctly in the interest of the mother that she becomes the beneficiary of it. Accordingly a contract by the putative father of an illegitimate child to provide for its support upon condition that bastardy proceedings will not be instituted is a compromise of civil injuries resulting from a criminal act, and not a contract to compound a criminal prosecution, and if it is fair and reasonable, it is in accord with the Bastardy Act and the public policy of the State.

Of course, a contract of a putative father to provide for the support of his illegitimate child must be based, like any other contract, upon sufficient consideration. The early English law made no distinction in regard to the sufficiency of a claim which the claimant promised to forbear to prosecute, as the consideration of a promise, other than the broad distinction between good claims and bad claims. No promise to forbear to prosecute an unfounded claim was sufficient consideration. In the early part of the Nineteenth Century, an advance was made from the criterion of the early authorities when it was held that forbearance to prosecute a suit which had already been instituted was sufficient consideration, without inquiring whether the suit would have been successful or not. Longridge v. Dorville, 5 B. & Ald. 117.

In 1867 the Maryland Court of Appeals, in the opinion delivered by Judge Bartol in Hartle v. Stahl, 27 Md. 157, 172, held: (1) that forbearance to assert a claim before institution of suit, if not in fact a legal claim, is not of itself sufficient consideration to support a promise; but (2) that a compromise of a doubtful claim or a relinquishment of a pending suit is good consideration for a promise; and (3) that in order to support a compromise, it is sufficient that the parties entering into it thought at the time that there was a bona fide question between them, although it may eventually be found that there was in fact no such question.

We have thus adopted the rule that the surrender of, or forbearance to assert, an invalid claim by one who has not an honest and reasonable belief in its possible validity is not sufficient consideration for a contract. 1 Restatement, Contracts, sec. 76(b). We combine the subjective requisite that the claim be bona fide with the objective requisite that it must have a reasonable basis of support. Accordingly a promise not to prosecute a claim which is not founded in good faith does not of itself give a right of action on an agreement to pay for refraining from so acting, because a release from mere annoyance and unfounded litigation does not furnish valuable consideration.

Professor Williston was not entirely certain whether the test of reasonableness is based upon the intelligence of the claimant himself, who may be an ignorant person with no knowledge of law and little sense as to facts; but he seemed inclined to favor the view that "the claim forborne must be neither absurd in fact from the standpoint of a reasonable man in the position of the claimant, nor, obviously unfounded in law to one who has an elementary knowledge of legal principles." 1 Williston on Contracts, Rev. Ed., sec. 135. We agree that while stress is placed upon the honesty and good faith of the claimant, forbearance to prosecute a claim is insufficient consideration if the claim forborne is so lacking in foundation as to make its assertion incompatible with honesty and a reasonable degree of intelligence. Thus, if the mother of a bastard knows that there is no foundation, either in law or fact, for a charge against a certain man that he is the father of the child, but that man promises to pay her in order to prevent bastardy proceedings against him, the forbearance to institute proceedings is not sufficient consideration.

On the other hand, forbearance to sue for a lawful claim or demand is sufficient consideration for a promise to pay for the forbearance if the party forbearing had an honest intention to prosecute litigation which is not frivolous, vexatious, or unlawful, and which he believed to be well founded. Snyder v. Cearfoss, 187 Md. 635, 643, 51 A.2d 264; Pullman Co. v. Ray, 201 Md. 268, 94 A.2d 266. Thus the promise of a woman who is expecting an illegitimate child that she will not institute bastardy proceedings against a certain man is sufficient consideration for his promise to pay for the child's support, even though it may not be certain whether the man is the father or whether the prosecution would be successful, if she makes the charge in good faith. The fact that a man accused of bastardy is forced to enter into a contract to pay for the support of his bastard child from fear of exposure and the shame that might be cast upon him as a result, as well as a sense of justice to render some compensation for the injury he inflicted upon the mother, does not lessen the merit of the contract, but greatly increases it. Hook v. Pratt, 78 N.Y. 371, 34 Am. Rep. 539; Hays v. McFarlan, 32 Ga. 699, 79 Am. Dec. 317.

A case in point is Pflaum v. McClintock, 130 Pa. 369, 18 A. 734. That was an action to collect a judgment bond which the defendant signed when he was in jail to settle a fornication and bastardy case. The defendant claimed that the bond was conditioned on the support of a child expected to be born, but that he was innocent of the charge, and that in fact the obligee had not given birth to any living child, but died without issue before the judgment was entered. The Supreme Court of Pennsylvania decided that the bond was supported by a good consideration.

Another analogous case is Thompson v. Nelson, 28 Ind. 431. There the plaintiff sought to recover back money which he had paid to compromise a prosecution for bastardy. He claimed that the prosecuting witness was not pregnant and therefore the prosecution was fraudulent. It was held by the Supreme Court of Indiana, however, that the settlement of the prosecution was a good consideration for the payment of the money and it could not be recovered back, inasmuch as it appeared from the evidence that the prosecution was instituted in good faith, and at that time there was reason to believe that the prosecuting witness was pregnant, although it was found out afterwards that she was not pregnant.

Likewise, in Heaps v. Dunham, 95 Ill. 583, 590, the Supreme Court of Illinois held that a man charged with bastardy may compromise the claim with the woman who claims to be pregnant, and if the man, after being arrested, enters into a settlement not induced by fraud or oppression and gives his promissory note for the benefit of the woman and child, such a contract is supported by a good consideration. In explanation of its ruling, the Court said:

But while there is great doubt from the evidence whether Lavina Snell was pregnant, yet so far as the charge of bastardy is concerned, as complainant voluntarily settled and gave his notes in settlement of the prosecution which had been commenced against him, he must be concluded by that settlement. When arrested on the charge he had the right to contest the case and require strict proof to sustain the charge, but under our statute a charge of this character may be settled between the prosecuting witness and defendant, and when a settlement has been made without fraud or oppression, we think it should be conclusive and binding between the parties.

In the case at bar there was no proof of fraud or unfairness. Assuming that the hematologists were accurate in their laboratory tests and findings, nevertheless plaintiff gave testimony which indicated that she made the charge of bastardy against defendant in good faith. For these reasons the Court acted properly in overruling the demurrer to the amended declaration and the motion for a directed verdict.

Finally, in attacking the action of the Court in overruling the motion for judgment n.o.v. or a new trial, defendant made the additional complaint that there was error in the charge to the jury. As we have said, the Court instructed the jury that defendant's acquittal in the Criminal Court was not binding upon the jury in the case before them. Defendant urged strongly that he had been acquitted by the Criminal Court in consequence of scientific findings from blood tests.

It is immaterial whether defendant was the father of the child or not. In the light of what we have said, we need not make any specific determination on this subject, as defendant took only one exception to the Court's charge, and his only objection was the general one that the charge did not refer to "a valid binding agreement in law."

The Court then gave the jury the following additional instruction:

Members of the Jury: Counsel for the defendant has asked me to add one point to the charge that I have just given you. He has asked me to instruct you that there must be a valid binding agreement.

There has been some testimony from the defendant that he was forced to make an agreement. In fact, I think in fairness to the defendant I should say that he definitely denies having made that agreement.

Now, there is a defense in the law of contracts called duress. If you enter into a contract as a result of coercion, or force or threats it might be an invalid agreement.

So that, in fairness to both sides, I add to my instruction that even if the defendant has admitted making an agreement—and I leave that to your recollection of the facts—if you feel that the agreement was invalid by reason of his having been forced to it, then there should not be such an agreement that he should be force[d] to adhere to it.

The Court then asked the attorneys if they were ready for argument. There was no further exception to the charge. Counsel on both sides informed the Court that they were ready to argue the case to the jury. Before the jury retires to consider its verdict, a party may object to any portion of any instruction given, or to any omission therefrom, or to the failure to give any instruction, stating distinctly the portion, or omission, or failure to instruct, to which he objects and the specific grounds of his objection. On appeal a party, in assigning error in the instructions, is restricted to (1) the particular portion of the instructions given, or the particular omission therefrom, or the particular failure to instruct, distinctly objected to before the jury retired, and (2) the specific grounds of objection distinctly stated at that time. Under our rules, no other errors or assignments of error in the instructions are considered by the Court of Appeals. General Rules of Practice and Procedure, part 3, subd. 3, rule 6; State Roads Commission of Maryland v. Berry, 208 Md. 461, 469, 118 A.2d 649, 653.

As we have found no reversible error in the rulings and instructions of the trial Court, we will affirm the judgment entered on the verdict of the jury.

Judgment affirmed, with costs.

3. Bartus v. Riccardi
55 Misc. 2d 3, 284 N.Y.S.2d 222 (1967)

Opinion

The plaintiff is a franchised representative of Acousticon, a manufacturer of hearing aids. On January 15, 1966, the defendant signed a contract to purchase a Model A-660 Acousticon hearing aid from the plaintiff. The defendant specified Model A-660 because he had been tested at a hearing aid clinic and had been informed that the best hearing aid for his condition was this Acousticon model. An ear mold was fitted to the defendant and the plaintiff ordered Model A-660 from Acousticon.

On February 2, 1966, in response to a call from the plaintiff the defendant went to the plaintiff's office for his hearing aid. At that time he was informed that Model A-660 had been modified and improved, and that it was now called Model A-665. This newer model had been delivered by Acousticon for the defendant's use. The defendant denies that he understood this was a different model number. The hearing aid was fitted to the defendant. The defendant complained about the noise, but was assured by the plaintiff that he would get used to it.

The defendant tried out the new hearing aid for the next few days for a total use of 15 hours. He went back to the hearing clinic, where he was informed that the hearing aid was not the model that he had been advised to buy. On February 8, 1966, he returned to the plaintiff's office complaining that the hearing aid gave him a headache, and that it was not the model he had ordered. He returned the hearing aid to the plaintiff, for which he received a receipt. At that time the plaintiff offered to get Model A-660 for the defendant. The defendant neither consented to nor refused the offer. No mention was made by either party about canceling the contract, and the receipt given by the plaintiff contained no notation or indication that the plaintiff considered the contract cancelled or rescinded.

The plaintiff immediately informed Acousticon of the defendant's complaint. By letter dated February 14, 1966, Acousticon, writing directly to the defendant, informed him that Model A-665 was an improved version of Model A-660, and that they would either replace the model that had been delivered to him or would obtain Model A-660 for him. He was asked to advise the plaintiff immediately of his decision so that they could effect a prompt exchange. After receiving this letter the defendant decided that he did not want any hearing aid from the plaintiff, and he refused to accept the tender of a replacement, whether it be Model A-665 or A-660.

The plaintiff is suing for the balance due on the contract. Although he had made a down payment of $80, the defendant made no claim for repayment of his down payment until the case was ready to go to trial. The plaintiff objected to the counterclaim as being untimely. There is nothing in the pleadings to show that such a claim had been previously made by the defendant and, therefore, the court will not consider any counterclaim in this matter.

The question before the court is whether or not the plaintiff, having delivered a model which admittedly is not in exact conformity with the contract, can nevertheless recover in view of his subsequent tender of the model that did meet the terms of the contract.

The defendant contends that since there was an improper delivery of goods, the buyer has the right to reject the same under sections 2-601 and 2-602 (subd. [2], par. [c]) of the Uniform Commercial Code. He further contends that, even if the defendant had accepted delivery, he may, under section 2-608 (subd. [1], par. [b]) of the Uniform Commercial Code, revoke his acceptance of the goods because "his acceptance was reasonably induced . . . by the seller's assurances." He also relies on section 2-711, claiming that he may recover not only the down payment but also consequential damages.

The defendant, however, has neglected to take into account section 2-508 of the Uniform Commercial Code which has added a new dimension to the concept of strict performance. This section permits a seller to cure a nonconforming delivery under certain circumstances. Subdivision (1) of this section enacts into statutory law what had been New York case law. This permits a seller to cure a nonconforming delivery before the expiration of the contract time by notifying the buyer of his intention to so cure and by making a delivery within the contract period. This has long been the accepted rule in New York. (Lowinson v. Newman, 201 App. Div. 266; Portfolio v. Rubin, 196 App. Div. 316.)

However, subdivision (2) of section 2-508 of the Uniform Commercial Code goes further and extends beyond the contract time the right of the seller to cure a defective performance. Under this provision, even where the contract period has expired and the buyer has rejected a nonconforming tender or has revoked an acceptance, the seller may "substitute a conforming tender" if he had "reasonable grounds to believe" that

the nonconforming tender would be accepted and "if he seasonably notifies the buyer" of his intention "to substitute a conforming tender." (51
N.Y. Jur., Sales, p. 41.)

This in effect extends the contract period beyond the date set forth
in the contract itself unless the buyer requires strict performance by including such a clause in the contract.

> The section [§2-508, subd. (2)] rejects the time-honored, and perhaps
> time-worn notion, that the proper way to assure effective results in com-
> mercial transactions is to require strict performance. Under the Code a
> buyer who insists upon such strict performance must rely on a special term
> in his agreement or the fact that the seller knows as a commercial matter
> that strict performance is required. (48 Cornell L.Q. 13; 29 Albany L. Rev.
> 260.)

This section seeks to avoid injustice to the seller by reason of a surprise rejection by the buyer. (Official Comment, McKinney's Cons. Laws
of N.Y., Book 62 1/2, Uniform Commercial Code, §2-508.)

An additional burden, therefore, is placed upon the buyer by this
section. "As a result a buyer may learn that even though he rejected or
revoked his acceptance within the terms of Sections 2-601 and 2-711, he
still may have to allow the seller additional time to meet the terms of the
contract by substituting delivery of conforming goods." (3 Bender's Uniform Commercial Code Serv., Sales and Bulk Transfers, §14-02[1][a][ii].)

Has the plaintiff in this case complied with the conditions of section
2-508?

The model delivered to the defendant was a newer and improved
version of the model that was actually ordered. Of course, the defendant
is entitled to receive the model that he ordered even though it may be
an older type. But, under the circumstances, the plaintiff had reasonable
grounds to believe that the newer model would be accepted by the defendant.

The plaintiff acted within a reasonable time to notify the defendant
of his tender of a conforming model. (Uniform Commercial Code, §1-
204.) The defendant had not purchased another hearing aid elsewhere.
His position had not been altered by reason of the original nonconforming tender.

The plaintiff made a proper subsequent conforming tender pursuant
to subdivision (2) of section 2-508 of the Uniform Commercial Code.

Judgment is granted to plaintiff.

4.   Schwinghammer v. Alexander
21 Utah 418, 446 P.2d 414 (1968)

Opinion

Plaintiffs commenced this action for damages for defective and incomplete construction of their home against the contractor-seller, Alex-

ander, and the mortgagee, Prudential. The trial court determined in the second cause of action that plaintiffs were third-party beneficiaries of an escrow agreement between Prudential and Alexander and awarded judgment to the plaintiffs. Prudential appeals.

In January 1965 plaintiffs executed an earnest money agreement with Alexander to purchase a home. Alexander agreed to complete the home including the unfinished basement area, which entailed the additional construction of a family room, two bedrooms and a bath.

Plaintiffs made an application to Prudential for a loan to finance their purchase. Prudential directed that an appraisal be made of the home as if the work were completed. The appraiser recommended the loan be approved upon the condition that $1900 be withheld to assure completion of the basement and installation of a garbage disposal in the kitchen sink. On March 3, 1965, the loan was closed, and plaintiffs authorized the payment of the proceeds to Alexander. However, Prudential, independently of plaintiffs' authorization to pay the funds and without their knowledge, insisted that an escrow agreement be executed, whereby Alexander deposited with Prudential $1900, with release thereof contingent upon the aforementioned items being satisfactorily completed. Completion was to be determined by inspection. Subsequently, and unknown to plaintiffs, Prudential made an inspection and found the basement completed and the disposal installed and released the funds to Alexander.

The trial court found that the escrow agreement was made for the express purpose of benefiting the plaintiffs, and the protection of Prudential's security was only incidental. The trial court determined that it was the intention of the parties to include the basement stairs with the work to be completed under the terms of the escrow agreement, although the stairs had been installed with covering prior to plaintiffs' and Alexander's execution of the earnest money agreement. By reason of the variation in the risers of the stairs, the trial court concluded that the stairs were incomplete and awarded plaintiffs, as third-party beneficiaries of the escrow agreement, judgment of $521 against Prudential.

On appeal, Prudential contends that the plaintiffs were, at most, incidental beneficiaries of the escrow agreement between Alexander and Prudential.

An incidental beneficiary acquires by virtue of the promise no right against the promisor or the promisee.

A third party who is not a promisee and who gave no consideration has an enforceable right by reason of a contract made by two others (1) if he is a creditor of the promisee or of some other person and the contract calls for a performance by the promisor in satisfaction of the obligation; or (2) if the promised performance will be of pecuniary benefit to him and the contract is so expressed as to give the promisor reason to know that such benefit is contemplated by the promisee as one of the motivating causes of his making the contract. A third party may be included within both of these provisions at once, but need not be. One who is included within neither of them has no right, even though performance will incidentally benefit him.

The term "incidental beneficiary" has been frequently used to denote a person who will be benefited by the performance of a contract in which he is not a promisee, but whose relation to the contracting parties is such that the courts will not recognize any legal right in him.

As the law has been developed in the decisions up to date, it is possible to say that the only third parties who have legal rights are the donees and the creditors of the promisee. If in buying the promise the promisee expresses an intent that some third party shall receive either the security of the executory promise or the benefit of performance as a gift, that party is a donee of either the contract right or of the promised performance or both. If, on the other hand, the promisee's expressed intent is that some third party shall receive the performance in satisfaction and discharge of some actual or supposed duty or liability of the promisee, the third party is a creditor beneficiary. All others who may in some way be benefited by performance have no rights and are called incidental beneficiaries. Incidental beneficiaries are all those who are not donees or creditors of the promisee.

Corbin illustrates an "incidental beneficiary" in Section 779D, pp. 43–46, in the following language:

> Where A owes money to a creditor C, or to several creditors, and B promises A to supply him with money necessary to pay such debts, no creditor can maintain suit against B on this promise. The same is true in any case where A is under a contractual duty to C the performance of which requires labor or materials, and B promises A to supply him such labor or material; C has no action against B on this promise. In such cases the performance promised by B does not itself discharge A's duty to C or in any other way affect the legal relations of C. It may, indeed, tend towards C's getting what A owes him, since it supplies A with the money or material that will enable A to perform, but such a result requires the intervening voluntary action of A. B's performance may take place in full without C's ever getting any performance by A or receiving any benefit whatever. In such cases, therefore, C is called an "incidental" beneficiary and is held to have no right.

In the instant action, are the plaintiffs donee or creditor beneficiaries? The promisor, Prudential, promised to pay a sum of money to Alexander, the promisee, upon his completion of the basement of the home and the installation of the disposal. Independently thereof, Alexander had an obligation to the plaintiffs to complete the home in accordance with the earnest money agreement. In the escrow agreement, Prudential did not promise to fulfill this obligation Alexander owed to plaintiffs. Furthermore, Prudential's payment of a sum of money in no way discharged Alexander's obligation to plaintiffs nor did it in any other way affect the legal relations between them; therefore, plaintiffs were not creditor beneficiaries. Nor is there anything to indicate that Alexander, in buying the promise of Prudential to pay a sum of money, expressed an intention that plaintiffs were to receive the benefit of Prudential's performance as a gift, thus disqualifying plaintiffs as donee-beneficiaries. We are compelled to conclude that plaintiffs were incidental beneficiaries under the escrow agreement, and the trial court erred in awarding them judgment against appellant, Prudential.

This case is reversed and remanded, with costs to appellant.

GLOSSARY

Acceptance: manifestation of assent in the manner requested or authorized by the offeror.

Accord and satisfaction: a special agreement in which the parties to a disputed contract agree to new terms in exchange for forbearing to sue under the original contract.

Antenuptial agreement: contract entered into prior to marriage determining the parties' rights on dissolution of the marriage; must be in writing to be enforceable.

Anticipatory breach: positive, unconditional, and unequivocal words that a party intends to breach his contractual obligations.

Arbitration: nonjudicial method of resolving legal disputes.

Assignee: transferee of contractual rights.

Assignment: transference of contractual rights by the promisee to a third party.

Assignor: transferor of a contractual right.

Attachment: the time a security interest becomes an inchoate right under Article IX of the UCC.

Auction with reserve: parties have the right to revoke any time before gavel comes down.

Auction without reserve: property owner relinquishes the right to revoke.

Battle of the forms: difference in forms used by merchants for sales agreements pursuant to Article II of the UCC.

Bilateral contract: a promise for a promise.

Breach of contract: failure of a promisor to fulfill a contractual obligation.

Caveat emptor: let the buyer beware.

Caveat venditor: let the seller beware.

Charitable subscription: promise to donate to a charity, given the enforceability of a contract under law.

Children of tender years: children between the ages of 7 and 14.

CIF: cost of insurance and freight.

Class: a group of persons identified as a group rather than as named individuals.

COD: cost on delivery, the moment when risk passes to the buyer.

Collateral: property subject of a security agreement under Article IX of the UCC.

Compensatory damages: standard measure of damages; puts the injured party in the same position he would have been in had the contract been fulfilled.

Condition: fact or event, the happening or nonhappening of which creates or extinguishes an absolute duty to perform.

Condition concurrent: promise to perform and performance occur simultaneously.

Condition precedent: fact or event that creates an absolute duty to perform.

Condition subsequent: fact or event that extinguishes as absolute duty to perform.

Conditional promise: a promise dependent on the happening or nonhappening of some event.

Consequential damages: damages above the standard measure due to special losses occasioned by the breach.

Consideration: a benefit conferred or a detriment incurred; a basic requirement of every valid contract.

Consignment contract: agreement whereby risk of loss to the subject goods remains with the seller until the buyer resells the goods.

Constructive condition: an implied-in-fact condition.

Contract: a legally enforceable agreement between two or more parties in which each agrees to give and receive something of legal value.

Contract of adhesion: a contract entered into where one party has an unfair bargaining advantage; voidable.

Contractual capacity: the legal ability to enter into a contractual relationship.

Contractual intent: the purposefulness of forming a contractual relationship.

Co-signer: person who agrees to be equally liable with a promisor under a contract.

Counteroffer: a variance in the terms of an offer that constitutes a rejection of the original offer and results in a new offer by the offeree to the original offeror.

Convenant: an absolute, unconditional promise to perform.

Cover: remedy whereby the buyer can purchase goods in substitution for the goods designated in a breached contract.

Cross-offer: see Counteroffer.

Damages: legal remedies; monetary awards.

Delegation: promisor having assistance in fulfilling contractual duties.

Divisible contract: contract capable of being broken down into several equal agreements.

Duress: force or coercion used to induce agreement to a contract.

Economic duress: threatening the loss of an economic benefit if the person refuses to contract.

Emancipation: a minor no longer under the legal care of an adult.

Equitable remedies: nonmonetary awards.

Equity: the branch of the legal system that deals with fairness and mercy.

Estoppel: equitable term; the doctrine bars certain actions in the interest of fairness.

Executed contract: a contract that is complete and final with respect to all of its terms and conditions.

Executory contract: a contract in which one or both of the parties still have obligations to perform.

Exemplary damages: additional monetary award designed to punish the breaching party.

Express condition: a condition created by the words of the parties.

Express contract: a contract manifested in so many words, oral or written.

Express waiver: a waiver occurring when the promisee specifically manifests an intention to forgive the other side's breach.

Express warranty: a guarantee created by words or conduct of the seller.

Ex ship: risk passes to buyer of the goods when the goods are offloaded from the means of conveyance.

FAS: free alongside; risk passes to buyer when goods are placed alongside the vessel used for transportation.

Financing statement: document filed in government office to protect a security interest under Article IX of the UCC.

Firm offer: Offer made by a merchant under the provisions of the UCC that cannot be revoked for a period of time.

Floating lien: security interest in after-acquired property.

FOB: free on board; risk passes to buyer when the goods are loaded on the vessel used to transport the goods.

Formal contract: historically, a written contract under seal; currently, any contract so designated by a state statute.

Fraud: a misrepresentation of a material fact made with the intent to deceive, relied on by the other party to his or her detriment.

Frustration of purpose: the purpose for which the contract was formed no longer exists.

Guarantee: promise to answer for the debts of another; must be in writing.

Guarantor: person who agrees to be responsible to answer for the debts of another should the debtor default.

Implied-in-fact condition: condition created by the reasonable expectation of the parties.

Implied-in-fact contract: a contract in which the promises of the parties are inferred from their actions as opposed to specific words.

Implied-in-law condition: a condition imposed by law in the interests of fairness.

Implied-in-law contract: see Quasi-contract.

Implied waiver: a waiver occurring when the promisee's actions imply an intention to forgive the other side's breach.

Implied warranty: guarantee created by operation of law.

Impossibility of performance: promisor's performance cannot be fulfilled due to outside forces.

Incidental beneficiary: person who benefits tangentially from a contract.

Informal contract: any nonformal contract.

Injunction: court order to stop engaging in a specific action.

Intended beneficiary: third party beneficiary.

Iron clad offer: offer under the UCC whose terms cannot be modified by the offeree.

Law: division of the legal system concerned with historical legal principles designed to provide equal treatment to all persons.

Legal remedies: monetary awards.

Limitation of damages: a contractual provision placing a ceiling on the amount of potential liability for breach of the contract.

Liquidated damages: a contractual provision providing a specified dollar amount for breach of the contract.

Mailbox rule: the acceptance of a bilateral contract is effective when properly dispatched by an authorized means of communication.

Majority: adulthood; above the legal age of consent.

Malum in se: bad in and of itself, against public morals.

Malum prohibitum: regulatory wrong; violates a statute.

Material breach: breach of contract that goes to the heart of the agreement.

Mechanic's lien: security interest given under common law to persons who repair property.

Mental duress: psychological threats used to induce a person to contract.

Merchant: under the UCC, any person who regularly trades in goods or who holds himself out as having knowledge peculiar to a specific good.

Minor breach: breach of contract that goes to an insignificant aspect of the agreement.

Minority: persons under the legal age of consent.

Mirror image rule: an acceptance must correspond exactly to the terms of the offer.

Misrepresentation: mistakes of a material fact relied on by the other party to his or her detriment; no intent to defraud.

Mistake: misconception of the subject matter of the contract.

Mitigation of damages: duty imposed on injured party to lessen, by reasonable means, the breaching party's liability.

Mutual assent: a meeting of the minds; agreeing to the same terms at the same time; the offer and acceptance combined.

Mutual mistake: misconception of the subject matter of a contract by both parties; makes the contract unenforceable.

Mutual rescission: agreement by both contracting parties to do away with the contract.

Mutuality of consideration: the bargain element of the contract; that each side must give and receive something of legal value.

Natural infant: a child under the age of seven.

Necessaries: food, clothing, shelter, and medical aid.

No arrival, no sale: risk passes to the buyer when the goods are tendered to the buyer.

Nominal consideration: consideration of insufficient legal value to support a contract.

Novation: substitution of a party to a contract; novated person takes over all rights and obligations under the contract.

Offer: a proposition made by one party to another manifesting a present intention to enter into a valid contract and creating a power in the other person to create a valid contract by making an appropriate acceptance.

Offeree: the person to whom an offer is made; the party who has the power to create a valid contract by making an appropriate acceptance.

Offeror: the person who initiates a contract by proposing the offer.

Operation of law: a manner in which rights and obligations devolve on a person without the act or cooperation of the party himself.

Option: a contract to keep an offer open for a specified time.

Output contract: an agreement whereby one person agrees to buy or sell all the goods produced by the other party.

Palimony: payment made to a person under certain circumstances pursuant to the break-up of a nonmarital relationship.

Parol evidence rule: oral testimony may not be used to vary the terms of a writing.

Perfect tender: Under the UCC the buyer's right to complete, not substantial, performance.

Perfection: method of creating and protecting a security interest under Article IX of the UCC.

Physical duress: threatening physical harm to force a person to contract.

Preexisting duty rule: promises to do what one is already legally bound to do is not consideration.

Prenuptial agreement: antenuptial agreement.

Principal-agent: an agent is one who acts for and on behalf of another, the principal, for the purpose of entering into contracts with third persons.

Promisee: the one who receives consideration in a bilateral contract.

Promisor: the one who gives consideration in a bilateral contract.

Promissory estoppel: doctrine in which promises not supported by consideration are given enforceability if the promisee had detrimentally relied on the promises.

Promissory note: promise to pay money; repayment of a loan.

Punitive damages: exemplary damages.

Purchase money security interest: security interest created in the person whose money was used to buy the collateral.

Quantum meruit: quasi-contractual award; value of the service performed.

Quantum valebant: quasi-contractual award; value of the good given.

Quasi-contract: a legal relationship that the courts, in the interests of fairness and equity, treat in a manner similar to a contractual relationship, but one in which no contract exists.

Quasi-contractual remedy: an equitable remedy involving a monetary award.

Quid pro quo: this for that; the mutuality of consideration.

Real party in interest: person with enforceable contractual rights.

Reformation: a court-ordered accord and satisfaction.

Rejection: to refuse an offer.

Release: contract relieving the promisor from an obligation under an existing contract.

Replevin: quitable remedy in which buyer reclaims property previously rejected.

Requirements contract: agreement whereby one person agrees to buy all his supplies from the other person.

Rescission and restitution: a court order revoking a contract that would be unduly burdensome to fulfill.

Reverse unilateral contract: a contract in which the performer, rather than the promisor, makes the offer.

Revocation: to recall an offer.

Rules of construction: guidelines used by the courts to interpret contractual provisions.

Sale on approval: risk passes to the buyer when the buyer receives and approves the goods.

Sale or return: risk passes to the buyer when the buyer receives the goods, but the buyer bears the cost of returning any goods of which she does not approve.

Secured transaction: any transaction, regardless of form, that intends to create a security interest in personal property or fixtures.

Security agreement: document signed by debtor and creditor naming the collateral and creating a security interest in said collateral.

Security interest: right acquired by a creditor to attach collateral in case of default by the debtor.

Severability: the ability to separate a contract into its legal and illegal portions.

Sham consideration: legally insufficient consideration used to mask a gift in words of contract.

Shipment contract: agreement whereby risk passes from seller to buyer when goods are transported by a third person under Article II of the UCC.

Specific performance: court order to perform contractual promises.

Speculative damages: damages that are not specifically provable.

Statute of Frauds: statute mandating that certain contracts must be in writing to be enforceable.

Strict liability: no standard of care; automatic liability if properly used goods do not meet warranties.

Substituted agreement: a new contract that incorporates the original contract in the new provisions.

Sufficiency of the consideration: doctrine that each party to a contract must contribute something of legal value for which he has bargained.

Supervening illegality: change in law that makes the subject matter of the contract illegal.

Temporary restraining order (TRO): preliminary step to an injunction.

Tender complete performance: being ready, willing, and able to perform.

Third party beneficiary contract: contract entered into for the purpose of benefiting someone not a party to the contract.

Third party creditor beneficiary: person who receives the benefit of a contract in order to extinguish a debt owed to him by the promisee.

Third party donee beneficiary: person who receives the benefit of a contract in order to receive a gift from the promisee.

Time of the essence clause: contractual clause in which a specified time for performance is made a key element of the contract.

Token chose: item of symbolic, rather than monetary, significance.

Undisclosed principal: a person, represented by an agent, who is party to a contract but has not revealed his or her identity to the other party.

Undue influence: mental duress by a person in a close and particular relationship to the innocent party.

Unenforceable contract: a contract that is otherwise valid but for breach of which there is no remedy at law.

Uniform Commercial Code (UCC): statutory enactment codifying certain areas of contract law, specifically with respect to sales contracts and security agreements.

Unilateral contract: a promise for an act.

Unilateral mistake: misconception of the subject matter of a contract by only one party to the contract; may be enforceable.

Usury: rate of interest higher than the rate allowed by law.

Valid contract: an agreement that meets all six contractual requirements.

Vested: having a legally enforceable right.

Void contract: a situation in which the parties have attempted to create a contract, but because one or more of the requisite elements are missing no contract exists.

Voidable contract: a contract that one party may avoid at his option without being in breach of contract.

Voluntary disablement: volitional act by a promisor making her obligation virtually incapable of being performed.

Waiver: forgiveness of a contractual obligation.

Warranty: guarantee made by the manufacturer or seller with respect to the quality, quantity, and type of good being sold.

Warranty of fitness for a particular use: guarantee that goods can be used for a specified purpose.

Warranty of merchantability: guarantee that goods can be used in their current condition.

Warranty of title: guarantee that seller has a title sufficient to transfer the goods to the buyer.

Index

Acceptance, 3
  bilateral contract, 58
  defined, 54
  mailbox rule, 59
  silence, 55
  termination of ability to accept, 62
  undisclosed principal, 57
  Uniform Commercial Code, 55
  unilateral contract, 61
  varying terms of offer, 54
  who may accept, 56
Accord and satisfaction, 90
  discharge of obligations, 272
Age
  contractual capacity, 114
Agent
  defined, 57
Alcohol
  contractual capacity, 116
Antenuptial agreement, 160
Arbitration, 198
  drafting simple contracts, 331
Assignment
  assignor, 241
  consent of the promisor, 242
  creating, 240
  defined, 240
  drafting simple contracts, 326
  effect of, 243
  estoppel, 244
  irrevocable, 243
  multiple assignees, 245

  novation, 244
  performance, 244
  token chose, 244
  writing, 244
Auction with reserve, 63
Auction without reserve, 63

Battle of the forms, 197
Benefit conferred, 82
Bilateral contract
  acceptance, 58
  mutuality of consideration, 82
  rejection, 60
  revocation, 63
Bilateral obligation, 6
Breach of contract
  discharge of obligations, 269

Charitable subscription, 91
Choice of law
  drafting simple contracts, 330
Compensatory damages, 288
Condition
  concurrent, 166
  constructive, 168
  defined, 164
  express, 167
  implied-in-fact, 167
  implied-in-law, 168
  precedent, 165
  subsequent, 166

Conditional contracts
　risk of loss, 200
Consequential damages, 290
Consideration, 3, 34
　accord and satisfaction, 90
　benefit conferred, 82
　charitable subscription, 91
　conditional promises, 88
　debtor's promises, 91
　defined, 81
　determining what is not
　　consideration, 83
　detriment incurred, 83
　formal contract, 93
　gift, 84
　guarantee, 92
　illusory promises, 85
　moral consideration, 84
　mutuality, 82
　nominal, 87
　past consideration, 84
　preexisting duty rule, 86
　promissory estoppel, 88
　sham, 88
　subject matter, 35
　sufficiency, 87
Constructive condition, 168
Contract
　acceptance, 3
　bilateral, 6
　consideration, 3
　contractual capacity, 4
　contractual intent, 5
　defined, 2
　enforceability, 11
　executed, 10
　executory, 10
　express, 7
　formal, 9
　implied, 7
　implied-in-fact, 7
　implied-in-law, 8
　informal, 9
　legality of subject matter, 4
　offer, 2
　quasi-contracts, 7
　requirements, 2
　timing, 10
　unenforceable, 12
　unilateral, 6
　valid, 11
　void, 11

　voidable, 11
Contract of adhesion, 137
Contracts not to be performed within
　one year, 161
Contractual capacity, 4, 114
　age, 114
　alcohol, 116
　drugs, 116
　mental capacity, 115
Contractual fraud
　elements, 134
Contractual intent, 5
　defined, 134
　duress, 136
　economic duress, 136
　fraud, 134
　mental duress, 137
　misrepresentation, 135
　mistake, 139
　physical duress, 136
Counteroffer, 54
Covenant
　defined, 157, 164

Damages
　compensatory, 288
　consequential, 290
　limitation of, 292
　liquidated, 291
　punitive, 290
　speculative, 291
Death of parties
　discharge of obligations, 274
Debtor's promises, 91
Delegation, 246
　drafting simple contracts, 327
Destination contracts
　risk of loss, 202
Detriment incurred, 83
Discharge of obligations, 263
　accord and satisfaction, 272
　agreement of parties, 271
　anticipatory breach, 267
　breach of contract, 269
　death of parties, 274
　destruction of subject matter, 274
　excuse of conditions, 264
　frustration of purpose, 275
　impossibility of performance,
　　273
　insolvency, 266

methods of, 264
modification, 273
mutual recission, 271
novation, 273
performance, 268
performance prevented, 265
release, 272
substituted agreement, 272
supervening illegality, 274
voluntary disablement, 266
Drafting simple contracts, 319
arbitration, 331
assignments, 326
checklist of clauses, 320
choice of law, 330
delegation, 327
description of consideration, 321
description of parties, 321
duration, 329
remedies, 330
risk of loss, 325
security agreement, 324
signatures, 332
special provisions, 328
submission to jurisdiction, 331
termination, 329
terminology, 327
Title to property, 325
waivers, 326
warranties, 324
Drugs
contractual capacity, 116
Duration
drafting simple contracts, 329
Duress, 136
contract of adhesion, 137
economic, 136
mental, 137
physical, 136

Economic duress, 136
Enforceability of contract, 11
Equitable remedies, 293
injunction, 294
quasi-contractual remedies, 296
reformation, 296
rescission and restitution, 295
specific performance, 294
Executed contract, 10
Executor's promise to pay
decedent's debts, 163

Executory contract, 10
Express condition, 167
Express contract, 7
Express waiver, 297
Express warranties, 198

Formal contract, 9, 93
Fraud, 134
Frustration of purpose
discharge of obligations, 275

Gambling, 112
Guarantee, 92, 162

Implied contract, 7
Implied waiver, 197
Implied warranties, 199
Implied-in-fact condition, 167
Implied-in-fact contract, 7
Implied-in-law condition, 168
Implied-in-law contract, 8
Impossibility of performance
discharge of obligations, 273
Informal contract, 9
Injunction, 294
Intent, 31

Jurisdiction
drafting simple contracts, 331

Leases, 196
Legality of subject matter, 4, 110
gambling, 112
licensing statutes, 112
malum in se, 110
malum prohibitum, 111
Statute of Frauds, 111
usury, 112
Licensing statutes, 112
Liquidated damages, 291

Mailbox rule, 59
rejection, 60
Malum in se, 110
Malum prohibitum, 111

Marriage, 160
Mental capacity
    contractual capacity, 115
Mental duress, 137
Mirror image rule, 55
Misrepresentation, 135
Mistake
    mutual mistake, 139
    unilateral mistake, 139
Mutual mistake, 139

Novation
    assignment, 244
    discharge of obligations, 273

Offer, 2
    acceptance. *See* Acceptance
    alternate offers, 37
    ambiguity, 36
    certainty, 33
    communication to offeree, 31
    defined, 30
    definiteness, 33
    essential terms, 33
    operation of law, 65
    parties, 38
    price, 34
    subject matter, 35
    termination, 65
    time of performance, 39
    varying terms of offer, 54
Operation of law, 65
Output contract, 37

Palimony, 161
Parol evidence rule, 169
Parties
    offer, 38
Perfect tender, 204
Physical duress, 136
Preexisting duty rule, 86
Prenuptial agreement, 160
Price, 34
Principal
    defined, 57
Principal-agent relationship, 57
Promissory estoppel, 88
Punitive damages, 290

Quantum meruit, 296
Quantum valebant, 297
Quasi-contract, 7
Quasi-contractual remedies, 296

Real estate, 159
Reformation, 296
Remedies, 202, 287
    arbitration, 198
    available to buyer, 204
    available to seller, 203
    drafting simple contracts, 330
    equitable. *See* Equitable remedies
    legal remedies. *See* Damages
Requirements contract, 38
Rescission and restitution, 295
Risk of loss, 200
    conditional contracts, 200
    destination contracts, 202
    drafting simple contracts, 325
    shipment contracts, 201
Rules of construction, 168

Sale of goods, 163
    background, 194
    battle of the forms, 197
    between merchants, 196
    express warranties, 198
    goods defined, 194
    implied warranties, 199
    leases, 196
    remedies, 203
    risk of loss, 200
    strict liability, 194
    warranties, 198
    warranty of title, 200
    written assurances, 205
Secured transactions
    defined, 206
    priorities, 210
Security agreement, 208
Security interest, 206
    attachment, 208
    perfection, 209
    requirements to create, 207
Shipment contracts
    risk of loss, 201
Signatures
    drafting simple contracts, 332
Specific performance, 294

Speculative damages, 291
Statute of Frauds, 111, 158
   antenuptial agreement, 160
   contracts not to be performed within
      one year, 161
   executor's promise to pay decedent's
      debts, 163
   guarantee, 162
   marriage, 160
   palimony, 161
   prenuptial agreement, 160
   real estate, 159
   sale of goods, 163
Subject matter, 35
   destruction, 274
   legality of. *See* Legality of
      subject matter
Supervening illegality
   discharge of obligations, 274

Termination
   drafting simple contracts, 329
Terminology, 327
Third party contracts, 231
   assignment. *See* Assignment
   beneficiary contracts, 232
   creditor beneficiary contracts, 234
   delegation, 246
   donee beneficiary contracts, 233, 237
   incidental beneficiaries, 234
   intended beneficiaries, 233
   promisee, 233
   promisor, 233
   real party in interest, 234
   vested, 235

Time of the essence clauses, 40
Timing of performance, 39
Title
   drafting simple contracts, 325

Undue influence, 137
Uniform Commercial Code (UCC), 40
   Article I, general provisions, 191
   Article II, sales. *See* Sale of goods
   Article IX, secured transactions. *See*
      Secured transactions
   background, 190
Unilateral contract
   acceptance, 61
   mutuality of consideration, 82
   revocation, 63
Unilateral mistake, 139
Unilateral obligation, 6
Usury, 112

Valid contract, 11
Vested, 235
Void contract, 11
Voidable contract, 11
   fraud, 136
   misrepresentation, 136

Waiver, 297
   drafting simple contracts, 326
Warranties, 198
   drafting simple contracts, 324
   express, 198
   implied, 199
   title, of, 200